MARRIAGE AND FAMILY
98/99

Twenty-Fourth Edition

Editor

Kathleen R. Gilbert
Indiana University

Kathleen Gilbert is an associate professor in the Department of Applied Health Science at Indiana University. She received her B.A. in Sociology and her M.S. in Marriage and Family Relations from Northern Illinois University. Her Ph.D. in Family Studies is from Purdue University. Dr. Gilbert's primary areas of interest are loss and grief in a family context, trauma and the family, family process, and minority families. She has published several books and articles in these areas.

D1444951

Annual Editions
A Library of Information from the Public Press
Dushkin/McGraw·Hill
Sluice Dock, Guilford, Connecticut 06437

Visit us on the Internet—http://www.dushkin.com/

The Annual Editions Series

ANNUAL EDITIONS, including GLOBAL STUDIES, consist of over 70 volumes designed to provide the reader with convenient, low-cost access to a wide range of current, carefully selected articles from some of the most important magazines, newspapers, and journals published today. ANNUAL EDITIONS are updated on an annual basis through a continuous monitoring of over 300 periodical sources. All ANNUAL EDITIONS have a number of features that are designed to make them particularly useful, including topic guides, annotated tables of contents, unit overviews, and indexes. For the teacher using ANNUAL EDITIONS in the classroom, an Instructor's Resource Guide with test questions is available for each volume. GLOBAL STUDIES titles provide comprehensive background information and selected world press articles on the regions and countries of the world.

VOLUMES AVAILABLE

ANNUAL EDITIONS

Abnormal Psychology
Accounting
Adolescent Psychology
Aging
American Foreign Policy
American Government
American History, Pre-Civil War
American History, Post-Civil War
American Public Policy
Anthropology
Archaeology
Astronomy
Biopsychology
Business Ethics
Canadian Politics
Child Growth and Development
Comparative Politics
Computers in Education
Computers in Society
Criminal Justice
Criminology
Developing World
Deviant Behavior
Drugs, Society, and Behavior
Dying, Death, and Bereavement

Early Childhood Education
Economics
Educating Exceptional Children
Education
Educational Psychology
Environment
Geography
Geology
Global Issues
Health
Human Development
Human Resources
Human Sexuality
International Business
Macroeconomics
Management
Marketing
Marriage and Family
Mass Media
Microeconomics
Multicultural Education
Nutrition
Personal Growth and Behavior
Physical Anthropology
Psychology
Public Administration
Race and Ethnic Relations

Social Problems
Social Psychology
Sociology
State and Local Government
Teaching English as a Second
    Language
Urban Society
Violence and Terrorism
Western Civilization, Pre-Reformation
Western Civilization, Post-Reformation
Women's Health
World History, Pre-Modern
World History, Modern
World Politics

GLOBAL STUDIES

Africa
China
India and South Asia
Japan and the Pacific Rim
Latin America
Middle East
Russia, the Eurasian Republics, and
    Central/Eastern Europe
Western Europe

Cataloging in Publication Data
Main entry under title: Annual Editions: Marriage and Family. 1998/99.
        1. Family—United States—Periodicals. 2. Marriage—United States—Periodicals. I. Gilbert, Kathleen,
comp. II. Title: Marriage and Family.
ISBN 0-697-39179-5   301.42'05   74-84596   ISSN 0272-7897

© 1998 by Dushkin/McGraw-Hill, Guilford, CT 06437, A Division of The McGraw-Hill Companies.

Twenty-Fourth Edition

Cover image © 1998 PhotoDisc, Inc.

Printed in the United States of America

 Printed on Recycled Paper

Editors/Advisory Board

Members of the Advisory Board are instrumental in the final selection of articles for each edition of ANNUAL EDITIONS. Their review of articles for content, level, currentness, and appropriateness provides critical direction to the editor and staff. We think that you will find their careful consideration well reflected in this volume.

EDITOR

Kathleen R. Gilbert
Indiana University

ADVISORY BOARD

Staff

Ian A. Nielsen, Publisher

To the Reader

In publishing ANNUAL EDITIONS we recognize the enormous role played by the magazines, newspapers, and journals of the *public press* in providing current, first-rate educational information in a broad spectrum of interest areas. Many of these articles are appropriate for students, researchers, and professionals seeking accurate, current material to help bridge the gap between principles and theories and the real world. These articles, however, become more useful for study when those of lasting value are carefully *collected, organized, indexed,* and *reproduced* in a *low-cost format,* which provides easy and permanent access when the material is needed. That is the role played by ANNUAL EDITIONS. Under the direction of each volume's *academic editor,* who is an expert in the subject area, and with the guidance of an *Advisory Board,* each year we seek to provide in each ANNUAL EDITION a current, well-balanced, carefully selected collection of the best of the public press for your study and enjoyment. We think that you will find this volume useful, and we hope that you will take a moment to let us know what you think.

The purpose of *Annual Editions: Marriage and Family 98/99* is to bring to the reader the latest thoughts and trends in our understanding of the family, to identify current concerns as well as problems and possible solutions, and to present alternative views of family process. The intent of this anthology is to explore intimate relationships as they are played out in marriage and family and, in doing this, to reflect the family's changing face.

The articles in this volume are taken from professional publications, semiprofessional journals, and popular lay publications aimed at both special populations and a general readership. The selections are carefully reviewed for their currency and accuracy. In some cases, contrasting viewpoints are presented. In others, articles are paired in such a way as to personalize the more impersonal scholarly information. In the current edition, a number of new articles have been added to reflect reviewers' comments. As the reader, you will note the tremendous range in tone and focus of these articles, from first-person accounts to reports of scientific discoveries as well as philosophical and theoretical writings. Some are more practical and applications-oriented, while others are more conceptual and research-oriented.

This anthology is organized to cover many of the important aspects of marriage and family. The first unit looks at varied perspectives on the family. The second unit examines the beginning steps of relationship building as individuals go through the process of exploring and establishing connections. In the third unit, means of finding and maintaining a relationship balance are examined. Unit four is concerned with crises and ways in which these can act as challenges and opportunities for families and their members. Finally, unit five takes an affirming view as it looks at families, now and into the future.

Instructors can use *Annual Editions: Marriage and Family 98/99* as a primary text for introductory marriage and family classes, particularly when they tie the content of the readings to basic information on marriage and family. This book can also be used as a supplement to update or emphasize certain aspects of standard marriage and family textbooks. Because of the provocative nature of many of the essays in this anthology, it works well as a basis for class discussion about various aspects of marriage and family relationships.

New to this edition of *Annual Editions: Marriage and Family* are *World Wide Web* sites that can be used to further explore topics addressed in the articles. These sites are cross-referenced by number in the *topic guide.*

I would like to thank everyone involved in the development of this volume. My appreciation goes to those who sent in *article rating forms* and comments on the previous edition as well as those who suggested articles to consider for inclusion in this edition. Finally, to all of the students in my Marriage and Family Interactions class who have contributed critiques of articles, I would like to say thanks.

Anyone interested in providing input for future editions of *Annual Editions: Marriage and Family* should complete and return the postage-paid *article rating form* at the end of this book. Your suggestions are much appreciated and contribute to the continuing high quality of this anthology.

Kathleen R. Gilbert
Editor

Contents

UNIT 1

Varied Perspectives on the Family

Five articles explore different views on where our images of family come from and how they are influenced by our life experiences as well as societal and cultural constraints.

The concepts in bold italics are developed in the article. For further expansion please refer to the Topic Guide and the Index.

UNIT 2

Exploring and Establishing Relationships

Twelve articles address factors that influence the formation of close relationships, both romantic and generative.

The concepts in bold italics are developed in the article. For further expansion please refer to the Topic Guide and the Index.

vi

The concepts in bold italics are developed in the article. For further expansion please refer to the Topic Guide and the Index.

UNIT 3

Finding a Balance: Maintaining Relationships

Eleven articles consider the complex issues related to keeping a relationship going. From marriage to parent/child relationships to sibling relationships, relationship maintenance requires thought and commitment from members.

The concepts in bold italics are developed in the article. For further expansion please refer to the Topic Guide and the Index.

UNIT 4

Crises— Challenges and Opportunities

A wide variety of crises,
normative and catastrophic,
are detailed in thirteen articles.
Ranging from broad cultural
factors impacting on families
to the intimate crises of
infidelity and divorce, these
articles provide accounts of
devastation and hope.

The concepts in bold italics are developed in the article. For further expansion please refer to the Topic Guide and the Index.

The concepts in bold italics are developed in the article. For further expansion please refer to the Topic Guide and the Index.

x

UNIT 5

Families, Now and Into the Future

Four articles examine
ways of establishing and/or
maintaining health and
healthy relationships
in families.

The concepts in bold italics are developed in the article. For further expansion please refer to the Topic Guide and the Index.

Topic Guide

This topic guide suggests how the selections in this book relate to topics of traditional concern to students and professionals involved with the study of marriage and family. It is useful for locating articles that relate to each other for reading and research. The guide is arranged alphabetically according to topic. Articles may, of course, treat topics that do not appear in the topic guide. In turn, entries in the topic guide do not necessarily constitute a comprehensive listing of all the contents of each selection. **In addition, relevant Web sites, which are annotated on pages 4 and 5, are noted in bold italics under the topic articles.**

TOPIC AREA	TREATED IN	TOPIC AREA	TREATED IN
Abuse	29. Behind Closed Doors 30. Things That Go Bump in the Home 31. Helping Children Cope with Violence *(1, 10, 11, 28, 33, 34)*	Communication	8. Back Off! 10. Staying Power 18. Peer Marriage 25. Effective Fathers 27. Grandparent Development and Influence 38. Lessons from Stepfamilies 40. Hard Lessons *(8, 9, 11, 20, 22, 24, 25, 26, 27, 28, 32, 33)*
Adoption	16. Lifelong Impact of Adoption *(22, 26, 33)*		
Aging	20. Receipts from a Marriage 27. Grandparent Development and Influence 39. Caregiving 43. What's Ahead for Families *(29, 30, 31, 38, 39)*	Culture	1. Way We Weren't 4. African American Families 10. Staying Power 13. Men, Sex, and Parenthood 19. For Better or Worse? 45. Rituals for Our Times *(7, 10, 11, 16, 19, 28, 39)*
Attachment	16. Lifelong Impact of Adoption 22. Healing Power of Intimacy 40. Hard Lessons *(22, 24, 26, 27, 28)*	Dating/Mate Selection	7. What Makes Love Last? *(14)*
Beliefs	13. Men, Sex, and Parenthood 18. Peer Marriage 19. For Better or Worse? 21. Work of Oneness 44. Rewriting Life Stories 45. Rituals for Our Times *(8, 9, 11, 22, 24, 26, 27, 28)*	Divorce	33. Beyond Betrayal 37. Should This Marriage Be Saved? 38. Lessons from Stepfamilies 43. What's Ahead for Families *(22, 24, 26, 27, 28, 32, 33, 39)*
Bereavement	12. Missing Children 16. Lifelong Impact of Adoption 40. Hard Lessons 41. How Kids Mourn *(35, 36)*	Family Systems	1. Way We Weren't 4. African American Families 18. Peer Marriage 21. Work of Oneness 26. Great Ages of Discovery 28. Sibling Connections 36. Remaking Marriage & Family 38. Lessons from Stepfamilies 44. Rewriting Life Stories 45. Rituals for Our Times *(7, 10, 19, 20, 22, 24, 26, 27, 28, 32, 33, 39)*
Biological Issues	6. Man's World, Woman's World? 11. Who Stole Fertility? 12. Missing Children 14. Artificial Womb Is Born 17. Fertile Minds *(8, 9, 12, 13, 14, 17, 19, 20)*		
		"Family Values" Conflict	1. Way We Weren't 19. For Better or Worse? *(20, 22, 24, 26, 28, 32, 33)*
Children and Child Care	5. Gay Families Come Out 15. What a Baby *Really* Costs 16. Lifelong Impact of Adoption 17. Fertile Minds 18. Peer Marriage 24. Myth of Quality Time 25. Effective Fathers 26. Great Ages of Discovery 27. Grandparent Development and Influence 29. Behind Closed Doors 32. Resilience in Development 41. How Kids Mourn *(18, 21, 22, 23, 24, 25, 26, 27, 28, 32, 33, 35)*	Finances	11. Who Stole Fertility? 15. What a Baby *Really* Costs 20. Receipts from a Marriage 43. What's Ahead for Families
		Future of Family	36. Remaking Marriage & Family 42. To See Your Future 43. What's Ahead for Families *(22, 23, 24, 26, 27, 28, 32, 33, 37, 38, 39)*

TOPIC AREA	TREATED IN	TOPIC AREA	TREATED IN
Gender and Gender Roles	2. Feminism & the Family 3. Among the Promise Keepers 6. Man's World, Woman's World 10. Staying Power 13. Men, Sex, and Parenthood 18. Peer Marriage 19. For Better or Worse? 25. Effective Fathers 30. Things That Go Bump in the Home 35. Myth of the Miserable Working Woman 36. Remaking Marriage & Family *(6, 7, 8, 9, 10, 11, 13, 19, 22, 24, 26, 28, 33, 39)*	**Parents/Parenting**	5. Gay Families Come Out 15. What a Baby *Really* Costs 18. Peer Marriage 20. Receipts from a Marriage 23. Parental Rights 24. Myth of Quality Time 25. Effective Fathers 37. Should This Marriage Be Saved? 38. Lessons from Stepfamilies *(6, 14, 15, 18, 21, 23, 26, 27, 28, 32, 33, 34)*
Grandparents	26. Great Ages of Discovery 27. Grandparent Development and Influence 43. What's Ahead for Families *(29, 30, 31, 35, 38, 39)*	**Poverty**	2. Feminism & the Family *(15, 21)*
Health Concerns	9. Choosing a Contraceptive 11. Who Stole Fertility? 12. Missing Children 13. Men, Sex, and Parenthood 14. Artificial Womb Is Born 39. Caregiving 40. Hard Lessons 42. To See Your Future *(8, 9, 11, 14, 15, 18, 20, 29, 31, 35, 38)*	**Pregnancy/Childbirth**	11. Who Stole Fertility? 12. Missing Children 13. Men, Sex, and Parenthood 14. Artificial Womb Is Born 15. What a Baby *Really* Costs *(12, 14, 15, 16, 18, 20)*
History	1. Way We Weren't 36. Remaking Marriage & Family 42. To See Your Future 44. Rewriting Life Stories	**Religion/Spirituality**	3. Among the Promise Keepers 21. Work of Oneness
		Remarriage	38. Lessons from Stepfamilies 43. What's Ahead for Families *(32, 33)*
Infidelity	33. Beyond Betrayal 34. Sex in America *(16, 22, 24, 32)*	**Resilience**	4. African American Families 32. Resilience in Development 38. Lessons from Stepfamilies 44. Rewriting Life Stories *(21, 22, 24, 26, 28, 32, 33)*
Intimacy/Romantic Love	7. What Makes Love Last? 8. Back Off! 18. Peer Marriage 19. For Better or Worse? 21. Work of Oneness 22. Healing Power of Intimacy 34. Sex in America *(14, 16, 19, 20, 22, 24, 26, 27, 34)*	**Sex/Sexuality**	6. Man's World, Woman's World? 9. Choosing a Contraceptive 11. Who Stole Fertility? 12. Missing Children 13. Men, Sex, and Parenthood 18. Peer Marriage 19. For Better or Worse? 33. Beyond Betrayal 34. Sex in America *(8, 9, 11, 12, 13, 14, 15, 16, 17, 18, 19, 20, 34, 39)*
Laws/Governmental Roles/Policy	2. Feminism & the Family 5. Gay Families Come Out 14. Artificial Womb Is Born 19. For Better or Worse? 23. Parental Rights *(5, 6, 8, 9, 11)*	**Siblings**	26. Great Ages of Discovery 28. Sibling Connections
		Values	1. Way We Weren't 3. Among the Promise Keepers 13. Men, Sex, and Parenthood 18. Peer Marriage 19. For Better or Worse? 21. Work of Oneness 37. Should This Marriage Be Saved? 40. Hard Lessons 45. Rituals for Our Times *(6, 7, 10, 16, 22, 24, 26, 35, 37, 39)*
Marriage	2. Feminism & the Family 7. What Makes Love last? 18. Peer Marriage 19. For Better or Worse? 20. Receipts from a Marriage 21. Work of Oneness 35. Myth of the Miserable Working Woman 37. Should This Marriage Be Saved? 38. Lessons from Stepfamilies 43. What's Ahead for Families *(14, 16, 22, 24, 28, 33, 34, 35, 37, 38, 39)*	**Work and Family**	18. Peer Marriage 24. Myth of Quality Time 35. Myth of the Miserable Working Woman 36. Remaking Marriage & Family 43. What's Ahead for Families *(9, 11, 14, 22, 24, 26, 28)*

Selected World Wide Web Sites for Annual Editions: Marriage and Family

All of these Web sites are hot-linked through the *Annual Editions* home page: *http://www.dushkin.com/annualeditions* (just click on this book's title). In addition, these sites are referenced by number and appear where relevant in the Topic Guide on the previous two pages.

Some Web sites are continually changing their structure and content, so the information listed may not always be available.

General Sources

1. American Psychological Association—*http://www.apa.org/psychnet/*—By exploring the APA's "PsychNET," you will be able to find links to an abundance of articles and other resources related to interpersonal relationships throughout the life span.

2. Encyclopedia Britannica—*http://www.ebig.com/*—This huge "Britannica Internet Guide" will lead you to a cornucopia of informational sites and reference sources on such topics as family structure and other social issues.

3. The Gallup Organization—*http://www.gallup.com/*—Open this Gallup Organization page for links to an extensive archive of public opinion poll results and special reports on many topics.

4. Penn Library: Sociology— *http://www.library.upenn.edu/resources/ social/sociology/sociology.html*—This site provides a number of indexes of culture and ethnic studies and statistical sources that are of value in studies of marriage and the family.

5. Social Science Information Gateway—*http://sosig.esrc.bris.ac.uk*—This is an online catalogue of thousands of Internet resources relevant to social science education and research. Every resource is selected and described by a librarian or subject specialist.

Varied Perspectives on the Family

6. American Studies Web—*http://www.georgetown.edu/crossroads/ asw/*—This eclectic site provides links to a wealth of resources on the Internet related to American studies, from gender studies to race and ethnicity. It is of great help when doing research in demography and population studies.

7. Anthropology Resources Page—*http://www.usd.edu/anth/*—Many cultural topics can be accessed from this site. Click on the links to find information about differences and similarities in values and lifestyles among the world's peoples.

8. Men's Health—*http://www.menshealth.com/new/guide/index.html*—This resource guide from *Men's Health* presents many links to topics about men and their concerns, from AIDS/STDs, to impotence, to vasectomy. It includes relationship and family issues.

9. Q Web Sweden: A Woman's Empowerment Base—*http://www. qweb.kvinnoforum.se/activity/thagemar.htm*—This site from a Swedish organization will lead you to a number of pages addressing women's health issues and discussing societal issues related to sex. It provides interesting cross-cultural perspectives.

10. U.S. Information Service—*http://www.usis.usemb.se/human/india. html*—Read this U.S. Department of State report on India's human-rights practices for an understanding into the issues that affect women's health and well-being in different parts of the world.

11. Women's Studies Resources—*http://www.inform.umd.edu/EdRes/ Topic/WomensStudies/*—This site provides a wealth of resources related to women and their concerns. You can find links to such topics as body image, comfort (or discomfort) with sexuality, personal relationships, pornography, and more.

Exploring and Establishing Relationships

12. Ask NOAH About Pregnancy: Fertility & Infertility—*http://www. noah.cuny.edu/pregnancy/fertility.html*—NOAH (New York Online Access to Health) seeks to provide relevant, timely, and unbiased health information for consumers. In this site, the organization presents extensive links to a variety of resources about infertility treatments and issues.

13. Bonobos Sex and Society—*http://soong.club.cc.cmu.edu/~julie/ bonobos.html*—This site, accessed through Carnegie Mellon University, contains an article explaining how a primate's behavior challenges traditional assumptions about male supremacy in human evolution. Guaranteed to generate spirited debate.

14. Go Ask Alice!—*http://www.columbia.edu/cu/healthwise/about.html*—This interactive site of the Columbia University Health Services provides discussion and insight into a number of personal issues of interest to college-age people—and those younger and older. Many questions about physical and emotional health and well-being in the modern world are answered.

15. Issue of Abortion in America—*http://caae.phil.cmu.edu/caae/ Home/Multimedia/Abortion/IssueofAbortion.html*—Open this site to learn about a CD-ROM that is being developed on "The Issue of Abortion in America." Reading the pages of this site (from the Carnegie Mellon University Center for the Advancement of Applied Ethics' Philosophy Department) will give you an introduction to important historical and social perspectives, legal issues, and medical facts related to the abortion debate.

16. The Kinsey Institute for Research in Sex, Gender, and Reproduction—*http://indiana.edu/~kinsey/*—The purpose of the Kinsey Institutes's Web site is to support interdisciplinary research and the study of human sexuality.

17. Mysteries of Odor in Human Sexuality—*http://www.pheromones. com/*—Keeping in mind that this is a commercial site with the goal of selling a book by James Kohl, look here to find topics of interest to nonscientists about pheromones. Check out the diagram of "Mammalian Olfactory-Genetic-Neuronal-Hormonal-Behavioral Reciprocity and Human Sexuality" for a sense of the myriad biological influences that play a part in sexual behavior.

18. Planned Parenthood—*http://www.plannedparenthood.org/*—Visit this well-known organization's home page for links to information on the various kinds of contraceptives (including outercourse and abstinence) and to discussions of other topics related to sexual and reproductive health.

19. The Society for the Scientific Study of Sexuality—*http://www.ssc. wisc.edu/ssss/*—The Society for the Scientific Study of Sexuality is an international organization dedicated to the advancement of knowledge about sexuality.

20. Sympatico: HealthyWay: Health Links—*http://www.ab.sympatico. ca/Contents/Health/GENERAL/sitemap.html*—This Canadian site meant for consumers will lead you to many links related to

sexual orientation. It also addresses aspects of human sexuality over the life span and reproductive health.

Finding a Balance: Maintaining Relationships

21. Child Welfare League of America—*http://www.cwla.org/*—The CWLA is the United States' oldest and largest organization devoted entirely to the well-being of vulnerable children and their families. This site provides links to information about such issues as teaching morality and values.

22. Coalition for Marriage, Family, and Couples Education—*http://www.smartmarriages.com/*—CMFCE is dedicated to bringing information about and directories of skill-based marriage education courses to the public. Nonpartisan and nonsectarian, it hopes to lower the rate of family breakdown through couple-empowering preventive education.

23. Family.com—*http://www.family.com/*—According to this site, Family.com is an online parenting service that offers comprehensive information and a supportive community for raising children.

24. Marriage and Family Therapy—*http://www.tamft.org/favmft.htm*—This site is maintained by the Tennessee Association for Marriage and Family Therapy. It is a link to many related resources on the Web.

25. The National Academy for Child Development—*http://www.nacd.org/*—This international organization is dedicated to helping children and adults reach their full potential. It presents links to various programs, research, and resources on many family topics.

26. National Council on Family Relations—*http://www.ncfr.com/*—This NCFR home page will lead you to valuable links to articles, research, and a raft of other resources on important issues in family relations, such as stepfamilies, couples, and children of divorce.

27. Positive Parenting—*http://www.positiveparenting.com/*—Positive Parenting is an organization dedicated to providing resources and information to make parenting rewarding, effective, and fun. This site provides a newsletter, an index of experts, chat groups, and links to many resources for families.

28. SocioSite—*http://www.pscw.uva.nl/sociosite/TOPICS/Women.html*—Open this site to gain insights into a number of issues that affect family relationships. It provides wide-ranging issues of women and men, of family and children, and more.

Crises: Challenges and Opportunities

29. Alzheimer's Association—*http://www.alz.org/*—The Alzheimer's Association is dedicated to researching the prevention, cures, and treatments of Alzheimer's disease and related disorders. It provides support and assistance to patients and their families.

30. American Association of Retired Persons—*http://www.aarp.org/*—The AARP, a major advocacy group for older people, includes among its many resources suggested readings and Internet links to organizations that deal with the health and social issues that may affect people and their families as they age.

31. Caregiver's Handbook—*http://www.acsu.buffalo.edu/~drstall/hndbk0.html*—This site is an online handbook for caregivers. Topics include nutrition, medical aspects, and liabilities of caregiving.

32. Children & Divorce—*http://www.hec.ohio-state.edu/famlife/divorce/*—Open this site to find links to articles and discussions of divorce and its effects on the family. Many bibliographical references are provided by the Ohio State University Department of Human Development and Family Science.

33. Parenting and Families—*http://www.cyfc.umn.edu/Parenting/parentlink.html*—By clicking on the various links, this site of the University of Minnesota's Children, Youth, and Family Consortium will lead you to many organizations and other resources related to divorce, single parenting, and stepfamilies, as well as information about other topics of interest in the study of marriage and family.

34. Sexual Assault Information Page—*http://www.cs.utk.edu/~bartley/saInfoPage.html*—This invaluable site provides dozens of links to information and resources on a variety of sexual assault–related topics, from child sexual abuse, to date rape, to incest, to secondary victims, to offenders. It also provides some material of interest in the pornography debate.

35. A Sociological Tour Through Cyberspace—*http://www.trinity.edu/~mkearl/index.html*—This extensive site, put together by Michael C. Kearl at Trinity University, provides essays, commentaries, data analyses, and links on such topics as death and dying, family, the sociology of time, social gerontology, social psychology, and many more.

36. Widow Net—*http://www.fortnet.org/~goshorn/WidowNet/*—Widow Net is an information and self-help resource for and by widows and widowers. The information is helpful to people of all ages, religions, and sexual orientation who have experienced a loss.

Families, Now and Into the Future

37. Economic Report of the President—*http://www.library.nwu.edu/gpo/help/econr.html*—This report includes current and anticipated trends in the United States and annual numerical goals concerning topics such as employment, income, and federal budget outlays. The database notes employment objectives for significant groups of the labor force.

38. National Institute on Aging—*http://www.nih.gov/nia/*—The NIA, one of the institutes of the U.S. National Institutes of Health, presents this page that leads to a variety of resources on health and lifestyle issues of interest to people as they grow older.

39. The North-South Institute—*http://www.nsi-ins.ca/info.html*—This site of the North-Site Institute—which works to strengthen international development cooperation and enhance gender and social equity—offers information on a variety of issues related to the family and social transitions that may affect us in the future.

We highly recommend that you review our Web site for expanded information and our other product lines. We are continually updating and adding links to our Web site in order to offer you the most usable and useful information that will support and expand the value of your Annual Editions. You can reach us at: *http://www. dushkin.com/annualeditions/.*

Varied Perspectives on the Family

Our image of what family is and what it should be is a powerful combination of personal experience, family forms we encounter, and attitudes we hold. Once formed, this image informs decision making and interpersonal interaction throughout our lives. It has far-reaching impacts: On an intimate level, it influences individual and family development as well as relationships both inside and outside the family. On a broader level, it affects social policy and programming.

In many ways, this image can be positive. It can act to clarify our thinking and facilitate interaction with like-minded individuals. It can also be negative, as it can narrow our thinking and limit our ability to see that other ways of carrying out the functions of family have value. Their very differentness makes them "bad." In this case, interaction with others can be impeded because of contrasting views.

This unit is intended to meet several goals with regard to perspectives on the family: (1) to sensitize the reader to sources of beliefs about the "shoulds" of the family—what the family should be and the ways in which family roles should be carried out, (2) to show how different views of the family can influence attitudes toward community responsibility and family policy, and (3) to show how views that dominate one's culture can influence awareness of ways of structuring family life.

First, the accuracy of our memories of "the good old days" is discussed by historian Stephanie Coontz in "The Way We Weren't: The Myth and Reality of the 'Traditional' Family." In "Feminism & the Family: An Indissoluble Marriage," Mary Ann Glendon argues that women, especially disadvantaged women, are at risk in families and that hope can be found in political activism to strengthen the position of women. The group profiled in "Among the Promise Keepers: An Inside Look at the Evangelical Men's Movement" has been controversial, as members have attempted to understand what it means to be a man at the turn of the century. In "African American Families: A Legacy of Vulnerability and Resilience," Beverly Greene debunks the stereotype of African American families as uniformly dysfunctional, presenting a picture of resilience and adaptive coping instead. The same debunking of myth can be seen in the final reading of this section, "Gay Families Come Out."

Looking Ahead: Challenge Questions

If you had the power to propose a government program to support today's families, what would it be? What image do you have of families that would take advantage of that program?

Discuss why you are—or are not—hopeful for the future of children and families. What can we learn from an accurate reading of history?

How would you go about expanding your ideas of what is acceptable in terms of family relationships and family roles? How far do you think you should go in this?

In what ways can we be responsive to the needs of members of society while also encouraging responsibility?

Several of the readings suggest that many of our ideas about families, past and present, are based on myth and stereotype. If this is true, how do we overcome it?

UNIT 1

The Way We Weren't

The Myth and Reality of the "Traditional" Family

Stephanie Coontz

Families face serious problems today, but proposals to solve them by reviving "traditional" family forms and values miss two points. First, no single traditional family existed to which we could return, and none of the many varieties of families in our past has had any magic formula for protecting its members from the vicissitudes of socioeconomic change, the inequities of class, race, and gender, or the consequences of interpersonal conflict. Violence, child abuse, poverty, and the unequal distribution of resources to women and children have occurred in every period and every type of family.

Second, the strengths that we also find in many families of the past were rooted in different social, cultural, and economic circumstances from those that prevail today. Attempts to reproduce any type of family outside of its original socioeconomic context are doomed to fail.

Colonial Families

American families always have been diverse, and the male breadwinner-female homemaker, nuclear ideal that most people associate with "the" traditional family has predominated for only a small portion of our history. In colonial America, several types of families coexisted or competed. Native American kinship systems subordinated the nuclear family to a much larger network of marital alliances and kin obligations, ensuring that no single family was forced to go it alone. Wealthy settler families from Europe, by contrast, formed independent households that pulled in labor from poorer neighbors and relatives, building their extended family solidarities on the backs of truncated families among indentured servants, slaves, and the poor. Even wealthy families, though, often were disrupted by death; a majority of colonial Americans probably spent some time in a stepfamily. Meanwhile, African Americans, denied the legal protection of marriage and parenthood, built extensive kinship networks and obligations through fictive kin ties, ritual co-parenting or godparenting, adoption of orphans, and complex naming patterns designed to preserve family links across space and time.

The dominant family values of colonial days left no room for sentimentalizing childhood. Colonial mothers, for example, spent far less time doing child care than do modern working women, typically delegating this task to servants or older siblings. Among white families, patriarchal authority was so absolute

From *National Forum: The Phi Kappa Phi Journal*, Summer 1995, pp. 11-14. © 1995 by Stephanie Coontz. Reprinted by permission.

that disobedience by wife or child was seen as a small form of treason, theoretically punishable by death, and family relations were based on power, not love.

The Nineteenth-Century Family

With the emergence of a wage-labor system and a national market in the first third of the nineteenth century, white middle-class families became less patriarchal and more child-centered. The ideal of the male breadwinner and the nurturing mother now appeared. But the emergence of domesticity for middle-class women and children depended on its absence among the immigrant, working class, and African American women or children who worked as servants, grew the cotton, or toiled in the textile mills to free middle-class wives from the chores that had occupied their time previously.

Even in the minority of nineteenth-century families who could afford domesticity, though, emotional arrangements were quite different from nostalgic images of "traditional" families. Rigid insistence on separate spheres for men and women made male-female relations extremely stilted, so that women commonly turned to other women, not their husbands, for their most intimate relations. The idea that all of one's passionate feelings should go toward a member of the opposite sex was a twentieth-century invention — closely associated with the emergence of a mass consumer society and promulgated by the very film industry that "traditionalists" now blame for undermining such values.

Early Twentieth-Century Families

Throughout the nineteenth century, at least as much divergence and disruption in the experience of family life existed as does today, even though divorce and unwed motherhood were less common. Indeed, couples who marry today have a better chance of celebrating a fortieth wedding anniversary than at any previous time in history. The life cycles of nineteenth-century youth (in job entry, completion of schooling, age at marriage, and establishment of separate residence) were far more diverse than they became in the early twentieth-century. At the turn of the century a higher proportion of people remained single for their entire lives than at any period since. Not until the 1920s did a bare majority of children come to live in a male breadwinner-female homemaker family, and even at the height of this family form in the 1950s, only 60 percent of American children spent their entire childhoods in such a family.

years as unhealthy. From this family we get the idea that women are sexual, that youth is attractive, and that marriage should be the center of our emotional fulfillment.

Even aside from its lack of relevance to the lives of most immigrants, Mexican Americans, African Americans, rural families, and the urban poor, big contradictions existed between image and reality in the middle-class family ideal of the early twentieth century. This is the period when many Americans first accepted the idea that the family should be sacred from outside intervention; yet the development of the private, self-sufficient family depended on state intervention in the economy, government regulation of parent-child relations, and state-directed destruction of class and community institutions that hindered the development of family privacy.

Not until the 1920s did a bare majority of children come to live in a male breadwinner-female homemaker family . . . .

From about 1900 to the 1920s, the growth of mass production and emergence of a public policy aimed at establishing a family wage led to new ideas about family self-sufficiency, especially in the white middle class and a privileged sector of the working class. The resulting families lost their organic connection to intermediary units in society such as local shops, neighborhood work cultures and churches, ethnic associations, and mutual-aid organizations.

As families related more directly to the state, the market, and the mass media, they also developed a new cult of privacy, along with heightened expectations about the family's role in fostering individual fulfillment. New family values stressed the early independence of children and the romantic coupling of husband and wife, repudiating the intense same-sex ties and mother-infant bonding of earlier

Acceptance of a youth and leisure culture sanctioned early marriage and raised expectations about the quality of married life, but also introduced new tensions between the generations and new conflicts between husband and wife over what were adequate levels of financial and emotional support.

The nineteenth-century middle-class ideal of the family as a refuge from the world of work was surprisingly modest compared with emerging twentieth-century demands that the family provide a whole alternative world of satisfaction and intimacy to that of work and neighborhood. Where a family succeeded in doing so, people might find pleasures in the home never before imagined. But the new ideals also increased the possibilities for failure: America has had the highest divorce rate in the world since the turn of the century.

In the 1920s, these contradictions created a sense of foreboding about "the future of the family" that was every bit as widespread and intense as today's. Social scientists and popular commentators of the time hearkened back to the "good old days," bemoaning the sexual revolution, the fragility of nuclear family ties, the cult of youthful romance, the decline of respect for grandparents, and the threat of the "New Woman." But such criticism was sidetracked by the stock-market crash, the Great Depression of the 1930s, and the advent of World War II.

Domestic violence escalated during the Depression, while murder rates were as high in the 1930s as in the 1980s. Divorce rates fell, but desertion increased and fertility plummeted. The war stimulated a marriage boom, but by the late 1940s one in every three marriages was ending in divorce.

The 1950s Family

At the end of the 1940s, after the hardships of the Depression and war, many Americans revived the nuclear family ideals that had so disturbed commentators during the 1920s. The unprecedented postwar prosperity allowed young families to achieve consumer satisfactions and socioeconomic mobility that would have been inconceivable in earlier days. The 1950s family that resulted from these economic and cultural trends, however, was hardly "traditional." Indeed it is best seen as a historical aberration. For the first time in 100 years, divorce rates dropped, fertility soared, the gap between men's and women's job and educational prospects widened (making middle-class women more dependent on marriage), and the age of marriage fell—to the point that teenage birth rates were almost double what they are today.

Admirers of these very *nontraditional* 1950s family forms and values point out that household arrangements and gender roles were less diverse in the 1950s than today, and marriages more stable. But this was partly because diversity was ruthlessly suppressed and partly because economic and political support systems for socially-sanctioned families were far more generous than they are today. Real wages rose more in any single year of the 1950s than they did in the entire decade of the 1980s; the average thirty-year-old man could buy a median-priced home on 15 to 18 percent of his income. The government funded public investment, home ownership, and job creation at a rate more than triple that of the past two decades, while 40 percent of young men were eligible for veteran's benefits. Forming and maintaining families was far easier than it is today.

Yet the stability of these 1950s families did not guarantee good outcomes for their members. Even though most births occurred within wedlock, almost a third of American children lived in poverty during the 1950s, a higher figure than today. More than 50 percent of black married-couple families were poor. Women were often refused the right to serve on juries, sign contracts, take out credit cards in their own names, or establish legal residence. Wife-battering rates were low, but that was because wife-beating was seldom counted as a crime. Most victims of incest, such as Miss America of 1958, kept the secret of their fathers' abuse until the 1970s or 1980s, when the women's movement became powerful enough to offer them the support denied them in the 1950s.

The Post-1950s Family

In the 1960s, the civil rights, antiwar, and women's liberation movements exposed the racial, eco-

nomic, and sexual injustices that had been papered over by the Ozzie and Harriet images on television. Their activism made older kinds of public and private oppression unacceptable and helped create the incomplete, flawed, but much-needed reforms of the Great Society. Contrary to the big lie of the past decade that such programs caused our current family dilemmas, those antipoverty and social justice reforms helped overcome many of the family problems that prevailed in the 1950s.

In 1964, after fourteen years of unrivaled family stability and economic prosperity, the poverty rate was still 19 percent; in 1969, after five years of civil rights activism, the rebirth of feminism, and the institution of nontraditional if relatively modest government welfare programs, it was down to 12 percent, a low that has not been seen again since the social welfare cutbacks began in the late 1970s. In 1965, 20 percent of American children still lived in poverty; within five years, that had fallen to 15 percent. Infant mortality was cut in half between 1965 and 1980. The gap in nutrition between low-income Americans and other Americans narrowed significantly, as a direct result of food stamp and school lunch programs. In 1963, 20 percent of Americans living below the poverty line had *never* been examined by a physician; by 1970 this was true of only 8 percent of the poor.

Since 1973, however, real wages have been falling for most Americans. Attempts to counter this through tax revolts and spending freezes have led to drastic cutbacks in government investment programs. Corporations also spend far less on research and job creation than they did in the 1950s and 1960s, though the average compensation to executives has soared. The gap between rich and poor, according to the April 17, 1995, *New York Times*, is higher in the United

States than in any other industrial nation.

Family Stress

These inequities are *not* driven by changes in family forms, contrary to ideologues who persist

tain families. According to an Associated Press report of April 25, 1995, the median income of men aged twenty-five to thirty-four fell by 26 percent between 1972 and 1994, while the proportion of such men with earnings below the poverty level for a family of four more than doubled to 32 percent. The fig-

America needs more than a revival of the narrow family obligations of the 1950s, whose (greatly exaggerated) protection for white, middle-class children was achieved only at tremendous cost to the women in those families and to all those who could not or would not aspire to the Ozzie and Harriet ideal. We need a concern for children that goes beyond the question of whether a mother is waiting with cookies when her kids come home from school. We need a moral language that allows us to address something besides people's sexual habits. We need to build values and social institutions that can reconcile people's needs for independence with their equally important rights to dependence, and surely we must reject older solutions that involved balancing these needs on the backs of women. We will not find our answers in nostalgia for a mythical "traditional family."

. . . romanticizing "traditional" families and gender roles will not produce the changes . . . that would permit families to develop moral and ethical systems relevant to 1990s realities.

in confusing correlations with causes; but they certainly exacerbate such changes, and they tend to bring out the worst in *all* families. The result has been an accumulation of stresses on families, alongside some important expansions of personal options. Working couples with children try to balance three full-time jobs, as employers and schools cling to policies that assume every employee has a "wife" at home to take care of family matters. Divorce and remarriage have allowed many adults and children to escape from toxic family environments, yet our lack of social support networks and failure to forge new values for sustaining intergenerational obligations have let many children fall through the cracks in the process.

Meanwhile, young people find it harder and harder to form or sus-

ures are even worse for African American and Latino men. Poor individuals are twice as likely to divorce as more affluent ones, three to four times less likely to marry in the first place, and five to seven times more likely to have a child out of wedlock.

As conservatives insist, there is a moral crisis as well as an economic one in modern America: a pervasive sense of social alienation, new levels of violence, and a decreasing willingness to make sacrifices for others. But romanticizing "traditional" families and gender roles will not produce the changes in job structures, work policies, child care, medical practice, educational preparation, political discourse, and gender inequities that would permit families to develop moral and ethical systems relevant to 1990s realities.

Stephanie Coontz teaches history and family studies at The Evergreen State College in Olympia, Washington. Her publications include *The Way We Never Were: American Families and the Nostalgia Trap* and *The Way We Really Are: Coming to Terms with America's Changing Families* (both published by Basic Books). She is a recipient of the Washington Governor's Writer's Award and the Dale Richmond Award of the American Academy of Pediatrics.

FEMINISM & THE FAMILY
An indissoluble marriage

Mary Ann Glendon

I n September 1995, I had the honor of heading the Vatican delegation to the United Nations' Fourth Conference on Women held in Beijing. The conference's mandate was "Action for Equality, Development, and Peace." To what extent the conference advanced that mandate is open to question. I will try to explain why we seem to have seen so little progress toward those goals.

Beijing and the Old Feminism

As news reports indicated, there were actually two women's conferences in China in September 1995: the official UN conference where delegates and negotiators from 181 member states produced the final version of the document known as the Beijing Program of Action; and a larger, more colorful, unofficial conference held several miles away. This second conference was the NGO conference (nongovernmental organizations). The official conference was attended by 5,000 persons; the NGO conference was attended by 30,000.

The word "conference" in both cases is somewhat misleading. UN conferences would be more accurately described as dispersed negotiating sessions. Their main aim is to put the final touches on a document that has been circulating for years in draft form. To do this, the delegates split up into groups to go over different sections of the document, paragraph by paragraph, trying to reach consensus on the

Mary Ann Glendon *is the Learned Hand Professor of Law at Harvard University. Her most recent book is* A Nation under Lawyers *(Harvard University Press). This article is adapted from a talk given to the Berkshire County Pregnancy Assistance Association.*

final text that will be submitted for approval when the whole group comes together on the last day. As for the so-called NGO conference with its 30,000 participants, you wouldn't be far wrong if you translated "conference" in that setting as "lobbyists' headquarters," and "NGO" as "special-interest group."

Like most UN conference documents, the statement that emerged after two weeks of negotiations was a set of nonbinding guidelines for future action. The Beijing statement set a UN record for length at 125 pages, single-spaced. The document contains many very fine proposals regarding women's access to education and employment, and the feminization of poverty. But it is marred by two serious defects.

The first is that the best parts of the Beijing program—especially the ones I just mentioned—are the most likely to remain dead letters because they require funding. If there was anything that united the rich countries at Beijing, it was their successful fight to keep out any language that would commit them to back up their fine promises with material resources.

The second defect also involves something that was left out. It is nothing short of amazing, in a world where over eight out of ten women have children, that a 125-page program of action produced at a *women's* conference barely mentions marriage, motherhood, or family life!

The reaction of most women to this document, I suspect, would be similar to that of a young Nigerian law student who wrote me recently. She couldn't afford to go to the conference, but she tried to follow it closely from afar. She was disappointed, she said, that the conference had paid so little attention to the problems that the majority of the world's women struggle with on a daily basis. She was surprised, for example, that the section on women's health was focused almost entirely on women's reproductive systems. She wondered why it didn't address the health of the whole woman, particularly the problems of poor nutrition, sanitation, and tropical disease that have a disproportionate impact on women. (Keep in mind that women and girls compose 70 percent of the world's poverty population.)

And even the treatment of reproductive health in the document is strange, since it focuses almost entirely on birth control and abortion—as though reproductive health did not include pregnancy and childbirth.

How are these omissions to be explained? For the answer, you only have to look at the original draft document prepared by the UN Committee on the Status of Women. In the few places where the drafting committee mentioned marriage, motherhood, or family life, these aspects of women's lives were described in a negative way—as sources of oppression, or as obstacles to women's progress. In other words, what we had to work with in Beijing was a document whose defects corresponded rather closely to the defects of 1970s' feminism. A negative attitude toward men and marriage and the same lack of attention to the problems of women who are mothers were starkly evident.

The conference document is not legally binding. It is in the form of "international standards" against which UN member states are supposed to measure their conduct. So why all the fuss and lobbying about a set of nonbinding guidelines?

The main reason is this: Government agencies and private foundations tend to use these UN documents (I should say, selected parts of these documents) to justify the way they run their foreign and domestic programs. That means that, when they announce policies and set conditions, they don't have to invoke the modern version of the golden rule ("We've got the gold, so we make the rules"). It sounds so much better to say: "We follow guidelines established by international consensus." *But the bottom line is that millions of people's lives are affected by a kind of rule-making as far removed as possible from public scrutiny and democratic participation.*

That fact makes these UN conferences magnets for all sorts of special-interest groups, especially those who want to do an end-run around ordinary political processes. It's tempting for them to try to plant their agendas in a long, unreadable document, behind closed doors at a conference held in some faraway place. (When I say closed doors, I mean that literally. All the negotiating sessions in Beijing were closed to the public and the press.)

The Beijing conference offers two lessons for those of us who are concerned with women's issues in the '90s. First, beware of policies manufactured far away from public scrutiny, and without input from the people most concerned. Second, it seems to me the conference was more about the women's ideology of the '70s than about women's issues in the '90s. Beijing was like a Woodstock reunion. Moreover,

it showed that the handwriting is on the wall for the peculiar form of feminism that held sway in the 1960s and 1970s. And the message on the wall is the same that was written in the Book of Daniel: "You have been weighed in the balance and found wanting."

That point was reinforced for me by the conversations I had with my students when I returned from Beijing. The very first question the women law students asked had never occurred to me. "What was the average age of the women at the conference?" Looking back, I realized that there was almost no one there under forty. Most were in their late forties, fifties, or sixties. Many, like Bella Abzug and Betty Friedan, were older.

Incidentally, I find it amusing that the attitudes of my women students' toward legendary figures like Abzug and Friedan are similar to the way my generation thought about Susan B. Anthony and the suffragettes. We admired them for securing the vote for women, but we didn't identify with them. To us, they seemed quaint, and a bit strange. Similarly, my students seem grateful to the second-wave women's movement for the educational and employment opportunities they now enjoy, but they're ready to move on to new frontiers. In the opinion polls of the '90s, when women are asked, "Do you consider yourself a feminist?" two-thirds of American women answer no. What's even more striking is the response of younger women. Among college women in their twenties, four out of five say they do not consider themselves feminists.

What is the message that large majorities of women are sending to organized feminism? Betty Friedan herself, I believe, has read it correctly. The message seems to be that official feminism hasn't been listening to the women who are too busy to be in movements, that it is out of touch with the real-life concerns of most women today. In a recent *New Yorker* article, Friedan urges feminists to wake up to the fact that "the most urgent concerns of women today are not gender issues but jobs and families." And whom did we see on the cover of *Time* magazine as the key voter in the 1996 elections? An exhausted, frazzled, working mother. The issue on her mind? Job and family.

I've observed a similar shift in attitude even among my career-oriented law students. Law schools were strongholds of feminism in the late '70s when women were a minority. But now that women make up nearly half the student body (and are more representative of the female population), I hear much more concern about how you can have a decent family life without suffering excessive career disadvantages. And, most significant of all, in my view, is that this worry seems to be bothering the young men almost as much as it concerns the women.

The signs of shifting attitudes among men lead to a point I'll discuss later on: the sense in which women's issues of the '90s are everybody's issues. But first, it must be noted that many issues confront men and women in significantly different ways, especially where the women concerned are, or hope to be, mothers. Let me give you some examples of that differential impact.

Women's Issues of the '90s

A major issue for the women's movement of the 1970s was the "gender gap" between men's and women's wages. You may recall we used to hear that for every dollar earned by a man, a woman made 60 cents. Today, women's opportunities have improved to the point where there is virtually no gender gap between the earnings of women and men *who have made similar life choices.* Among young adults who have never had children, women's earnings are now nearly 98 percent of men's earnings.

But something is wrong with that picture. Why do we talk about women in the abstract when the great majority of women (about 85 percent in the United States) are mothers? The women who are disadvantaged in the workplace are not women in the abstract, but women who are raising children. And the real income gap in this country is between child-raising families and other types of households.

Another good example of the different form that the

> *Motherhood in our society is a pretty risky occupation. Ironically, women in the abstract have never had more rights, but rarely has the position of mothers been more precarious.*

work-family dilemma takes for men and women is what happens when a child-raising family is broken up by divorce. (Keep in mind here that the majority of all divorces, 57 percent, involve couples with children under sixteen.) There is no doubt that the rise in divorce has had a disproportionate effect on women. After divorce it is nearly always the mother who remains primarily responsible for the physical care of the children; the father's standard of living typically rises, while that of the mother and children declines—in all too many cases below the poverty line.

To put it another way, motherhood in our society is a pretty risky occupation. Ironically, women in the abstract have never had more rights, but rarely has the position

of mothers been more precarious. Women have tried to protect themselves and their children against the risks they face in two ways: They're having fewer children, and they're maintaining at least a foothold in the labor force even when their children are very young. But that strategy still does not protect them very well against what we might call the four deadly Ds: disrespect for unpaid work in the home; disadvantages in the workplace for anyone who takes time out for family responsibilities; divorce; and destitution, a condition that afflicts so many female-headed families.

As if that were not enough, many women now find themselves facing what might be called "Work-Family Dilemma II": no sooner has the last child left home than the needs of aging parents start the process of juggling job and family responsibilities all over again.

The fact is that we are in a situation where the experience of past generations gives little guidance. Now that most women are in the labor force, no one has yet come up with a good solution to the problem of who performs the caretaking work for children and for the elderly that women used to do, for free. The idea of some social conservatives is that women should "just stay home" (unless they're welfare mothers, in which case off to work they must go). I can't help thinking that the "just stay home" idea is a bit like what the chicken said to the pig when they were trying to think what they could give Old MacDonald for a birthday present. The chicken said: "How about a nice breakfast of bacon and eggs—I'll provide the eggs and you give the bacon." You can see why the pig was not enthusiastic about that division of labor.

Another set of problems that will have a disparate impact on women is just beginning to come into view. Thanks to medical advances, we have never had such a large elderly population. As you know, that group includes more women than men. At the same time, we know that much of the burden of supporting that population will fall on the shoulders of a labor force that is growing proportionately smaller.

Against that background, a real concern about the assisted-suicide movement is the pressure that is going to be exerted on elderly people in failing health to cease using up scarce resources. When you consider that three out of four poor Americans over sixty-five are women, you can see that this is yet another issue that is everybody's issue, but that will affect women in a special way. It is sobering to think that more than two-thirds of the people Dr. Jack Kevorkian has helped to die are women.

Assisted suicide also involves the political problem mentioned earlier in connection with Beijing—the question of who settles whose hash. The "right to die" (like the right to abortion) is being pushed mainly by the kind of people who are accustomed to having a lot of control over their lives. The outcome of the debate over this issue is likely to be determined by judges—who are also people who are used to having a lot of control over their lives.

To privileged folks, the right to die may look like an aspect of personal freedom—a way of feeling in control until the very end. In the case of such people, it may well work out that way. But how is it going to work out for the less fortunate, the people who are in the most danger of being regarded as burdensome to their families and a drag on the taxpayers of the welfare state? What is a "right to die" for some may well become a "duty to die" for others. And if that happens, women, again, will be most affected.

Consider the ways in which, despite the disparate impact on women, all these problems are everybody's problems. One of the main sources of discontent with the old feminism was the way it set women and men at odds with one another. Now we're beginning to realize that we're all in this thing together. In the world of work, men as well as women are increasingly chafing under pressures to put the demands of the job ahead of the needs of their families. Both men and women are increasingly realizing that feminists have always had a strong point when they complained that society gives little respect or security to people who make sacrifices for their children and families. Ironically, the '70s feminists bought into that disrespect. By treating marriage and motherhood as obstacles to women's progress, they actually helped to reinforce the idea that the only work that counts is work for pay outside the home.

But while feminists were maintaining, correctly, that society doesn't respect work in the home, things were changing in the workplace outside the home. In all too many ways the new globalized economy is sending the same message to working men and women that society once sent to homemakers: that they and the work they do are not worthy of much respect.

Monsignor George Higgins, a longtime advocate of the rights of workers, asked some important questions in a recent speech. When a profitable company "downsizes," doesn't that tell dedicated employees that their years of service don't really count for much? When employees' wages stagnate while their companies prosper, aren't working people being told that their effort and skill aren't valued? And when benefits like health insurance and pensions are cut back, doesn't that tell working people that nobody cares what happens when they get sick and old? To those questions, you might add: What scale of values rewards some CEOs to the tune of $200 million a year (head of Disney) while moms and dads must work harder than ever to counter a relative decline in real family income?

All these are men's and women's issues. They are family issues. They are issues about what kind of society we want to try to hand on to future generations. Something is wrong when most jobs are too rigidly structured to accommodate family responsibilities. Something is wrong when we frame laws and policies as though human beings existed to serve the economy, rather than the other way round. In the long run, that's not even good for the economy. To spell out the obvious: a healthy economy requires a certain kind of work force, with certain skills and qualities of character. And those qualities—honesty, a work ethic, and the ability to cooperate with others—are going to be acquired, for the most part, in the nation's families or not at all.

Having said that, it is not easy to imagine what can be done about all this. Some factors, such as worldwide economic developments, may be outside the control of any one country. Other factors, let's admit it, are more related to the materialistic excesses of a consumer society than to basic family needs. We Americans do have a tendency to want to "have it all." But anyone who has tried to combine work and family life knows that we can't have it all. You're always shortchanging somebody somewhere—one day it's the job, the next it's your spouse, or your children. The grown-up question is not can all our dreams come true. The real question is whether we can do better than we're doing now. Is it possible to harmonize women's and men's roles in social and economic life with their desires (and their children's needs) for a decent family life?

I would say it's possible—but that the prospects are dim, unless society as a whole is prepared to recognize that when mothers and fathers raise their children well, they are not just doing something for themselves and their own children, but for all of us. Governments, private employers, and fellow citizens would all have to recognize that we all owe an enormous debt to parents who do a good job raising their children under today's difficult conditions. There's something heroic about the everyday sacrifices that people have to make these days just to do the right thing by their nearest and dearest.

What is to be done?

The above observations bring me to the realm of politics. I want to focus on one basic problem: the problem of how American men and women can gain a say in the decisions that shape their lives and livelihoods—a voice in our jobs, in our children's education, in our communities, and in the direction our country is taking.

Is that problem soluble? A glance around the social landscape is not particularly reassuring. Something is terribly wrong when Americans from every viewpoint and every walk of life are beginning to feel that the forces that govern our economic and political lives have spun out of control; and when parents feel that they are losing the struggle for the hearts and minds of their own children.

There has been much speculation about why Americans seem uninterested in voting and in the electoral process generally. That disaffection just might have something to do with the perception that both political parties are out of touch with citizens' deepest concerns. Reporting on political party finances shows that that common perception isn't uninformed. Both political parties are heavily financed by big business—the Democrats by the kinds of businesses that make their livings from government, and the Republicans by the kinds of businesses that just want government to butt out. Yes, the Democrats throw a few crumbs to working men and women. Yes, the Republicans throw a few crumbs to those who are concerned about the moral fabric of society. But it's been a long time since either party has done much for constituents whose main concerns are a decent job and decent conditions for raising a family.

My one suggestion for a possible solution to this problem is likely to make many people groan, but I can see no other alternative. Simply put, more of us have to take a more active role in politics. Frustration with a distant, unresponsive government is nothing new in America. Indeed, this nation was founded in the rejection of unresponsive government. The constitutional convention in Philadelphia produced an ingenious design for a republic with democratic elements. (Not a pure democracy, but a republic in which the democratic elements were extremely important.) To protect those democratic elements, the Bill of Rights specified that all powers not expressly delegated to the federal government, or forbidden to the states, are reserved to the states and the people. That's the forgotten part of the Bill of Rights—the Tenth Amendment. You'll wait a long time before you hear a peep about the powers reserved to the people from the groups that are self-appointed defenders of our civil liberties. Yet what liberty is more basic than the freedom to participate in setting the conditions under which we live, work, and raise our families?

Now it seems that many people are tempted to give up on the idea that we, especially at the local level, can help to make things better. They're tempted to give up on the idea that we could ever take back democratic institutions; that we could ever restore decision-making power to the many who have the most to lose from the few who have the most to gain. But, to be honest, the women and men who have gone before us often faced much greater challenges than we do now. Do we really want to be the generation who didn't even try to turn things around? After all, this isn't Eastern Europe where the men and women who toppled authoritarian regimes are now struggling to build democratic government from scratch. We have the machinery at hand. We've had it for over 200 years. It's rusty, but it's there. Let's use it. □

AMONG THE
PROMISE KEEPERS

NEW AGE JOURNAL
Jeff Wagenheim

An inside look at the evangelical men's movement

The jam-packed stadium is a stunning spectacle of men, smiling and back-slapping men, cheering and foot-stomping men, good old boys alongside bad-looking hombres. There are father and son pairs everywhere—some with Dad in his 30s, others in which Junior looks to be about that age. There are bearded, scraggly bikers in black leather, their Harleys parked out in the lot—probably right next to the Chrysler minivans that brought in the groups of clean-scrubbed athletic types dressed in caps and T-shirts bearing football team insignias, looking like they've come to Texas Stadium to root for its home team, the Dallas Cowboys.

But this crowd's Sunday hero doesn't wear shoulder pads and a helmet. That point is being made loud and clear by a chant arising from one section of sideline seats and rocking the place all the way to the upper deck: "We love Jesus, yes we do," a thousand men are proclaiming in one voice. "*We* love Jesus, how 'bout *you*?" Cheers of spirited affirmation explode from the other sideline, followed by an answer: "*We* love Jesus, yes we do . . ."

Promise Keepers is a puzzle. What to make of an organization that seems to combine the men's movement of Robert Bly with the conservative Christianity of Pat Robertson? Perhaps this Bible-based work fills a void for men who feel safer in the sanctity of their inner holy man than in the company of that threatening wild man. But could the group also be a shrewdly disguised vehicle for furthering the political agenda of the religious right?

Promise Keepers was founded in 1990 by Bill McCartney, who until recently served as head coach of the University of Colorado football team. With the same fiery faithfulness he used to evaluate the Buffaloes into college football's elite, McCartney has transformed his weekly prayer and fellowship group of 72 men into an organization that today has twice that many *employees*. After holding men's conferences in Boulder in each of its first three summers and achieving its goal of filling 50,000-seat Folsom Field in 1993, Promise Keepers took the show on the road in 1994, reaching nearly 300,000 men in seven stadiums around the country. The 1995 schedule included 13 stadium-sized events that attracted more than 700,000 men. The organization is trying to ride its runaway momentum to draw a million men to a gathering in Washington in 1996.

How to explain this group's burgeoning growth? Looking for answers, I bought a copy of *Seven Promises of a Promise Keeper*, a collection of essays that has become the Promise Keepers' second bible. Though most of what the book's numerous contributors write is loving, commitment-affirming guidance, there are passages here and there that you definitely won't find excerpted in *Ms.* magazine.

Instructing husbands how to reclaim their manhood, for instance, pastor Tony Evans writes: "The first thing you do is sit down with your wife and say something like this: 'Honey, I've made a terrible mistake. I've given you my role. I gave up leading this family, and I forced you to take my place. Now I must reclaim that role.' Don't misunderstand what I'm saying here. I'm not suggesting that you *ask* for your role back, I'm urging you to *take it back*.... Be sensitive. Listen. Treat the lady gently and lovingly. But *lead*!"

That's a stance that spooks feminists. And gays are nervous about the ramifications of the group's position statement that "homosexuality violates God's creative design for a husband and a wife and . . . is a sin." Protests have dogged each summer's Promise Keepers gathering in Boulder, the acrimony coming to a head in 1993 when the group filled Folsom Field for the first time.

What brought out the opposition, I suspect, was not the essays in *Seven Promises* or even what was being said at the gatherings so much as the controversial politics of Bill McCartney. The charismatic coach first made headlines back in the mid-'80s when he battled the American Civil Liberties Union over his practice of leading the team in pregame prayer. His notoriety reached a peak in 1992 during the debate over Amendment 2, a state ballot question aimed at blocking civil rights guarantees for gays and lesbians. After McCartney authorized the amendment's

resentative Patricia Schroeder (D-Colo.) called McCartney a "self-anointed ayatollah."

But McCartney seems to be more enigma than ayatollah. At the same time that he was taking his civil rights–denying stance regarding gays, he was a vocal and demonstrative supporter of racial equality—the only head coach in Division I-A, in fact, to have on his staff as many black coaches as white. And when he resigned in January 1995 and his longtime assistant Bob Simmons was passed over for a less-experienced white replacement, McCartney sided with an unlikely ally, the Reverend Jesse Jackson, in charging racism.

I was guessing that Promise Keepers, McCartney's current focus, was similarly complex. There was only one way to find out what was really going on.

The unmoving line of cars ahead of me must extend all the way to the gates of heaven. At least it seems that way. It's 9 o'clock on a Saturday morning in October, I've just hit a freeway ramp traffic jam at the Texas Stadium exit, and from the looks of things I ought to be inside for the second day of the event by, oh, around noon.

On the radio I hear that chant: "*We* love Jesus, yes we do . . ." I park my car and walk the half-mile to the stadium. Surveying the scene outside, I notice that there are no protesters. No message-toting airplane circling the stadium. Well, there are two signs: I NEED TICKETS, held by a guy who looks like he thinks he's outside a Dead show, and MEN OF GOD: I NEED A JOB, held by a neatly dressed black man of 40 or so who is offered encouragement by men in the passing, mostly white, crowd.

In the parking lots nearest the main stadium gates are a few large tents—one for registration (a surprisingly rea-

---

What to make of an organization that seems to combine the men's movement of Robert Bly with the conservative Christianity of Pat Robertson?

---

sponsor, Colorado for Family Values, to use his name and affiliation on its fund-raising letters, the university received complaints about this apparent violation of policy. The coach agreed to ask the anti–gay rights crusaders to drop his name from their printed materials and called a news conference to make the announcement. There, McCartney proceeded to urge Coloradans to support Amendment 2 and termed homosexuality "an abomination of almighty God." This prompted campus protests and a reprimand from the university president. U.S. Rep-

sonable $55, including two meals), one for dispensing literature about related organizations (Christian Men's Network, Focus on the Family, etc.), one for selling Promise Keepers books and merchandise. These tents and other projects of the day—such as setting up 45,000 box lunches—are being run almost exclusively by women. "We're all here as volunteers supporting this ministry and the men in our lives," says the middle-aged woman behind the cash register. "I'm here with my husband. This is his second event, and after the last one he was a changed person. Attentive. Positive attitude. Closer to God. So I'm happy to help an organization that has had such a positive effect on our marriage."

As I finally enter the stadium, Christian Men's Network president Edwin Cole steps to the microphone and launches into a fire-and-brimstone sermon preaching celibacy until marriage. For a while Cole sounds—dare I say it?—positively feminist as he talks about how respect for women is lost when a man is pursuing sex without love. Then, suddenly, per Cole's request, dozens of young men all around the stadium are standing to take a vow of chastity, and nearby men are moving closer to them to lay a hand of support on their bodies, all heads nodded in prayer.

The only overtly political statement of the weekend comes in the conference's very first speech, by pastor Greg Laurie. "When a man makes a promise to his wife—a marriage vow—and doesn't keep it, he is teaching her not to trust him," he says. "And isn't it true that we have a problem like this with some of our leaders today?" Wild applause. "I see some of you are ahead of me," says Laurie with a smile.

That shared humor at the president's expense reveals something about these men that I have trouble overlooking: When push comes to shove, these and the thousands of other Promise Keepers are likely to pull voting-

nication. This doesn't look like a bunch of guys working toward becoming tyrants in their households.

Throughout the weekend, as conference speakers delve deeper and deeper into issues that tear couples and families apart—a husband or father being emotionally distant or neglecting his responsibilities are among the common ones—I notice that some of the men seem to be fighting back tears, while a few have no fight left: They're crying freely as the men around them offer the comfort of a touch, an embrace, or a quiet word.

Near the end of the weekend, when Chuck Swindoll, president of the Dallas Theological Seminary, leads the men through the seven promises that this conference is all about, there's a hush in the stadium. He explains, step by step, precisely what it means for a man to commit himself to, say, "pursuing vital relationships with a few other men, understanding that he needs brothers to help him keep his promises." The discussion-and-response process is slow and thoughtful, and it downshifts noticeably when Swindoll gets to Promise Number Six: "A Promise Keeper is committed to reaching beyond any racial and denominational barriers to demonstrate the power of biblical unity."

"This one may be an especially difficult one for men raised in the South," Swindoll says. "So think about it, and

---

I'm stunned by all the heartfelt discussions of romance and communication. This doesn't look like a bunch of guys working toward becoming tyrants in their households.

---

booth levers to abolish abortion or curtail gay rights. Ultimately, these men are a voting bloc—an evangelical Christian voting bloc.

Still, this *is* a complex gathering. Gary Smalley—the president of Today's Family, whom you may have seen on late-night cable TV hawking his better-relationships videotape series through infomercials featuring couples such as Kathie Lee and Frank Gifford—is responsible for one of the most moving moments of the weekend. At the time I am standing in the press box, high above the playing field. Smalley is finishing up on the topic of expressiveness in marriage, and he asks the men to break into groups of four or five to discuss pet peeves and possibilities.

In small groups, the men come alive—even in the press box, where a couple of small groups form to discuss marital issues. I've never seen reporters participate in anything like this. For the next 15 minutes I'm stunned by all the heartfelt discussions of romance and commu-

do not commit to this or any promise unless you can keep it. This is what being a Promise Keeper is all about."

The organization does take an uncharacteristically progressive approach to the difficult issue of racial reconciliation. "I've been at Promise Keepers meetings where men have broken down and cried and renounced their prejudice and hatred," says the Reverend Edgar Vann Jr., pastor of the Second Ebeneezer Baptist Church in Detroit. "You just don't often see that in the church."

After spending a weekend with Promise Keepers, I believe that the organization's commitment to these issues is sincere. I was made to feel accepted in my every contact with the Promise Keepers staff, conference participants, and Christian reporters in the press box—even after I would identify myself as an editor at, gulp, *New Age Journal*.

Still, whenever a Promise Keeper drew me into a discussion—on anything from culture to theology—I would get the feeling I was talking to a brick wall. A friendly and talkative brick wall, but an unmovable object nonetheless. It was either his Scripture-based worldview—homosexuality as an abomination, the husband as "leader" in the home—or . . . *splat*.

Promise Keepers president Randy Phillips maintains that that "leadership" role is deeper and better than male chauvinism. "It comes down to whether you understand what it is to be a spiritual leader, which we define in the person of Jesus Christ," he says. "What did Jesus do to respond to the needs of others? He gave his life for others. So, from a biblical perspective, a spiritual leader is not one who lords authority over others; spiritual leadership is the absolute commitment to serve and to honor. It means involving yourself in the life of your wife, hearing her needs and responding to those needs, just like Jesus responded to our needs. . . . There is responsibility in providing spiritual initiative and there is authority in carrying out those responsibilities, but it is expressed through a servant's heart."

With rhetoric like that, notes the Reverend Priscilla Inkpen, a United Church of Christ minister from Boulder who has been one of the group's more prominent opponents, "It's difficult to be 100 percent critical of the Promise Keepers. I think they are speaking to an important need: for men to take responsibility. A lot of men need to learn that, and Promise Keepers seems to be touching a nerve with many. But . . . you have to ask: What nerve are they touching? Is it men's hunger to be present in their relationships with their wives and children? Or is it the hunger to be on top?"

Jeff Wagenheim is a contributing editor of New Age Journal.

African American Families

A Legacy of Vulnerability and Resilience

African Americans, despite a legacy of stigmatizing psychological folklore and an antagonistic environment manifested in centuries of racial discrimination, display an undeniable development of adaptive coping strategies and resilience. Understanding the realities in the lives of contemporary African American families requires an examination of the history of African Americans in the United States.

Beverly Greene

African Americans are one of the oldest and largest groups of persons of color in the United States. The first census in 1790 counted 760,000 African Americans. By 1990, over 30,000,000 were counted. African Americans are descendants of people who belonged to the tribes of the West African coast and were the primary objects of the U.S. slave trade. Many African Americans have Native American and European ancestry as well.

They are perhaps the only ethnic group in the United States whose immigration was wholly involuntary. Entry into the United States was not, as it was for members of white ethnic groups and other groups of persons of color, the result of an effort to better their circumstances or find a more advantageous political climate than their homeland could offer. Instead of bettering their circumstances, their forced departure from the West African coast resulted in pervasive losses. Aside from the loss of life for many, there was a loss of community, the loss of original languages, and the loss of status as human beings for those who survived the Atlantic Passage.

As slaves, literally deprived of all human rights, they were to provide free labor and were bought and sold as any other commodity. Their children were salable commodities as well. In this system, family attachments were routinely ignored as slaves were transported, sold, and regarded as livestock with no regard for their family or important emotional ties. In this context, slave families came to place less emphasis on the role of biological parents because most children were separated from and not raised by them. Rather, children were informally "adopted" and raised by other people in their immediate community in extended rather than nuclear family arrangements. These extended family arrangements are still a prominent feature of contemporary African American families and may be considered a major survival tool.

The struggles of African Americans are often viewed as if they ended with emancipation. This belief ignores over a century more of legal racial discrimination that led to the civil rights struggles which reached a peak in the 1950s and 1960s. Even in the wake of legislation designed to make racial discrimination illegal, discrimination in more subtle, institutionalized forms still operates to this day in ways that continue to challenge the optimal physical, psychological, and economic well-being of African Americans.

Characteristics of African American Families

Characteristics of contemporary African American families represent an interaction of African cultural derivatives, the need to adapt to a racially antagonistic environment, and the influence of American cultural imperatives. They include extended networks of kinship between family members and persons who are not blood-related in complex networks of obligation and support. African Americans as a group are geographically and socioeconomically diverse. However, they share both cultural origins and the need to manage the anxieties and prejudices of a dominant group that is culturally different and that discriminates against African Americans both actively and passively on the basis of race. In some form, all African Americans must make psychological sense out of their disparaged condition, deflect hostility from the dominant group, and negotiate racial barriers under a wide range of circumstances. If the group is to survive, the members must teach their children to do so as well.

In this regard, African American parents have a special task and a unique stressor that are not shared by their white counterparts.

These consist of the special things they must do to prepare their children to function in an adaptive fashion without internalizing the dominant culture's negative messages about African American people. In *Children of Color*, Allen and Majidi-Ahi note that teaching African American children how to cope with racism represents a socialization issue that exemplifies all that is distinct about the African American experience in America. A major component of this experience entails the task of communicating to African American children the racial realities and dangers of the world, how to correctly identify and

cope with the resulting barriers, and how to seek support for the feelings evoked when confronting these barriers.

Succeeding Against Odds

Despite many historical and contemporary obstacles, African Americans have succeeded against many overwhelming odds in every generation. African American families are an important source of socialization and support for their members and can be an important translator of the dominant culture for African American children. At its best, this system teaches African American children to imitate and function in the dominant culture without believing that its demeaning images of African Americans are true.

Another role of the family is to pass along different kinds of successful coping strategies against racism. One strategy, the heightened sensitivity to the potential for exploitation by white persons, has been referred to by Grier and Cobbs in *Black Rage* as cultural paranoia. While this heightened sensitivity often has been pathologized by the dominant culture, it is a realistic and adaptive way of approaching situations that have frequently been antagonistic. Hopson and Hopson in *Different and Wonderful* suggest that another important coping strategy and a major source of psychological

. . . all African Americans must make psychological sense out of their disparaged condition, deflect hostility from the dominant group, and negotiate racial barriers under a wide range of circumstances.

resilience is reflected in the sharing of African cultural derivatives with children while encouraging them to take pride in their ancestry. In *Long Memory*, Mary Berry and John Blassingame note that each generation of African Americans prepares the next for survival in a society that devalues them by passing along "searing vignettes" about what has preceded them. They view this process as a long collective memory that is in and of itself an instrument of survival.

African American families must do all of these things in addition to providing the normal range of basic necessities that all families must provide for their children. In the context of a racist society, however, African American families' ability to do this may be compromised by the institutional barriers that providers in the family invariably confront. In these scenarios there may be a drain on the family's emotional and material resources, making the extended family structure an important resource in this regard. Sharing the burden of child care and child rearing helps to ease this burden in many families and can be seen as an example of resilience.

Multiple Mothering

In *Black Families*, Nancy Boyd-Franklin gives one example of this in what she describes as "multiple mothering." "Multiple mothers" refers to grandmothers, aunts, cousins, close friends, or people considered "kin" to a child's mother. They need not be biologically related. These multiple mothers provide

emotional safety valves, sounding boards, and alternative role models to children while often providing their real mothers with important tangible support in the form of child care. These arrangements also emphasize the important role for elder members of the family and the importance of their connection to members of the next generation. It is important to remember this extended family structure when viewing "single-parent families." The fact that African American families may deviate in structure from the White Anglo Saxon Protestant norm does not warrant pathologizing them or presuming that this deviation accounts for family problems.

In what appear to be many

single-parent families, extensive networks of other family members, family friends, neighbors, and others are routinely involved in the caretaking of children. Hence, the unmarried status of the mother does not automatically tell us what the rest of the family structure is like. The single-parent family as a large and diverse group among African Americans is not synonymous with teenaged or underaged mothers. Becoming a parent before one is biologically and emotionally mature, or when it interferes with important developmental tasks of the parent, is certainly not what is recommended. Rather, I suggest that African American family structures be viewed as perhaps having a wider range of flexibility in what is available to its members, reflected

The single-parent family as a large and diverse group among African Americans is not synonymous with teenaged or underaged mothers.

in a wider range of persons, in addition to biological parents, involved in parenting roles.

Gender Role Flexibility

Robert Hill, in *The Strengths of Black Families*, identifies major characteristics of African American families: strong kinship bonds, a strong achievement motivation, a strong religious and spiritual orientation, and a strong work orientation. Hill views these characteristics as strengths that have helped African Americans survive and function under difficult circumstances. He further cites gender-role flexibility as an important and adaptive characteristic of African

American families. This flexibility in gender roles is explained in part as a derivative of the value of interdependence among group members, typical of Western African precolonial cultures, that is unlike the value of rugged individualism of the West. It is also a function of the need to adapt to racism in the United States in many different ways.

One of the features that distinguished African American women from their white counterparts was their role as workers. Aside from being brought into the country as slaves whose primary function was to work, the status of African American women as slaves superseded their status as women. Hence they were not given the courtesies of femininity that were routinely accorded white women. Conventions of femininity considered many forms of labor that were routine for white males inappropriate for white females. Slavery deprived African American women of this protection, and as such their roles as workers did not differ from those of African American males. Hence at the very outset, rigid gender-role stratification among African Americans was not permitted. Later, because African American men faced significant racial barriers in the workplace and could not fit the idealized image of the Western male provider, women were forced to work to help support the home. Thus, the dominant cultural norm of women remaining in the home while men worked outside the home was never a practical reality for African American families.

This does not mean that there is no sexism within African American families. Tensions are often produced when African American men internalize the dominant culture's value of male domination and female subordination. Working women become the targets of African American male frustration rather than institutional racism. Despite such occurrences, flexibility in gender roles represents another example of an adaptive strategy that has contributed to the survival of African American families.

Summary

African American families have functioned under a legacy of challenges to their survival, beginning with slavery when families were not allowed to exist and when they were continually disrupted by abrupt and permanent separations. Surviving these disruptions, African American families have continued to demonstrate their flexibility and resilience under many adverse circumstances. It is not surprising that many African American families would be in crisis, given the range of routine assaults they face. What is more surprising is that many of these families display a remarkable legacy of adaptive strengths. James Comer, in *Maggie's American Dream*, reminds us that what we learn from survivors will tell us more about the circumvention of problems than will an exclusive focus on victims. African Americans are, if anything, survivors of historical and contemporary circumstances that may increase their vulnerability. However, as survivors they have much to teach us about resilience.

Beverly Greene is a professor of psychology at St. John's University and a clinical psychologist in private practice in New York City. A Fellow of the American Psychological Association and the recipient of national awards for her distinguished professional contributions, she is a coeditor of *Women of Color: Integrating Ethnic and Gender Identities in Psychotherapy*.

Gay Families Come Out

SAME-SEX PARENTS are trying to move out of the shadows and into the mainstream. Will they—and their kids—be accepted?

By Barbara Kantrowitz

THERE WERE MOMENTS IN Claire's childhood that seemed to call for a little . . . ingenuity. Like when friends came over. How could she explain the presence of Dorothy, the woman who moved into her Chicago home after Claire's dad left? Sometimes Claire said Dorothy was the housekeeper; other times she was an "aunt." In the living room, Claire would cover up the titles of books like "Lesbian Love Stories." More than a decade later, Claire's mother, Lee, recalls silently watching her daughter at the bookcase. It was, she says, "extremely painful to me." Even today, Lee and Claire—now 24 and recently married—want to be identified only by their middle names because they're worried about what their co-workers might think.

Hundreds of miles away, a 5-year-old girl named Lily lives in a toy-filled house with her mommies—Abby Rubenfeld, 43, a Nashville lawyer, and Debra Alberts, 38, a drug- and alcohol-abuse counselor who quit working to stay home. Rubenfeld and Alberts don't feel they should have to hide their relationship. It is, after all, the '90s, when companies like IBM offer gay partners the same benefits as husbands and wives, and celebrity couples like Melissa Etheridge and Julie Cypher proudly announce their expectant motherhood.

Lily was conceived in a very '90s way; her father, Jim Hough, is a gay lawyer in New York who once worked as Rubenfeld's assistant and had always wanted to have kids. He flew to Nashville and the trio discussed his general health, his HIV status (negative) and logistics. They decided Rubenfeld would bear the child because Alberts is diabetic and pregnancy could be dangerous. They all signed a contract specifying that Hough has no financial or legal obligation. Then Rubenfeld figured out when she would be ovulating, and Hough flew down to donate his sperm so Alberts could artificially inseminate her at home. Nine months later, Lily was born.

Two daughters, two very different families. One haunted by secrecy, the other determined to be open. In the last few years, families headed by gay parents have stepped out of the shadows and moved toward the mainstream. Researchers believe the number of gay families is steadily increasing, although no one knows exactly how many there are. Estimates range from 6 million to 14 million children with at least one gay parent. Adoption agencies report more and more inquiries from prospective parents—especially men—who identify themselves as gay, and sperm banks say they're in the midst of what some call a "gayby boom" propelled by lesbians.

But being open does not always mean being accepted. Many Americans are still very uncomfortable with the idea of gay parents—either because of religious objections, genuine concern for the welfare of the children or bias against homosexuals in general. In a recent NEWSWEEK survey, almost half of those polled felt gays should not be allowed to adopt, although 57 percent thought gays could be just as good at parenting as straight people. Despite the tolerance of big companies like IBM, most gay partners do not receive spousal health benefits. Congress recently passed—and President Clinton signed—a bill allowing states to ban same-sex marriages. Only 13 states specifically permit single lesbians or gay men to adopt, according to the Lambda Legal Defense and Education Fund, a gay-rights advocacy group. Even then, usually only one partner is the parent of record—leaving the other in legal limbo. Courts have allowed adoptions by a second parent (either gay or straight) in some of those states, although the law is still in flux. In California, for example, Gov. Pete Wilson has been lobbying hard against his state's fairly open procedure for second-parent adoptions.

Dealing with other people's prejudices continues to be a rite of passage for children in gay families. Merle, 14, lives north of Boston with her mother, Molly, and her mother's partner, Laura. Over the years she has learned to ignore the name-calling—gay, queer, faggot—from kids who know her mother is a lesbian and assume she must be one, too (as far as she knows, she isn't). And there are other painful memories, like the time in fifth grade when a friend suddenly "changed her mind" about sleeping over. Merle later learned that the girl's parents had found out about Molly and Laura and wouldn't let their daughter associate with Merle. One day in sixth-grade health class, the teacher asked for examples of different kinds of families. When Merle raised her hand and said, "lesbian," the teacher responded: "This is such a nice town. There wouldn't be any lesbians living here."

Gays say they hope that being honest with the outside world will ultimately increase tolerance, just as parenthood makes them feel more connected to their communities. "It sort of gets you into the Mom and Dad clubs of America," says Jenifer Firestone, a lesbian mother and gay-family educator in Boston. Having a child can also repair strained family relations; mothers and fathers who may have once turned their backs on gay sons and daughters often find it emotionally impossible to ignore their grandchildren.

Still, the outlook for children in this new generation of gay families is unclear. Only a few have even reached school age, so there are no long-term studies available of what the effects of growing up in such a family might be. Researchers do have some data on kids who grew up about the same time that Claire was living with Lee and Dorothy in Chicago. Most were born to a married mother and father who later split up. If the children were young, they generally wound up living with their mother, as did the majority of children of divorce. Pressures were often intense. The children worried about losing friends, while the mothers worried about losing custody if anyone found out about their sexual orientation. Yet despite these problems, the families were usually emotionally cohesive. In a comprehensive 1992 summary of studies of gay parenting, psychologist Charlotte Patterson of the University of Virginia concluded that the children are just as well adjusted (i.e., they do not have any more psychological problems and do just as well in school) as the offspring of heterosexual parents. The studies also show that as adults, they are no more likely to be gay than are children of straight parents.

The new generation of gay parents is far more diverse and will be harder to analyze. Often they are already in stable partnerships when they decide to start a family. They include lesbian couples who give birth through artificial insemination (the donors can be friends or anonymous contributors to a sperm bank); gay dads who adopt, hire surrogate mothers or pair up with lesbian friends to co-parent, and the more traditional—in this context, at least—parents who started out in heterosexual unions.

Usually they try to settle in a relatively liberal community within a large urban area like Boston, Chicago or Los Angeles, where their children will be able to mix with all kinds of families. They often join one of the many support groups that have been springing up around the country, like Gay and Lesbian Parents Coalition International or COLAGE, an acronym for Children of Lesbians and Gays Everywhere. The support groups form a kind of extended family, a shelter against the often hostile outside world.

A decade ago, when gay parents routinely hid their sexual orientation, the issues of differences rarely came up in school. But now gay parents say they try to be straightforward from the first day of class. Marilyn Morales, 34, and her partner, Angela Diaz, 37, live on Chicago's Northwest Side with their son, Christopher, 6, and their 4-month-old daughter, Alejandra, both conceived through artificial insemination. Registering Christopher for school proved to be an education for everyone. Because Morales appeared to be a single mother, a school official asked whether the family was receiving welfare. When Morales explained the situation, the woman was clearly embarrassed. "People don't know how to react," says Diaz. At Christopher's first soccer game, Diaz had to fill out a form that asked for "father's name." She scratched out "father's name"

and wrote "Marilyn Morales." Both Morales and Diaz feel Christopher is more accepted now. "At birthday parties people say, 'Here comes Christopher's moms'," says Morales. Dazelle Steele's son Kyle is a friend of Christopher's, and the two boys often sleep over at each other's home. "They're such great parents," Steele says of Diaz and Morales. "Their actions spoke louder to me than rhetoric about their political decisions."

To the parents, each new encounter can feel like coming out all over again. Brian and Bernie are a Boston-area couple who don't want their last names used because they are in the process of finalizing the adoptions of two boys, ages 12 and 6. A few years ago, Brian dreaded meeting the older boy's Cub Scout leader because the man had actively tried to block a sex-education curriculum in the schools. But his son Ryan wanted badly to join the Scouts, and Brian felt he needed to tell the man that the boy's parents were gay. As it turned out, the session went better than Brian had expected. "People challenge themselves, and people grow," Brian says. But, he adds, "as out as I am, I still feel the blood pressure go up, I sweat profusely, I'm red in the face as I tell him I'm gay, that I have a partner and that Ryan has two dads. I always think how it looks to Ryan. I'm always hoping he doesn't see me sweat."

Even in the relatively more tolerant '90s, gay parents "always feel threatened," says April Martin, a New York family therapist who is also a lesbian mother and the author of "The Lesbian and Gay Parenting Handbook." "How can you feel secure when it's still legal for someone to tear apart your family?" The parents are haunted by such well-publicized legal cases as the 1995 Virginia Supreme Court ruling that Sharon Bottoms was an unfit parent because she is a lesbian; she had to surrender custody of her 5-year-old son, Tyler, to her mother. In Florida this summer, the state appeals court ruled that John Ward, who was convicted of murdering his first wife in 1974, was a more fit parent than his ex-wife Mary, a lesbian.

Catherine Harris, 41, a university administrator in Boston, knows only too well the pain of these legal battles. Ten years ago, she was married and the mother of a toddler daughter, Tayler. Then she fell in love with Paula Vincent, now 38, a nurse-midwife. During the divorce Harris's husband fought for custody of Tayler, and Harris's parents, who disapproved of her new identity as a lesbian, testified against her. Her ex-husband won.

Harris is still on rocky terms with her parents and her ex-husband, but she and Vincent have started a new family of their own that now includes Sora, 7, and her twin siblings, Kaelyn and Marilla, 22 months. In contrast to Tayler, Sora knows her biological father only as "the donor." She has seen the vial his sperm came in and knows that her biological mother, Vincent, and Harris chose him because—according to the questionnaire he filled out at the sperm bank—he was well educated, spiritual and optimistic. "I don't really want a dad," says Sora. "I like having two moms."

But problems can arise even in the most innocent situations. Wayne Steinman and Sal Iacullo didn't truly understand their fragile footing until Labor Day weekend a few years ago, when they drove to Disney World from their home in New York City. As they passed through Virginia, Steinman was at the steering wheel; Iacullo was in the back seat with their adopted daughter, Hope, now 9. They noticed a pickup truck sticking close to them, and when they pulled off the highway to get lunch the truck followed. Just as they were getting ready to pay the bill, two highway patrolmen walked in and started questioning them. The driver of the pickup had called the cops because he suspected the fathers of kidnapping. Fortunately, Steinman and Iacullo were able to convince the patrolmen that they were, in fact, Hope's parents. "From that point on, we carried the adoption papers in our pockets," says Iacullo.

Legalities aside, gay parents—and those who disapprove of gay families—are also concerned about issues of the children's emotional development. Most same-sex parents say they make a special effort to ensure that their kids learn to relate to adults of the opposite sex. Their situation is not that different from that of heterosexual single parents, and the solution is often the same:

persuading aunts, uncles or grandparents to be part of their children's lives. Hope Steinman-Iacullo, for example, often visits with her grandmother, her aunts and her teenage cousins. "There are a lot of female role models," says Iacullo.

Psychologists say the best time to tell kids how their families are different is either in childhood or in late adolescence. Young adolescents—from about ages 11 to 15—are particularly vulnerable because they are struggling with their own issues of sexual identity. George Kuhlman and his ex-wife shared joint custody of their daughter, Annie, who was 13 when their marriage fell apart in the early 1980s. But although Annie talked to her father nearly every day of her life, he never told her he was gay. "Several of my friends and even family members had been of the opinion that there might be some real psychological damage and some anger if I didn't make the disclosure," says Kuhlman, now 49 and the ethics counsel for the American Bar Association in Chicago. "That was the bear breathing down my neck." But the timing never seemed right.

Then, one day when Annie was a college freshman, he called to say goodbye as he was about to head off for a Caribbean vacation with a male friend. "She just said, 'Dad, I know. I've known for a long time . . . I just thought you and Tom would have a much nicer time and a happier vacation if you know that I knew and I love you.' I pretty much fell to pieces." Annie, now 24, says she is happy she learned about her father when she was an adult. His sexuality isn't an issue now, she says. "When you have a dedicated parent, it matters less."

And, ultimately, it is the quality of the parenting—not the parents' lifestyle—that matters most to kids. Sexual orientation alone doesn't make a person a good or bad parent. In Maplewood, N.J., Charlie and Marc are raising 17-month-old Olivia, whom they adopted. Last Christmas she had a lead role in their church's holiday pageant. "So you had a little Chinese girl of two gay parents who was the baby Jesus," says Charlie. Adds Marc: "It gives a whole new meaning to the word 'Mary'." As she gets older, Charlie and Marc say, they'll explain to Olivia why her family is unusual. "I think Olivia is so lucky to have the opportunity to be different," says Marc. "And that's what I intend to teach her."

With KAREN SPRINGEN *in Chicago,* CLAUDIA KALB
in Boston, MARC PEYSER *in New York,*
MARK MILLER *in Los Angeles*
and DANIEL GLICK *in Denver*

Exploring and Establishing Relationships

Emotions, Relating, and Mating (Articles 6–8)
Gender and Sexuality in Relationships (Articles 9 and 10)
Conception and Pregnancy (Articles 11–14)
The Next Generation (Articles 15–17)

By and large, humans are social animals, and as such, we seek out meaningful connections with other humans. John Bowlby, Mary Ainsworth, and others have proposed that this drive toward connection is biologically based and is at the core of what it means to be human. However it plays out in childhood and adulthood, the need for connection, to love and be loved, is a powerful force moving us to establish and maintain close relationships.

As we explore various possibilities, we engage in the complex business of relationship building. In this business, many processes simultaneously occur: Messages are sent and received; differences are negotiated; assumptions and expectations are or are not met. The ultimate goals are closeness and continuity.

How we feel about others and what we see as essential to these relationships play an important role in our establishing and maintaining relationships. In this unit, we look at factors that underlie the establishment of relationships as well as the beginning stages of relationships.

The first section takes a broad look at factors that influence the building of meaningful relationships and at the beginning stages of adult relationships. The first two essays explore the nature of love itself. "Man's World, Woman's World? Brain Studies Point to Differences" discusses research that suggests that gender differences may begin with brain differences. "What Makes Love Last?" considers different ways in which love is played out in long-term relationships. In "Back Off!" Geraldine Piorkowski suggests that, just as time together is important for a relationship, so too do individuals need time alone for themselves.

In the second section, two important aspects of adult relationships are explored, gender and sexuality. Particular attention is given to the idea of responsibility to oneself and others in acting out our sexuality. Joseph Anthony, in "Choosing a Contraceptive," looks at the strengths and weaknesses of contraceptives available in the United States. Then, in "Staying Power: Bridging the Gender Gap in the Confusing '90s," Melinda Blau looks at gender and promotes the idea of a less traditional approach to gender roles.

The third section explores conception and pregnancy, as well as the struggle many couples face as they attempt to conceive. The first two articles address infertility. "Who Stole Fertility?" looks at the prevalence of infertility in the United States as well as the tremendous stress that infertile couples face. "Missing Children: One Couple's Anguished Attempt to Conceive" chronicles one couple's ongoing, grief-filled struggle to conceive a child. The next article takes an international perspective on pregnancy and pregnancy decision making. Aaron Sachs, in "Men, Sex, and Parenthood in an Overpopulating World," contends that it is essential to involve men in the pregnancy decision-making process. In the final article in this section, "The Artificial Womb Is Born," Perri Klass looks into the future of conception and pregnancy and considers possible technological advancements in this area.

In the final section, building new family relationships is explored. Readers of "What a Baby *Really* Costs" may find themselves amazed at the high cost of having an uncomplicated birth. Adoption, another way of creating parent-child bonds, is addressed in "The Lifelong Impact

of Adoption." Marlou Russell provides a cautionary look at the long-term impacts, particularly those related to a sense of loss, that are found among those who have been touched by adoption. The complexity of a baby's brain and the many ways in which brain development is influenced are addressed in the final article, "Fertile Minds" by J. Madeleine Nash.

Looking Ahead: Challenge Questions

What is your definition of love? How do you know you are in love? How do you know you love someone? What does it take for you to believe someone loves you? What can you do when love fades?

What do you look for in a mate? Would you be willing to settle for less? Why or why not?

What are your beliefs about appropriate sexual behavior in intimate relationships? Whose responsibility is contraception? Would you feel comfortable discussing this with your partner? Why or why not?

What are appropriate gender roles? What is appropriate behavior in these roles? What would your response be if you encountered someone behaving in a way you found inappropriate for the role?

Do you see children as a part of your life? Why or why not? Discuss whether or not you would consider adoption.

How do children enrich a relationship? What are the drawbacks of having children? What are the responsibilities associated with parenthood? If you do have children, how will it affect you and your relationship with your partner?

Man's World, Woman's World? Brain Studies Point to Differences

Gina Kolata

Dr. Ronald Munson, a philosopher of science at the University of Missouri, was elated when Good Housekeeping magazine considered publishing an excerpt from the latest of the novels he writes on the side. The magazine eventually decided not to publish the piece, but Dr. Munson was much consoled by a letter from an editor telling him that she liked the book, which is written from a woman's point of view, and could hardly believe a man had written it.

New scanner finds more evidence of how the sexes differ in brain functions.

It is a popular motion: that men and women are so intrinsically different that they literally live in different worlds, unable to understand each other's perspectives fully. There is a male brain and a female brain, a male way of thinking and a female way. But only now are scientists in a position to address whether the notion is true.

The question of brain differences between the sexes is a sensitive and controversial field of inquiry. It has been smirched by unjustifiable interpretations of data, including claims that women are less intelligent because their brains are smaller than those of men. It has been sullied by overinterpretations of data, like the claims that women are genetically less able to do everyday mathematics because men, on average, are slightly better at mentally rotating three dimensional objects in space.

But over the years, with a large body of animal studies and studies of humans that include psychological tests, anatomical studies, and increasingly, brain scans, researchers are consistently finding that the brains of the two sexes are subtly but significantly different.

Now, researchers have a new non-invasive method, functional magnetic resonance imaging, for studying the live human brain at work. With it, one group recently detected certain apparent differences in the way men's and women's brains function while they are thinking. While stressing extreme caution in drawing conclusions from the data, scientists say nonetheless that the groundwork was being laid for determining what the differences really mean.

"What it means is that we finally have the tools at hand to begin answering these questions," said Dr. Sally Shaywitz, a behavioral scientist at the Yale University School of Medicine. But she cautioned: "We have to be very, very careful. It behooves us to understand that we've just begun."

The most striking evidence that the brains of men and women function differently came from a recent study by Dr. Shaywitz and her husband, Dr. Bennett A. Shaywitz, a neurologist, who is also at the Yale medical school. The Shaywitzes and their colleagues used functional magnetic resonance imaging to watch brains in action as 19 men and 19 women read nonsense words and determined whether they rhymed.

In a paper, published in the Feb. 16 issue of Nature, the Shaywitzes reported that the subjects did equally well at the task, but the men and women used different areas of their brains. The men used just a small area on the left side of the brain, next to Broca's area, which is near the temple. Broca's area has long been thought to be associated with speech. The women used this area as well as an area on the right side of the brain. This was the first clear evidence that men and women can use their brains differently while they are thinking.

Another recent study, by Dr. Ruben C. Gur, the director of the brain behavior laboratory at the University of Pennsylvania School of Medicine, and his colleagues, used magnetic resonance imaging to look at the metabolic activity of the brains of 37 young men and 24 young women when they were at rest, not consciously thinking of anything.

In the study, published in the Jan. 27 issue of the journal Science, the investigators found that for the most part, the brains of men and women at rest were indistinguishable from each other. But there was one difference, found in a brain structure called the limbic system that regulates emotions. Men, on average, had higher brain activity in the more ancient and primitive regions of the limbic system, the parts that are more involved with action. Women, on average, had more activity in the newer and more complex parts of the limbic

From the *New York Times*, February 28, 1995, pp. C1, C7. © 1995 by The New York Times Company. Reprinted by permission.

system, which are involved in symbolic actions.

Men have larger brains; women have more neurons.

Dr. Gur explained the distinction: "If a dog is angry and jumps and bites, that's an action. If he is angry and bares his fangs and growls, that's more symbolic."

Dr. Sandra Witelson, a neuroscientist at McMaster University in Hamilton, Ontario, has focused on brain anatomy, studying people with terminal cancers that do not involve the brain. The patients have agreed to participate in neurological and psychological tests and then to allow Dr. Witelson and her colleagues to examine their brains after they die, to look for relationships between brain structures and functions. So far she has studied 90 brains.

Several years ago, Dr. Witelson reported that women have a larger corpus callosum, the tangle of fibers that run down the center of the brain and enable the two hemispheres to communicate. In addition, she said, she found that a region in the right side of the brain that corresponds to the region women used in the reading study by the Shaywitzes was larger in women than in men.

Most recently, Dr. Witelson discovered, by painstakingly counting brain cells, that although men have larger brains than women, women have about 11 percent more neurons. These extra nerve cells are densely packed in two of the six layers of the cerebral cortex, the outer shell of the brain, in areas at the level of the temple, behind the eye. These are regions used for understanding language and for recognizing melodies and the tones in speech. Although the sample was small, five men and four women, "the results are very, very clear," Dr. Witelson said.

Going along with the studies of brain anatomy and activity are a large body of psychological studies showing that men and women have different mental abilities. Psychologists have consistently shown that men, on average, are slightly better than women at spatial tasks, like visualizing figures rotated in three dimensions, and women, on average, are slightly better at verbal tasks.

Dr. Gur and his colleagues recently looked at how well men and women can distinguish emotions on someone else's face. Both men and women were equally adept at noticing when someone else was happy, Dr. Gur found. And women had no trouble telling if a man or a woman was sad. But men were different. They were as sensitive as women in deciding if a man's face was sad—giving correct responses 90 percent of the time. But they were correct about 70 percent of the time in deciding if women were sad; the women were correct 90 percent of the time.

"A woman's face had to be really sad for men to see it," Dr. Gur said. "The subtle expressions went right by them."

Studies in laboratory animals also find differences between male and female brains. In rats, for example, male brains are three to seven times larger than female brains in a specific area, the preoptic nucleus, and this difference is controlled by sex hormones that bathe rats when they are fetuses.

"The potential existence of structural sex differences in human brains is almost predicted from the work in other animals," said Dr. Roger Gorski, a professor of anatomy and cell biology at the University of California in Los Angeles. "I think it's a really fundamental concept and I'm sure, without proof, that it applies to our brains."

But the question is, if there are these differences, what do they mean?

Dr. Gorski and others are wary about drawing conclusions. "What happens is that people overinterpret these things," Dr. Gorski said. "The brain is very complicated, and even in animals that we've studied for many years, we don't really know the function of many brain areas."

This is exemplified, Dr. Gorski said, in his own work on differences in rat brains. Fifteen years ago, he and his colleagues discovered that males have a comparatively huge preoptic nucleus and that the area in females is tiny. But Dr. Gorski added: "We've been studying this nucleus for 15 years, and we still don't know what it does. The most likely explanation is that it has to do with sexual behavior, but it is very, very difficult to study. These regions are very small and they are interconnected with other things." Moreover, he said, "nothing like it has been shown in humans."

And, with the exception of the work by the Shaywitzes, all other findings of differences in the brains or mental abilities of men and women have also found that there is an amazing degree of overlap. "There is so much overlap that if you take any individual man and woman, they might show differences in the opposite direction" from the statistical findings, Dr. Gorski said.

Dr. Munson, the philosopher of science, said that with the findings so far, "we still can't tell whether the experiences are different" when men and women think. "All we can tell is that the brain processes are different," he said, adding that "there is no Archimedean point on which you can stand, outside of experience, and say the two are the same. It reminds me of the people who show what the world looks like through a multiplicity of lenses and say, 'This is what the fly sees.'" But, Dr. Munson added, "We don't know what the fly sees." All we know, he explained, is what we see looking through those lenses.

Some researchers, however, say that the science is at least showing the way to answering the ancient mind-body problem, as applied to the cognitive worlds of men and women.

Dr. Norman Krasnegor, who directs the human learning and behavior branch at the National Institute of Child Health and Human Development, said the difference that science made was that when philosophers talked about mind, they "always were saying, 'We've got this black box.' " But now, he said, "we don't have a black box; now we are beginning to get to its operations."

Dr. Gur said science was the best hope for discovering whether men and women inhabited different worlds. It is not possible to answer that question simply by asking people to describe what they perceive, Dr. Gur said, because "when you talk and ask questions, you are talking to the very small portion of the brain that is capable of talking." If investigators ask people to tell them what they are thinking, "that may or may not be closely related to what was taking place" in the brain, Dr. Gur said.

On the other hand, he said, scientists have discovered that what primates perceived depends on how their brains function. Some neurons fire only in response to lines that are oriented at particular angles, while others seem to recognize faces. The world may well be what the philosopher Descartes said it was, an embodiment of the workings of the human mind, Dr. Gur said. "Descartes said that we are creating our world," he said. "But there is a world out there that we can't know."

Dr. Gur said that at this point he would hesitate to baldly proclaim that men and women inhabit different worlds. "I'd say that science might be leading us in that direction," he said, but before he commits himself he would like to see more definite differences in the way men's and women's brains function and to know more about what the differences mean.

Dr. Witelson cautioned that "at this point, it is a very big leap to go from any of the structural or organizational differences that were demonstrated to the cognitive differences that were demonstrated." She explained that "all you have is two sets of differences, and whether one is the basis of the other has not been shown." But she added, "One can speculate."

Dr. Witelson emphasized that in speculating she was "making a very big leap," but she noted that "we all live in our different worlds and our worlds depend on our brains.

"And," she said, "if these sex differences in the brain, with 'if' in big capital letters, do have cognitive consequences, and it would be hard to believe there would be none, then it is possible that there is a genuine difference in the kinds of things that men and women perceive and how these things are integrated. To that extent it may be possible that in some respects there is less of an easy cognitive or emotional communication between the sexes as a group because our brains may be wired differently."

The Shaywitzes said they were reluctant even to speculate from the data at hand. But, they said, they think that the deep philosophical questions about the perceptual worlds of men and women can eventually be resolved by science.

"It is a truism that men and women are different," Dr. Bennett Shaywitz said. "What I think we can do now is to take what is essentially folklore and place it in the context of science. There is a real scientific method available to answer some of these questions."

Dr. Sally Shaywitz added: "I think we've taken a qualitative leap forward in our ability to ask questions." But, she said, "the field is simply too young to have provided more than a very intriguing appetizer."

Approaches to Understanding Male-Female Brain Differences

Studies of differences in perception or behavior can suggest how male and female thinking may diverge; studies of structural or metabolic differences can suggest why. But only now are differences in brain organization being studied.

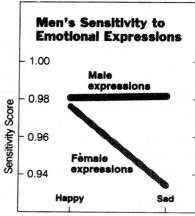

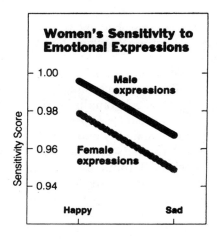

A study compared how well men and women recognized emotions in photos of actors portraying happiness and sadness. Men were equally sensitive to a range of happy and sad faces in men but far less sensitive to sadness in women's faces.

The women in the study were generally more sensitive to happy faces than to sad ones. They were also better able to recognize sadness in a man's face. For both sexes, sensitivity scores reflected the percent of the time the emotion was correctly identified.

**PSYCHOLOGISTS
AT THE "LOVE LAB"
ARE USING SCIENCE
TO UNCOVER THE
REAL REASON
WHY MARRIAGES
SUCCEED OR FAIL.**

What Makes Love Last?

Alan AtKisson

Alan AtKisson is a writer, songwriter, and consultant living in Seattle, Washington. He and partner, Denise Benitez, recently celebrated their ninth wedding anniversary by hiking in the North Cascades.

My old friends Karen and Bill, married since 1955, recently celebrated another anniversary. "I wore the same nightgown I wore on our wedding night," confessed Karen to me over the phone. "Just as I have every anniversary for thirty-nine years."

"I wore pajamas on our wedding night," offered Bill. "But last night I didn't wear nothin'." They laughed, and even over three thousand miles of telephone wire I felt the strength of their love for one another.

Long-lasting marriages like Bill's and Karen's are becoming increasingly rare. Not only do more than 50 percent of all first marriages in the United States end in divorce (make that 60 percent for repeat attempts), but fewer people are even bothering to tie the slippery knot in the first place. One fourth of Americans eighteen or older—about 41 million people—have never married at all. In 1970, that figure was only one sixth.

But even while millions of couples march down the aisle only to pass through the therapist's office and into divorce court, a quiet revolution is taking place when it comes to understanding how long-term love really works. Inside the laboratories of the Family Formation Project at the University of Washington in Seattle—affectionately dubbed the Love Lab—research psychologists are putting our most cherished relationship theories under the scientific microscope. What they're discovering is that much of what we regard as conventional wisdom is simply wrong.

"Almost none of our theory and practice [in marital therapy] is founded on empirical scientific research," contends the Love Lab's head, John Gottman, an award-winning research psychologist trained both as a therapist and a mathematician. Indeed, it is this lack of solid research, Gottman believes, that contributes to a discouraging statistic: for 50 percent of married couples who enter therapy, divorce is still the end result.

Gottman believes that, although relationship counseling has helped many people, much of it just doesn't work. Not satisfied with warm and fuzzy ideas about how to "get the love you want," Gottman is scouting for numbers, data, *proof*—and he's finding it.

From *New Age Journal*, September/October 1994, pp. 74-79, 146-148. © 1994 by New Age Publishing, Inc. Reprinted by permission.

For the past twenty years, in a laboratory equipped with video cameras, EKGs, and an array of custom-designed instruments, Gottman and his colleagues have been intensely observing what happens when couples interact. He watches them talk. He watches them fight. He watches them hash out problems and reaffirm their love. He records facial expressions and self-reported emotions, heart rhythms and blood chemistry. He tests urine, memories, and couples' ability to interpret each other's emotional cues. Then he pours his data, like so many puzzle pieces, into a computer. The resulting picture, he says, is so clear and detailed it's like "a CAT scan of a living relationship." [See "Putting Love to the Test," at right.]

What Gottman and his colleagues have discovered—and summarized for popular audiences in a new book, *Why Marriages Succeed or Fail* (Simon & Schuster) —is mind-boggling in its very simplicity. His conclusion: Couples who stay together are . . . well . . . *nice* to each other more often than not. "[S]atisfied couples," claims Gottman, "maintained a five-to-one ratio of positive to negative moments" in their relationship. Couples heading for divorce, on the other hand, allow that ratio to slip below one-to-one.

If it ended there, Gottman's research

Fighting, whether rare or frequent, is sometimes the healthiest thing a couple can do for their relationship.

might remain just an interesting footnote. But for him and his colleagues, this discovery is just the beginning. In fact, Gottman's novel and methodical approach to marriage research is threatening to turn much of current relationship therapy on its head. He contends that many aspects of wedded life often considered critical to long-term success— how intensely people fight; whether they face conflict or avoid it; how well they solve problems; how compatible they are socially, financially, even sexually

—are less important than people (including therapists) tend to think. In fact, Gottman believes, none of these things matter to a marriage's longevity as much as maintaining that crucial ratio of five to one.

If it's hard to believe that the longevity of your relationship depends primarily on your being five times as nice as you are nasty to each other, some of Gottman's other conclusions may be even more surprising. For example:

❤ Wildly explosive relationships that vacillate between heated arguments and passionate reconciliations can be as happy—and long-lasting—as those that seem

more emotionally stable. They may even be more exciting and intimate.

❤ Emotionally inexpressive marriages, which may seem like repressed volcanoes destined to explode, are actually very successful—so long as the couple maintains that five-to-one ratio in what they do express to each other. In fact, too much emotional catharsis among such couples can "scare the hell out of them," says Gottman.

❤ Couples who start out complaining about each other have some of the most stable marriages over time, while those who don't fight early on are more likely to hit the rocky shoals of divorce.

Putting Love to the Test

How the "Love Lab" researchers decode blood, sweat, and tears.

THE STUDIO APARTMENT IS TINY, BUT IT affords a great view of Seattle's Portage Bay. The ambiance is that of a dorm room tastefully furnished in late-'80s Sears, Roebuck. A cute kitchen table invites you to the window. A Monet print graces one wall. Oh, and three video cameras—suspended from the ceiling like single-eyed bats—follow your every move.

Welcome to the "Love Lab," wherein Professor John Gottman and a revolving crew of students and researchers monitor the emotions, behaviors, and hormones of married couples. Today, lab coordinator Jim Coan—a calm, clear-eyed, pony-tailed young man in Birkenstocks who started out as a student volunteer three years ago—is giving me the tour.

The Love Lab is actually two labs. I have entered through the "Apartment Lab," whose weekly routine Coan describes: A volunteer couple arrives on a Sunday morning, prepared to spend the day being intensely observed (for which they are modestly compensated). Special microphones record every sound they make; videotape captures every subtle gesture. The only true privacy is found in the bathroom, but even there science has a presence: A cooler by the toilet has two

little urine collection bottles, today marked "Bill" and "Jeannie."

At the end of a relaxed day doing whatever they like (and being watched doing it), the couple welcomes a house guest—a psychologist who listens to the story of how they met, fell in love, and began building a life together. This "oral history," which most people greatly enjoy telling, will later be closely scrutinized: Gottman and company have learned that how fondly a couple remembers this story can predict whether they will stay together or divorce.

Then, after a sleep-over on the Lab's hide-a-bed (cameras and microphones off) and a blood sample, a technician takes the pair out for breakfast, gives them their check, and sends them on their way. The videotapes will later be analyzed in voluminous detail. Every affectionate gesture, sarcastic jab, or angry dispute will be recorded and categorized using Gottman's "specific affect" emotional coding system (the lab folks call it SPAFF for short). At the same time, the couple's blood and urine will be sent to another lab and tested for stress hormone levels. Finally, in four years or so (depending on the study), the lab will follow up with the

♥ Fighting, whether rare or frequent, is sometimes the healthiest thing a couple can do for their relationship. In fact, blunt anger, appropriately expressed, "seems to immunize marriages against deterioration."

♥ In happy marriages, there are no discernible gender differences in terms of the quantity and quality of emotional expression. In fact, men in happy marriages are more likely to reveal intimate personal information about themselves than women. (When conflict erupts, however, profound gender differences emerge.)

♥ Men who do housework are likely to have happier marriages, greater physical health, even better sex lives than men who don't. (This piece of news alone could cause a run on aprons.)

♥ Women are made physically sick by a relentlessly unresponsive or emotionally contemptuous husband. Gottman's researchers can even tell just how sick: They can predict the number of infectious diseases women in such marriages will suffer over a four-year period.

♥ How warmly you remember the story of your relationship foretells your chances for staying together. In one study that involved taking oral histories from couples about the unfolding of their relationship, psychologists were able to predict—with an astonishing 94 percent accuracy—which couples would be divorced within three years.

THE THREE VARIETIES OF MARRIAGE

In person, Gottman is a fast-talking, restless intellect, clearly in love with his work. Now in his late forties and seven years into a second marriage (to clinical psychologist Julie Schwartz), he seems very satisfied. Yet, in his book, he sheds

---

couple to see if they're still together—and take another look at the data they gathered to see if a predictable pattern can be discerned.

OTHER COUPLES WHO VISIT THE FAMILY Formation Project, as the "Love Lab" is more formally known, merely pass the pleasant apartment on their way to a less cozy destination: the "Fixed Lab." Here they are seated ("fixed") in plain wooden chairs and hooked up with a dizzying array of instruments—EKG electrodes, finger-pulse detectors, and skin galvanometers ("a fancy word for sweat detectors," says Coan). A thick black spring stretched across their chests registers breathing. Their chair itself is a "jiggleometer," recording every fidget and tremor.

A "facilitator" first interviews the pair about what issues cause conflict in their marriage, then gets them talking about the most contentious ones. Video cameras focus on the couple's faces and chests. Computers track the complex streams of data coming in through the sensors and displays them on a color monitor in a rainbow of blips and graphs.

After fifteen minutes of surprisingly "normal" and often emotional conversation, the couple are stopped by the facilitator, who plays back the videotape for them. While watching, each partner rates his or her own emotional state at every moment during the conversation, using a big black dial with a scale running from "extremely negative" through "neutral" to "extremely positive." Then the pair watch the tape again, this time in an attempt to similarly judge their partner's emotional state (with widely varying levels of success).

Later, students trained by Coan will review the tape using a specially designed dial and the SPAFF coding system, to chart the feelings being displayed. It's eerie to see the range of human emotional expression represented on a high-tech instrument panel: disgust, contempt, belligerence, domination, criticism, anger, tension, tense humor ("very popular, that one," Coan tells me), defensiveness, whining, sadness, stonewalling, interest, validation, affection, humor, joy, and positive or negative surprise (students made Gottman aware of the two different kinds). In the middle is a neutral setting for when couples are merely exchanging information without noticeable emotion.

BACK IN THE APARTMENT LAB, COAN SHOWS me videos of couples who have agreed to be involved with the media. Two young parents from Houston discuss the stress around caring for their new baby, and Coan gives me the play-by-play: "He's being very defensive here" or "See that deep sigh? She's feeling sad now" or "Now that was a nice validation."

Coan says that most people seem to enjoy the lab experience—and even get some benefit from it (though it's not meant to be therapeutic). Amazingly, even with sensors attached to their ears and fingers and chests, the couples seem to forget that they're being watched. They giggle and cry and manage to create a genuine closeness while fixed under a physiological microscope.

"It's a real privilege to work here," Coan says thoughtfully. Even in a short visit, I feel it too. The observation of intimacy, both its joy and its pain, is more than just scientific video voyeurism. It's as though the love these couples are trying so devotedly to share with each other seeps out of the box, a gift to the watchers.

— A. A.

the mantle of guru in the first sentence: "My personal life has not been a trail of great wisdom in understanding relationships," he says. "My expertise is in the scientific observation of couples."

Gottman began developing this expertise some twenty years ago, when a troubled couple who came to him for help didn't respond well to conventional therapy. In frustration, Gottman suggested that they try videotaping the sessions. "Both the couple and I were astonished by the vividness and clarity on the tape of the pattern of criticism, contempt, and defensiveness they repeatedly fell into," he recalls. "It shocked them into working harder . . . [and] it gave me my life's work."

Struck by the power of impartial observation, Gottman became fascinated with research. His goal: to systematically describe the differences between happy and unhappy couples, and from those observations develop a scientific theory capable of predicting marital success. This seemed a daunting task, both because "marriage is so subjective" and because "personality theory, in psychology, has been a failure at predicting anything."

The result of Gottman's passion is a veritable mountain of data: tens of thousands of observations involving thousands of couples, gathered by the Love Lab's researchers and stored in its computer data-bases. The geography of that mountain reveals a surprising pattern: Successful marriages come in not one but three different varieties, largely determined by how a couple handles their inevitable disagreements. Gottman calls these three types of stable marriages *validating, volatile,* and *conflict-avoiding.*

Validating couples are what most people (including most therapists) have in mind when they think of a "good marriage." Even when these couples don't agree, they "still let their partner know that they consider his or her opinions and emotions valid." They "compromise often and calmly work out their problems to mutual satisfaction as they arise." And when they fight, they know how to listen, acknowledge their differences, and negotiate agreement without screaming at each other. "These couples," Gottman notes, "look and sound a lot like two psychotherapists engaging in a dialogue."

But where modern therapy often goes wrong, says Gottman, is in assuming that this is the only way a marriage can work—and trying to force all couples

Couples who start out complaining about each other have some of the most stable marriages over time.

into the validating mold. While "viewing this style of marriage as the ideal has simplified the careers of marital therapists," it hasn't necessarily helped their clients, he says, who may fall into the other two types of stable pattern.

Volatile couples, in contrast to validating ones, thrive on unfiltered emotional intensity. Their relationships are full of angry growls and passionate sighs, sudden ruptures and romantic reconcilia-

Men who do housework are likely to have happier marriages, greater physical health, even better sex lives than men who don't.

tions. They may fight bitterly (and even unfairly), and they may seem destined for divorce to anyone watching them squabble. But Gottman's data indicate that this pessimism is often misplaced: These couples will stay together if "for every nasty swipe, there are five caresses." In fact, "the passion and relish with which they fight seems to fuel their positive interactions even more." Such couples are more romantic and affectionate than most—but they are also more vulnerable to a decay in that all-important five-to-one ratio (and at their worst, to violence). Trying to change the style of their relationship not only isn't necessary, Gottman says, it probably won't work.

Nor will conflict-avoiding couples, the third type of stable marriage, necessarily benefit from an increase in their emotional expression, he says. Gottman likens such unions to "the placid waters of a summer lake," where neither partner wants to make waves. They keep the peace and minimize argument by constantly agreeing to disagree. "In these relationships, solving a problem usually means ignoring the difference, one partner agreeing to act more like the other . . . or most often just letting time take its course." The universal five-to-one ratio must still be present for the couple to stay together, but it gets translated into a

Four Keys to a Happy Relationship

DESPITE ALL HIS SOPHISTICATED ANALYSIS of how relationships work (and don't work), researcher John Gottman's advice to the lovelorn and fight-torn is really quite simple.

LEARN TO CALM DOWN.
This will cut down on the flooding response that makes further communication so difficult. "The most brilliant and philosophically subtle therapy in the world will have no impact on a couple not grounded in their own bodies to hear it," he says. Once couples are calm enough, suggests Gottman, they can work on three other basic "keys" to improving their relationship.

LEARN TO SPEAK AND LISTEN NONDEFENSIVELY.
This is tough, Gottman admits, but defensiveness is a very dangerous response, and it needs to be interrupted. One of the most powerful things you can do—in addition to working toward the ideal of listening with empathy and speaking without blame—is to "reintro-

much smaller number of swipes and caresses (which are also less intensely expressed). This restrained style may seem stifling to some, but the couple themselves can experience it as a peaceful contentment.

Things get more complicated when the marriage is "mixed"—when, say, a volatile person marries someone who prefers to minimize conflict. But Gottman suggests that, even in these cases, "it may be possible to borrow from each marital style and create a viable mixed style." The most difficult hurdle faced by couples with incompatible fighting styles lies in confronting that core difference

duce praise and admiration into your relationship." A little appreciation goes a long way toward changing the chemistry between people.

VALIDATE YOUR PARTNER.
Validation involves "putting yourself in your partner's shoes and imagining his or her emotional state." Let your partner know that you understand how he or she feels, and why, even if you don't agree. You can also show validation by acknowledging your partner's point of view, accepting appropriate responsibility, and apologizing when you're clearly wrong. If this still seems too much of a stretch, at least let your partner know that you're *trying* to understand, even if you're finding it hard.

PRACTICE, PRACTICE, PRACTICE.
Gottman calls this "overlearning," doing something so many times that it becomes second nature. The goal is to be able to calm yourself down, communicate nondefensively, and validate your partner automatically—even in the heat of an argument.

and negotiating which style (or combination of styles) they will use. If they can't resolve that primary conflict, it may be impossible to tip the overall balance of their relational life in the direction of five-to-one.

The important thing here is to find a compatible fighting style—not to stop fighting altogether. Gottman is convinced that the "one" in that ratio is just as important as the "five": "What may lead to temporary misery in a marriage —disagreement and anger—may be healthy for it in the long run." Negativity acts as the predator in the ecosystem of marriage, says Gottman. It's the lion that feeds on the weakest antelopes and makes the herd stronger. Couples who never disagree at all may start out happier than others, but without some conflict to resolve their differences, their marriages may soon veer toward divorce because their "ecosystem" is out of balance.

THE FOUR HORSEMEN OF THE APOCALYPSE

Even the most stable marriages of any style can fall apart, and Gottman and company have observed an all-too-predictable pattern in their decline and fall. He likens the process to a cascade—a tumble down the rapids—that starts with the arrival of a dangerous quartet of behaviors. So destructive is their effect on marital happiness, in fact, that he calls these behaviors "The Four Horsemen of the Apocalypse."

The first horseman is criticism: "attacking someone's personality or character" rather than making some specific complaint about his or her behavior. The difference between saying, say, "I wish you had taken care of that bill" (a healthy and specific complaint) and "You never get the bills paid on time!" (a generalizing and blaming attack) is very significant to the listener. Criticism often engenders criticism in return and sets the stage for the second horseman: contempt.

"What separates contempt from criticism," explains Gottman, "is the intention to insult and psychologically abuse your partner." Negative thoughts about the other come out in subtle put-downs, hostile jokes, mocking facial expressions, and name-calling ("You are such an idiot

around money"). By now the positive qualities that attracted you to this person seem long ago and far away, and instead of trying to build intimacy, you're ushering in the third horseman.

Defensiveness comes on the heels of contempt as a seemingly reasonable response to attack—but it only makes things worse. By denying responsibility, making excuses, whining, tossing back counter-attacks, and other strategies ("How come I'm the one who always pays the bills?!"), you just accelerate your speed down river. Gottman also warns that it's possible to skip straight to the third horseman by being oversensitive about legitimate complaints.

Once stonewalling (the fourth horseman) shows up, things are looking bleak. Stonewallers simply stop communicating, refusing to respond even in self-defense. Of course, all these "horsemen" drop in on couples once in a while. But when a partner habitually shuts down and withdraws, the final rapids of negativity (what Gottman calls the "Distance and Isolation Cascade") can quickly propel the marriage through whirlpools of hopelessness, isolation, and loneliness over the waterfall of divorce. With the arrival of the fourth horseman, one or both partners is thinking negative thoughts about his or her counterpart most of the time, and the couple's minds—as well as their bodies—are in a perpetual state of defensive red alert.

The stress of conflict eventually sends blood pressure, heart rate, and adrenaline into the red zone—a phenomenon Gottman calls *flooding*. "The body of someone who feels flooded," he writes, "is a confused jumble of signals. It may be hard to breathe. . . . Muscles tense up and stay tensed. The heart beats fast, and it may seem to beat harder." Emotionally, the flooded person may feel a range of emotions, from fear to anger to confusion.

The bottom line is that flooding is physically uncomfortable, and stonewalling becomes an attempt to escape that discomfort. When flooding becomes chronic, stonewalling can become chronic, too. Eighty-five percent of the time the stonewaller (among heterosexual couples) is the man. The reason for this gender discrepancy is one of many physiological phenomena that Gottman sees as critical to understanding why mar-

Women are made physically sick by a relentlessly unresponsive or emotionally contemptuous husband. Gottman's researchers can even tell just how sick.

riages go sour, and what people can do to fix them.

Though flooding happens to both men and women, it affects men more quickly, more intensely, and for a longer period of time. "Men tend to have shorter fuses and longer-lasting explosions than women," says Gottman. Numerous observations in the laboratory have shown that it often takes mere criticism to set men off, whereas women require something at least on the level of contempt. The reasons for this are left to speculation. "Probably this difference in wiring had evolutionary survival benefits," Gottman conjectures. An added sensitivity to threats may have kept males alert and ready to repel attacks on their families, he suggests, while women calmed down more quickly so they could soothe the children.

Whatever its origin, this ancient biological difference creates havoc in contemporary male-female relationships, because men are also "more tuned in to the internal physiological environment than women," Gottman reports. (For example, men are better at tapping along with their heartbeat.) Men's bodily sensitivity translates into greater physical discomfort during conflict. In short, arguing hurts. The result: "Men are more likely to withdraw emotionally when their bodies are telling them they're upset." Meanwhile, "when men withdraw, women get upset, and they pursue [the issue]"—which gets men more upset.

Here is where physiology meets sociology. Men, says Gottman, need to rely on physiological cues to know how they're feeling. Women, in contrast, rely on social cues, such as what's happening in the conversation.

In addition, men are trained since early

childhood not to build intimacy with others, while women "are given intense schooling on the subject" from an equally early age. Socially, the genders are almost totally segregated (in terms of their own choices of friendships and playmates) from age seven until early adulthood. Indeed, it would seem that cross-gender relationships are set up to fail. "In fact," Gottman writes, "our upbringing couldn't be a worse training ground for a successful marriage."

Yet the challenge is far from insurmountable, as millions of marriages prove. In fact, Gottman's research reveals that "by and large, in happy marriages there are *no* gender differences in emotional expression!" In these marriages, men are just as likely to share intimate emotions as their partners (indeed they may be more likely to reveal personal information about themselves). However, in unhappy marriages, "all the gender differences we've been talking about

Men's bodily sensitivity translates into greater physical discomfort during conflict. The result: Men are more likely to withdraw emotionally.

emerge"—feeding a vicious cycle that, once established, is hard to break.

Married couples who routinely let the Four Horsemen ransack their living rooms face enormous physical and psychological consequences. Gottman's studies show that chronic flooding and negativity not only make such couples more likely to get sick, they also make it very difficult for couples to change how they relate. When your heart is beating rapidly and your veins are constricting in your arms and legs (another evolutionary stress response), it's hard to think fresh, clear thoughts about how you're communicating. Nor can the brain process new information very well. Instead, a flooded person

relies on "overlearned responses"—old relationship habits that probably just fan the flames.

All this physiological data has enormous implications for relationship therapists as well as their clients. Gottman believes that "most of what you see currently in marital therapy—not all of it, but most of it—is completely misguided."

For example, he thinks it's an exercise in futility when "the therapist says 'Calm down, Bertha. Calm down, Max. Let's take a look at this and analyze it. Let's remember the way we were with our mothers.' Bertha and Max can do it in the office because he's doing it for them. But once they get home, and their heart rates get above 100 beats per minute, whew, forget about it."

Teaching psychological skills such as interpreting nonverbal behavior also misses the mark. "We have evidence that husbands in unhappy marriages are terrible at reading their wives' nonverbal behavior. But they're great at reading other people's nonverbal behavior. In other words, they have the social skills, but they aren't using them." The problem isn't a lack of skill; it's the overwhelming feelings experienced in the cycle of negativity. Chronic flooding short-circuits a couple's basic listening and empathy skills, and it undermines the one thing that can turn back the Four Horsemen: the repair attempt.

HEADING OFF DISASTER

Repair attempts are a kind of "meta-communication"—a way of talking about how you're communicating with each other. "Can we please stay on the subject?" "That was a rude thing to say." "We're not talking about your father!" "I don't think you're listening to me." Such statements, even when delivered in a grouchy or complaining tone, are efforts to interrupt the cycle of criticism, contempt, defensiveness, and stonewalling and to bring the conversation back on track.

"In stable relationships," explains Gottman, "the other person will respond favorably: 'Alright, alright. Finish.' The agreement isn't made very nicely. But it does stop the person. They listen, they accept the repair attempt, and they actually change" the way they're relating.

Repair attempts are "really critical," says Gottman, because "everybody screws up. Everybody gets irritated, defensive, contemptuous. People insult one another," especially their spouses. Repair attempts are a way of saying "we've got to fix this before it slides any deeper into the morass." Even people in bad marriages make repair attempts; the problem is, they get ignored.

Training people to receive repair attempts favorably—even in the middle of a heated argument—is one of the new frontiers in relationship therapy. According to Gottman, "Even when things are going badly, you've got to focus not on the negativity but on the repair attempt. That's what couples do in happy mar-

Even people in bad marriages make repair attempts; the problem is, they get ignored.

riages." He's convinced that such skills can be taught: One colleague has even devised a set of flash cards with a variety of repair attempts on them, ranging from "I know I've been a terrible jerk, but can we take this from the top?" to "I'm really too upset to listen right now." [See Upfront, July/August 1993.] Even in mid-tempest, couples can use the cards to practice giving, and receiving, messages about how they're communicating.

Breaking the Four Horsemen cycle is critical, says Gottman, because "the more time [couples] spend in that negative perceptual state, the more likely they are to start making long-lasting attributions about this marriage as being negative." Such couples begin rewriting the story of how they met, fell in love, made commitments. Warm memories about how "we were so crazy about each other" get replaced with "I was *crazy* to marry him/her." And once the story of the marriage has been infected with negativity, the motivation to work on its repair declines. Divorce becomes much more likely (and predictable—consider that 94 percent accuracy rate in the oral history study).

Of course, not all relationships can, or should, be saved. Some couples are trapped in violent relationships, which "are in a class by themselves." Others may suffer a fundamental difference in their preferred style—validating, volatile, or conflict-avoidant—that leaves them stuck in chronic flooding. With hard work, some of these marriages can be saved; trying to save others, however, may do more harm than good.

In the end, the hope for repairing even a broken marriage is to be found, as usual, in the courage and effort people are willing to invest in their own growth and change. "The hardest thing to do," says Gottman, "is to get back to the fundamentals that really make you happy." Couples who fail to do this allow the Four Horsemen to carry them far from the fundamentals of affection, humor, appreciation, and respect. Couples who succeed cultivate these qualities like gardeners. They also cultivate an affirming story of their lives together, understanding that that is the soil from which everything else grows.

The work may be a continuous challenge, but the harvest, as my long-married friends Bill and Karen would say, is an enormous blessing: the joy in being truly known and loved, and in knowing how to love.

The Lovers' Library

A slew of new books appearing in 1994 address some of the most entrenched problems facing long-term lovers:

■ *Hot Monogamy: Essential Steps to More Passionate, Intimate Lovemaking,* by Patricia Love and Jo Robinson (Dutton, 1994). This is a wonderful guide to enriching your sex life in a host of imaginative ways, and to reducing the shame and anxiety caused by differences in sexual appetite. (Also available as an excellent workshop on cassette from The Sounds True Catalog, 800-333-9185.)

■ *When Opposites Attract: Right Brain/ Left Brain Relationships and How to Make Them Work,* by Rebecca Cutter (Dutton, 1994). A very helpful and thorough guide to dealing with the wide range of problems that can stem from fundamental differences in brain wiring.

■ *The Couple's Comfort Book: A Creative Guide for Renewing Passion, Pleasure, and Commitment,* by Jennifer Louden (HarperSanFrancisco, 1994). A highly usable compendium of nurturing and imaginative things to do together, cross-referenced so you can hop around the book and design your own program of relationship rebirth.

BACK OFF!

We're putting way too many expectations on our closest relationships. It's time to retreat a bit. Consider developing same-sex friendships. Or cultivating a garden. Whatever you do, take a break from the relentless pursuit of intimacy.

Geraldine K. Piorkowski, Ph.D.

You can't miss it. It's the favorite topic of Oprah and all the other talk shows. It's the suds of every soap opera. And I probably don't have to remind you that it's the subject of an extraordinary number of self-help books. Intimate relationships. No matter where we tune or turn, we are bombarded with messages that there is a way to do it right, certainly some way of doing it better—if only we could find it. There are countless books simply on the subject of how to communicate better. Or, if it's not working out, to exit swiftly.

We are overfocused on intimate relationships, and I question whether our current preoccupation with intimacy isn't unnatural, not entirely in keeping with the essential physical and psychological nature of people. The evidence suggests that there is a limit to the amount of closeness people can tolerate and that we need time alone for productivity and creativity. Time alone is necessary to replenish psychological resources and to solidify the boundaries of the self.

All our cultural focus on relationships ultimately has, I believe, a negative impact on us. It causes us to look upon intimate relationships as a solution to all our ills. And that only sets us up for disappointment, contributing to the remarkable 50 percent divorce rate.

Our overfocus on relationships leads us to demand too much of intimacy. We put all our emotional eggs in the one basket of intimate romantic relationships. A romantic partner must be all things to us—lover, friend, companion, playmate, and parent.

We approach intimate relationships with the expectation that this new love will make up for past letdowns in life and love. The expectation that this time around will be better is bound to disappoint, because present-day lovers feel burdened by demands with roots in old relationships.

We expect unconditional love, unfailing nurturance, and protection. There is also the expectation that the new partner will make up for the characteristics we lack in our own personality—for example, that he or she will be an outgoing soul to compensate for our shyness or a goal-oriented person to provide direction in our messy life.

If the personal ads were rewritten to emphasize the emotional expectations we bring to intimacy, they would sound like this. "WANTED: Lively humorous man who could bring joy to my gloomy days and save me from a lifetime of depression." Or, "WANTED: Woman with self-esteem lower than mine. With her, I could feel superior and gain temporary boosts of self-confidence from the comparison."

From my many years as a clinical psychologist, I have come to recognize that intimacy is not an unmitigated good. It is not only difficult to achieve, it is treacherous in some fundamental ways. And it can actually harm people.

The potential for emotional pain and upset is so great in intimate relationships because we are not cloaked in the protective garb of maturity. We are unprotected, exposed, vulnerable to hurt; our defenses are down. We are wide open to pain.

Intuitively recognizing the dangers involved, people normally erect elaborate barriers to shield themselves from closeness. We may act superior, comical, mysterious, or super independent because we fear that intimacy will bring criticism, humiliation, or betrayal—whatever an earlier relationship sensitized us to. We develop expectations based on what has happened in our lives with parents, with friends, with a first love. And we often act in anticipation of these expectations, bringing about the result we most want to avoid.

The closer we get to another person, the greater the risks of intimacy. It's not just that we are more vulnerable and defenseless. We are also more emotionally unstable, childish, and less intelligent than in any other situation. You may be able to run a large company with skill and judgment, but be immature, ultrasensitive, and needy at home. Civilized rules of conduct often get suspended. Intimacy is both unnerving and baffling.

HEALTHY RETREATS

Once our fears are aroused in the context of intimacy, we tend to go about calming them in unproductive ways. We make excessive demands of our partner, for affection, for unconditional regard. The trouble is, when people feel demands are being made of them, they tend to retreat and hide in ways that hurt their partner. They certainly do not listen.

Fears of intimacy typically limit our vulnerability by calling defensive strategies into play. Without a doubt, the defense of choice against the dangers of intimacy is withdrawal. Partners tune out. One may retreat into work. One walks out of the house, slamming the door. Another doesn't call for days. Whatever the way, we spend a great deal of time avoiding intimacy.

After many years of working with all kinds of couples, I have come to believe that human nature dictates that intimate relationships have to be cyclical.

When one partner unilaterally backs off, it tends to be done in a hurtful manner. The other partner feels rejected, uncared about, and unloved. Typically, absolutely nothing gets worked out.

However, avoidance is not necessarily unhealthy. Partners can pursue a time out, where one or both work through their conflict in a solitary way that is ultimately renewing. What usually happens, however, is that when partners avoid each other, they are avoiding open warfare but doing nothing to resolve the underlying conflicts.

Fears of intimacy can actually be pretty healthy, when they're realistic and protective of the self. And they appear even in good relationships. Take the fears of commitment that are apt to surface in couples just before the wedding. If they can get together and talk through their fears, then they will not scare one another or themselves into backing off permanently.

After many years of working with all kinds of couples, I have come to believe that human nature dictates that intimate relationships have to be cyclical. There are limitations to intimacy and I think it is wise to respect the dangers. Periods of closeness have to be balanced with periods of distance. For every two steps forward, we often need to take one step back.

An occasional retreat from intimacy gives individuals time to recharge. It offers time to strengthen your sense of who you are. Think of it as constructive avoidance. We need to take some emphasis off what partners can do for us and put it on what we can do for ourselves and what we can do with other relationships. Developing and strengthening same-sex friendships, even opposite-sex friendships, has its own rewards and aids the couple by reducing the demands and emotional expectations we place on partners.

In our culture, our obsession with romantic love relationships has led us to confuse all emotional bonds with sexual bonds, just as we confuse infatuation with emotional intimacy. As a result, we seem to avoid strong but deeply rewarding emotional attachments with others of our own sex. But having recently lost a dear friend of several decades, I am personally sensitive to the need for emotionally deep, same-sex relationships. They can be shared as a way of strengthening gender identity and enjoying rewarding companionship. We need to put more energy into nonromantic relationships as well as other activities.

One of the best ways of recharging oneself is to take pleasure in learning and spiritual development. And there's a great deal to be said for spending time solving political, educational, or social ills of the world.

Distance and closeness boundaries need to be calibrated and constantly readjusted in every intimate relationship. Such boundaries not only vary with each couple, they change as the relationship progresses. One couple may maintain their emotional connection by spending one evening together a week, while another couple needs daily coming together of some sort. Problems arise in relationships when partners cannot agree on the boundaries. These boundaries must be jointly negotiated or the ongoing conflict will rob the relationship of its vitality.

S.O.S. SIGNALS

When you're feeling agitated or upset that your partner is not spending enough time with you, consider it a signal to step back and sort out internally what is going on. Whether you feel anxiety or anger, the emotional arousal should serve as a cue to back off and think through where the upset is coming from, and to consider whether it is realistic.

That requires at least a modest retreat from a partner. It could be a half hour, or two hours. Or two days—whenever internal clarity comes. In the grip of emotion, it is often difficult to discriminate exactly which emotion it is and what its source is. "What is it I am concerned about? Is this fear realistic considering Patrick's behavior in the present? He's never done this to me before, and he's been demonstrating his trustworthiness all over the place, so what am I afraid of? Is it coming from my early years of neglect with two distant parents who never had time for me? Or from my experiences with Steve, who dumped me two years ago?"

Introspective and self-aware people already spend their time thinking about how they work, their motives, what their feelings mean. Impulsive people will have a harder time with the sorting-out process. The best way to sort things out is to pay attention to the nature of the upset. Exactly what you are upset about suggests what your unmet need is, whether it's for love, understanding, nurturance, protection, or special status. And once you identify the need, you can figure out its antecedents.

The kinds of things we get upset about in intimacy tend to follow certain themes. Basically, we become hurt or resentful because we're getting "too much" or "too little" of something. Too many demands, too much criticism, too much domination. Or the converse, too little affectional, conversational, or sexual attention (which translates into "you don't feel I'm important" or "you don't love me"). Insufficient empathy is usually voiced as "you don't understand me," and too little responsibility translates into failure to take on one's share of household and/or financial tasks. All these complaints require some attention, action, or retreat.

SHIFTING GEARS

It's not enough to identify the source of personal concern. You have to present your concerns in a way your partner can hear. If I say directly to my partner, "I'm afraid you're going to leave me," he has the opportunity to respond, "Darling, that's not true. What gave you that idea?" I get the reassurance I need. But if I toss it out in an argument, in the form of "you don't care about me," then my partner's emotional arousal keeps him from hearing me. And he is likely to back away—just when I need reassurance most.

If people were aware that intimate relationships are by nature characterized by ambivalence, they would understand the need to negotiate occasional retreats. They wouldn't feel so threatened by the times when one partner says, "I have to be by myself because I need to think about my life and where I'm going." Or "I need to be with my friends and spend time playing." If people did more backing off into constructive activities, including time to meditate or to play, intimate relationships would be in much better shape today.

If couples could be direct about what they need, then the need for retreat would not be subject to the misrepresentation that now is rampant. The trouble is, we don't talk to each other that openly and honestly. What happens is, one partner backs off and doesn't call and the partner left behind doesn't know what the withdrawal means. But he or she draws on a personal history that provides room for all sorts of negative interpretations, the most common being "he doesn't care about me."

No matter how hard a partner tries to be all things to us, gratifying all of another's needs is a herculean task—beyond the human calling. Criticism, disappointment, and momentary rejection are intrinsic parts of intimate life; developing a thicker skin can be healthy. And maintaining a life apart from the relationship is necessary. Energy invested in other people and activities provides a welcome balance.

GOOD-ENOUGH INTIMACY

Since our intimate partner will never be perfect, what is reasonable to expect? The late British psychiatrist D. W. Winnicott put forth the idea of "good-enough mothering." He was convinced that mothering could never be perfect because of the mother's own emotional needs. "Good-enough mothering" refers to imperfect, though adequate provision of emotional care that is not damaging to the children.

In a similar vein, I believe there is a level of imperfect intimacy that is good enough to live and grow on. In good-enough intimacy, painful encounters occasionally occur, but they are balanced by the strength and pleasures of the relationship. There are enough positives to balance the negatives People who do very well in intimate relationships don't have a perfect relationship, but it is good enough.

The standard of good-enough intimacy is essentially subjective, but there are some objective criteria. A relationship must have enough companionship, affection, autonomy, connectedness, and separateness, along with some activities that partners engage in together and that they both enjoy. The relationship meets the needs of both partners reasonably well enough, both feel reasonably good about the relationship. If one person is unhappy in the relationship, then by definition it is not good enough for them.

People looking for good-enough intimacy are bound to be happier than those seeking perfect intimacy. Their expectations are lower and more realistic. Time and time again, those who examine the intricacies of happiness have found the same thing—realistic expectations are among the prime contributors to happiness.

CHOOSING A CONTRACEPTIVE

What's Best for You?

Joseph Anthony

Joseph Anthony is a Contributing Editor at AMERICAN HEALTH.

If you've been frustrated by a lack of contraceptive choices, there's good news: In the last couple of years, several new forms of contraception specifically, the long-lasting, hormone-based products Depo-Provera and Norplant and the female condom have been approved for use in the U.S., which means that we're finally catching up with the rest of the world. Depo-Provera and Norplant have been in use in other countries for years. But much ballyhooed new methods, such as contraceptive "vaccines" and a male birth control pill, are still probably a decade or more away.

Why? Manufacturers worry about boycotts and other protests from the religious right and antiabortion activists. And, says Dr. Michael Policar, vice president for medical affairs at the Planned Parenthood Federation of America, "the threat of litigation has had an incredibly chilling effect on contraceptive development in the last 10 years."

What are in the pipeline are mostly variations on existing themes—a two-capsule Norplant (instead of today's six); redesigned, baggier male condoms that promise greater comfort; intrauterine devices (IUD's) that release hormones; barrier methods that release spermicides, creams or gels with anti-HIV as well as antisperm properties; and perhaps some new injectables. There has also been some movement toward making the Pill available over the counter (without a prescription), although the Food and Drug Administration (FDA) is not currently considering any formal proposals to do so.

Here's a rundown on newly available methods of birth control, followed by more-established and better-known alternatives.

THE FEMALE CONDOM: This device looks like a large, floppy tube closed at one end. Marketed by Wisconsin Pharmacal under the name Reality, the polyurethane barrier (thinner, stronger and a better conductor of heat than latex) was approved by the FDA last May. Like other barrier methods this one can take some time and patience to use correctly. The device has two

rings, one around the outer rim and one inside. The inner ring is designed to fit over the cervix, anchored in place behind the pubic bone, like a diaphragm. The outer ring covers the labia and the base of the penis during intercourse. Some women have complained that the condom can rise into the vagina if not sufficiently lubricated; it can also twist around if not inserted properly.

The one-year failure rate with "typical use" is high, estimated at 21% to 26%, which means that about one in four women using it may become pregnant over the course of a year. (The pregnancy rate for "perfect use" would be much lower—about 5%.)

DEPO-PROVERA: This injectable prescription contraceptive, first available in New Zealand in 1969 and subsequently used by 30 million women in 90 countries, was finally approved in the U.S. in late 1992. One injection of this synthetic version of the female hormone progesterone every three months blocks ovulation.

The drug, which provides no protection against sexually transmitted diseases (STD's), may cause irregular periods, and women may not regain fertility until six to 12 months after they stop taking it.

Side effects of Depo-Provera are similar to those of other hormonal contraceptives and may include weight gain, headaches and fatigue. Women usually experience some irregular bleeding or spotting during the first months of use. On the plus side, studies by the World Health Organization have found a link between Depo-Provera use and a reduced risk of cancer of the endometrium (the lining of the uterus).

NORPLANT: This implant of six thin capsules, placed under the skin of a woman's arm, releases the hormone levonorgestrel, which keeps the body from producing the hormones necessary for ovulation. Norplant is effective for up to five years.

The implant was approved after two decades of testing on more than 50,000 women. More than 900,000 American women have received Norplant since it was introduced in February of 1991 by U.S. distributor Wyeth-Ayerst Laboratories. It's not appropriate for women who have liver disease, blood clots, inflammation of the veins or a history of breast cancer, or for those who are breast-feeding in the first six weeks after delivery. Fertility returns soon after the implant is removed.

The most common side effect of Norplant is irregular menstrual bleeding during the first six months after implantation. Norplant provides no STD protection.

Wyeth-Ayerst Laboratories has been charging $365 for Norplant in the U.S. (With doctor's fees, Norplant generally costs between $500 and $800.) After congressional hearings last year revealed that the drug sells for as little as $23 in other countries, the company announced that the price to public clinics would be lowered in 1995. But company officials won't comment on what the new price will be.

STERILIZATION: Every year more than 600,000 women in the U.S. have their fallopian tubes surgically blocked or severed, thus preventing eggs from reaching the uterus. About 25% of all women at risk of pregnancy (sexually active, heterosexual and fertile) aged 15 to 50 have had this procedure, called a tubal ligation; among such women 35 to 44 the number soars to more than 60%, according to the Alan Guttmacher Institute, a nonprofit group studying contraceptive issues. In addition, each year about half a million American men have vasectomies, in which the tube that carries sperm from the testes is cut and sealed. Vasectomy, which is performed under local anesthesia, carries less surgical risk than tubal ligation, which requires general anesthesia.

Both forms of sterilization are more than 99% effective and virtually permanent. (Though surgical sterilizations can sometimes be reversed—the success rate for such procedures is better for vasectomies than for tubal ligations—but anyone contemplating surgical sterilization is generally advised to consider the operation irreversible.)

ORAL CONTRACEPTIVES: Commonly known as the Pill, oral contraceptives, which suppress ovulation, are the most popular form of birth control for women in the U.S. About 28% of American women at risk of pregnancy between 15 and 44 use oral contraceptives. Fewer than 1% of women using oral contraceptives properly will become pregnant in the course of a year.

Literally hundreds of studies over the past four decades have attempted to analyze the effect of the Pill on women's health. No solid connections between taking the Pill and getting breast cancer have been made. The Pill does appear to increase the risk of blood clots, heart attack and stroke for women over 35 who smoke. The authors of *Contraceptive Technology,* a leading reference manual in the field, characterize the risk for non-smokers and smokers under 35 as relatively minor.

While the Pill has been linked to circulatory problems in women who have high cholesterol, hypertension or any heart or vascular disease, as well as those who have a family history of heart disease, oral contraceptives also have been associated with several health *benefits.* Some studies indicate that birth control pills can actually reduce a woman's chances of developing ovarian or endometrial cancer, as well as lower her risk of pelvic inflammatory disease. Women taking the Pill also have fewer ovarian cysts and benign breast tumors than other women.

There are more than a dozen side effects attributed to the Pill, including breast tenderness, fluid retention, weight gain and headaches.

BARRIER METHODS: Condoms, diaphragms, cervical caps, sponges and spermicides all operate on the same basic principle: preventing sperm from reaching an egg. Latex condoms have the added benefit of providing the most protection against STD's, although all barrier methods, even spermicides, are thought to provide some protection when used properly.

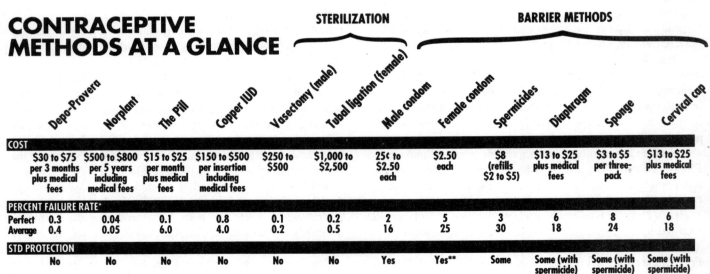

CONTRACEPTIVE METHODS AT A GLANCE

	Depo-Provera	Norplant	The Pill	Copper IUD	Vasectomy (male)	Tubal ligation (female)	Male condom	Female condom	Spermicides	Diaphragm	Sponge	Cervical cap
					STERILIZATION		BARRIER METHODS					
COST	$30 to $75 per 3 months plus medical fees	$500 to $800 per 5 years including medical fees	$15 to $25 per month plus medical fees	$150 to $500 per insertion including medical fees	$250 to $500	$1,000 to $2,500	25¢ to $2.50 each	$2.50 each	$8 (refills $2 to $5)	$13 to $25 plus medical fees	$3 to $5 per three-pack	$13 to $25 plus medical fees
PERCENT FAILURE RATE*												
Perfect	0.3	0.04	0.1	0.8	0.1	0.2	2	5	3	6	8	6
Average	0.4	0.05	6.0	4.0	0.2	0.5	16	25	30	18	24	18
STD PROTECTION	No	No	No	No	No	No	Yes	Yes**	Some	Some (with spermicide)	Some (with spermicide)	Some (with spermicide)

*Estimated percentage of women who get pregnant unintentionally in the first year of use. "Perfect use" is calculated from pregnancies occurring among couples who use the method correctly each time they have intercourse; "average use" combines perfect use figures with pregnancies occurring among couples who use the method sporadically or incorrectly.

**Although the female condom does provide protection against sexually transmitted diseases (STD's), its manufacturer is required by the Food and Drug Administration to note that for "highly effective protection" against STD's, including AIDS, it is important to use latex condoms for men.

FAILURE RATE DATA: ALAN GUTTMACHER INSTITUTE. FEMALE CONDOM FAILURE RATES: WISCONSIN PHARMACAL.

RU-486 and MORNING-AFTER TREATMENTS

Women who fear they may have become pregnant because they experienced condom rupture or otherwise engaged in unprotected intercourse have a little-publicized "morning-after," or postcoital, contraceptive option. Take what Dr. Felicia Stewart, director of research for the Sutter Medical Foundation in Sacramento, Calif., calls emergency contraceptive pills as soon as possible after the unprotected intercourse but no later than 72 hours afterward.

The "emergency pills" are regular birth control pills, but taken in two larger-than-usual doses (the second 12 hours after the first). The number of pills per dose depends on the brand: two Ovral, or four Lo/Ovral, Nordette, Levlen or yellow-colored Triphasil or Tri-Levlen (the yellow versions of both are the strongest formulas). By taking a larger-than-normal dose of birth control pills, you'll disrupt your body's natural hormone patterns, thereby reducing your chances of becoming pregnant by about 75%.

Obviously, the morning-after option shouldn't be looked at as a regular birth control method—it's a one-time emergency measure. And the procedure may not be suitable for women suffering from severe liver disease, blood clots or other circulation problems. Up to half of all women using this approach report short-term nausea or vomiting.

The drug RU-486, which prevents a fertilized egg from implanting itself in the uterine wall, might also find a secondary use as a morning-after contraceptive if it's approved for sale in the U.S. A University of Edinburgh study published in *The New England Journal of Medicine* found that if taken within 72 hours of unprotected sexual intercourse, RU-486 also prevents pregnancy. The women surveyed in the study reported much milder side effects than those taking birth control pills as morning-after measures.

Last year RU-486 manufacturer Roussel-Uclaf announced it would grant U.S. rights to the drug to the nonprofit research organization the Population Council, which would market and test the drug. As of the beginning of this year, however, the final details of the agreement had not been ironed out.

The main side effects of barrier methods are allergies or sensitivity to latex or spermicides. (The sponge is off-limits to women who have had toxic shock syndrome.)

INTRAUTERINE DEVICES (IUD's): IUD's are placed in a woman's uterus, where they prevent pregnancy by interfering with sperm transport and egg fertilization. The Dalkon Shield gave IUD's a terrible name in this country during the 1980s. After more than 10,000 lawsuits over pelvic inflammatory disease linked to the shield, IUD's have fallen out of favor. Fewer than 2% of women in the U.S. currently use them, a fact some experts regard as unfortunate.

"Compare that to around 30% of the women in Finland who choose an IUD," says Dr. Daniel Mishell, chairman of obstetrics and gynecology at the University of Southern California School of Medicine. "The IUD is effective and is one of the least expensive forms of long-term contraception, but it is also one of the least used in the U.S. because of the perception that it is dangerous." Recent studies have shown modern copper IUD's present little, if any risk of pelvic inflammatory disease.

The only IUD's currently sold in the U.S. are the Copper T-380A, which can be used for up to eight years, and the Progestasert, which releases progesterone and can be used for up to one year.

What form of contraception is right for you? People who have new or multiple partners have to be concerned about STD's as well as pregnancy. That means they should use condoms for maximum STD protection. A survey of 678 women receiving Norplant in Texas indicated that about half who had previously used condoms intended to keep doing so at least some of the time. "Until the last few years, nobody even *asked* questions about whether women using a hormonal contraceptive like Norplant would also continue to use barrier methods like condoms," says Margaret Frank, a contraceptive researcher at the University of New Haven in Connecticut and coauthor of the Texas study. People in monogamous, long-term relationships shouldn't have to worry about diseases and may focus instead on effective contraception.

But there's no way of saying that any one choice is "best." "Some women are going to get along really well with a particular method, and that's great," says *Contraceptive Technology* coauthor Dr. Felicia Stewart, director of research for the Sutter Medical Foundation, a managed-care organization in Sacramento, Calif. "If you have a method that is a comfortable fit with your hormonal makeup or your anatomy and your habits, then that method is fine for you. Trying, to say there's one best method is just ridiculous."

Staying Power

Bridging the Gender Gap in the Confusing '90s

Melinda Blau

Melinda Blau is the author of Families Apart: Ten Keys to Successful Co-Parenting.

Karen Mason*, 40, considers herself lucky. "I have a husband who's a real parent—kissy-huggy with the kids. And three nights a week he cooks dinner so I can be on the swim team."

Yet even this seeming paragon of a modern husband continues to exhibit what she considers to be typically male characteristics. Peter, 40, isn't much of a talker, Karen notes wistfully, and yes, he likes sex whereas she likes romance. And sometimes Karen gets frustrated because her husband just doesn't seem to focus when it comes to the house and children.

When they got married, Karen and Peter were determined not to be bound by traditional gender-role assumptions—that he would bring home the bacon and she would cook it. Peter, a salesman, shared the housework and put in almost equal time with their first child. But then the demands of Peter's work increased, a second child arrived and the couple's time together began to slip away.

Even though Peter is a far cry from

Couples' names and some identifying details have been changed.

his own father, who wasn't home much or "always had his head in the newspaper," some evenings Peter understands how his dad must have felt. "I like to bury myself in the TV," he admits. "I'm exhausted at night." Karen agrees that Peter "is doing his best" but says she's sometimes saddened by what she perceives as their real gender differences.

Many '90s couples are grappling with new ways of being men and women. At the same time that expectations and demands have changed for both, the popular press suggests the battle of the sexes may never end because men and women are irreconcilably different. Books proclaim that *Men Are From Mars, Women Are From Venus,* and personal accounts highlight the issues on which couples differ: Communication (she wants more talk; he wants more action). Intimacy (she needs to relax to have sex; he needs sex to relax). Division of household labor and child care (she says she does more; he talks about how much he does). Money and careers (she says he doesn't value her job as much as his; he notes that he makes more money).

Yet despite these differences, the fact that men and women can transcend traditional gender roles indicates that many of these distinctions may be more a result of socialization than biology. "Men are not emotionally defective monsters, and women aren't depen-

dent, helpless creatures," says psychologist Susan Johnson at the University of Ottawa in Ontario.

While researchers debate the contributions of nature and nurture to gender differences, family therapists suggest we examine why couples become polarized in the first place. Boston psychologist Kathy McMahon notes that "gender rage," as she calls it, stands for the disappointment couples feel when reality doesn't live up to expectations.

Dr. McMahon offers a typical scenario: Both parents work, and their child gets sick. In a spirit of fairness, they decide to split caretaking, but by the end of the week, they're fighting about who does what around the house. The problem, says McMahon, is that neither has a model for this new behavior—Mom working when a child is sick, Dad staying home—and they can't buck their inner cultural imprinting. When it's time for Mom to go to work, she feels guilty for not living up to her role as mother. And Dad's upset because he's not living up to his role as provider.

Today's couples, say the experts, must acknowledge their unconscious expectations and speak up before gender rage erodes their relationship. "This is not so much about understanding differences," says family therapist Jo-Ann Krestan, "as it is about holding partners equally accountable for the quality of life in a family. Sharing responsibility doesn't mean the husband saying, 'Honey, I'll cook tonight—where's the stove?'"

In essence, men and women usually want the same things from a relationship: closeness, support, respect, fairness, healthy children, a nice home and longevity. But, says California psychologist Lonnie Barbach, co-author of *Going the Distance,* they often differ about how to achieve these things and don't necessarily talk productively with each other about them.

Couples who talk about their needs and feelings fare far better than those who don't. But the longer people stay together, the less time they spend thinking and talking about their relationship, says University of Michigan psychologist Linda Acitelli. Complaining about a spouse's behavior doesn't count. Relationship work, Dr. Acitelli says, is like car maintenance—for safety's sake, you shouldn't wait until the vehicle breaks down.

The process of divvying up both practical *and* emotional responsibilities should be worked out thoughtfully. Some couples allocate chores arbitrarily, according to what has to be done; others earmark assignments based on preference. However it's done, structure—a chart or other means of clarifying who does what—can be helpful.

New York City designer Sara Roark, 41, and her husband, Carl, 42, an architect, drew up a "contract" and even included their four-year-old son, Orin. The major headings represent a bird's-eye view of what it takes to run a house and a family: meals and dishes, laundry, school, shopping, housecleaning, home maintenance, car, mail, finances, medical care, lifestyle decisions and leisure time.

At first the Roarks wanted to keep the assignments objective, but they wound up basing certain responsibilities on each person's skills and availability. "I took over more of the financial things, because it took me less time. My husband is more of a morning person, so he gets Orin ready for school, while I do more of the night things."

To a woman who complains that she's always in charge or that her husband does less than she does, Krestan would say it's her own fault for doing his share. "Sometimes you just have to leave his empty yogurt container on the kitchen counter. Throw it away and you cripple his ability to notice empty yogurt containers in the future."

Indeed, Sara Roark had to redefine "what needs to be done" and to accept the fact that things might not be done the way she'd do them, or when. "It's tough to let go. Sometimes when I come home late, I find that he's given our son crackers and cheese and put him to bed. A lot of women just take over at that point."

Dr. Ron Taffel, a New York City family therapist, concurs: "The biggest complaint I hear from men is, 'She wants me to do it, but when I do, she criticizes me.'" Our society, he explains, puts each member in a no-win situation. "The woman feels responsi-

Arguments over dirty dishes are signs of deeper issues.

ble for how the house looks and how the kids turn out. Society will hold her accountable, so she feels driven to be in charge. And even though the man may want to participate as an equal, he often feels like he has a boss."

Taffel's prescription goes beyond chores: Couples must also reserve time every night for reviewing the day. "One couple began to talk for 15 minutes each night after the kids went to bed about what happened with each other and with their sons. It made them feel more in synch."

While women typically will participate in such sessions, men are generally more resistant. Men tend to focus on what's in front of them, Taffel explains. "When they leave the office, they don't want to talk about work, and when the children finally are in bed, they don't want to talk about them. I try to get them to realize that the more they separate the different aspects of their lives, the more they end up zoning out in front of the TV or walking out on wives who want to talk."

Dave Goodrich, 34, an estate manager in Indianapolis, was happy to share the housework and child care for his two sons. But intimacy was another matter. "When Annie first complained that she was always the one to initiate conversations about our relationship, I was very defensive," he admits. "Guys don't talk about those kinds of things. We had a number of conversations, till

all hours of the night. Now I understand where she's coming from. It's hard sometimes, but I really make an attempt to share the emotional work of our marriage too."

Annie Goodrich, 37, a teacher, realizes that her attitude also made a difference. "In the beginning I would yell and scream, which just pushed him further away. I finally realized that when we had an argument, he needed a cooling-off period before he could talk."

Certainly, it takes perseverance—not

HOW TO CLOSE THE GAP

Get honest before you get angry: Something deeper than dry cleaning is probably bothering you.
Establish systems for sharing chores and child care.
Negotiate the division of labor *and* the division of love.
Don't get locked into your role: Try swapping responsibilities on occasion.
Express your emotional needs and expectations and really listen to your partner.
Review the cultural messages of your childhood to help understand the conflicts inherent in your new roles.
Give each other time to change; don't monitor or criticize.
Accept your differences and applaud each other's strengths.
Protect your intimate time together.

---

the same as nagging—to get some men to talk. More important, it requires the woman to speak honestly about what she needs, not rant about what her spouse is doing wrong. In most relationships, in fact, both partners are usually afraid of intimacy; the fear just looks different on men and women. As Dr. Johnson points out, "To love and to be intimately connected is to be incredibly at risk." A woman may believe she's doing "relationship work" because she starts conversations, but if she doesn't allow herself to be vulnerable and doesn't take responsibility for her own feelings, she may be dodging intimacy by focusing on him. Unexpressed feelings can contaminate a relationship—and obscure the real issues. Arguments over dirty dishes, vacuuming or food shopping or even a partner's infidelity are usually symptoms of deeper problems.

After two children and 14 years of marriage, Dana Berk, 37, finally had to confront why she felt so depressed, so sexually apathetic, so envious of other couples. It had nothing to do with chore wars. "Over the years, without realizing it, Hal and I had both shut down."

Realizing she was attracted to another man was Dana's wake-up call. Rather than act on impulse, she decided to talk to her husband. "It was brutal having to express our bottled-up feelings. I have tremendous gratitude because he was wonderful in terms of being able to face the issues, deal with the pain and support me. We had many talks late into the night. There was anger, but we also cried a lot. I even have a sex drive now, and there's a passion in our relationship that's deeper than we ever had. I think we've really learned how to be there for each other."

Dave and Annie Goodrich learned to be there for each other through a series of crises—beginning with Annie's miscarriage—that made their different styles pale in comparison with their ability to share life's hard knocks. "When we lost the baby, Dave really let go," Annie says. "He knew that we both had to talk about it. When I developed an eating disorder, he was really supportive. Then our youngest was born with a birth defect. Just knowing we can talk about it makes it bearable."

Successful couples constantly and consciously nurture their relationship. "The need to protect intimacy—their time with each other—is central to being together," stresses Taffel, "all the way from having conversations without being interrupted to having weekends together without the kids. When that starts to disappear, it's dangerous; the reservoir dips too low."

Taffel suggests creating rituals. One couple he knows takes a brief walk after dinner. The Roarks try to set aside a portion of every weekend for themselves. The Goodriches try to get away one weekend a month.

Of course, some gender differences will persist: She may not feel as comfortable being away from the kids; he may never be as observant. But such issues don't have to be divisive if you remember to reserve time to be alone together and if you appreciate your common victories instead of bemoaning each other's failings.

"Your partner is probably not going to get it the first time," Dr. Barbach emphasizes. "Acknowledge small changes, even if they're not perfect." Whether your differences are over housework, child care or emotions, she adds, "really value what each of you gives." In some areas, one person probably is more proficient. "If you're better at bringing romance into your relationship, do it."

Last year Karen Mason did just that. On Peter's 40th birthday, she "surprise kidnapped" him for a weekend alone, planning the whole thing meticulously, down to taking his clothes "bit by bit" so she could pack their suitcase. "He was so appreciative," she recalls, "but he admitted that he could never have done it for me. He wouldn't have thought of all the details."

Karen is satisfied, however, because Peter is a loving husband and father who can tolerate that her idea of a great birthday present is to go away *with* the kids. Thus the Masons have reached a workable détente. "As I get older, I realize there are some real differences between men and women," says Karen, "and I'm happier when I accept it."

Who Stole Fertility?

CONTRARY TO POPULAR BELIEF, THERE IS NO INFERTILITY CRISIS SWEEPING THE NATION. WE'VE JUST LOST ALL CONCEPTION OF WHAT IT TAKES TO CONCEIVE. REPRODUCTIVE TECHNOLOGY HAS MADE US IMPATIENT WITH NATURE. SO FOR INCREASING NUMBERS OF COUPLES THE CREATION OF A NEW HUMAN BEING HAS BECOME A STRANGELY DEHUMANIZING PROCESS.

VIRGINIA RUTTER

My great-aunt Emily and great-uncle Harry never had kids, and nobody in our family talked about it. Growing up, I knew not to ask. It would have been impolite, as crass as asking about their income or their weight. The message was clear: If they didn't have kids, they couldn't have them, and talking about it would only be humiliating.

How times have changed. Today, a couple's reproductive prospects—or lack of them—are not only apt to be a conversation topic at your average dinner party, they're the subject of countless news stories illustrating our nationwide infertility "crisis."

In an infertility cover story last year, *Newsweek* reported that more than 3 million American couples would seek procreative help in 1995. Diagnostic tests, hormone treatments, fertility drugs, and assisted-reproduction techniques with names like in vitro fertilization (IVF), gamete intrafallopian transfers (GIFT), intrauterine insemination (IUI), zygote intrafallopian transfer (ZIFT), intracytoplasmic sperm injection (ICSI)—to name the top five procedures—have become as much a part of the reproductive process as the more poetic aspects of family making. While some of those 3 million–plus couples were legitimate candidates for the host of high-tech options now available to them, most wound up needing only low-tech assistance, such as boxer shorts instead of briefs.

Earlier this year, in a four-part series, the *New York Times* reported on the fertility industry's growth and the increased competition among clinics.

And that's how an infertility crisis is created and perpetuated. For contrary to popular belief, infertility rates are not on the rise. Creighton University sociologist Shirley Scritchfield, Ph.D., says that American infertility rates have not increased during the past three decades: In 1965, the infertility rate for the entire U.S. population was around 13.3 percent; in 1988, it was 13.7 percent. According to the U.S. Office of Technology Assessment, infertility rates for married women have actually *decreased* from 11.2 percent in 1965 to a little less than eight percent in 1988. These rates even include the "subfecund," the term used to describe people who have babies, just not as many as they want as quickly as they want. This means that more than 90 percent of couples have as many babies—or more than as many babies—as they want.

LETTING NATURE TAKE ITS COURSE

Rather than an infertility crisis, what we have is a society that's allowed technology to displace biology in the reproductive process, in effect dehumanizing the most human of events. At the very least, this means stress replaces spontaneity as women become tied to thermometers—constantly checking to see when they're ovulating—while men stand by waiting to give command performances. At the most, it involves women and men subjecting themselves to invasive procedures with high price tags. Whatever happened to love and romance and the idea of letting nature take its course? Instead, we seem to have embraced the idea that science, not sex, provides the best chance for producing biological children. Technicians have stolen human reproduction. And there are some 300 fertility clinics—with annual revenues of $2 billion—to prove it.

Infertility has become big business, one that's virtually exempt from government regulation. And it's not for the faint of heart—or pocketbook (see "Bucks for Babies"). But all the hype has made us lose sight of what it really takes to make a baby. Conception takes time. Infertility is classically defined as the inability to conceive or carry a baby to term after one year of unprotected sex two to three times a week. On average, it takes less time for younger (in their 20s) would-be parents than older (in their 30s) ones; as couples move through their 30s, experts suggest staying on the course for two years. But even couples in their reproductive prime—mid- to late 20s—need around eight months of sex two to three times a week to make a baby. (Last December, the New England Journal of Medicine reported that healthy women are most fertile, and therefore most likely to conceive, when they have intercourse during the six-day period leading up to ovulation.)

The correlation between how often a couple has sex and the speed with which they succeed in conceiving may seem obvious. But psychologist and University of Rochester Medical School professor Susan McDaniel, Ph.D., says she counseled one infertile couple for six months

The confidence we have in preventing pregnancies has given us a false sense of control over our fertility.

before discovering they had only been having sex once or twice a month!

Of course, these days the one thing many prospective parents feel they don't have is time. During the baby boom, couples began having children at about age 20. But by 1980—when women were in the workforce in record numbers and putting off motherhood—10.5 percent of first births were to women age 30 and older. By 1990, 18 percent of first births were to women age 30 and up. Because more would-be parents are older and hear their biological clocks ticking, they're more likely to become impatient when they don't conceive instantly. But how much of a factor is age in the conception game? Men have fewer age-related fertility problems than women do. The quality of their sperm may diminish with age; when they reach their 50s, men may experience low sperm motility (slow-moving sperm are less likely to inseminate).

After about age 37, women's eggs tend to show their age and may disintegrate more easily. This makes it increasingly difficult for women to conceive or maintain a pregnancy. That's not to say there's anything unusual about a 40-year-old woman having a baby, however. Older women have been having children for eons—just not their first ones. In many cultures, the average age of a last child is around age 40.

Some older women may even be as fertile as their younger sisters. A 40-year old woman who has been taking birth control pills for a good part of her reproductive life—thus inhibiting the release of an egg each month—may actually benefit from having conserved her eggs, says Monica Jarrett, Ph.D., a professor of nursing at the University of Washington. She may even have a slight edge over a 40-year-old mother with one or two children trying to conceive.

"Focusing on aging as the primary source of infertility is a distraction." says Scritchfield. "Age becomes a factor when women have unknowingly always been infertile. These are women who, even if they'd tried to get pregnant at age 20 or 27, would have had difficulty despite the best technology."

GENDER POLITICS AND INFERTILITY

Some feminists suggest all this talk of infertility is part of a backlash, an effort

Who Is Infertile?

Although infertility rates are not on the rise overall, Creighton University sociologist Shirley Scritchfield, Ph.D., points out that they are rising among some subgroups of the population: all young women between the ages of 20 and 24 and women of color. She says this is due to an increase in sexually transmitted diseases (STDs) among the young. STDs, including chlamydia, gonorrhea, and genital warts, can permanently harm reproductive organs. Pelvic inflammatory disease, which women can develop as a consequence of other STDs, is perhaps most responsible for infertility in young women, in part because it—as well as other STDs—often goes undetected.

With few records having been kept, it's difficult to determine whether male infertility is on the rise. A 1992 study by

Norwegian scientists looked at semen quality over the past 50 years by pooling the evidence available from earlier research. They concluded that, in general, sperm counts had decreased.

Rebecca Sokol, M.D., professor of medicine and obstetrics/gynecology at the University of Southern California, says that while the Norwegian study reports a significant reduction in sperm counts over half a century, the reductions are not "clinically significant." That is, if sperm counts have decreased over time—and many scientists do not agree that they have—they've simply gone from a very high count to moderate levels.

"We're exposed to higher levels of estrogens than ever before; we inject cows and other animals with estrogens and estrogen-like hormones to keep them healthy. There isn't any data that directly proves this alters sperm counts, but we know an increase in estrogens in men is toxic to sperm. The theory is that in some way, this low-grade constant exposure to estrogen is ultimately altering sperm."

to drive women out of the boardroom and back into the nursery. While there may be some truth to this, it's only part of the story. The fertility furor is also a result of increasing expectations of control over nature by ordinary men and women.

Ironically, the growing intolerance for the natural course of conception stems from technological advances in contraception. Birth control is more reliable than ever. The confidence we have in preventing pregnancies has given us a false sense of control over our fertility. "People have the idea that if they can prevent conception, then they should also be able to conceive when they want to," says McDaniel.

This illusory sense of control, says Judith Daniluk, Ph.D., a University of British Columbia psychologist and fertility researcher, weighs most heavily on women. "Women are told that if they miss taking even one birth control pill, they risk becoming pregnant. This translates into feeling extremely responsible when it comes to getting pregnant, too."

If we've let technicians steal fertility from us, perhaps it's because it was up for grabs. Until recently, infertility was considered a woman's problem rather than a couple's problem. In the 1950s, physicians and psychologists believed that women whose infertility couldn't be explained were "suppressing" their true femininity. Of course, in those days men were rarely evaluated; the limited technology available focused mostly on women.

When a couple steps into the infertility arena today, both partners receive

An overestimation of success rates by the technofertility industry hooks couples in.

full evaluations—in theory. In practice, however, this doesn't always happen because technology is such that even a few sperm from an infertile man are enough for high-tech fertilization. About 40 percent of infertility is the result of "female factors"—problems with hormones, eggs, or reproductive organs. Another 40 percent is explained by "male factors"— problems with low sperm count or slow-moving sperm. The remaining 20 percent is unexplained or due to factors in both partners. There may be an immune problem, where the sperm and egg are "allergic" to each other. Advances— such as ICSI, a way of injecting a single sperm into an egg during IVF—have been made to get around this immune system clash. Advances have also been made in understanding male infertility, including treatments for low sperm motility that involve extracting sperm directly from the testes. But the bulk of fertility treatments still focus on women.

Women also tend to "carry" the issue for a couple, says McDaniel. "As much as men are invested in having children, they don't have to think about it, or perhaps be as conscious of it—because women are so focused on the problem. It makes

sense, then, that when it comes to an infertility workup, men will often be the ones to put on the brakes. If both partners were running headlong onto the conveyor belt of technology, there'd be a mess. So what happens—largely because of sex roles—is women become advocates of the process, and men, who may be more ambivalent, question it and wonder whether it's time to stop."

Women will go so far as to protect their partner from the diagnostic process, as well as treatment, observes Daniluk. She says they'll even shield their partner from blame when he's the infertile one.

COMPELLED TO PRODUCE

Regardless of its cause, infertility is a profound blow to people's sense of self, who they are, and who they think they should be. To understand just how devastating infertility is, it helps to know why we want babies in the first place.

"The most essential thing the human animal does is reproduce," insists anthropologist Helen Fisher, Ph.D., author of *Anatomy of Love*. Citing survival of the species as the reason why our drive to reproduce is so strong, Fisher says it's not surprising that couples will go to great emotional and financial lengths to conceive. "The costs of reproducing have always been great. The time-consuming and costly procedures a modern couple uses to pursue their reproductive ends may never be as costly as it was on the grasslands of Africa, when women regularly died in childbirth."

Fisher says men, too, feel obliged to plant their seed or die out, so they'll work very hard to sire and raise their own kids.

B ucks for Babies

The fertility industry may boast of its dedication to bringing healthy babies into the world, but in reality, it appears to be interested in producing only *wealthy* ones.

A thorough fertility workup to diagnose the source of a couple's problem can take up to two months and cost from $3,000 to $8,000. That's just for starters. For a simple procedure, like hormone shots to stimulate egg production, it's $2,300 per cycle. Expect to pay $10,000 for one round of in vitro fertilization (IVF). About 30,000 women a year attempt pregnancy via IVF. Intracytoplasmic sperm injection, where doctors inject a single sperm into an egg, adds $1,000 to the price of IVF. A procedure requiring an egg donor (in demand among older mothers) runs from $8,500 to $16,000—per cycle. A varicocelectomy, to correct varicose veins around the testicles, costs $3,500. Few health plans include coverage for fertility treatment. Even when insurance does kick in, it doesn't cover all of the direct costs, to say nothing of the many indirect costs, including lost income from missed work and child care expenses.

They aren't exempt from social pressures either. "Male sexuality has always been tied to potency," says William Doherty, Ph.D., a professor of family social science at the University of Minnesota. "The slang term for male infertility is 'shooting blanks.' After all, what good is a man if he can't reproduce? That's probably why we've blamed women for infertility for millennia. It's too humiliating for men."

Animal instincts may provide the primal motivation for having kids. But notions of masculinity and femininity are another big influence. Infertility taps into our deepest anxieties about what it is to be a man or a woman, a core part of our identity. McDaniel says many of the infertile women she sees speak of feeling incomplete. They also talk about a loss of self-confidence and a sense of helplessness and isolation. Women still get the message that much of their femaleness is derived from motherhood—more so than men are taught their maleness is tied to fatherhood. Losing the dream of motherhood may fill a woman with such grief that she'll consciously avoid the places kids populate. It's a loss that can be difficult to share because it's the death of something that never was.

Infertile men also experience a loss, says McDaniel. They, too, may insulate themselves from the world of kids. They may be even less likely than women, says Doherty, to talk about their sad feelings. "Men feel if they're not able to pass on their seed, they're not living up to what's expected of them as men," says Andrew McCullough, M.D., director of the Male Sexual Health and Fertility Clinic at New York University Medical Center.

Parental expectations are yet another powerful reason people feel the procreational pull. "When it comes to having kids," says McDaniel, "there can be a lot of familial pressure. If you don't have them, everybody wonders why."

TECHNOFERTILITY TAKES OVER

With all of these pressures to produce, is it any wonder couples get caught up in the technofertility maze? Seduced by well-meaning doctors who hold out hope and the availability of all kinds of treatments, two vulnerable people—alone—are left to decide how much re-productive assistance they will or won't accept. There are no guidelines.

It wasn't until about their seventh year of fertility treatments that a physician finally sat Steve and Lori down and told them that their chances of having a baby were slim, given their ages—37 and 32—and their efforts until that point. Steve had had a varicocele, a twisting of veins in the testicles, and Lori had had various explorations of her ovaries by endoscopy in search of ovarian cysts, plus two failed IVFs.

"It turned out that my wife's gynecologist wasn't really competent to tell us about fertility treatments," Steve says. "It ended up being like going to the Motor Vehicle Bureau. First, they tell you to take care of one thing, but it turns out you need to take care of something else. Then they tell you to go do a third thing. You wind up moving from place to place with no particular plan. It's rare that you get a doctor who explains in plain English what's going on and helps you evaluate your choices. Instead of talking with Lori and me and asking us what was in our hearts, they were saying, 'Okay, you want a baby, how can we make one for you?'"

Even as they went through test after test, procedure after procedure, it seemed at least semicomical to them: drives at the crack of dawn to a distant clinic, painful shots Steve was obliged to administer to Lori, even a "hamster penetration" test that involved Steve producing a sperm sample to see whether his sperm could penetrate a hamster's egg. All of it was very difficult to resist. "I think it was partly the adventure that kept us going," Steve says. "Once you commit and say you're going to give it a go, you don't want to stop midstream. There's always the chance that it might work. I mean, medicine is fantastic; you take some pills, stick some stuff in you, and maybe you get a baby."

Fertility treatments are so technically focused, says McDaniel, that people's feelings get left behind. She advocates a more human "biopsychosocial" approach. "Couples' emotional needs should dictate the pacing and decision making as they move up the pyramid of technological possibilities. But in some, maybe even most clinics, little or no attention is paid to the process, only the possible product. As a result, the patients suffer."

Even under normal circumstances, conception is immaculate—it tends to clean all else out of the mind. Whenever people begin to plan a family, says McDaniel, their worldview narrows. But with technofertility, a couple's worldview can narrow to the exclusion of all else. Because the outcome is the entire focus, fertility treatments intensify our instincts to give birth and nurture a baby. So the very technology that disregards couples' emotions also heightens their desire to nurture. For women, especially, maternal instincts are intensified by all-consuming fertility treatments that leave little time for anything else and cause women to define themselves solely as mothers.

Indeed, as soon as prospective parents seek help, statistics and biology become the focus. Before long, they're up on the latest research and talking in terms of "control groups," "statistical significance," and "replication." The walls of fertility clinics are plastered with pictures of newborns, and staffers and customers alike speak endlessly about "take-home baby rates," the bottom line when it comes to success. But take-home baby rates are more than numbers. They represent people's hopes for a family.

As a result, couples undergoing intensive fertility treatments lose their wide-angle perspective on life. They may fall behind in their careers and cut themselves off from friends and family, all in the narcissistic pursuit of cloning their genes. Technology may provide us with the illusion that it's helping us control our reproductive fate, but in reality, it just adds to the narcissism. "The higher tech the treatment, the more inwardly focused couples become," says Doherty.

"Biological connections are so strongly emphasized in our culture that it's hard not to become self-absorbed," Steve explains. "You even see it in the adoption process. Couples are often concerned that the kids they adopt have similar characteristics to their own. But the truth is, kids are kids." (Steve and Lori have since adopted a baby.)

An overestimation of success rates by the technofertility industry hooks couples in and fuels the narcissism. Fertility clinics typically report about a 25 percent success rate. But this rate is usually calculated after clinics have screened out the

How Couples Cope with Infertility

In general, couples without children are more likely to split up than partners with children, reports demographer Diane Lye, Ph.D., a professor of sociology at the University of Washington. What about mates who can't have kids, or who want them but encounter difficulties? Researchers don't know about the ones who don't seek fertility treatment—and who tend to be poor. But Lauri Pasch, Ph.D., a psychologist and fertility researcher at the University of California at San Francisco, did study 50 couples who, on average, had been trying to get pregnant for two years. She says infertile couples going for fertility treatment tend to have higher rates of marital satisfaction than the rest of the population.

"Most couples who seek fertility treatment are committed enough to their relationship that they will go through pain and suffering to have a child together," says Pasch. And if they have the skills to address their problem, their relationships tend to become stronger—even if they never have a baby."

So what kind of skills does a couple confronting infertility need? Mates with matching coping styles do best, says Pasch, who points out that infertility, like other major stressors, tends to bring out people's natural ways of coping. "Couples who have similar ways of living with problems and relieving their distress are better off than those with different styles," says Pasch. "Both might be support seekers, or both might be private and keep to themselves. So long as they both go about things in the same way."

Pasch finds that spouses who rely on emotional expression can do harm to their relationship. That's because they tend to let their feelings out *at* their partner rather than sharing them *with* him or her. (So much for the old saw that talking things out always makes them better.) "In this destructive communication pattern, one person eventually demands and one withdraws," says Pasch. "One member of the couple pressures for change, while the other one withdraws, refusing to discuss the problem."

Though which partner demands and which one withdraws can shift, typically women are the ones who demand more, and men are the ones who withdraw. In the case of an infertile couple, the woman may get alarmed sooner than her husband about not being able to have children. But they may switch roles, and she may become more resigned to it while he becomes more concerned and wants to start treatment. Either way, the couple is at odds.

Tammy and Dan, the parents of two children—the products of five IVFs and eight years of fertility treatments—were just such a couple. "I was the leader, taking care of everything," says Tammy. Her daily routine included being at the fertility clinic at 6:30 every morning for blood tests, and returning every afternoon for more exams. Once she became pregnant, she had to stay in bed practically from the day she conceived until the day her children were born.

"When you're trying to get pregnant, it becomes your whole focus. Everything you do is planned around it. You are told what to do every day, and you can't do very much. Then, all of a sudden, you realize you have focused your whole life on getting pregnant and not on your relationship. After our second child was born, and we didn't have a crisis to deal with every day, it was difficult being normal."

The emotional climate becomes even more difficult when one partner chooses to withdraw from the entire fertility process. Psychologist Susan McDaniel, Ph.D., of the University of Rochester School of Medicine, saw one couple where the wife underwent extensive tests to see whether she was infertile. Her husband, meanwhile, could never seem to make it to the urologist to be tested. He couldn't tolerate the idea that his sperm count might be low. Of course, his wife was furious. She had gone through painful and stressful—not to mention expensive—workups. When her husband finally went to the urologist, he couldn't produce a sperm sample. When he finally did, it turned out he was the infertile one. Both partners had trouble understanding what the prospect of infertility was like for the other one. Eventually, they decided to get a divorce.

most hopeless cases. The true rate—which counts everyone who has sought reproductive help and which considers live births rather than pregnancies as success—is closer to half, Scritchfield says. "Unfortunately, this isn't what the public hears. If we were really concerned about infertility, we would be working on preventive measures. That's not addressed by biomedical entrepreneurs because they don't deal with people, just body parts."

Yet technofertility can create such stress in a couple that it can come close to undoing their relationship—the raison d'être for baby making. McDaniel remembers one couple who were at complete odds, having come to see her a year after having undergone five years of unsuccessful fertility treatments. The woman still hoped technology could help them, but the man felt his wife had gone too far; the procedures were invasive and the lack of results too painful. Attempting to protect both of them from any more disappointment, he insisted they stop.

The husband questioned why they'd ever gotten involved in the first place, and the wife felt unsupported by his reaction. No one at the fertility clinic had helped them work through any of their reactions. In therapy with McDaniel, they ultimately admitted to themselves—and to each other—what their expectations had been and the anxiety and grief they felt over the loss of an easy pregnancy. Then they decided to adopt.

Given the single-mindedness of baby making, adding infertility and technology to the mix creates the perfect recipe for obsession. But it's an obsession only for the rich. Which means having a baby becomes a luxury that many truly infertile couples, who might otherwise make wonderful parents, will never be able to afford.

MISSING CHILDREN

One couple's anguished attempt to conceive
By Bob Shacochis

One morning last April, groaning with self-reproach but not yet contrite, I woke up in an unfamiliar place, somewhere I had never slept before yet nevertheless under my own roof. I had done this maybe a half dozen times in the two decades my wife and I had been together—abandoned her, crying and curled into herself, in the bed we shared and exiled myself to a spare room or downstairs couch, tugging a stubborn blanket of fury over my head like a temporary shroud.

The image of bedtime estrangement—a potent domestic cliché—evokes fault even in the absence of fault, but the tension between us that had erupted the night before into a matched set of absurd accusations had nothing whatsoever to do with infidelity and everything to do with faith: faith that, despite the odds, we could survive as a couple even as we confronted the defeat not of romance but of the garden of our mutual flesh. For during the past eight years, while America cried crocodile tears over the apparent dissolution of its families, my wife and I had knocked our heads against emotional and physiological brick walls trying to manufacture a family of our own. We had tried our very best to heed Babe Ruth's stalwart advice—"Never let the fear of striking out get in your way"—but if baby making were baseball, our team was now playing its final season, and the last game was all but over.

Early on in our life together, my wife had decided to avoid pregnancy, which is not the same as the desire to remain childless, although that's how it had seemed to me at the time, back at the beginning of the 1980s, when I was in my early thirties and first raised the subject of children with the woman I lived with and loved. More than wanting the freedom to anchor herself in a career, she simply didn't wish to be pregnant, she told me, ever; pregnancy was synonymous with trauma, perhaps even self-destruction. And although I was alarmed by her rhetorical absolutism, I was also willing to tell myself that this was not her final word on procreation, that the subject could be deferred without disadvantage and then favorably resolved—that, like all things, it would be held accountable to its own season.

Still, my literary and biological clocks had apparently been set to the same mean time, synchronized to similar imperatives, and it made full sense to me that my first breaks as a writer, when I began faintly scratching the fact of my existence on the palisades of the external world, coincided with the wistful clarification of my desire for offspring—on one of many levels, the impulse to secure readers, to pitch a rock into the generational pool and contemplate the concentric rings that ripple through a self when one's blood-past has made a concerted effort to speak to the future. This was a gift I myself had not inherited (only the dimmest record of my peasant ancestors survived), and, for reasons of self-admiration, I envied my future progeny, whom I hoped I might one day engage, through my writing if nothing else, on terms so intimate that the existential distance between parent and child would compress to mere logistics, and never would I be mistaken for a stranger but recognized as a fellow traveler.

Although children arrive on earth adorned with metaphorical ribbons of immortality, a life with a child is, finally, only a life of days actually lived. Shakespeare's third sonnet, which warns "Die single, and thine image dies with thee," is

Bob Shacochis, a contributing editor of Harper's Magazine, *is working on a book about the U.S. intervention in Haiti. His most recent article for the magazine, "The Immaculate Invasion," appeared in the February 1995 issue. A different version of this essay will appear in* Family, *to be published by Pantheon Books.*

quaint and sentimental, vulnerable to the vicious paradox of time and the technological eternities, illusory and fleeting, that proliferate across the surface of contemporary life. Beyond the increasingly bad moral premise of the biblical command to go forth and multiply, the rationales for having children felt rather metaphysically arbitrary to me, weighted with self-love and often preempted by accident, but there were lines in the sonnet that struck me with the force of crippling hunger, lines that made me imagine one day seeing the face of my wife in the face of my son or daughter—"Thou art thy mother's glass, and she in thee/Calls back the lovely April of her prime." If my words were meant to reproduce myself, my corporeal seed had a loftier, more lovesick goal: to reproduce my wife. And although I understood this was, in its most gentle form, the ideal scenario of love, and most represented my preference, it was, I had to concede, only one of many variations on the theme of parenthood.

For if love itself were a destiny, like geography or genetics, once a child washed ashore in your life, was it really so important where that child came from, did it matter how it arrived? The shape of her eyes, the color of his skin? Maybe, I told myself, yet maybe not. Which is to say, however much I wanted a child, I didn't feel bound to any specifics or obligated to motivations that reared inward, back to the barn of DNA. Nor did I believe that having children was what it meant to grow up, or that having children was an innately self-magnifying event for an adult rather than, as is sometimes the case, pathetically self-subverting. We weren't, to our knowledge, fundamentally lonely, needy, or incomplete people, my wife and I; we could discern no gap in our collective psyche that needed to be repaired by a child. Yet if procreation was not the zenith of an individual's existence, it was still an immense and astonishing opportunity. Why ignore a vital clause in the divine contract, not necessarily between men and women but between humanity and life? Why show up at the celebration empty-handed, with nothing to give back to that from which you have taken?

If, for the moment, my wife resisted the appeal of kids underfoot, fine, because as the years passed our life was whole without them. So when, at her prompting, we stopped using contraceptives, it seemed to me we had tacitly decided to wait and see what happened, and this rearrangement seemed a workable balance between what chance found and determination might deliver. I told myself that, regardless of what either of us intended, someday an alarm clock would ring, wake my wife from her reluctance, rouse me from my dreamy ambivalence, and we would consciously, conclusively, propel ourselves into the future and mate. And it did, in fact, happen . . . the way sadness happens, the way it takes up permanent residence in your life. One heartbreak and then another, and then that's it: something precious has receded, beyond reach, forever.

Sooner or later, I suspected, the focus would sharpen, and so it did on Christmas Eve, 1988, in a cabin in the Uinta Mountains of Utah. My wife and I found ourselves trapped in a blizzard with Tyrone, our aging Irish setter, our surrogate son. He was dying, and as I watched his labored breathing, I hated myself for removing him from the old-dog comforts of Florida to expose him to this terrible blast of cold. Finally my wife insisted we buck up, drink a bottle of wine, try to enjoy the meal I had cooked on this damaged but still sacrosanct occasion, and then afterward, the Christmas treat she had been anticipating all day: we'd repair to bed and listen to our friend Ron Carlson on National Public Radio, reading his beguiling short story "The H Street Sledding Record."

But as the moment approached, the radio's reception tore away into tatters of static, and my wife howled. It was Ron himself who had lent us the cabin; there was a copy of his collection, *The News of the World,* there. My wife announced she would read the story herself, out loud. Shivering on a couch across the room, she began. The story is about a young couple in Salt Lake City who each Christmas Eve go sledding with their daughter. It's a law, I think, not of life but of humanity, that you create your own myths, find things to believe in, things smaller than God but larger than a credit card, in order to inhabit a loving universe, and this fictional family's annual attempt at the H Street sledding record—the moment the daughter wedges herself between her mother and father atop the sled and they accelerate into the snowy darkness—becomes the defining rite of their union. My wife kept her composure until the last two paragraphs, when her voice began to waver: "Now the snow spirals around us softly. I put my arms around my family and lift my feet onto the steering bar."

I watched dismayed as my wife locked up in agony on the final lines, the book slipping from her hands. "I want my own daughter," she said, her voice barely audible. She lifted her head, her lower lip trembling, and looked at me. "I want my own daughter," she cried adamantly, as if suddenly understanding that she had been opposed in this desire and it was time to fight back against whatever it was within her fate that had designed this prohibition. "God! God *damnit,* where is my little girl?" I leapt up from the bed to rock her in my arms while she exhausted herself into sleep. She was thirty-five years old. I was thirty-seven. This was the Christmas when my wife and I realized there was indeed a missing person in our life together, and this was the moment we began the enormously difficult quest to track and rescue that person, that child, from the wilderness of our shared imagination.

That Christmas also marked the end of our biological innocence, our sense of ourselves as autonomous beings patterned by the mystery of creation rather than, after technology's sublime seduction, mere organic systems as readily manipulated as the electrical impulses inside a machine. And although this is a story that has counted and recounted its years, its blood cycles, begging an ending that never arrives, becoming a small, private tale of weariness and despair, but equally of tenacity and hope, it is also, and primarily, a travelogue about a journey we took into the kingdom of science and beyond. I couldn't tell you what this other place was called, the world beyond the envelope of empirical remedy, but its cities are named Dream and Myth, Angel and Supplication, and its central crossroads are named Anything You Want and Delusion.

A few weeks after we returned from Utah, we lost Tyrone, our alter ego: the purest, simplest, and most viscerally consistent reflection of our joy in togetherness. Tyrone had been with us since the early days of our relationship. We, a childless couple, were not and had never been two, always three. I didn't expect our lives would ever be the same. For weeks I sat mourning in a chair, stupefied by the awful, intolerable emptiness of the house, and yet I thought I didn't want another dog; maybe now was the time to seize complete freedom, take advantage of our lack of responsibility for another life, however much I savored the clarity and mechanisms of such responsibility. My wife coaxed me back to my senses. It was time, she finally said, to go on.

We got a new pup, very much like obtaining a new chamber for one's heart, and now implicit in my wife's domestic building code was a clause acknowledging that our relationship had been rezoned for kids. "You're sure?" I was compelled to ask. We had been together thirteen years, and after our first year, when she had told me she never wanted to be pregnant and told me why, I told myself to be patient and never pressed the issue. She is a remarkable woman, beautiful and strong, an intelligent and mature woman who, as a junior in high school in the late 1960s, was out

of it enough to get unwittingly pregnant. This happened before *Roe v. Wade,* and her parents, as you might imagine, reacted in a manner that could not have been mistaken as sympathetic. In order to have a legal abortion she had to be declared mentally unfit by not one but two psychiatrists, and so her folks dragged her off to the shrinks, then dumped her alone at Columbia Hospital for Women in Washington, D.C. My dear girl. No one thought to tell her what was about to happen, that the fetus was too far advanced for traditional intervention and instead would require a saline-solution abortion, actually a method of inducing labor, and its result would not necessarily be immediate. The OB/GYN doctors pumped my wife, who was once this frightened girl, full of salt water, and then housed her away in a room for three days, waiting for her body to evict the child, which it did on the fourth day, her womb evacuating its voluminous contents onto the tile floor. She was sixteen years old and five months' pregnant and alone. I never knew this girl, but I knew and loved the woman she had become, and if what had happened to the girl was something that the woman could not overcome, I understood, however helpless I felt in that understanding.

Now I needed reaffirmation of her own certainty, her willingness to push off from shore into the unknown and its surprising challenges, especially now that she was enrolled in law school, and yeah, she answered, she was sure. For the next two years we did what, conventionally, you do: we threw away the condoms and f___ed. Beyond the customary rewards of lovemaking, nothing happened, although there were subtle changes in our conjugal pattern, a density that clustered around significant days of the month. I developed a keener sense of my wife's bodily rhythms, the tempo between ovulation and menses, and now I awoke to the *peep* of her digital thermometer as she tracked the rise and fall in her temperature that would signal the ovaries' release of eggs into the fallopian tubes. Without urgency, we went about our lives, conscious of our agenda but not (yet) neurotically enthralled by the process. We had set up shop, we were open for business, we had a modest goal, one customer was all it would take to measure success in our enterprise, we were frustrated but not alarmed, yet in the back of our minds, increasing in frequency, was an unsettling echo: *Nothing's happening.*

For baby boomers approaching middle age, the narrative of baby making has been ironically reversed, and frolicsome screwing no longer can be relied upon. The goddess Technologia is not now the protector but the enhancer—the madam, the pimp—here in the brothel of reproductive science, with its endless promises of redemption.

T HAT CHRISTMAS

MARKED THE END OF OUR

BIOLOGICAL INNOCENCE

We had been living in Florida only a few years; my wife needed a trustworthy gynecologist. Female friends recommended a specialist, the best in town—let's call him Dr. Cautious—and, after an examination, which revealed no obvious cause for her inability to get knocked up, my wife became his patient. I soon fell victim to the diagnostic chronology and became suspect

On videotape, my wife's uterus was being scorched by a laser

number one, ordered to sample the male version of the small but memorable humiliations commonplace to women in the literal maintenance of their inner lives. What I mean is, I had to provide semen for analysis—ejaculate into a jar, a dubious, shabby pleasure. How absurd the moment: the cold glass cunt, the quick indifferent hand, the presentation to a technician of this pathetic colloid specimen.

Several days later, we received the results. On the face of it, the news was somewhat of a relief. The analysis suggested that I might be the bump in our reproductive road, a condition easily repaired: no hot baths, boxer shorts, and, to compensate for my smoking, large doses of vitamins B and C. After two weeks of this regimen, it was clear my semen was adequate, and we were instructed to have sexual intercourse, after which my wife had to throw on her clothes and rush to the gynecologist's office for an appalling postcoital examination meant to determine if her body, reacting to my sperm, was issuing the wrong chemical signals, treating the pearly troops like hostile invaders. But no, nothing was amiss, we were all friends here in the birth canal. Dr. Cautious was cautiously optimistic. My wife and I allowed ourselves a half dozen months of mindless normalcy, bed-wise, before we were forced again to admit the obvious, only this time the obvious echoed with unsuspected depth and darker meaning. As two halves of a projected whole, we were failing to come together, turned back from our greatest ambition as a couple. We were failing to connect, not with eternity but with the present, the here and now, and the danger in that was a sense of self-eradication.

While Dr. Cautious stoically advised patience, my wife, tentatively at first, tried to convince him that what she felt instinctively was true—that she was walking around with a rare disease, nonsymptomatic endometriosis—and although she won this battle, she lost the war. Who would not agree that one level of hell is exclusively reserved for the insurance companies, medicine's border guards, who cast a beastly eye upon all would-be

immigrants. Finally Dr. Cautious acquiesced to exploratory surgery, but our health insurance company responded with Las Vegas rules: if surgery identified a problem, they'd pay; if surgery was inconclusive, the $10,000 cost would have to come somehow from our own empty pockets. Lacking hard evidence that anything was wrong, the gamble seemed foolhardy indeed, and it took a full year, another year of futility, to switch our policy to a more magnanimous HMO.

Exploratory laparoscopy confirmed my wife's worst suspicion: the most severe class of endometriosis had gummed up her reproductive tract, and fibroid tumors as well as scarring condemned her to permanent infertility without corrective surgery. Good news, sort of; the procedure had a high success rate, but the preparation for it was a hormonal nightmare: my wife was made to endure two months of chemically induced menopause designed to shrink the marble-size growths and thus facilitate their removal. The operation was, in fine postmodern fashion, videotaped, so that later my wife and I could review it at home, watch in macabre fascination her uterus being scorched by a laser. "Look," came Dr. Cautious's laconic voice-over, "there's your gall bladder."

Five months later, my wife was pronounced fit, and a month after that she waved in front of me a little plastic stick from a home pregnancy test. Pregnant. I cheered, of course, I felt a surge of joy, yet no true sensation of accomplishment, knowing full well we would have to hold our breath as we crossed the immeasurable distance between a blue line on a stick and the deliverance of a child. A month later my wife returned home euphoric after her first sonogram, waving the indecipherable image of our embryonic union—a fingernail-size fishbaby. I couldn't relate to the linear storm of squiggles, which seemed of secondary importance to the sea change in my wife's demeanor. She had never felt better, she claimed, she had never felt this good in all her life. I soon found her on the phone, talking excitedly with her friends, her sisters, her mother, and I told her perhaps she should wait until the end of the first trimester to spread the happy news, but she couldn't contain her jubilation, she wanted to share the hard-won moment with those who loved her, and if the unthinkable happened, then, she thought naively, she would share the pain of that moment too.

The following month, December, I was on assignment in northeastern India, waiting for the sun to rise over southwestern China and burst forth among the peaks of the Himalayan range that dominated the near horizon, a mammoth uplift of the earth's crust culminating in the five summits of the world's third-highest, and most sacred, mountain—Kangchenjunga. As I climbed out of my jeep, something amazing happened. A shooting star blazed down, burning *below* Kangchenjunga's 28,099-foot summit, streaking down perhaps another mile before it extinguished. I was dumbstruck for a moment, and then I blurted out to my companions, "That was about my child." In the days ahead I would recount the story of the shooting star, and my listeners would congratulate me on such a lucky omen. Within a few weeks I would receive their letters at home in Florida, prayers that all was well with the child, that my first-born would be a son, but by then I knew that the very hour I had seen the star flame across the face of Kangchenjunga, halfway around the earth, the fetus had died and my wife was in the midst of a miscarriage.

Twelve months of rueful insularity passed, the condolences of our friends and relatives met by my wife's self-imposed silence. Faith returned us to the bedroom and failure returned us to another Christmas, another cascade of tears. I was caught by surprise and sat down next to my suddenly bawling wife on the sofa. "Honey, what's wrong?" I asked, embracing her. "The baby died a year ago today," she wailed. I didn't quite understand and stupidly asked, "What baby?" The truth was, I had never permitted myself to imagine the child that had inhabited her womb for a scant three months, a most ephemeral bond between us, tissue-thin, and prematurely ruptured. I had stored away my acceptance until I saw her belly inflate, until the day she placed my hand on its roundness to feel the first kick. Of course I knew the fetus had existed, but other than the enigmatic experience on the mountaintop in India I had not connected with that existence, and for me this shadow-child remained shapeless, faceless, and nameless, forever lost in the cosmic mail, something that had profoundly inspired us but had come no closer to our lives than a falling star.

But for my wife it was different: she had acknowledged this baby's presence in her breasts, her toes, her skin; and when its thimble of life had spilled—not a miscarriage technically but a death that would have to be cleaned away in the hospital—she had known that too, before any doctor's confirmation.

There were cognitive and psychological issues I came to realize were not mine and never would be, given my gender and its biological limitations. In the ongoing rehearsals for parenthood I was conception's silent partner, a passive investor, spermatologically speaking, whereas my wife was the line producer, subject to the paralyzing responsibilities of opening night. Awash in melancholy, I watched the burden of doubt crease her face. She felt under siege by the possibility that her continuing infertility would defeat our relationship: Was she dispensable? Would I awake one morning as merciless as Henry VIII? Such questions seemed anachronistic and landed like punches on my heart, yet it was true that it became more and more difficult to conceal my dissatisfaction with the progress of the campaign. Dr. Cautious ordered more tests, but to me his stewardship seemed defined by infuriating hesitation. Let's find out where we're going and get there, I lobbied my wife. All problems ought to have solutions.

As the year went by I was often on the road, one of us parachuting in on the other the days she ovulated. The schedule grew tedious, but there was a certain harried romance to it all. In six months we made love in Florida, London, New York, Missouri, and twice in Washington, D.C. My wife had finished law school and landed herself a demanding job as a staff attorney in the Florida State Senate drafting First Amendment legislation, her area of expertise, but she made no secret of her loneliness, falling asleep twenty-five out of every thirty days sandwiched between our two new dogs but otherwise deserted, and my guilt whispered to me: *give her a child to keep her company.*

Instead of abandoning hope, we amended it, developing contingency plans. We began to speak about adoption matter-of-factly, with an explicit though not fully parsed understanding that we would stay the biological course, run with the trickle of our luck until the trickle ran dry. Adoption was and always had been our safety net, and we in fact considered it a second act, a sequel; once we got rolling we were going to fill up the house. Whenever I headed overseas, before she kissed me goodbye, my wife would say in a fanciful voice, "Bring me home a baby," and I knew she meant it. First, though, we were going to expend all biological options like a twelve-step recovery program: one day at a time.

That summer I went to Haiti to cover the U.S. military intervention, traveling between the island and Florida for the next eighteen months. Dr. Cautious injected dye into my wife's womb, discovering a blockage of scar tissue in one fallopian tube and clear sailing in the other. I was made to jerk off into more bottles, then more tests, more pale assurances. My wife was beginning to feel like a tawdry lab experiment, and I frankly was getting fed up, not with her but with Dr. Cautious.

One night I returned from Haiti and found my wife in bed, her face swollen from weeping. She didn't often cry, and never for sentimental reasons. It was her habit to put on a brave face, to cloak her tribulations behind false cheer. Once or twice a year her suffering would overflow the cup of its solitude, and this was one of those times. Someone close to us had died in an accident, another was terminally ill, and her sister, she had just learned, had breast cancer. "I've been lucky," she told me bitterly, the tears streaming down her face. "There's tragedy in every life, but I've been spared. My tragedy is to have no children. I waited too long for everything."

Never had I heard my wife venture so near to self-pity, either before or since. Our struggle wasn't making either of us strong, only resigned, our hearts slowed by sadness. Her words frightened me, and their wretched poignancy galvanized me into action. Our advance to the next level was long overdue, and I insisted on accompanying her to a consultation with Dr. Cautious. Was I pushing this beyond her capacity and desire? No, she said, this is what she wanted, too. But no matter how much a couple discusses such things, the right and the wrong of a decision are never easily determined or entirely resolved. At the gynecologist's office, I listened to him murmur the platitudes of his profession—"just keep trying, hope for the best"—and I felt my pulse rise in reaction to the complacency of this well-intentioned but uninvested man. "This is no good, and I want it to stop," I said. I was now forty-three years old, my wife was forty-two, and time was the luxury of other, younger couples. "What do you want to do?" he asked, and we left with a referral to the fertility clinic at the University of Florida.

On the morning of our appointment in the summer of 1995, we drove to the Park Avenue Women's Center in Gainesville, Florida, where we sat in a waiting room filled with madonnas and infants, inhaling the postnatal smells—diapers and talcum and milky vomit—of our imagined destiny. We were fetched to an interview room and introduced to Ginny, a compassionate nurse who would serve as our guardian and guide into the enchanted forest of in vitro fertilization. The questions were common sense, the literature lucid and comprehensive—ovulation induction, egg retrieval, fertilization, embryo transfer, egg donation, and cryopreservation of "surplus embryos."

Ginny explained success rates: IVG—25.3 percent; egg donor IVF—43 percent. A roll of the dice, we were told, but also a "realistic option for many infertile couples who might otherwise never become pregnant." A doctor came in to scan our medical histories, cluck over our age, and close the deal. "I recommend we proceed aggressively," he said, and despite my wife's apprehension, I seconded the motion. Ginny returned to discuss the finances: in the next eight months, in $5,000 increments, we would empty our savings account, take out a bank loan, and borrow against my future earnings.

After we were both tested for AIDS, my wife underwent a pelvic exam. I was directed to the bathroom, given old copies of *Playboy*—erotic white noise—and told to masturbate. This fatuous, unwanted pleasure was my one sacrifice on the altar of fertility, a free ride compared with where my wife now stood poised, a seasoned veteran of repeated bodily invasions, on the feudal threshold of new tortures. We reunited in an examination room, where Ginny began un-

capping syringes and lining up innocuous vials of saline solution. Once we started down this path, I would be called upon to give my wife a monthlong sequence of daily injections in the ass, with a needle the length of my middle finger, and now Ginny was going to teach me how to do it. She demonstrated how to mix the hormones, fill the syringe, tap it free of air bubbles, jab it to the hilt into an orange. There was a pamphlet Ginny showed me, with a line drawing of a woman's backside, identifying the half-dollar size area on each buttock that could safely receive the needle without injuring the sciatic nerve.

"Okay," said Ginny, "let's have your wife lie down and pull up her skirt." I felt a flush of vertigo. "You're kidding," I protested, but of course she wasn't: this was my only opportunity to get it right with the proper supervision, and as I leaned over my wife's butt with the gleaming needle, I told Ginny I didn't want to do this. "Just plunge it straight in like a dart," Ginny coaxed, and so I did, horrified as I watched my wife grimace, her hands contract, and her knuckles whiten, and as soon as I removed the needle from her flesh I lay down atop her, aggrieved, kissing her cheek and apologizing. Teamwork, I thought, had never been so ruthless. Ginny had been a paragon of empathy, though, and I thanked her. "You have the perfect job," I said ignorantly, "bringing so much joy into people's lives." She brightened for a moment, but then her eyes turned doleful, her mouth grim. "Yes," she said, "but when it doesn't work it can be devastating."

We soon would be well educated in the exact nature and magnitude of that devastation. Mid-August I was back in Haiti, and my wife began self-injecting Lupron, a drug that produced hot flashes and insomnia, into her abdominal wall to suppress and then synchronize egg development in her ovaries. A few weeks later I was home in time to begin turning her backside into a pincushion, shooting doses of Pergonal and Metrodin, to begin stimulating egg development, into her buttocks morning and night. Neither of us was brave about the hateful needles, and the tension between us rose; under the stress of hurting her, I'd yell, she'd weep, and for a month the process itself made us adversaries. We both lived in dread of the injections. Frequent blood tests, which turned her arms black-and-blue, and ultrasound exams, in which she was painfully prodded by a wand inserted into her cervix, multiplied the hellishness of her torment.

Finally, when her ovarian follicles had achieved the optimal size, I shot her up with a hormone to trigger ovulation and we drove to Shands Hospital in Gainesville to be "harvested." For the second time in our lives, I impregnated my wife, although this time fertilization occurred in a petri dish, at the hands of Jack the white-coated embryologist, who, like a reincarnation of a nineteenth-century Fabergé artisan, further manipulated the cluster of cells in a new technique called "assisted hatching" and painstakingly abraded the shell of each embryo with an acid solution in order that it better adhere to the uterine lining. Two days later four embryos were placed inside a Teflon catheter and transferred into my wife's womb. We drove home. By the time she dragged herself to the clinic for a pregnancy test, the results were moot, because two days earlier, in a gush of tears and blood, whatever children who would ever unite our separate DNA structures, marry the essence of our flesh, and blend our natures into the next generation of us had vanished back into the unknowable starry night of nothingness. We were permitted two more attempts by the wizards of reproduction, both aborted early in the game when it was clear that my wife's body would not respond to the drugs.

This time, fertilization occurred in a petri dish

It seems it's always meant to be December, and I am always meant to be away, when the news that fractures the foundation of our lives arrives. I called her from Haiti and listened quietly to her ragged, fatigue-ridden voice. Ginny had phoned that afternoon: my wife's ovarian reserve was depleted, her infertility was irreversible, she was biologically incapable of procreation and permanently exiled from the purest form of motherhood, though not from motherhood itself.

I came back home to watch my wife, shattered and bereft, decorate the Christmas tree, to rise early in the morning, day after day, to bake cookies for the holidays—*to bake and bake and bake and bake*. What was she going to say, what words would she use to describe her anguish, to tell me what was going on in her mind, to explain what happens to the heart when a woman's reproductive time runs the course of its season? And what more could I do than promise her, with a lover's force of conviction, that another Christmas would not pass without a child in the house?

Time in season, mine; time out of season, hers. How do you reconcile this severance, the split that occurs in a couple's imagination when what ends for the female continues on for the male? For a man, history's answer, unlike technology's, had been brutally simple: choose between the barren woman and your unborn children. But science had rolled the dilemma between its magician's fingers and come up with another option.

The April argument that sent me trudging to the guest room dispersed much, if not all, of the pressure that had built between us as we ventured further on the thin ice of possibility, loaded down with the weight of our decision to proceed with our fourth in vitro fertilization attempt. I had been afraid that my wife was balking at this, her final commitment in her role as immaculate guinea pig, afraid I had somehow coopted her into agreeing to try something she didn't want to do—accept the oocyte of another woman into her womb. It was the most delicate of issues, and I thought I had given my wife plenty of room to arrive at her own decision. Six months earlier she had said she would consider egg donorship only when it was clear that all other options had been foreclosed. If she said no, that would be okay; we would redirect our dwindling money, time, and energy toward adoption. What she said she expressed rather bluntly—"At least we'll know half of what we get, right?"—and whatever her doubts, she still wanted to seize this last chance to carry a child. But this would be it; for my wife the process had escalated toward the time when she **would hand herself back to nature and be at peace, beyond reproach, beyond the secular optimism of machines and the artifice of miracles.**

It was stress, not the strategy itself, that caused our freefall into that April night's hostility—a silly detail, the timing of a phone call to Ginny—but by the next day the conflict was forgotten, and the following month the last

These were angels dancing on the head of the embryologist's pin

xeroxed calendar—OVULATION INDUCTION/ ASSISTED HATCHING—taped to the refrigerator came down, a calendar similar to its three predecessors, each an anxious countdown through the spectrum of faith and the torment of science to the imagined felicities of maternity, and each climaxing with the death of hope. It was hope, more than anything else, that my wife most feared these days.

The next morning we were in Gainesville, in an operating room at the university's hospital. High-intensity lights, state-of-the-art computer-age electronics. Everyone was in green surgical scrubs except for my wife, who was draped in a flimsy institutional gown, prone on the table. Her feet were placed flat, and her legs were bent at the knees, a drape spread from one kneecap to the other, making an open-ended tent between her thighs. Her expression was upbeat, but in the far, courageous recesses of her eyes, under the surface of her resilient smile, I could see the look of someone persecuted over and over again with no possibility of escape.

The three faces of the stork—the doctor, Ginny the nurse coordinator, the embryologist—hovered over the table, gaily inspecting what my wife held in her hand: objects, icons, fertility fetishes—things she kept in a yogurt container. Her desperate cocktail of beliefs. There was a walnut-size clay sculpture of a Paleolithic Venus—the prototypical earth mother—sent by her ill sister in San Francisco. In a doll-size leather pouch, a saint's medal, perhaps the Virgin Mary with child, carried throughout World War II by the father of a friend who herself had two IVF daughters. In a spice bottle, several grams of holy dirt, said to produce miracles of healing, that my wife had scooped up from the floor of the mission chapel in Chimayo, New Mexico. On a chain around her neck she wore an evil eye I brought her from Turkey, her schoolgirl confirmation cross, a prelapsarian mosquito embedded in amber, and a small ring of happiness jade, a gift from a friend in China. Here on the frontier of neo-primitivism and the techno-voodoo of the new millennium, I couldn't resist a wisecrack. "Hey, she's even got a chicken's head from last night's sacrifice," I joked.

"You don't notice them pooh-poohing any of it," protested my wife.

"Why not?" said the embryologist. "You don't really think we have all the answers, do you? Who knows how all of this really happens?"

Collectively, we were all trying to ignore how bizarre this was—so weird it made me spin, the moments when I contemplated what we were doing. In my own hand I held a questionnaire filled out by the anonymous twenty-three-year-old woman with whom, two days previously, I had had test-tube sex. There was a cover page, a profile of the donor—short, "attractive," in Ginny's eyes, of German descent, a college graduate, a family history of heart problems—and on it, a statement of motivation that both intrigued and baffled me: "She wants to do something nice." Something *nice*? The language of altruism struck me as girlish and archaic. The night before I had dreamed about this young woman I will never meet; we sat in a room together and talked, although I couldn't remember what we said. At breakfast before coming to the hospital, I told my wife about the dream. "What did she look like, what color was her hair?" she asked (Ginny had told us the donor's hair was dark blonde). "Not really dark blonde," I said to my wife. "It had red undertones." Now, as I flipped through the questionnaire, my wife placed her finger on the page, pointing to a box stating the woman's hair color: strawberry blonde.

This is the part my wife prefers that I not write

about—not the quirky, clutching mysticism but the enormously complicated choice of egg donorship, which neither of us had ever suspected would elicit such callous response from our closest friends. *Why would you want to do that?!* they challenged my wife on the telephone. Almost invariably these were women with their own children, women whose souls had never been lacerated by the psychic catastrophe of infertility, women who would never know the toll of our quest to have what for them was so easily given, women who would never blink at the mention of a sperm bank. Their swift, unthinking judgment brought out the devil in me: in my fantasies I took away their children, then proposed a deal—they could have them back, altered yet recognizable; their children would more or less look and act as they always had, yet they would no longer possess their maternal genes. It would be as though I had given them the opportunity to bear their own stepchildren in their wombs. That, or never see them again. What do you suppose they would choose?

The doctor pushed a button; above my wife's head, a television monitor descended from the ceiling, and there, on the screen, in translucent cabbage-green monochromatic simplicity, were the magnified kids, in truth no larger than the molecules of ink in the very tip of my pen, poised to write the word "gestation," the word "family." Three perfect human embryos in colloidal suspension: one five-cell cluster and two four-cell motes that, within the next few minutes, would be implanted into my wife. I studied the images with a mixture of awe and alienation. These were fairies, I suppose, angels dancing on the head of the embryologist's pin. More idea than substance, spirits videotaped on the cusp of potentiality, not quite of this world, clinging to the slightest speck of flesh in transition from nonexistence to being.

On the OR boom box, Jimmy Durante was singing "Make Someone Happy." The doctor had his head between my wife's legs. The embryologist approached with a stainless-steel cylinder in his hands, something that resembled a cake-frosting applicator. The doctor fed the tube's catheter past my wife's cervix, the embryologist unscrewed a cap at the top of the cylinder, and gravity nudged the embryos home. "We don't want to see you coming back out of there," Jack told the fairies, "for nine more months."

A Saturday afternoon, ten days later, the beginning of Memorial Day weekend, last May 25. We were nervous wrecks, my wife and I. She had spent the morning sweeping the patio, then making mango sorbet and baking almond cookies for a dinner party we would host that night. A few moments earlier I had asked her how she was feeling and she said, "Weird," but there was no way to gauge the significance of this, and she went upstairs to lie down. In two more days—Monday—she would go to the hospital for a pregnancy test, if she could hold out that long. In the newspaper that morning I had read that on this day, sixty-one years ago, the great Babe Ruth hit the final home run of his career. That's something, I told myself, feeling a pang of encouragement.

Writers are perpetually giving birth to the vastly extended family of their characters. Sometimes, at night in the bathtub, I say their names, testing their appeal, the weight and music of the life-creating sounds: Kyra, Catherine, Jerusha, Jack, Sam—Sammy? Who are these people? I wonder to myself, trying to visualize their every detail. Sometimes they fall out of the cradle of my mind into a quasi-immortal existence on the page. The other night, though, I said their names and knew differently. Kyra, Catherine, Jerusha, Jack, Sam—Sammy? These are the children who will not come to me, to us, our ever wayward children.

Because it was a holiday, not business as usual at the chain of clinics and hospitals she depended on, my wife had meticulously prearranged the logistics of that Monday, Memorial Day, to avoid a breakdown in the lines of communication. After my wife's morning blood test, the clinic in our hometown would call in the results to the answering machine at the Park Avenue Women's Center in Gainesville; the on-call (but off-site) nurse who was substituting for Ginny would telephone the machine, listen to the record-

ing, and then contact us with the news before noon. That's not how it went, however, because instead of phoning Gainesville as we had planned, the clinic that performed the blood test sent a fax to an empty office, and by noon, when we hadn't heard anything, my wife called the clinic, where the technician confirmed that the results had been "sent" to the women's center hours ago but refused to tell her anything else. She screamed in frustration and fear.

"Go run some errands, I said, shoving her out the door. "And by the time you get back they'll have called."

But no one called, and when she returned I watched my wife flip out, flinging the packages she carried into a window, knocking things off countertops, hitting back at me as I tried to subdue her, refusing any attempt at consolation, until finally her uncontainable hysteria imploded and she stumbled vacantly up the stairs to bed. I spent the remainder of that afternoon on the phone; finally I connected with an on-duty IVF doctor at Shands Hospital, and after he had phoned me back with the results of my wife's blood test I opened a bottle of wine, took a glass from the cupboard, climbed the stairs, and have never felt so dead as when I stood by our bedside and watched my wife face me and saw, *still*, the quick, up-turned hope that was there, shining through the pain, as she turned to hear what I would say.

Sometimes I have to hold my wife harder than I ever dreamed or wanted, and repeat—as I have throughout the worst moments of the years behind us—a faith-borne cruelty, telling her yet again that this story has a happy ending.

Men, Sex, *and* Parenthood *in an* Overpopulating World

Because women bear the primary responsibility for childrearing and family life in every country, they are also presumed to bear the primary responsibility for excess population growth. But family planning is unlikely to succeed—and population is unlikely to stabilize—until men share fully in those responsibilities.

Aaron Sachs

Aaron Sachs is a staff researcher at the Worldwatch Institute.

In almost all mammalian species, the male lives the life of a philanderer. From pandas to pumas, mammalian fathers tend to abandon their mate right after conception, leaving to the mother the entire burden of childrearing. The very classification "mammal" refers to a mother's independent capacity to nurse her babies: it's always the female bear that people see feeding, training, and protecting the cubs.

But human males are different. From the beginning, they have tended to stay with their mates and their children, and today many anthropologists and biologists believe that men's participation in the family played a critical role in the evolution of *homo sapiens'* most distinctive features, especially our capacity for psychosocial development. The children of very few other species, over the millennia, have been lucky enough to receive the attention of two caring adults.

Unfortunately, as human culture continues to evolve, more and more men are breaking with tradition and shirking their childrearing responsibilities. And the world's women and children are bearing the costs of this neglect. According to Judith Bruce, a senior associate at the Population Council in New York, the amount of time contributed by mothers to childcare is commonly seven times greater than that contributed by fathers, and the mothers' share only seems to be increasing. While important social revolutions in the industrialized world have begun to free women from an imposed dependence on men, some husbands and fathers are using this broadening of women's opportunities as an excuse to contribute less time and money to their families. By 1980, for instance, American men aged 20 to 49 were spending almost 50 percent less time living with their young children than they were in 1960. In less developed countries, even when there is a long tradition of male financial contributions to the family, men often abandon their wives and children because of increasing economic pressures: fewer and fewer are able to succeed as breadwinners. A recent Chilean study of low-income adolescent couples and their first-born children found that, by the children's sixth birthday, 42 percent of the fathers were providing no child support whatsoever.

Male sexual behavior, too, puts a strain on society: besides the indirect stresses caused by men's failure to avoid fathering children they might not be able to support later, their higher fertility levels contribute disproportionately to population growth. Because men stay fertile much longer than women do, and because they tend to be more promiscuous, the average man, by the end of his lifetime, is responsible for more children than the average woman. In the 18th century, a Moroccan emperor had reportedly fathered more than 1,000 children by the time he turned 50. Though childrearing is becoming more expensive and parents are finding themselves with fewer resources to pass on to their children (whether in the form of cash or land), many men have continued to have large families. In some sub-Saharan African countries, the average man wants to have more than 10

Of 333 fathers with eight-year-old children, only 22 percent were still living with their child.

children, in part because large families serve as cultural symbols of a man's virility and wealth. Consequently, under male-dominated social systems that tend not to hold fathers accountable for the well-being of their children, the women of the Third World are increasingly finding themselves doing hard labor for food as well as walking several miles every day for water and fuelwood—all with babies on their backs or at their breasts.

Society has long expected women to take ultimate responsibility for the duties of raising a family. Currently in the United States, fathers head only one of every 40 single-parent households: men just aren't expected to juggle childcare and a job. Single women often end up simply raising their children by themselves, whether or not they have access to resources. In all parts of the world, both women and children would no doubt be better off if women faced fewer barriers to economic independence—and if men fulfilled their familial obligations. According to a recent study in Barbados, of 333 fathers with eight-year-old children, only 22 percent were still living with their child, and the children of the fathers who stayed were doing significantly better in school than all the others. And in the Chilean study, children's diets and nutrition levels tended to be much healthier when their fathers were living at home.

Men's failure to embrace their familial responsibilities begins with a failure to acknowledge that families get started through sex. A growing body of sociological research suggests that a family's eventual size and welfare depend largely on how the father and mother interact in bed—that men who are attentive to their partner's concerns tend later to be attentive to their family's concerns. Unfortunately, many men continue to see sex not as a shared experience but as their prerogative, as simply an opportunity to fulfill their desires. When interviewed by the demographer Alex Chika Ezeh, men in Ghana explained bluntly that their large families reflected, most of all, their desire to assert their culturally sanctioned sexual dominance over their wives. "The woman has no right to choose the number [of children] she prefers," said one man, "since it is you, the man, who decides when to have sex with her."

Over the past decade, then, many advocates for women's and children's welfare have turned to fam-

ily planning as a way of addressing men's irresponsibility. And many family planning organizations, in turn, have recognized a need to supplement their efforts to provide women with safe, appropriate contraception with efforts to educate men. In the mid-1980s, for instance, the poster campaigns of many national-level affiliates of the International Planned Parenthood Association (IPPF) targeted men's sexual attitudes quite explicitly. They attempted to make men empathize with women, to help them understand that, though they themselves do not get pregnant, they do have a role in reproduction.

Family planners reason that if men take full responsibility for their potential to procreate by participating in family planning, then each of the children they do father will be both expected and wanted—and presumably they will father only the number of children for whom they are able to provide. No culture directly encourages men not to care about their families, after all. Emphasizing male responsibility in family planning, therefore, is a key to getting men both to fulfill their broader responsibilities as husbands and fathers and to contribute their fair share to population stabilization.

THE HIGHER FERTILITY OF MEN

Of course, family planning is still, at heart, a women's issue. The development of the birth control pill, the IUD, and safe methods of female sterilization have remained the most important and revolutionary innovations in the history of family planning, because they finally gave a significant number of women control over their own fertility. After all, as Margaret Sanger, America's family planning pioneer of the early 20th century, frequently noted, it is the woman who risks her life in childbirth. Even at the end of the 20th century, maternal mortality rates remain high in the developing world. In Afghanistan and Sierra Leone, for instance, according to the World Health Organization (WHO), one mother dies for every 100 live births—a rate 250 times higher than that of some European countries. And many maternal deaths in developing countries are attributed by WHO to excessive childbearing.

The focus of family planning policies and programs, then, should not be shifted away from women, but rather broadened to include men as well. Though the importance of female methods of birth control seems to lie in their very independence from male influence, and though many women would not be using contraception were it not for private, female-only clinics, the exclusion of men from family planning has also had some negative consequences for women that were not foreseen by many activists. "Putting all the responsibility onto women," says Gill Gordon of IPPF's AIDS prevention unit, "has the effect of marginalizing men and making them *less* likely to behave responsibly." In many places where female birth control methods predominate, the connection between sexuality and reproduction has disappeared in the minds of many men, and they simply haven't had to confront or even consider the very serious reasons women might have for wanting to limit their childbearing. Though giving all women control over their fertility would be a significant accomplishment, it would not insure their well-being, or the well-being of any children they might eventually want to have.

The reality in many developing countries is that if a man's wife resists childbearing, he will often simply withdraw his financial support and marry another woman. Even worse, many men have resorted to violence in order to keep their wives from using contraception. One recent study showed that more than 50 percent of Mexican women using state-sponsored birth control services do so secretly, for fear of being physically abused by their husbands. A woman's ability to regulate her own fertility is often contingent upon her partner's recognition of her right to do so—which means that family planners need to work that much harder to make men empathize with women and understand their own responsibilities.

Changing men's sexual attitudes in a patriarchal world is delicate, time-consuming, expensive work, and the cost-effectiveness of education campaigns aimed at men is always difficult to measure, since progress is inevitably so slow. It would be a mistake, then, to let male-focused policies and programs take away any of the already limited resources currently devoted to women and family planning. But changing men's attitudes about familial decision-making is still crucial, especially since men currently tend to be responsible for more children than do women. All around the developing world, the population pressures caused by high fertility are contributing at least indirectly to problems as varied as wood and water shortages, joblessness, inadequate sanitation, the spread of infectious diseases, and the accumulation of waste—all of which have a direct impact on families. And, if current demographic trends continue, the globe's current population of almost 5.6 billion will probably have risen to about 8.4 billion by 2025. Ninety-five percent of those new babies will be born in the Third World.

Traditionally, population programs and policies have held women responsible for high fertility, at least implicitly. For years, national censuses and surveys did not even consider men's fertility. A country's fertility rate—the target of most programs and policies—is always measured as the average *female* fertility rate, because women are the ones who actu-

MEN HAVE MORE CHILDREN

Average Number of Living Children of Men and Women over 50, Selected Countries in Sub-Saharan Africa.

COUNTRY	MEN	WOMEN	PERCENTAGE BY WHICH MALE RATE IS HIGHER
CAMEROON	8.1	4.8	69
NIGER	6.7	4.9	37
KENYA	9.6	7.9	22
GHANA	8.5	7.4	15

Source: Demographic and Health Surveys

ally have children. Over the last decade, however, as demographers have begun to provide more relevant data, population policies guided solely by analyses of women's fertility have begun to seem less appropriate. Especially in societies where polygyny is common, family planning programs would do better to focus on men, since most of the excess childbearing in such societies can be traced to sexual pairings of older men—who might be able to provide child support for only a few more years—with much younger women. In Kenya, Ghana, and Cameroon, for instance, married men over the age of 50, who might continue to father children until their death, tend to have between eight and 10 living children. Married women at the end of their reproductive years report having five to eight.

THE POLITICS OF CONTRACEPTION

Since so many men in the developing world are so strongly predisposed to reject family planning, and since progress in changing their attitudes is so hard to measure in the short term, Third World development experts have tended to focus their family-planning efforts on couples who are already interested in limiting childbearing. Most development funders like to support programs that aspire to deliver a certain number of contraceptives to a certain number of people and achieve a measurable decline in fertility. And, without question, expanding access to birth control devices is crucial in the struggle both to improve women's and children's health and welfare and to help stabilize the world's burgeoning population. A 1992 study by Population Action International (then called the Population Crisis Committee) found 22 countries in which men and women still have no access, in effect, to birth control information or services. The contraceptive prevalence rate—or percentage of married women of reproductive age (15 to 49) using birth control—has surpassed 50 percent in a few countries in Latin America and Asia, but in sub-Saharan Africa, for example, it averages only 14 percent.

Simply flooding developing nations with contraceptives will go only so far, however. To make a significant contribution to population stabilization on a global scale, family planning programs will have to change people's attitudes, and especially men's attitudes, about the number of children they want to have. Unfortunately, in addition to the broad social and cultural factors that discourage men from participating in family planning, there are several more intimate factors about which men tend to express concern. Some men worry, for instance, that their wives would become promiscuous if provided with the means of preventing pregnancy. More generally, many men fear—probably with good reason—that, whether or not their wives ended up using birth control for extramarital affairs, the simple fact that it would allow them to assert a new form of control over sex and their bodies would probably change the power dynamics of the marriage. And men often have genuine concerns about the threats to their partner's health that many contraceptive devices are reputed to pose. Some of their fears—about pelvic inflammatory disease from IUDs, and nausea and headaches from the pill—are valid, while others—that the pill causes arthritis and sterility—are myths perpetuated by failings in information and education systems.

Men usually have even stronger negative feelings about the three birth control methods commonly thought of as male-initiated—withdrawal, the condom, and vasectomy. Withdrawal and the condom represent an unreasonable sacrifice of sexual pleasure to many men. Family planning field workers commonly report that suggestions of condom use are most often greeted with smiles and quickly composed maxims, such as "You can't wash your feet with your socks on," or "That would be like eating a sweet with the wrapper still on it." Vasectomies are even less acceptable in many parts of the developing world, because it seems highly unnatural to many men to have surgery on their sexual organ, or because they don't understand exactly what the operation entails. In the Sudan, 34 percent of male participants in a recent study thought that getting a vasectomy was equivalent to being castrated.

Many of these concerns could be easily overcome, though, since they stem from simple gaps in information or services. Family planning programs that cater to the specific concerns of men, and that offer a wider selection of contraceptive options, with complete explanations of their risks and how they are to be used, could make converts of millions. Already, more men than ever before are at least considering the use of family planning, if only, in many cases, for spacing their children further apart.

In the early 1970s, surveys of men in sub-Saharan Africa showed consistently that more than half fervently disapproved of birth control. In the 1990s, though, outright rejection of contraception is rare even in this region. Approval ratings are still low in some countries, such as Mali, where only 17 percent of men aged 20 to 55 support family planning; but in Burundi, for instance, male approval has soared to 94 percent. In 10 other recent Third World surveys cited in a paper written by Cynthia Green for WHO, countries reported contraceptive approval rates among men of between 56 percent and 96 percent. Of course, a positive survey response hardly guarantees that a man will practice contraception, but it is a first step. Some men have even begun to express a more philosophical attitude about so sensitive an issue as female promiscuity. If a woman "wants to go out," noted a member of a 1989 focus group in Burkina Faso, "whether she takes the pill or not, she can go out." And a young telephone operator in Quito, Ecuador, went so far as to connect family planning with shared parental responsibility: "Even if you have enough money to ensure the children have a good education, they probably suffer from lack of attention if there are too many. And men here never help the women at home—she has to do everything. These kinds of decisions must be taken together by the man and the wife."

JUST FOR MEN

One way for a man to begin sharing the burden of planning and caring for a family is to offer to use a male method of birth control. Unfortunately, though, because contraceptive research has always been guided by the assumption that contraception is woman's work, men's options remain limited. While women theoretically have access to several modern, semi-permanent but fully reversible methods, ranging from the pill and the IUD to Norplant and injectables such as Depo-Provera, research on modern methods for men seems to have stopped at vasectomy. The IPPF's *Medical Bulletin* estimates that "only approximately 8 percent of the world contraceptive budget is spent on the development of male methods." It is true that certain chemical methods just aren't well suited to male physiology: developing a "male pill," for instance, would mean finding a way of blocking the ongoing production of millions of sperm without blocking the production of male hormones, a task much more daunting than chemically blocking the production of one egg every month. "Physically," however, as Elaine Lissner, the director of the Male Contraception Information Project in Santa Cruz, points out, "it's easier to stop millions of sperm than one egg. The sperm all travel through the vas deferens, a small, easily accessed tube, where they can be incapacitated or blocked." In any case, family planning researchers have hardly even begun to develop the potential range of useful contraceptive services for men.

Meanwhile, about one quarter of the world's couples who are currently using contraception rely on male methods. Withdrawal is perhaps the most dubious birth control method, with a failure rate of about 18 percent. But it has a long and notable history. Withdrawal was especially important in the 19th century during Europe's massive demographic transition to replacement-level fertility (when each man and woman have, on average, just two surviving children). The men of the Victorian era, perhaps aided by a pervasive cultural prudery, present the ultimate example of male responsibility, remembering their duty to their family even at the height of passion. Today, withdrawal still provides a free, safe method of birth control for about 15 million couples in the developing world who perhaps have no other options.

Vasectomy remains an important birth control method for men who don't want any more children. Because so many births are accidental, and because sterilization is almost 100 percent successful as a birth control method, the average vasectomy in the developing world is thought to prevent about two births. More reproductive health clinics are expanding their services and offering comprehensive vasectomy programs. PRO-PATER, in Sao

Of 204 published references on the Latin American family, only two discussed the role of fathers.

Paulo, Brazil, has been particularly successful in attracting men, thanks to a carefully planned, high-profile outreach program. Its staffers go to workplaces to talk about family planning with men in settings where they feel at ease. The clinic also runs a series of television advertisements that describe vasectomy as "an act of love" and reassure men that it does not affect sexual functioning—a key strategy with male sterilization. Nick Danforth, men's programs advisor for the Association of Voluntary Surgical Contraception in New York, likes to point out that although vasectomy—increasingly performed without a scalpel—is technically simpler, safer, and quicker than female sterilization, it is still used only a third as often.

Overall, condom use is probably the most significant male method, because it is not only cheap, easy, highly effective, and free of side effects, but it is also the one contraceptive additionally capable of preventing the spread of sexually transmitted diseases (STDs), including AIDS. Unfortunately, the condom's association with disease makes it that much more controversial as a birth control device. Many men and women, especially in regions where STDs have become widespread, take suggestions of condom use as insults: the person making the suggestion is either admitting that he or she might have a disease or expressing the fear that his or her partner might have a disease. In both cases, the implication is that someone has been unfaithful. For this reason, many couples feel uncomfortable about even acquiring condoms. "The condom is not seen as a contraceptive like, for example, the pill," explains a 50-year-old man in Burkina Faso. "It has come with AIDS. . . . If you want a condom, then that means you want to have an affair. So you have to get it via a third person. You cannot go yourself." Obtaining condoms may be even more problematic for women, because of the double standard operating in so many cultures. Men are expected to be discreet if they want to be promiscuous, but women are simply not expected to be promiscuous. Many women, intimidated by such strong stigmatization and by their male-dominated societies, end up risking pregnancy and disease rather than risking their partner's wrath by asking him to use a condom.

As with all male methods, condoms leave the woman in a particularly vulnerable situation: she

MEN *WANT* MORE CHILDREN

Average Number of Desired Children of Men and Women, Selected Countries in Sub-Saharan Africa.

COUNTRY	MEN	WOMEN	PERCENTAGE BY WHICH MALE RATE IS HIGHER
CAMEROON	11.2	7.3	53
NIGER	12.6	8.5	48
GHANA	7.6	5.3	43
BURUNDI	5.5	5.5	0
KENYA	4.8	4.8	0

Source: Demographic and Health Surveys

must depend on her partner to use them, and use them correctly. But AIDS is making condoms increasingly important to women's health in the developing world. HIV is passed much more easily from a man to a woman than from a woman to a man, and it has already infected a significant portion of the adult, heterosexual population in Africa and Asia, where prostitution and male promiscuity are common. For now, women have to rely on male condoms for their safety, and while the female condom might give women slightly more control, using it will still probably entail complicated sexual negotiations. It is essential, then, that men acknowledge the sensitivity of the situation and take the lead in encouraging condom use. Perhaps family planners and AIDS activists can join forces to produce education campaigns that will help to inform couples about the specifics of sexually transmitted diseases and their consequences, and help to dissipate sexual tensions by allowing partners to anticipate and understand each other's anxieties.

In the end, a willingness to participate in sexual and familial decisions as a concerned, forthcoming, equal partner is the real key to male responsibility. More than being willing to use a male method of birth control, men have to be willing to listen—to learn how to be sensitive to their partners' health, welfare, and desires. As Mary Daly, a leader of the modern feminist movement, has remarked, true responsibility is defined by an ability to be responsive.

NOT-SO-GREAT EXPECTATIONS

In almost all matters of policy, the family is defined as the mother-child unit: policymakers and program directors forget about gender dynamics, or simply don't expect men to take part. All too often, well-intentioned representatives of industrialized countries simply press packages of pills into the outstretched palms of Third World women, "as if women alone," in the words of the Population Council's Judith Bruce, "could bring about fertility decline, and as if their sexual and parental roles were determined autonomously." The United Nations Educational, Scientific, and Cultural Organization (UNESCO) recently asked a sociologist to do a review of the current literature on the Latin American family. Of the 204 documents she examined, only two mention fatherhood or the situation of men.

In the 1990s, men's family planning and parenting responsibilities need to be explicitly defined. A logical starting point would be prioritizing the goal of establishing paternity and enforcing child support payments—as leaders have in Nigeria, where, according to the new national population policy,

children have a legal claim on their father's time and money. Even in so "advanced" a country as the United States, where most of the so-called "deadbeat dads"—fathers who have abandoned their partner and child to the welfare system—could actually afford to pay child support, only about 18 percent do.

Changes in men's roles will not emerge quickly or with anything resembling ease. In some places, as economies modernize, the direct costs of childrearing—from medicines and nutritious foods to schooling fees—are increasing, and familial resources are getting tight. Instead of having smaller families, though, many fathers simply shift the financial burden to the mother or the older children. And even when men genuinely want to act more responsibly, they sometimes believe they are unable to because of certain social and economic factors that continue to be neglected by policymakers. Both fathers and mothers, for instance, feel in many cases that children provide them with their only means of achieving economic and social security. And many fathers insist that they would have fewer children if they could be sure that more of them would survive: a study by the World Bank revealed that, on average, the prevention of 10 infant deaths results in one to five fewer births. But fathers in sub-Saharan Africa, where the infant mortality rate has remained as deplorably high as 10 percent—compared to one percent in the industrialized world—feel that they cannot afford to take chances with their fertility. And some fathers are contributing no financial resources to their children simply because they have none to give. Often they are desperately searching for work, perhaps in a far-off city.

YOU REAP WHAT YOU SOW

Still, educational efforts—ideally in tandem with pointed policy initiatives that force men to take up some of the economic burden of raising children—have considerable potential. If more field workers sought out men and provided them with better information, they would surely have more influence over men's family planning decisions. Good strategies for increasing male responsibility range from integrating family planning into community development programs to integrating sex and gender education into primary school systems. A recent IPPF report stated that, in general, field workers have had the most success changing men's attitudes and behavior through peer counseling: when men felt they were being advised by people who really identified with their concerns, whether sexual or financial, they were much more likely to respond favorably to suggestions of taking on more familial responsibility.

In Colombia, men started turning out in droves at vasectomy clinics modeled after Sao Paulo's PRO-PATER when male clinicians began offering more reproductive health services, including urological exams, infertility treatment, and sexuality counseling. Between 1985 and 1987 the number of vasectomies being performed quadrupled in Bogota and increased tenfold in Medellin.

The National Family Planning Council of Zimbabwe ran an intensive media campaign in 1989 designed specifically to increase men's responsibility in family planning and encourage joint decision making among couples. Male educators gave a series of 80 informational and motivational talks, and an entertaining serial drama about the consequences of irresponsible sexual and familial behavior was broadcast over the radio twice a week for six months, reaching about 40 percent of the country's men. By the end of the campaign, 61 percent of the men who had tuned in to "Akarumwa Nechekuchera"—variously translated as "Man is his own worst enemy" or "You reap what you sow"—reported a change in their attitudes about their families, and 17 percent of the men who had attended at least one talk reported that they actually started using a family planning method. Most importantly, the number of men saying that family planning decisions ought to be made jointly by husband and wife had risen by 40 percent: the council's educational programs were getting men and women to talk.

Some fatalists argue that because of undeniable evolutionary and physiological differences between men and women, men aren't likely ever to take much responsibility as parents: they are no better than all the other mammalian males. But such arguments overlook thousands of years of male contributions to family welfare—from big-game hunting to protection, wage earning, counseling, mentoring, and even nurturing. Men have the potential to participate fully in planning and raising a family. It is only because they have society's implicit permission that some men still limit their participation to the act of sex.

The Artificial Womb Is Born

At birth, fathers are merely bystanders. Someday, mothers may be, too. By Perri Klass

"One by one the eggs were transferred from their test-tubes to the larger containers; deftly the peritoneal lining was slit, the morula dropped into place, the saline solution poured . . . and already the bottle had passed on through an opening in the wall, slowly on into the Social Predestination Room."—Aldous Huxley, "Brave New World"

The artificial womb exists. In Tokyo, researchers have developed a technique called EUFI—extrauterine fetal incubation. They have taken goat fetuses, threaded catheters through the large vessels in the umbilical cord and supplied the fetuses with oxygenated blood while suspending them in incubators that contain artificial amniotic fluid heated to body temperature.

With these new technologies come ethical questions so potent that the very inventors of these miracles seem half-afraid of where we may be heading.

Yoshinori Kuwabara, chairman of the Department of Obstetrics and Gynecology at Juntendo University in Tokyo, has been working on artificial placentas for a decade. His interest grew out of his clinical experience with premature infants, and as he writes in a recent abstract, "It

---

Perri Klass's most recent book is "Baby Doctor." She is a pediatrician at Boston Medical Center.

goes without saying that the ideal situation for the immature fetus is growth within the normal environment of the maternal organism."

Kuwabara and his associates have kept the goat fetuses in this environment for as long as three weeks. But the doctor's team ran into problems with circulatory failure, along with many other technical difficulties. Pressed to speculate on the future, Kuwabara cautiously predicts that "it should be possible to extend the length" and, ultimately, "this can be applied to human beings."

For a moment, as you contemplate those fetal goats, it may seem a short hop to the Central Hatchery of Aldous Huxley's imagination. In fact, in recent decades, as medicine has focused on the beginning and end stages of pregnancy, the essential time inside the woman's body has been reduced. We are, however, still a long way from connecting those two points, from creating a completely artificial gestation. But we are at a moment when the fetus, during its obligatory time in the womb, is no longer inaccessible, no longer locked away from medical interventions.

The future of human reproductive medicine lies along the speeding trajectories of several different technologies. There is neonatology, accomplishing its miracles at the too-abrupt end of gestation. There is fetal surgery, intervening dramatically during pregnancy to avert the anomalies that kill and cripple newborns. There is the technology of assisted reproduction, the in-vitro fertilization and gamete retrieval-and-transfer fireworks of the last 20 years. And then, inevitably, there is genetics. All these technologies are essentially new, and with them come ethical questions so potent that the very inventors of these miracles seem half-afraid of where we may be heading.

Between Womb and Air

Modern neonatology is a relatively short story: a few decades of phenomenal advances and doctors who resuscitate infants born 16 or 17 weeks early, babies weighing less than a pound. These very low-birthweight babies have a survival rate of about 10 percent. Experienced neonatologists are extremely hesitant about pushing the boundaries back any further; much research is aimed now at reducing the severe morbidity of these extreme preemies who do survive.

"Liquid preserves the lung structure and function," says Thomas Shaffer, professor of physiology and pediatrics at the School of Medicine at Temple University. He has been working on liquid ventilation for almost 30 years. Back in the late 1960's, he looked for a way to use liquid ventilation to prevent decompression sickness in deep-sea divers. His technology was featured in the book "The Abyss," and for the movie of that name, Hollywood built models of the devices Shaffer had envisioned. As a postdoctoral student in physiology, he began working with premature infants. Throughout gestation, the lungs are filled with the appropriately named fetal lung fluid. Perhaps, he thought, ventilating these babies with a liquid that held a lot of oxygen would offer a gentler, safer way to take these immature lungs over the threshold toward the necessary goal of breathing air. Barotrauma, which is damage done to the lungs by the forced air banging out of the ventilator, would thus be reduced or eliminated.

Today, in Shaffer's somewhat labyrinthine laboratories in Philadelphia, you can come across a ventilator with pressure settings that seem astoundingly low; this machine is set at pressures that could never force air into stiff newborn lungs. And then there is the long bubbling cylinder where a special fluorocarbon liquid can be passed through oxygen, picking up and absorbing quantities of oxygen molecules. This machine fills the lungs with fluid that flows into the tiny passageways and air sacs of a premature human lung.

Shaffer remembers, not long ago, when many people thought the whole idea was crazy, when his was the only team working on filling human lungs with liquid. Now, liquid ventilation is cited by many neonatologists as the next large step in treating premature infants. In 1989, the first human studies were done, offering liquid ventilation to infants who were not thought to have any chance of survival through conventional therapy. The results were promising, and bigger trials are now under way. A pharmaceutical company has developed a fluorocarbon liquid that has the capacity to carry a great deal of dissolved oxygen and carbon dioxide—every 100 milliliters holds 50 milliliters of oxygen. By putting liquid into the lung, Shaffer and his colleagues argue, the lung sacs can be expanded at a much lower pressure.

"I wouldn't want to push back the gestational age limit," Shaffer says. "I want to eliminate the damage." He says he believes that this technology may become the standard. By the year 2000, these techniques may be available in large centers. Pressed to speculate about the more distant future, he imagines a premature baby in a liquid-dwelling and a liquid-breathing intermediate stage between womb and air: "Immersed in fluid—that would eliminate insensible water loss—you would need a sophisticated temperature-control unit, a ventilator to take care of the respiratory exchange part, better thermal control and skin care."

The Fetus as Patient

The notion that you could perform surgery on a fetus was pioneered by Michael Harrison at the University of California in San Francisco. Guided by an improved ultrasound technology, it was he who reported, in 1981, that surgical intervention to relieve a urinary track obstruction in a fetus was possible.

"I was frustrated taking care of newborns," says N. Scott Adzick, who trained with Harrison and is surgeon in chief at the Children's Hospital of Philadelphia.

When children are born with malformations, damage is often done to the organ systems before birth; obstructive valves in the urinary system cause fluid to back up and destroy the kidneys, or an opening in the diaphragm allows loops of intestine to move up into the chest and crowd out the lungs. "It's like a lot of things in medicine," Adzick says, "if you'd only gotten there earlier on, you could have prevented the damage. I felt it might make sense to treat certain life-threatening malformations before birth."

Adzick and his team see themselves as having two patients, the mother and the fetus. They are fully aware that once the fetus has attained the status of a patient, all kinds of complex dilemmas result. Their job, says Lori Howell, coordinator of Children's Hospital's Center for Fetal Diagnosis and Treatment, is to help families make choices in difficult situations. Terminate a pregnancy, sometimes very late? Continue a pregnancy, knowing the fetus will almost certainly die? Continue a pregnancy, expecting a baby who will be born needing very major surgery? Or risk fixing the problem in utero and allow time for normal growth and development?

The first fetal surgery at Children's Hospital took place seven months ago. Felicia Rodriguez, from West Palm Beach, Fla., was 22 weeks pregnant. Through ultrasound, a congenital cystic adenomatoid malformation had been diagnosed in the fetus. The malformation, a mass growing in the chest, would compress the fetal heart, backing up the circulation, killing the fetus and possibly putting the mother into congestive heart failure.

When the fetal circulation started to back up, Rodriguez flew to Philadelphia. The surgeons made a Caesarean-type incision. They performed a hysterotomy by opening the uterus quickly and bloodlessly, and then opened the amniotic sac and brought out the fetus's arm, exposing the relevant part of the chest. The mass was removed, the fetal chest was closed, the amniotic membranes sealed with absorbable staples and glue, the uterus was closed and the abdomen was sutured. And the pregnancy continued—with special monitoring and continued use of drugs to prevent premature labor. The uterus, no longer anesthetized, is prone to contractions. Rodriguez gave birth at 35 weeks' gestation, 13 weeks after surgery, only 5 weeks before her due date. During those 13 weeks, the fetal heart pumped normally with no fluid backup, and the fetal lung tissue developed properly. Roberto Rodriguez 3d was born this May, a healthy baby born to a healthy mother.

This is a new and remarkable technology. Children's Hospital of Philadelphia and the University of California at San Francisco are the only centers that do these operations, and fewer than a hundred have been done. The research fellows, residents working in these labs and training as the next generation of fetal surgeons, convey their enthusiasm for their field and their mentors in everything they say. When you sit with them, it is impossible not to be dazzled by the idea of what they can already do and by what they will be able to do. "When I dare to dream," says Theresa Quinn, a fellow at Children's Hospital, "I think of intervening before the immune system has time to mature, allowing for advances that could be used in organ transplantation to replacement of genetic deficiencies."

But What Do We Want?

Eighteen years ago, in-vitro fertilization was tabloid news: test-tube babies! Now IVF is a standard therapy, an insurance wrangle, another medical term instantly understood by most lay people. Enormous advertisements in daily newspapers offer IVF, egg-donation programs, even the newer technique of ICSI—intracytoplasmic sperm injection—as consumer alternatives. It used to be, for women at least, that genetic and gestational motherhood were one and the same. It is now possible to have your own fertilized egg carried by a surrogate or, much more commonly, to go through a pregnancy carrying an embryo formed from someone else's egg.

Given the strong desire to be pregnant, which drives many women to request donor eggs and go through biological motherhood without a genetic connection to the fetus, is it really very likely that any significant proportion of women would take advantage of an artificial womb? Could we ever reach a point where the desire to carry your own fetus in your own womb will seem a willful rejection of modern health and hygiene, an affected earth-motherism that flies in the face of common sense—the way I feel about mothers in Cambridge who ostentatiously breast-feed their children until they are 4 years old?

"I would argue that God in her wisdom created pregnancy so Moms and babies could develop a relationship before birth," says Alan Fleischman, professor of pediatrics at Albert Einstein College of Medicine in New York, who directed the neonatal program at Montefiore Medical Center for 20 years.

Mary Mahowald, a professor at the MacLean Center for Clinical Medical Ethics at the University of Chicago, and one of her medical students surveyed women about whether they would rather be related to a child gestationally or genetically, if they couldn't choose both. A slight majority opted for the gestational relationship, caring more about carrying the pregnancy, giving birth and nursing than about the genetic tie. "Pregnancy is important to women," Mahowald says. "Some women might prefer to be done with all this—we hire our surrogates, we hire our maids, we hire our nannies—but I think these things are going to have very limited interest."

Susan Cooper, a psychologist who counsels people going through infertility workups, isn't so sure. Yes, she agrees, many of the patients she sees have "an intense desire to be pregnant—but it's hard to know whether that's a biological urge or a cultural urge."

And Arthur L. Caplan, director of the Center for Bioethics at the University of Pennsylvania, takes it a step further. Thirty years from now, he speculates, we will have solved the problem of lung development; neonatology will be capable of saving 15- and 16-week-old fetuses. There will be many genetic tests available, easy to do, predicting the risks of acquiring late-onset diseases, but also predicting aptitudes, behavior traits and aspects of personality. There won't be an artificial womb available, but there will be lots of prototypes, and women who can't carry a pregnancy will sign up to use the prototypes in experimental protocols. Caplan also predicts that "there will be a movement afoot which says all this is unnecessary and unnatural, and that the way to have babies is sex and the random lottery of nature—a movement with the appeal of the environmental movement today." Sixty years down the line, he adds, the total artificial womb will be here. "It's technologically inevitable. Demand is hard to predict, but I'll say significant."

It all used to happen in the dark—if it happened at all. It occurred well beyond our seeing or our intervening, in the wet, lightless spaces of the female body. So what changes when something as fundamental as human reproduction comes out of the closet, so to speak? Are we, in fact, different if we take hands-on control over this most basic aspect of our biology? Should we change our genetic trajectory and thus our evolutionary path? Eliminate defects or eliminate differences—or are they one and the same? Save every fetus, make every baby a wanted baby, help every wanted child to be born healthy—are these the same? What are our goals as a society, what are our goals as a medical profession, what are our goals as individual parents—and where do these goals diverge?

"The future is rosy for bioethicists," Caplan says.

What a baby *really* costs

Grab that calculator and see what you can expect to spend during your child's first year.

Jessica Rosenthal Benson and Maija Johnson

The average first baby costs his parents approximately $8,000 by the time he celebrates his first birthday, according to the Family Economics Research Group of the U.S. Department of Agriculture (USDA). But your cost may be much more or less than that: Where you live, how many gifts you receive, and how much you can afford, or want, to spend are just a few of the factors involved in the accounting. Plus, what you dub a lifesaver may be considered an unnecessary expenditure by another parent.

One cost that the USDA omits is that of prenatal care and delivery—an average $4,720 for a normal pregnancy and birth, and $7,826 if a cesarean is needed. These numbers, however, don't shed much light on actual regional costs. An uncomplicated pregnancy and birth in New York City might cost $10,000, while in Oregon the cost could be half that amount.

In addition to taking into account regional costs, you should check your health-insurance policy. Traditional fee-for-service plans often do not reimburse obstetrical costs until after the delivery. And under some insurance plans, well-baby care is not covered.

Once they are home with their baby, many new parents are surprised how the cost of indispensable items, such as diapers, adds up, not to mention the cost of incidentals, such as film. And then there are the totally unexpected expenses, such as take-out food. "My husband and I were too overwhelmed to go grocery shopping and prepare meals, so we ordered in a lot," says Nancy Brower, of Madison, Wisconsin.

New parents may also face a jump in housing costs. Depending on whether you are decorating a nursery, remodeling, or moving to a bigger home, the cost of making room for a baby can range from under $100 to thousands of dollars.

In compiling these lists, we discovered that calculating costs for the first year is tricky at best. Besides some of the variables already mentioned, manufacturer and store prices vary widely, as does product quality. Nevertheless, you an use the lists, or individual items within them, to get an idea of how much you can expect to spend during your baby's first year of life. And no parent has ever been known to complain that having a child wasn't worth the expense!

Feeding

Breast-feeding:
4 nursing bras, $52–$116
360 disposable bra pads for early months, $40
Breast pump, $26–$165
Lactation consultant, $0–$225
6 waterproof lap pads, $8
6 bibs, $6–$46
total: $132–$600

Bottle-feeding:
8 eight-ounce bottles, $9–$28
4 four-ounce bottles, $4–$14
18 nipples, $21–56
Formula, $616–$956
Bottle and nipple brush, $1–$2
6 waterproof lap pads, $8
6 bibs, $6–$46
total: $665–$1,110

Solids:
24 boxes of infant cereal, $24–$30
432 jars of baby food, $127–$217
156 jars of infant juice, $42–$73
Food grinder, $8
Feeding dish, $2–$9
3 baby spoons, $4–$8
3 training cups, $5–$13
6 large bibs, $15–$51
High chair, $25–$100
Hook-on chair, $28–$35
total: $280–$544

Dressing

Chest of drawers, $200–$350
20 undershirts, $36–$125
6 "onesies" or bodysuits, $19–$36
4 drawstring nightgowns, $20–$28
6 pairs of pajamas, $20–$69
10 stretchies, coveralls, or creepers, $90–$200
2 pairs of overalls, $32–$80
7 jumpsuits, $133–$280
6 tops, $54–$78
4 pairs of pants, $28–$36
2 dresses, $34–$56
4 pairs of booties, $16–$18
8 pairs of socks, $8–$10
1 pair of walking shoes, $25–$32
3 sweaters, $30–$60
3 sunsuits, $30–$63
2 cool-weather hats, $4–$10
1 sunbonnet, $4–$5
1 snowsuit, $48–$60
2 jackets, $64–$120
total: $895–$1,716

Bathing and skin care

Baby bathtub, $10–$20
Baby bath seat, $13–$15
6 washcloths, $4–$9
6 hooded bath towels, $48–$60
2 containers of liquid baby soap, $5
Baby shampoo, $3–$4
Baby lotion, $2
Baby powder or cornstarch, $2–$3
Baby oil, $2–$3
Baby nail clippers, $2
Isopropyl rubbing alcohol, $1
520 cotton balls, $10–$11
Baby brush and comb, $2–$14
total: $104–$149

Diapering

Home-laundered:
4-dozen cloth diapers, $36–$432
Water, utilities, laundry products, $243
Diaper pail, $8–$20
12 diaper pins, $2–$6
18 pairs of waterproof pants, $24–$90
4,160 diaper wipes, $156
Diaper-rash ointment, $3–$4
Changing pad, $9–$30
Changing table, $70–$100
total: $551–$1,081

Diaper service:
Weekly supply of cloth diapers for one year, $552–$803
Diaper pail, $8–$20
12 diaper pins, $2–$6
18 pairs of waterproof pants, $24–$90
4,160 diaper wipes, $156
Diaper-Rash ointment, $3–$4
Changing pad, $9–$30
Changing table, $70–$100
total: $824–$1,209

Disposable diapers:
2,600 diapers for one year, $676–$884
Diaper pail, $8–$20
360 diaper-pail liners, $29
4,160 diaper wipes, $156
Diaper-rash ointment, $3–$4
Changing pad, $9–$30
Changing table, $70–$100
total: $951–$1,223

Outings

Infant car seat, $30–$83
Convertible car seat, $40–$118
Stroller, $20–$200
Soft front carrier, $15–$40
Metal-framed back carrier, $30–$89
Diaper bag, $7–$20
Stroller bag, $8–$9
Travel bassinet, $45
Portable crib, $70–$142
total: $265–$746

Sleeping

Crib, $100–$600
Mattress, $20–$200
2 waterproof mattress covers, $6–$12
2 quilted mattress pads, $4–$16
6 fitted sheets, $54–$80
6 receiving blankets, $24–$48
3 crib blankets, $27–$57
Quilt or comforter, $17–$21
Bumper pads, $23–$30
Dust ruffle, $16–$20
Night-light, $4–$5
Musical mobile, $25–$30
total: $320–$1,119

Playing

Infant seat, $25–$50
Play yard, $47–$120
Baby swing, $24–$110
Toys, $143
total: $239–$423

Child care

One parent cares for child: $0 (does not account for loss of income if this parent has left a full-time job)
Day-care center: $3,326
Family day care: $2,650
At-home sitter: $3,703
Relative: $2,151
Occasional baby-sitter: $448
If these numbers seem particularly low or high to you, keep in mind that they are national averages. Fees vary according to region. For example, fees in the Northeast and West are relatively higher than in the South and Midwest. Centers in the Northeast average $4,534 per year, while centers in the South cost about $2,683.

Health care and safety

Well-baby care, $617
Vitamin and mineral supplements, $80
Thermometer, $2–$10
Liquid acetaminophen, $4–$6
Nasal aspirator, $2
Cool-mist humidifier, $15–$150
Syrup of ipecac, $2–$3
8 pacifiers, $8–$22
Nursery monitor, $29–$49
2 safety gates, $30–$80
Smoke detector (includes battery), $12–$25
Safety gadgets (such as outlet covers and latches), $20–$130
total: $821–$1,174

Nice-to-haves

Cradle, $69–$100
Household help, $3,265–$11,821
35-mm camera, $50–$1,250
14 rolls of film, $52–$62
Film processing, $61–$122
Camcorder, $700–$2,300
22 camcorder tapes, $77–$242
Washing machine, $280–$900
Clothes dryer, $249–$799
Cordless phone, $59–$280
total: $4,862–$17,876

Grand total

From the low end to the high end, here is what your bottom-line expenses—excluding childbirth and child-care costs—could amount to:
total: $3,607–$26,080

Cost Cutters

Gifts and hand-me-downs.
Clothing can be a big expense, but there is good news: You'll probably receive some clothing as gifts—and more as hand-me-downs—which will help cut costs.

Secondhand equipment.
If you are given—or if you buy—a used piece of baby equipment, you must be absolutely sure that it is in good condition and safe for your child to use. For a free safety checklist called *Safe and Sound for Baby,* send a self-addressed, business-size envelope to the Juvenile Products Manufacturers Association, Public Informa- tion, 2 Greentree Centre, Box 955, Marlton, NJ 08053.

Free or at cost.
There are programs that offer car seats, either free or at cost. Your health-insurance carrier or the hospi- tal where you plan to deliver may provide such a service.

Renting.
Breast pumps can be rented. To locate a rental station near you, call Ameda/ Egnell, Inc., at 1-800-323-8750; or call Medela at 1-800-TELL-YOU (call collect from Illinois, Alaska, or Ha- waii at 815-363-1166).

—J.R.B. and M.J.

The Lifelong Impact of ADOPTION

In many cases, birthparents have trouble dealing with giving up their offspring; adoptees want to know more about their biological roots and genetic history; and adoptive parents are being confronted with issues concerning the raising of their adopted children that no one had warned them about.

Marlou Russell

Dr. Russell is a clinical psychologist in private practice in Santa Monica, Calif., specializing in adoption. She is an adoptee who has been reunited with her birthmother and two brothers.

IMAGINE BEING an adoptive parent who has gone through years of infertility treatment. You recently have adopted an infant and are at a party with it. Someone exclaims, "What a cute baby. Why, I didn't even know you were pregnant!" You wonder if you need to explain.

Now, try to imagine being a birthmother who relinquished a child 25 years ago. You since have married and had two more offspring. You strike up a conversation with someone you've just met. She asks, "How many children do you have?" You hesitate for a moment, then answer, "Two."

Finally, imagine that you were adopted as an infant. You have an appointment to see a new physician for the first time. When you arrive at the office, you are given a two-page form asking for your medical history. When you meet the doctor, he asks, "Does cancer run in your family?" You respond, "I don't know."

The adoption triad has three elements: the adoptive parent or parents, the birthparents, and the adoptee. All members are

necessary and all depend on each other, as in any triangle.

There have been many changes in adoption over the years. The basic premise of adoption in the past was that it was a viable solution to certain problem situations. The infertile parents wanted a child; a birthparent was pregnant and unable to raise her offspring; and the infant needed available parents. It was thought that all the triad members would get their needs met by adoption. The records were amended, sealed, and closed through legal proceedings, and the triad members were expected never to see each other again.

It was discovered, however, that there were problems with closed adoption. Some birthparents began having trouble "forgetting" that they had had a child and were finding it hard "getting on with their lives," as suggested by those around them. There were adoptees who wanted to know more about their biological roots and had questions about their genetic history. Some adoptive parents were having difficulties raising their adopted children and were being confronted with parenting issues that no one had told them about.

Clinicians and psychotherapists became involved because more and more adopted children were being brought in for psychotherapy and being seen in juvenile deten-

tion facilities, inpatient treatment centers, and special schools. Questions began to be raised about the impact and process of closed adoption.

From these questions, it became clear that there are new basic tenets in adoption. One is that adoption usually is a second choice for all the triad members. For example, most people don't imagine that they will grow up, get married, and adopt children. They expect that they will grow up, get married, and have kids of their own. Girls and/or women also don't expect to get pregnant and give their child to strangers to raise.

Coping with loss

A second basic tenet of adoption is that it involves loss for all involved. A birthparent loses a child; the adoptee loses biological connections; and infertile adoptive parents lose the hope for biological children. Those indirectly involved in adoption also experience loss. The birthparents' parents lose a grandchild, while the siblings of the birthparent lose a niece or nephew.

Since loss is such a major part of adoption, grieving is a necessary and important process. The five stages of normal grief and mourning, as set forth by psychologist

From *USA Today Magazine*, July 1994, pp. 50-51. © 1994 by the Society for the Advancement of Education. Reprinted by permission.

Elisabeth Kübler-Ross, are denial—feeling shocked, numbed, and detached; anger—maintaining that the situation is unfair; bargaining—wanting to make a deal or trade-off; depression—feeling helpless and hopeless; and acceptance—integrating and resolving the loss enough to function.

For triad members, grief holds a special significance. They may not even be aware that they are grieving or mourning their loss. Adoption can create a situation where grieving is delayed or denied. Because adoption has been seen as such a positive solution, it may be difficult for a triad member to feel that it is okay to grieve when everything is "working out for the best."

There are no rituals or ceremonies for the loss of adoption. In the case of death, society provides the rituals of funerals and the gathering of people to support the person who is mourning. If the adoption process is secret, as was the case in many adoptions of the past, there is even less opportunity for mourning. In addition, with adoption, much attention is given to the next step of raising the child or getting on with one's life.

Some triad members resolve their grief by trying to find the person they are grieving for. Search and reunion offers the opportunity to address the basic and natural curiosity that all people have in their inheritance and roots. The missing pieces can be put in the puzzle, and lifelong questions can be answered. In addition, there is an empowering aspect to search and reunion and an internal sense of timing that brings with it a feeling of being in control and trusting one's own judgment. For most people who search, knowing—even if they find uncomfortable information—is better than not knowing.

Whether someone actively searches or not, there usually is some part of the person that is searching internally. A common experience among adoptees and birthparents is scanning crowds, looking for someone who could be their parent or their child. Even triad members who say they aren't interested in seeking will express curiosity and react to the idea of search and reunion.

What holds many triad members back from searching or admitting they are doing so is the fear of causing pain to one of the other triad members. Adoptees may worry about hurting their adoptive parents' feelings and appearing to be ungrateful, while birthparents may be concerned that their child wasn't told of the adoption or that he or she will reject them.

Reunion between triad members is the beginning of a previous relationship. It is where fantasy meets reality. Reunions impact all triad members and those close to them. As with other relationships, there has to be nurturing, attention, and a respect for people's boundaries and needs. Reunions and the interactions within them show that adoption was not just a simple solution, but a process that has lifelong impact.

FERTILE MINDS

From birth, a baby's brain cells proliferate wildly,
making connections that may shape a lifetime of experience.
The first three years are critical

By J. MADELEINE NASH

RAT-A-TAT-TAT. RAT-A-TAT-TAT. RAT-A-tat-tat. If scientists could eavesdrop on the brain of a human embryo 10, maybe 12 weeks after conception, they would hear an astonishing racket. Inside the womb, long before light first strikes the retina of the eye or the earliest dreamy images flicker through the cortex, nerve cells in the developing brain crackle with purposeful activity. Like teenagers with telephones, cells in one neighborhood of the brain are calling friends in another, and these cells are calling their friends, and they keep calling one another over and over again, "almost," says neurobiologist Carla Shatz of the University of California, Berkeley, "as if they were autodialing."

But these neurons—as the long, wiry cells that carry electrical messages through the nervous system and the brain are called—are not transmitting signals in scattershot fashion. That would produce a featureless static, the sort of noise picked up by a radio tuned between stations. On the contrary, evidence is growing that the staccato bursts of electricity that form those distinctive rat-a-tat-tats arise from coordinated waves of neural activity, and that those pulsing waves, like currents shifting sand on the ocean floor, actually change the shape of the brain, carving mental circuits into patterns that over time will enable the newborn infant to perceive a father's voice, a mother's touch, a shiny mobile twirling over the crib.

Of all the discoveries that have poured out of neuroscience labs in recent years, the finding that the electrical activity of brain cells changes the physical structure of the brain is perhaps the most breathtaking. For the rhythmic firing of neurons is no longer assumed to be a by-product of building the brain but essential to the process, and it begins, scientists have established, well before birth. A brain is not a computer. Nature does not cobble it together, then turn it on. No, the brain begins working long before it is finished. And the same processes that wire the brain before birth, neuroscientists are finding, also drive the explosion of learning that occurs immediately afterward.

At birth a baby's brain contains 100 billion neurons, roughly as many nerve cells as there are stars in the Milky Way. Also in place are a trillion glial cells, named after the Greek word for glue, which form a kind of honeycomb that protects and nourishes the neurons. But while the brain contains virtually all the nerve cells it will ever have, the pattern of wiring between them has yet to stabilize. Up to this point, says Shatz, "what the brain has done is lay out circuits that are its best guess about what's required for vision, for language, for whatever." And now it is up to neural activity—no longer spontaneous, but driven by a flood of sensory experiences—to take this rough blueprint and progressively refine it.

During the first years of life, the brain undergoes a series of extraordinary changes. Starting shortly after birth, a baby's brain, in a display of biological exuberance, produces trillions more connections between neurons than it can possibly use. Then, through a process that resembles Darwinian competition, the brain eliminates connections, or synapses, that are seldom or never used. The excess synapses in a child's brain undergo a draconian pruning, starting around the age of 10 or earlier, leaving behind a mind whose patterns of emotion and thought are, for better or worse, unique.

Deprived of a stimulating environment, a child's brain suffers. Researchers at Baylor College of Medicine, for example, have found that children who don't play much or are rarely touched develop brains 20% to 30% smaller than normal for their age. Laboratory animals provide another provocative parallel. Not only do young rats reared in toy-strewn cages exhibit more complex behavior than rats confined to sterile, uninteresting boxes, researchers at the University of Illinois at Urbana-Champaign have found, but the brains of these rats contain as many as 25% more synapses per neuron. Rich experiences, in other words, really do produce rich brains.

The new insights into brain development are more than just interesting science. They have profound implications for parents and policymakers. In an age when mothers and fathers are increasingly pressed for time—and may already be feeling guilty about how many hours they spend away from their children—the results coming out of the labs are likely to increase concerns about leaving very young children in the care of others. For the data underscore the importance of hands-on parenting, of finding the time to cuddle a baby, talk with a toddler and provide infants with stimulating experiences.

The new insights have begun to infuse new passion into the political debate over early education and day care. There is an urgent need, say child-development experts, for preschool programs designed to boost the brain power of youngsters born into impov-

 From *Time*, February 3, 1997, pp. 48-56. © 1997 by Time Inc. Magazine Company. Reprinted by permission.

erished rural and inner-city households. Without such programs, they warn, the current drive to curtail welfare costs by pushing mothers with infants and toddlers into the work force may well backfire. "There is a time scale to brain development, and the most important year is the first," notes Frank Newman, president of the Education Commission of the States. By the age of three, a child who is neglected or abused bears marks that, if not indelible, are exceedingly difficult to erase.

But the new research offers hope as well. Scientists have found that the brain during the first years of life is so malleable that very young children who suffer strokes or injuries that wipe out an entire hemisphere can still mature into highly functional adults. Moreover, it is becoming increasingly clear that well-designed preschool programs can help many children overcome glaring deficits in their home environment. With appropriate therapy, say researchers, even serious disorders like dyslexia may be treatable. While inherited problems may place certain children at greater risk than others, says Dr. Harry Chugani, a pediatric neurologist at Wayne State University in Detroit, that is no excuse for ignoring the environment's power to remodel the brain. "We may not do much to change what happens before birth, but we can change what happens after a baby is born," he observes.

Strong evidence that activity changes the brain began accumulating in the 1970s. But only recently have researchers had tools powerful enough to reveal the precise mechanisms by which those changes are brought about. Neural activity triggers a biochemical cascade that reaches all the way to the nucleus of cells and the coils of DNA that encode specific genes. In fact, two of the genes affected by neural activity in embryonic fruit flies, neurobiologist Corey Goodman and his colleagues at Berkeley reported late last year, are identical to those that other studies have linked to learning and memory. How thrilling, exclaims Goodman, how intellectually satisfying that the snippets of DNA that embryos use to build their brains are the very same ones that will later allow adult organisms to process and store new information.

As researchers explore the once hidden links between brain activity and brain structure, they are beginning to construct a sturdy bridge over the chasm that previously separated genes from the environment. Experts now agree that a baby does not come into the world as a genetically preprogrammed automaton or a blank slate at the mercy of the environment, but arrives as something much more interesting. For this reason the debate that engaged countless generations of philosophers—whether nature or nurture calls the shots—no longer interests most scientists. They are much too busy chronicling the myriad ways in which genes and the en-

vironment interact. "It's not a competition," says Dr. Stanley Greenspan, a psychiatrist at George Washington University. "It's a dance."

THE IMPORTANCE OF GENES

THAT DANCE BEGINS AT AROUND THE THIRD week of gestation, when a thin layer of cells in the developing embryo performs an origami-like trick, folding inward to give rise to a fluid-filled cylinder known as the neural tube. As cells in the neural tube proliferate at the astonishing rate of 250,000 a minute, the brain and spinal cord assemble themselves in a series of tightly choreographed steps. Nature is the dominant partner during this phase of development, but nurture plays a vital supportive role. Changes in the environment of the womb—whether caused by maternal malnutrition, drug abuse or a viral infection—can wreck the clockwork precision of the neural assembly line. Some forms of epilepsy, mental retardation, autism and schizophrenia appear to be the results of developmental processes gone awry.

But what awes scientists who study the brain, what still stuns them, is not that things occasionally go wrong in the developing brain but that so much of the time they go right. This is all the more remarkable, says Berkeley's Shatz, as the central nervous system of an embryo is not a miniature of the adult system but more like a tadpole that gives rise to a frog. Among other things, the cells produced in the neural tube must migrate to distant locations and accurately lay down the connections that link one part of the brain to another. In addition, the embryonic brain must construct a variety of temporary structures, including the neural tube, that will, like a tadpole's tail, eventually disappear.

What biochemical magic underlies this incredible metamorphosis? The instructions programmed into the genes, of course. Scientists have recently discovered, for instance, that a gene nicknamed "sonic hedgehog" (after the popular video game Sonic the Hedgehog) determines the fate of neurons in the spinal cord and the brain. Like a strong scent carried by the wind, the protein encoded by the hedgehog gene (so called because in its absence, fruit-fly embryos sprout a coat of prickles) diffuses outward from the cells that produce it, becoming fainter and fainter. Columbia University neurobiologist Thomas Jessell has found that it takes middling concentrations of this potent morphing factor to produce a motor neuron and lower concentrations to make an interneuron (a cell that relays signals to other neurons, instead of to muscle fibers, as motor neurons do).

Scientists are also beginning to identify some of the genes that guide neurons in

their long migrations. Consider the problem faced by neurons destined to become part of the cerebral cortex. Because they arise relatively late in the development of the mammalian brain, billions of these cells must push and shove their way through dense colonies established by earlier migrants. "It's as if the entire population of the East Coast decided to move en masse to the West Coast," marvels Yale University neuroscientist Dr. Pasko Rakic, and marched through Cleveland, Chicago and Denver to get there.

But of all the problems the growing nervous system must solve, the most daunting is posed by the wiring itself. After birth, when the number of connections explodes, each of the brain's billions of neurons will forge links to thousands of others. First they must spin out a web of wirelike fibers known as axons (which transmit signals) and dendrites (which receive them). The objective is to form a synapse, the gap-like structure over which the axon of one neuron beams a signal to the dendrites of another. Before this can happen, axons and dendrites must almost touch. And while the short, bushy dendrites don't have to travel very far, axons—the heavy-duty cables of the nervous system—must traverse distances that are the microscopic equivalent of miles.

What guides an axon on its incredible voyage is a "growth cone," a creepy, crawly sprout that looks something like an amoeba. Scientists have known about growth cones since the turn of the century. What they didn't know until recently was that growth cones come equipped with the molecular equivalent of sonar and radar. Just as instruments in a submarine or airplane scan the environment for signals, so molecules arrayed on the surface of growth cones search their surroundings for the presence of certain proteins. Some of these proteins, it turns out, are attractants that pull the growth cones toward them, while others are repellents that push them away.

THE FIRST STIRRINGS

UP TO THIS POINT, GENES HAVE CONTROLLED the unfolding of the brain. As soon as axons make their first connections, however, the nerves begin to fire, and what they do starts to matter more and more. In essence, say scientists, the developing nervous system has strung the equivalent of telephone trunk lines between the right neighborhoods in the right cities. Now it has to sort out which wires belong to which house, a problem that cannot be solved by genes alone for reasons that boil down to simple arithmetic. Eventually, Berkeley's Goodman estimates, a human brain must forge quadrillions of connections. But there are only 100,000 genes in human DNA. Even though half these genes—some 50,000—appear to be dedicated to constructing and maintaining the nervous system, he observes, that's not enough to specify more than a tiny fraction of the connections required by a fully functioning brain.

In adult mammals, for example, the axons that connect the brain's visual system arrange themselves in striking layers and columns that reflect the division between the left eye and the right. But these axons start out as scrambled as a bowl of spaghetti, according to Michael Stryker, chairman of the physiology department at the University of California at San Francisco. What sorts out the mess, scientists have established, is neural activity. In a series of experiments viewed as classics by scientists in the field, Berkeley's Shatz chemically blocked neural activity in embryonic cats. The result? The axons that connect neurons in the retina of the eye to the brain never formed the left eye–right eye geometry needed to support vision.

But no recent finding has intrigued researchers more than the results reported in October by Corey Goodman and his Berkeley colleagues. In studying a deceptively simple problem—how axons from motor neurons in the fly's central nerve cord establish connections with muscle cells in its limbs—the Berkeley researchers made an unexpected discovery. They knew there was a gene that keeps bundles of axons together as they race toward their muscle-cell targets. What they discovered was that the electrical activity produced by neurons inhibited this gene, dramatically increasing the number of connections the axons made. Even more intriguing, the signals amplified the activity of a second gene—a gene called CREB.

The discovery of the CREB amplifier, more than any other, links the developmental processes that occur before birth to those that continue long after. For the twin processes of memory and learning in adult animals, Columbia University neurophysiologist Eric Kandel has shown, rely on the CREB molecule. When Kandel blocked the activity of CREB in giant snails, their brains changed in ways that suggested that they could still learn but could remember what they learned for only a short period of time. Without CREB, it seems, snails—and by extension, more developed animals like humans—can form no long-term memories. And without long-term memories, it is hard to imagine that infant brains could ever master more than rudimentary skills. "Nurture is important," says Kandel. "But nurture works through nature."

EXPERIENCE KICKS IN

WHEN A BABY IS BORN, IT CAN SEE and hear and smell and respond to touch, but only dimly. The brain stem, a primitive region that controls vital functions like heartbeat and breathing, has completed its wiring. Elsewhere the connections between neurons are wispy and weak. But over the first few months of life, the brain's higher centers explode with new synapses. And as dendrites and axons swell with buds and branches like trees in spring, metabolism soars. By the age of two, a child's brain contains twice as many synapses and consumes twice as much energy as the brain of a normal adult.

University of Chicago pediatric neurologist Dr. Peter Huttenlocher has chronicled this extraordinary epoch in brain development by autopsying the brains of infants and young children who have died unexpectedly. The number of synapses in one layer of the visual cortex, Huttenlocher reports, rises from around 2,500 per neuron at birth to as many as 18,000 about six months later. Other regions of the cortex score similarly spectacular increases but on slightly different schedules. And while these microscopic connections between nerve fibers continue to form throughout life, they reach their highest average densities (15,000 synapses per neuron) at around the age of two and remain at that level until the age of 10 or 11.

This profusion of connections lends the growing brain exceptional flexibility and resilience. Consider the case of 13-year-old Brandi Binder, who developed such severe epilepsy that surgeons at UCLA had to remove the entire right side of her cortex when she was six. Binder lost virtually all the control she had established over muscles on the left side of her body, the side controlled by the right side of the brain. Yet today, after years of therapy ranging from leg lifts to math and music drills, Binder is an A student at the Holmes Middle School in Colorado Springs, Colorado. She loves music, math and art—skills usually associated with the right half of the brain. And while Binder's recuperation is not 100%—for example, she has never regained the use of her left arm—it comes close. Says UCLA pediatric neurologist Dr. Donald Shields: "If there's a way to compensate, the developing brain will find it."

What wires a child's brain, say neuroscientists—or rewires it after physical trauma—is repeated experience. Each time a baby tries to touch a tantalizing object or gazes intently at a face or listens to a lullaby, tiny bursts of electricity shoot through the brain, knitting neurons into circuits as well defined as those etched onto silicon chips. The results are those behavioral mileposts that never cease to delight and awe parents. Around the age of two months, for example, the motor-control centers of the brain develop to the point that infants can suddenly reach out and grab a nearby object. Around the age of four months, the cortex begins to refine the connections needed for depth perception and binocular vision. And around the age of 12 months, the speech centers of the brain are poised to produce what is perhaps the most magical moment of childhood: the first word that marks the flowering of language.

When the brain does not receive the right information—or shuts it out—the result can be devastating. Some children who display early signs of autism, for example, retreat from the world because they are hypersensitive to sensory stimulation, others because their senses are underactive and provide them with too little information. To be effective, then, says George Washington University's Greenspan, treatment must target the underlying condition, protecting some children from disorienting noises and lights, providing others with attention-grabbing stimulation. But when parents and therapists collaborate in an intensive effort to reach these abnormal brains, writes Greenspan in a new book, *The Growth of the Mind* (Addison-Wesley, 1997), three-year-olds who begin the descent into the autistic's limited universe can sometimes be snatched back.

Indeed, parents are the brain's first and most important teachers. Among other things, they appear to help babies learn by adopting the rhythmic, high-pitched speaking style known as Parentese. When speaking to babies, Stanford University psychologist Anne Fernald has found, mothers and fathers from many cultures change their speech patterns in the same peculiar ways. "They put their faces very close to the child," she reports. "They use shorter utterances, and they speak in an unusually melodious fashion." The heart rate of infants increases while listening to Parentese, even Parentese delivered in a foreign language. Moreover, Fernald says, Parentese appears to hasten the process of connecting words to the objects they denote. Twelve-month-olds, directed to "look at the ball" in Parentese, direct their eyes to the correct picture more frequently than when the instruction is delivered in normal English.

In some ways the exaggerated, vowel-rich sounds of Parentese appear to resemble the choice morsels fed to hatchlings by adult birds. The University of Washington's Patricia Kuhl and her colleagues have conditioned dozens of newborns to turn their heads when they detect the *ee* sound emitted by American parents, vs. the *eu* favored by doting Swedes. Very young babies, says Kuhl, invariably perceive slight variations in pronunciation as totally different sounds. But by the age of six months, American babies no longer react when they hear variants of *ee*, and Swedish babies have become impervious to differences in *eu*. "It's as though their brains have formed little magnets," says Kuhl, "and all the sounds in the vicinity are swept in."

TUNED TO DANGER

EVEN MORE FUNDAMENTAL, SAYS Dr. Bruce Perry of Baylor College of Medicine in Houston, is the role parents play in setting up the neural circuitry that helps children regulate their responses to stress. Children who are physically abused early in life, he observes, develop brains that are exquisitely tuned to danger. At the slightest threat, their hearts race, their stress hormones surge and their brains anxiously track the nonverbal cues that might signal the next attack. Because the brain develops in sequence, with more primitive structures stabilizing their connections first, early abuse is particularly damaging. Says Perry: "Experience is the chief architect of the brain." And because these early experiences of stress form a kind of template around which later brain development is organized, the changes they create are all the more pervasive.

Emotional deprivation early in life has a similar effect. For six years University of Washington psychologist Geraldine Dawson and her colleagues have monitored the brain-wave patterns of children born to mothers who were diagnosed as suffering from depression. As infants, these children showed markedly reduced activity in the left frontal lobe, an area of the brain that serves as a center for joy and other lighthearted emotions. Even more telling, the patterns of brain activity displayed by these children closely tracked the ups and downs of their mother's depression. At the age of three, children whose mothers were more severely depressed or whose depression lasted longer continued to show abnormally low readings.

Strikingly, not all the children born to depressed mothers develop these aberrant brain-wave patterns, Dawson has found. What accounts for the difference appears to be the emotional tone of the exchanges between mother and child. By scrutinizing hours of videotape that show depressed mothers interacting with their babies, Dawson has attempted to identify the links between maternal behavior and children's brains. She found that mothers who were disengaged, irritable or impatient had babies with sad brains. But depressed mothers who managed to rise above their melancholy, lavishing their babies with attention and indulging in playful games, had children with brain activity of a considerably more cheerful cast.

When is it too late to repair the damage wrought by physical and emotional abuse or neglect? For a time, at least, a child's brain is extremely forgiving. If a mother snaps out of her depression before her child is a year old, Dawson has found, brain activity in the left frontal lobe quickly picks up. However, the ability to rebound declines markedly as a child grows older. Many scientists believe that in the first few years of childhood there are a number of critical or sensitive periods, or "windows," when the brain demands certain types of input in order to create or stabilize certain long-lasting structures.

For example, children who are born with a cataract will become permanently blind in that eye if the clouded lens is not promptly removed. Why? The brain's visual centers require sensory stimulus—in this case the stimulus provided by light hitting the retina of the eye—to maintain their still tentative connections. More controversially, many linguists believe that language skills unfold according to a strict, biologically defined timetable. Children, in their view, resemble certain species of birds that cannot master their song unless they hear it sung at an early age. In zebra finches the window for acquiring the appropriate song opens 25 to 30 days after hatching and shuts some 50 days later.

WINDOWS OF OPPORTUNITY

WITH A FEW EXCEPTIONS, THE WINDOWS OF opportunity in the human brain do not close quite so abruptly. There appears to be a series of windows for developing language. The window for acquiring syntax may close as early as five or six years of age, while the window for adding new words may never close. The ability to learn a second language is highest between birth and the age of six, then undergoes a steady and inexorable decline. Many adults still manage to learn new languages, but usually only after great struggle.

The brain's greatest growth spurt, neuroscientists have now confirmed, draws to a close around the age of 10, when the balance between synapse creation and atrophy abruptly shifts. Over the next several years, the brain will ruthlessly destroy its weakest synapses, preserving only those that have been magically transformed by experience. This magic, once again, seems to be encoded in the genes. The ephemeral bursts of electricity that travel through the brain, creating everything from visual images and pleasurable sensations to dark dreams and wild thoughts, ensure the survival of synapses by stimulating genes that promote the release of powerful growth factors and suppressing genes that encode for synapse-destroying enzymes.

By the end of adolescence, around the age of 18, the brain has declined in plasticity but increased in power. Talents and latent tendencies that have been nurtured are ready to blossom. The experiences that drive neural activity, says Yale's Rakic, are like a sculptor's chisel or a dressmaker's shears, conjuring up form from a lump of stone or a length of cloth. The presence of extra material expands the range of possibilities, but cutting away the extraneous is what makes art. "It is the overproduction of synaptic connections followed by their loss that leads to patterns in the brain," says neuroscientist William Greenough of the University of Illinois at Urbana-Champaign. Potential for greatness may be encoded in the genes, but whether that potential is realized as a gift for mathematics, say, or a brilliant criminal mind depends on patterns etched by experience in those critical early years.

Psychiatrists and educators have long recognized the value of early experience. But their observations have until now been largely anecdotal. What's so exciting, says Matthew Melmed, executive director of Zero to Three, a nonprofit organization devoted to highlighting the importance of the first three years of life, is that modern neuroscience is providing the hard, quantifiable evidence that was missing earlier. "Because you can see the results under a microscope or in a PET scan," he observes, "it's become that much more convincing."

What lessons can be drawn from the new findings? Among other things, it is clear that foreign languages should be taught in elementary school, if not before. That remedial education may be more effective at the age of three or four than at nine or 10. That good, affordable day care is not a luxury or a fringe benefit for welfare mothers and working parents but essential brain food for the next generation. For while new synapses continue to form throughout life, and even adults continually refurbish their minds through reading and learning, never again will the brain be able to master new skills so readily or rebound from setbacks so easily.

Rat-a-tat-tat. Rat-a-tat-tat. Rat-a-tat-tat. Just last week, in the U.S. alone, some 77,000 newborns began the miraculous process of wiring their brains for a lifetime of learning. If parents and policymakers don't pay attention to the conditions under which this delicate process takes place, we will all suffer the consequences—starting around the year 2010.

Finding a Balance: Maintaining Relationships

Marriage and Other Committed Relationships (Articles 18–22)
Relationships between Parents and Children (Articles 23–25)
Siblings and Grandparents: Other Family Relationships (Articles 26–28)

And *they lived happily ever after . . . "* The romantic image conjured up by this well-known final line from fairy tales is not reflective of the reality of family life and relationship maintenance. The belief that somehow love alone should carry us through is pervasive. In reality, relationship maintenance takes dedication, hard work, and commitment.

We come into relationships, regardless of their nature, with fantasies about how things ought to be. Spouses, parents, children, siblings, and others—all family members have at least some unrealistic expectations about each other. It is through the negotiation of their lives together that they come to work through these expectations and replace them with other, hopefully more realistic ones. By recognizing and acting on their own contribution to the family, members can set and attain realistic family goals. Tolerance and acceptance of differences can facilitate this process, as can competent communication skills. Along the way, family members need to learn new skills and develop new habits of relating to each other. This will not be easy, and, try as they may, not everything will be controllable. Factors both inside and outside the family may impede their progress.

From the start, the expectations both partners have of their relationship have an impact, and the need to negotiate differences is a constant factor. Adding a child to the family affects the lives of parents in ways that they could previously only imagine. Feeling under siege, many parents struggle to know the right way to rear their children. These factors can all combine to make child rearing more difficult than it might otherwise have been. Other family relationships also evolve, and in our nuclear family-focused culture, it is possible to forget that family relationships extend beyond those between spouses and parents and children.

The initial section presents a variety of aspects regarding marital and other committed, long-term relationships. The first article focuses on the multiple and often competing roles played by today's couples, who hope to fulfill individual as well as couple needs. It is a difficult balancing act to cope with the expectations and pressures of work, home, children, and relational intimacy. One possibility, presented by Pepper Schwartz, is a "Peer Marriage," in which couples create a truly egalitarian relationship. The reader will see that there are both positive and negative aspects to such a marriage. In the next reading in this section, "For Better or Worse?" Jonathan Rauch recommends marriage as a stabilizing force in relationships, for gay and lesbian couples as well as for those who are heterosexual. Margaret Ambry, in "Receipts from a Marriage," addresses the shifting pattern of spending habits that couples face throughout their marriage. Marriages are increasingly seen as requiring more than an emotional and intellectual commitment. "The Work of Oneness: How to Make Marriage a Sacred Union" presents an alternative view—one of marriage as a sacred union, spiritual in its basis. At the same time, relationships benefit us in more ways than mere social contact, and Bill Thomson, in "The Healing Power of Intimacy," identifies several ways in which we benefit, physically, through intimate relationships.

The next section examines the parent/child relationship. The first article, "Parental Rights: An Overview," is a provocative piece on the rights of parents to make decisions about their children's welfare. In "The Myth of Quality Time," Laura Shapiro questions another myth, the idea that parents' relationships with children can be scheduled into specific times of intense communication between parent and child. The next reading, "Effective Fathers: Why Are Some Dads More Successful than Others?" offers a look at fathers who have been successful in their role.

The final section expands our view beyond spousal and parent-child relationships to other family relationships. Here, we explore those of siblings and the "grand" alliance—between grandparents and their grandchidren. "The Great Ages of Discovery" explores the influence of siblings and grandparents, as well as others, on child de-

velopment. Then, in "Grandparent Development and Influences," Robert Strom and Shirley Strom extends this exploration. Laura Markowitz, in "Sibling Connections," reports on this relationship and its impact on children's development and ability to relate to others. Although raised in the same family, children do not experience identical family influence. Each child goes through a different interactive process in the family, and as a result, each can have a radically different family experience.

Looking Ahead: Challenge Questions

When you think of a marriage, what do you picture? What are your expectations of your (future) spouse? What are your expectations of yourself? What and how much are you willing to give to your marriage? Who, in your opinion, should get married?

How is your experience of committed relationships influenced by those you saw while growing up? How do those relationships affect your own willingness to enter a committed relationship?

How should each spouse behave in a marriage? How are men's and women's roles the same or different?

What do you expect parenthood to be like? What have you learned in talking with your parents or other parents about their expectations and experiences? Why should you share parenting tasks with your spouse or partner? Why would you want or not want to have a child by yourself? Do you believe that fathers and mothers should have different roles?

What differences have you seen in the ways in which siblings are treated in families? Why do you think this is so? What is the best way to rear children? Why should one focus on equal treatment of children?

What is the influence of siblings and grandparents on children as they grow up? What is the experience of growing up as the sole child in a family? What would it be like to grow up without the influence of grandparents?

PEER MARRIAGE

What does it take to create a truly egalitarian relationship?

PEPPER SCHWARTZ

Pepper Schwartz, Ph.D., is a professor of sociology and an author. Address: University of Washington, Seattle, Washington, 98195. Her latest book is Peer Marriage: How Love Between Equals Really Works *(Free Press, 1994).*

WHEN I TOLD PEOPLE THAT I WAS beginning a research study of couples who evenly divided parenting and housework responsibilities, the usual reaction was mock curiosity—how was I going to find the three existing egalitarian couples in the universe? Despite several decades of dissecting the sexism and inequities inherent in traditional marriage, as a society, we have yet to develop a clear picture of how more balanced marital partnerships actually work. Some critics even argue that the practice of true equality in marriage is not much more common today than it was 30 years ago. In fact, authors like Arlie Hochschild have suggested that women's liberation has made prospects for equity worse. The basic theme of her provocative book, *The Second Shift,* is that women now have two jobs—their old, traditional marital roles and their new responsibilities in the work force. A look at the spectacular divorce rates and lower marriage rate for successful women provides further fuel for the argument that equality has just brought wives more, not less, burdens.

All of this figured heavily in my own commitment to exploring the alternative possibilities for marital partnership. Ten years ago this began with *American Couples: Money, Work and Sex*, a study I did with Philip Blumstein that compared more than 6,000 couples—married, cohabiting, gay males and lesbians—looking for, among other things, what aspects of gendered behavior contributed to relationship satisfaction and durability. This study contained within it a small number of egalitarian couples, who fascinated and inspired me. We discussed them rather briefly in the book, but our editor encouraged us to make them the subject of a second study that would examine how couples manage to sustain an egalitarian partnership over time. Unfortunately, my co-author was not able to continue the project and it was not until three years ago that I began the research on what I came to call Peer Marriage. I began looking for couples who had worked out no worse than a 60-40 split on childrearing, housework and control of discretionary funds and who considered themselves to have "equal status or standing in the relationship."

I started out interviewing some of the couples originally studied for *American Couples* and then, using what sociologists call a "snowball sample," I asked those couples if they knew anyone else like themselves that I could interview. After talking to a few couples in a given network, I then would look for a different kind of couple (different class, race, educational background, etc.) in order to extend the range of my sample. I interviewed 57 egalitarian couples, but even after the formal study was over, I kept running into couples that fit my specifications and did 10 more partial interviews.

While initially my design included only Peer Marriages, I also began to interview a lot of couples who others thought to be egalitarian, but who did not meet my criteria. Instead of throwing them out of the sample, I used them as a base of comparison, dividing them into two additional categories: "Traditionals" and "Near Peers." Traditionals were couples in which the man usually had veto power over decision-making (except with the children) and in which the wife felt that she did not have—nor did she want—equal status. The Near Peers were couples who, while they believed in equality, felt derailed from their initial goal of an egalitarian marriage because of the realities of raising children and/or the need or desire to maximize male income. As a result, the husband could not be anywhere near as participatory a father as the couple had initially envisioned. These two groups proved to be a fortuitous addition to the design. It is some-

 From *The Family Therapy Networker*, September/October 1994, pp. 57-61, 92. © 1994 by the Family Therapy Networker, Inc. Reprinted by permission.

times hard to understand what peer couples are doing that allows them to fulfill an egalitarian agenda without understanding what keeps other couples from doing the same.

Even though I consider myself to be in a Peer Marriage, I found many surprises among the Peer Couples I studied. Of course, as a researcher, one is never supposed to extrapolate from one's own experience, but it is almost impossible not to unconsciously put one's presuppositions into the hypothesis phase of the research. Clearly, people make their marital bargains for many different reasons, and face different challenges in sustaining them. Here are some of the discoveries I made that I thought might be of use to therapists.

I ASSUMED MOST COUPLES WOULD, like myself, come to egalitarianism out of the women's movement or feminist ideology. Nevertheless, while approximately 40 percent of the women and about 20 percent of the men cited feminism and a desire to be in a non-hierarchical relationship, the majority of couples mentioned other reasons. These included a desire to avoid parental models that they found oppressive in their own upbringing, the *other* partner's strong preference for an egalitarian marriage, some emotional turmoil that had led to their rethinking their relationship, or an intense desire for co-parenting. Women in particular often mentioned their own parents as a negative model. One woman said, "I want a husband who knows how to pack his own suitcase, who puts away his own clothes, who can't tell me to shut up at will . . . My mother may have been happy with this kind of marriage, but I'm still angry at my father for treating my mother like that—and angry at her for letting him." A 25-year-old husband told me, on a different theme, "My main objective in having an equal relationship was not to be the kind of father I had. I want my kids to know me before they are adults. I want them to be able to talk to me. I want them to run to me if they hurt themselves. I want our conversations to be more than me telling them they could do better on a test or that I was disappointed they didn't make the team. I want to be all the things to my kids that my dad was not. I want us to have hugged many, many times and not just on birthdays or their wedding day."

Quite a few men in Peer Marriages said they really had no strong feelings about being in either traditional or egalitarian marriages, but had merely followed their wives' lead. Typical of this group was a high school basketball coach who said he had had a very traditional first marriage because that was the only arrangement that he and his wife could envision even when it wasn't working. But when he met his current wife, a policewoman who had been single quite a while, her demands for equality seemed perfectly reasonable to him. He just, more or less, fell into line with his future wife's ideas about the relationship. Many of these men told me they had always expected a woman to be the emotional architect of a relationship and were predisposed to let her set the rules.

Most of the couples, however, did have strong ideas about marriage and placed particular emphasis on equity and equality. Even if they didn't start out with a common agenda, most ended up sharing a high degree of conscious purpose. People's particular personal philosophies about marriage mattered less than the fact that their philosophies differentiated their family from a culture that reinforced the general belief that equality is neither possible nor even in the long-term interests of couples. Many people talked about how easy it is to slide into old and familiar roles or follow economic opportunities that started to whittle away at male participation in childrearing. It takes an intense desire to keep a couple on the nontraditional track and a clear sense of purpose to justify the economic sacrifices and daily complications it takes to co-parent. As one wife of 10 years said, "We always try to make sure that we don't start getting traditional. It's so easy to do. But we really want this extraordinary empathy and respect we have. I just know it wouldn't be there if we did this marriage any other way."

I MPORTANT AS RELATIONSHIP IDE-ology is, Peer Marriages depend at least as much on coordinating work with home and childraising responsibilities and not letting a high earner be exempt from daily participation. Previous research had shown me the connection between a husband's and wife's relative income and their likelihood of being egalitarian. So I assumed that most of the couples I interviewed would be working couples, and have relatively similar incomes. This was mostly true, although I was struck by the couples who were exceptions. Four husbands in the study had non-working wives. The men didn't want to dominate those relationships because they felt very strongly that money did not legitimately confer power. For example, one husband had inherited a great deal of money but didn't feel it was any more his than his wife's. She stayed at home with the children, but he took over in the late afternoon and on weekends. He also was the primary cook and cleaner. In another case, a husband who earned a good deal more than his wife put all the money in a joint account and put investments in her name as well as his. Over time, she had assets equal to his. While these triumphs over income differentials were exceptions, it did make me respect the fact that truly determined couples could overcome being seduced by the power of economic advantage.

However, many Peer Marriages had a significant income differential and husbands and wives had to negotiate a lot just to make sure they didn't fall into the trap of letting the higher earner be the senior decision-maker. Even more tricky, according to many, was not letting work set the emotional and task agenda of the household. The couples needed to keep their eyes on what was the tail and what was the dog so that their relationship was not sidetracked by career opportunities or job pressures. Many Peer Couples had gone through periods in which they realized that they were beginning to have no time for each other, or that one of them was more consistently taking care of the children while the other was consumed with job demands. But what distinguished those couples from more traditional marriages was that they had a competing ideology of economic or career success that guided them when their egalitarianism began to get out of kilter.

One husband, who had an architectural practice designing and building airports, had begun to travel for longer and longer periods of time until it was clear that he was no longer a true co-parent or a full partner in the marriage. After long and painful discussions, he quit his job and opened up a home office so he could spend more time with his wife and children. Both partners realized this would cause some economic privations and, in fact, it took the husband five years to get a modestly successful practice going while the wife struggled to support the family. Without minimizing how tough this period had been, the couple felt they had done the right thing. "After all," the husband said, "we saved our marriage."

This attitude helped explain another surprise in this study. I had presumed that most of the Peer Marriages I would find would be yuppie or post-yuppie couples, mostly young or baby boom professionals who were "having it all." In fact, most of them were solidly middle class: small-business owners, social workers, school-teachers, health professionals (but not

There was an unexpected down side for the couples who did manage to co-parent. I was unprepared for how often Peer Couples mentioned serious conflict over childrearing.

●

doctors). Apparently, people on career fast tracks were less willing to endanger their potential income and opportunities for promotion. There may be childrearing Peer Marriages out there comprised of litigators, investment bankers and brain surgeons—but I didn't find them. The closest I came to finding fast trackers in a Peer Marriage and family were high-earning women who had husbands who were extremely pleased with their partner's success and were willing to be the more primary parent in order to support her career.

When these women negotiated issues with their husbands in front of me, they seemed more sensitive about their husbands' feelings than men of comparable accomplishment with lower earning wives. For example, they did not interrupt as much as high-earning men in traditional marriages, and they seemed to quite consciously not pull rank when I asked them jointly to solve a financial problem. They told me, however, that they consciously had to work at being less controlling than they sometimes thought

they deserved to be. A very successful woman attorney, married to another, significantly-less-prominent attorney, told me that they had some problems because he wasn't used to picking up the slack when she was called away suddenly to represent a Fortune 500 company. She found herself battling her own ambitions in order to be sensitive to his desire for her to let up a bit. As she noted, "We [women] are not prepared to be the major providers and it's easy to want all the privileges and leeway that men have always gotten for the role. But our bargain to raise the kids together and be respectful of one another holds me back from being like every other lawyer who would have this powerful a job. Still, it's hard."

The other fast track exception was very successful men in their second marriages who had sacrificed their first in their climb to the top. Mostly these were men who talked about dependent ex-wives, their unhappiness at paying substantial support and their determination not to repeat the mistakes of their first marriages. One 50-year-old man, who had traveled constantly in his first marriage raising money for pension funds, told me he was through being the high earner for the company and wanted more family time in the second part of his life. As he put it, "I consciously went looking for someone who I could spend time with, who I had a lot in common with, who would want me to stop having to be the big earner all the time. I don't want to die before I've been a real partner to somebody who can stand on her own two feet . . . and I've been a real father."

When I first realized how often the desire to co-parent led couples into an egalitarian ideology, I thought this might also lead couples to prioritize their parenting responsibilities over their husband-and-wife relationship. But these were not marriages in which husbands and wives called each other "Mom" and "Dad." For the most part, these couples avoided the rigidly territorial approach I saw in Traditional and Near Peer marriages. In both of these types of couples, I observed mothers who were much more absorbed in their children, which both partners regarded as a primarily female responsibility. As a result, women had sole control over decisions about their children's daily life and used the children as a main source of intimacy, affection and unshared secrets. They related stories about things the children told them that "they would never dare tell their father." While quite a few of the mothers talked about how "close" their husbands were with their children, they would also,

usually in the same story, tell me how much closer their children were with them. What surprised me was that while these traditional moms complained about father absence, very few really wanted to change the situation. Most often, it was explained that, while it would be great to have their husband home, they "couldn't afford it." But of course "afford" is a relative term and I sensed that the women really did not want the men interfering with their control over parenting. Or they would have liked more fatherly engagement but definitely not at the cost of loss of income. One young, working Near Peer Couple with four kids was discussing the husband's lesser parenting responsibilities with me when he said, "You know, I could come home early and get the kids by 3:30. I'd like to do that." The wife's response was to straightforwardly insist that with four kids going to private school, his energies were best used paying for their tuitions. She preferred a double shift to a shared one because her financial priorities and her vision of what most profited her children were clear.

But there was an unexpected downside for the couples who did manage to co-parent. I was unprepared for how often Peer Couples mentioned serious conflict over childrearing. Because each partner felt very strongly about the children's upbringing, differences of opinion were not easily resolved. As one peer wife said, "We are both capable of stepping up to the line and staying there screaming at each other." Another husband said, "If you only talked to us about how we deal with disagreements about the kids, you might think we were a deeply conflicted marriage. We're not. But unfortunately, we have very different ideas about discipline and we can get pretty intense with one another and it might look bad. We went to counseling about the kids and this therapist wanted to look at our whole relationship and we had to say, 'You don't get it. This really is the only thing we argue about like this.'"

Peers may, in fact, have more conflict about children than more Traditional partners because unlike Traditional Marriage, there is no territory that is automatically ceded to the other person and conflict cannot be resolved by one person claiming the greater right to have the final word. Still, while a majority of Peer Couples mentioned fights over child-related decisions, there were only a few Peer Marriages where I wondered if these arguments threatened the relationship. In the majority of them, the couples talked about how they ultimately, if not in the heat of battle, followed their usual pattern of talking until agreement was reached. What usually forced them to continue to communicate and reach a joint answer was their pledge to give the other partner equal standing in the relationship. Occasionally, a few people told me, they just couldn't reach a mutually satisfying answer and let their partner "win one" out of trust in his or her good judgement, not because they agreed on a given issue.

The couples that I felt might be in more trouble had recurring disagreements that they were never able to resolve over punishments, educational or religious choices or how much freedom to give kids. Furthermore, in each instance at least one partner said that the other partner's approach was beginning to erode the respect that made their relationship possible. Moreover, this particular kind of conflict was deeply troubling since many of them had organized their marriage around the expectation of being great co-parents. It may be that co-parenting requires that parenting philosophies be similar or grow together. Co-parents may have a particular need for good negotiating and communication skills so that they can resolve their differences without threatening the basis of their relationship.

IN CONTRAST WITH TRADITIONAL or Near Peer Couples, the partners in Peer Marriages, never complained about lack of affection or intimacy in their relationships. What they did mention, that other couples did not, was the problem of becoming so familiar with each other that they felt more like siblings than lovers. Some researchers have theorized that sexual arousal is often caused or intensified by anxiety, fear and tension. Many others have written about how sexual desire depends on "Yin" and "Yang"—mystery and difference. And quite a few women and men I talked to rather guiltily confessed that while they wanted equal partners, all their sexual socialization had been to having sex in a hierarchical relationship: Women had fantasies of being "taken" or mildly dominated; men had learned very early on that they were expected to be the orchestrators of any given sexual encounter and that masculinity required sexual directiveness. For men, sexual arousal was often connected with a strong desire to protect or control.

Peer couples complained that they often forgot to include sex in their daily lives. Unlike Traditional or Near Peers, their sexual frequency did not slow down because of unresolved issues or continuing anger, at least not in any systematic ways. These couples may start to lose interest in sex even more than the other kinds of marriages because sex is not their main way of getting close. Many Traditional and some Near Peer Couples mentioned that the only time they felt that they got through to each other was in bed. Perhaps the more emotional distance couples feel with one another, the larger the role sexuality plays in helping them feel they still have the capacity for intimacy. Being less dependent on this pathway to intimacy, partners in Peer Marriage may be more willing to tolerate a less satisfactory sexual relationship.

One husband, who worked with his wife in their own advertising firm, even talked about having developed "an incest taboo," which had led to the couple entering therapy. They were such buddies during the daytime, he had trouble treating her as anything else in the evening. The therapist this couple consulted encouraged them to assume new personas in the bedroom. For example, he told them to take turns being the dominant partner, to create scenarios where they created new characters and then behaved as they thought the person they were impersonating would behave. He gave them "homework," such as putting themselves in romantic or sexy environments and allowing themselves to imagine meeting there the first time. The wife was encouraged to dress outrageously for bed every now and then; the husband occasionally to be stereotypically directive. The therapist reminded both partners that their emotional bargain was safe: they loved and respected each other. That meant they could use sex as recreation, release and exploration. They were good pupils and felt they had really learned something for a lifetime.

In another couple, it was the wife who mentioned the problem. Her husband had been the dominant partner in his previous marriage and had enjoyed that role in bed. However, she liked more reciprocity and role-sharing in sex, so he tried to be accommodating. However, early on in the relationship he began treating her, as she put it, "too darn respectfully... it was almost as if we were having politically correct sex... I had to remember that he wasn't my brother and it was okay to be sexually far out with him."

On the other hand, Peer Couples with satisfying sexual relationships often mentioned their equality as a source of sexual strength. These couples felt their emotional security with one another allowed them to be more uninhibited and made sex more likely since both people were responsible for making it happen.

Women with unhappy sexual experiences with sexist men mentioned that for the first time in their lives they could use any sexual position without worrying about any larger meaning in the act. Being on the bottom just meant being on the bottom; it was not about surrendering in more cosmic ways. Being a sex kitten was a role for the evening—and not part of a larger submissive persona.

Many of the Peer Couples I interviewed had terrific sexual lives. The women, especially, felt they had finally met men with whom they could be vulnerable and uninhibited. As one woman said, "I used to be a real market for women's books. I wanted men who fit the stereotype of Clark Gable or Kevin Costner—few words, and when they are delivered, they are real ringers, and there is a lot of eye contact and passion, and that's about as much talking as you get. Maybe it was dating all these guys who were really like that, but even as fantasy objects, I got tired of men who didn't want to explore a feeling or who were only loving when they had a hard-on. I fell in love the first time sharing *Prince of Tides* with the guy I was dating, and fell in love with Eric [her husband] over a discussion of *Eyes on the Prize*. The sexy thing was the conversation and the quality of our mind... I can't imagine anything more boring or ultimately unsexy than a man—and I don't care if he looked like Robert Redford and earned like Donald Trump—who had nothing to say or if he did, didn't get turned on by what I was saying."

Equality brings with it the tools to have a great erotic relationship and also, at the same time, the pitfalls that can lead to sexual boredom. If couples learn that their sexual lives need not be constrained by any preconceived idea of what is "egalitarian sex" or appropriate sexual roles, there is no reason that their equality can't work for them. But couples who cannot separate their nights and days, who cannot transcend their identities in everyday life, may need guidance from a knowledgeable counselor.

WHAT ENABLES COUPLES TO SUS-tain a style of egalitarian relationship in a world that encourages families to link their economic destiny with the male's career and casts women in an auxiliary worker role so that they can take responsibility for everyday childcare and household chores? In Peer Couples, a sense of shared purpose helps guide the couple back to why they are putting up with all the problems that come from putting together a new model of relationship without societal or familial supports.

Peer Couples may start to lose interest in sex even more than couples in other kinds of marriages because sex is not their main way of getting close.

●

Otherwise it is all too easy for mothers to fall in love with their children and assume primary responsibility for their upbringing or for men to allow their careers to sweep them out of the home, away from their children and back into the more familiar territory they have been trained to inhabit. When this begins to happen, a couple's ideology, almost like an organization's mission statement, helps remind them what their central goal is: the marital intimacy that comes from being part of a well-matched, equally empowered, equally participatory team.

But avoiding traditional hierarchy involves a constant struggle to resist the power of money to define each partner's family roles. Peer Couples continually have to evaluate the role of work in their

lives and how much it can infringe on parenting and household responsibilities. If one partner earns or starts to earn a lot more money, and the job starts to take up more time, the couple has to face what this means for their relationship—how much it might distort what they have set out to create.

Peer Couples check in with each other an extraordinary amount to keep their relationship on track. They each have to take responsibility for making sure that they are not drifting too far away from reciprocity. Peer Couples manage to maintain equity in small ways that make sure the balance in their marriage is more than an ideology. If one person has been picking up the kids, the other is planning their summer activities and getting their clothes. Or if one partner has been responsible lately for making sure extended family members are contacted, the other person takes it over for a while. If one partner really decides he or she likes to cook, then the other partner takes on some other equally functional and time-consuming job. There's no reason that each partner can't specialize, but both are careful that one of them doesn't take over all the high-prestige, undemanding jobs while the other ends up with the classically stigmatized assignments (like cleaning bathrooms, or whatever is personally loathed by that person).

Besides monitoring jobs and sharing, couples have to monitor their attitude. Is the wife being treated as a subordinate? Does one person carry around the anger so often seen in someone who feels discounted and unappreciated? Is one person's voice considered more important than the other person's? Is the relationship getting distant and is the couple starting to lead parallel lives? Do they put in the time required to be best friends and family collaborators? Are they treating each other in the ways that would support a non-romantic relationship of freely associating friends?

There is nothing "natural" or automatic about keeping Peer Marriages going. There will be role discomfort when newly inhabiting the other gender's world. That is why some research shows that men who start being involved with a child from prenatal classes on show more easy attachment and participation in childrear-

ing activities later. While men become comfortable with mothering over time, some need a lot of help. Children will sense who is the primary parent and that will be the person to whom they run, make demands, and from whom they seek daily counsel. One direct way of helping fathers evaluate how they are doing is to help the partners measure how much the children treat them as equally viable sources of comfort and help.

Likewise, being a serious provider is a responsibility some women find absolutely crushing. Most middle-class women were raised to feel that working would be voluntary. After they have made a bargain to do their share of keeping the family economically afloat, they may regret the pressures it puts on them. The old deal of staying at home and being supported can look pretty good after a bad day at the office. But only the exceptional relationship seems to be able to make that traditional provider/mother deal for very long and still sustain a marriage where partners have equal standing in each other's eyes. Couples have to keep reminding themselves how much intimacy, respect and mutual interest they earn in exchange for learning new roles and sustaining the less enjoyable elements of new responsibilities.

Couples who live as peers often attract others like themselves and the building of a supportive community can modify the impact of the lack of support in the larger world. Like-minded others who have made similar decisions help a lot, especially when critical turning points are reached: such as re-evaluating a career track when it becomes painfully clear that it will not accommodate Peer Family life.

This study yielded no single blueprint for successful Peer Marriage. As in all couples, partners in Peer Marriages require a good measure of honesty, a dedication to fair play, flexibility, generosity and maturity. But most of all, they need to remember what they set out to do and why it was important, at least for them. If they can keep their eyes and hearts on the purpose of it all—if we help them do that—more Peer Marriages will endure and provide a model for others exploring the still-unchartered territory of egalitarian relationships.

The case for gay (and straight) marriage.

FOR BETTER OR WORSE?

Jonathan Rauch

JONATHAN RAUCH is the author of *Demosclerosis: The Silent Killer of American Government* (Random House).

Whatever else marriage may or may not be, it is certainly falling apart. Half of today's marriages end in divorce, and, far more costly, many never begin—leaving mothers poor, children fatherless and neighborhoods chaotic. With timing worthy of Neville Chamberlain, homosexuals have chosen this moment to press for the right to marry. What's more, Hawaii's courts are moving toward letting them do so. I'll believe in gay marriage in America when I see it, but if Hawaii legalizes it, even temporarily, the uproar over this final insult to a besieged institution will be deafening.

Whether gay marriage makes sense—and whether straight marriage makes sense—depends on what marriage is actually for. Current secular thinking on this question is shockingly sketchy. Gay activists say: marriage is for love, and we love each other, therefore we should be able to marry. Traditionalists say: marriage is for children, and homosexuals do not (or should not) have children, therefore you should not be able to marry. That, unfortunately, pretty well covers the spectrum. I say "unfortunately" because both views are wrong. They misunderstand and impoverish the social meaning of marriage.

So what is marriage for? Modern marriage is, of course, based upon traditions that religion helped to codify and enforce. But religious doctrine has no special standing in the world of secular law and policy (the

"Christian nation" crowd notwithstanding). If we want to know what and whom marriage is for in modern America, we need a sensible secular doctrine.

At one point, marriage in secular society was largely a matter of business: cementing family ties, providing social status for men and economic support for women, conferring dowries, and so on. Marriages were typically arranged, and "love" in the modern sense was no prerequisite. In Japan, remnants of this system remain, and it works surprisingly well. Couples stay together because they view their marriage as a partnership: an investment in social stability for themselves and their children. Because Japanese couples don't expect as much emotional fulfillment as we do, they are less inclined to break up. They also take a somewhat more relaxed attitude toward adultery. What's a little extracurricular love provided that each partner is fulfilling his or her many other marital duties?

In the West, of course, love is a defining element. The notion of life-long love is charming, if ambitious, and certainly love is a desirable element of marriage. In society's eyes, however, it cannot be the defining element. You may or may not love your husband, but the two of you are just as married either way. You may love your mistress, but that certainly doesn't make her your spouse. Love helps make sense of marriage emotionally, but it is not terribly important in making sense of marriage from the point of view of social policy.

If love does not define the purpose of secular marriage,

what does? Neither the law nor secular thinking provides a clear answer. Today marriage is almost entirely a voluntary arrangement whose contents are up to the people making the deal. There are few if any behaviors that automatically end a marriage. If a man beats his wife, which is about the worst thing he can do to her, he may be convicted of assault, but his marriage is not automatically dissolved. Couples can be adulterous ("open") yet remain married. They can be celibate, too; consummation is not required. All in all, it is an impressive and also rather astonishing victory for modern individualism that so important an institution should be so bereft of formal social instruction as to what should go on inside of it.

Secular society tells us only a few things about marriage. First, marriage depends on the consent of the parties. Second, the parties are not children. Third, the number of parties is two. Fourth, one is a man and the other a woman. Within those rules a marriage is whatever anyone says it is.

Perhaps it is enough simply to say that marriage is as it is and should not be tampered with. This sounds like a crudely reactionary position. In fact, however, of all the arguments against reforming marriage, it is probably the most powerful.

Call it a Hayekian argument, after the great libertarian economist F.A. Hayek, who developed this line of thinking in his book *The Fatal Conceit.* In a market system, the prices generated by impersonal forces may not make sense from any one person's point of view, but they encode far more information than even the cleverest person could ever gather. In a similar fashion, human societies evolve rich and complicated webs of nonlegal rules in the form of customs, traditions and institutions. Like prices, they may seem irrational or arbitrary. But the very fact that they are the customs that have evolved implies that they embody a practical logic that may not be apparent to even a sophisticated analyst. And the web of custom cannot be torn apart and reordered at will because once its internal logic is violated it falls apart. Intellectuals, such as Marxists or feminists, who seek to deconstruct and rationally rebuild social traditions, will produce not better order but chaos.

So the Hayekian view argues strongly against gay marriage. It says that the current rules may not be best and may even be unfair. But they are all we have, and, once you say that marriage need not be male-female, soon marriage will stop being anything at all. You can't mess with the formula without causing unforeseen consequences, possibly including the implosion of the institution of marriage itself.

However, there are problems with the Hayekian position. It is untenable in its extreme form and unhelpful in its milder version. In its extreme form, it implies that no social reforms should ever be undertaken. Indeed, no laws should be passed, because they interfere with the natural evolution of social mores. How could Hayekians abolish slavery? They would probably note that slavery violates fundamental moral principles. But in so doing they would establish a moral platform from which to judge social rules, and thus acknowledge that abstracting social debate from moral concerns is not possible.

If the ban on gay marriage were only mildly unfair, and if the costs of changing it were certain to be enormous, then the ban could stand on Hayekian grounds. But, if there is any social policy today that has a fair claim to be scaldingly inhumane, it is the ban on gay marriage. As conservatives tirelessly and rightly point out, marriage is society's most fundamental institution. To bar any class of people from marrying as they choose is an extraordinary deprivation. When not so long ago it was illegal in parts of America for blacks to marry whites, no one could claim that this was a trivial disenfranchisement. Granted, gay marriage raises issues that interracial marriage does not; but no one can argue that the deprivation is a minor one.

To outweigh such a serious claim it is not enough to say that gay marriage might lead to bad things. Bad things happened as a result of legalizing contraception, but that did not make it the wrong thing to do. Besides, it seems doubtful that extending marriage to, say, another 3 or 5 percent of the population would have anything like the effects that no-fault divorce has had, to say nothing of contraception. By now, the "traditional" understanding of marriage has been sullied in all kinds of ways. It is hard to think of a bigger affront to tradition, for instance, than allowing married women to own property independently of their husbands or allowing them to charge their husbands with rape. Surely it is unfair to say that marriage may be reformed for the sake of anyone and everyone except homosexuals, who must respect the dictates of tradition.

Faced with these problems, the milder version of the Hayekian argument says not that social traditions shouldn't be tampered with at all, but that they shouldn't be tampered with lightly. Fine. In this case, no one is talking about casual messing around; both sides have marshaled their arguments with deadly seriousness. Hayekians surely have to recognize that appeals to blind tradition and to the risks inherent in social change do not, a priori, settle anything in this instance. They merely warn against frivolous change.

So we turn to what has become the standard view of marriage's purpose. Its proponents would probably like to call it a child-centered view, but it is actually an anti-gay view, as will become clear. Whatever you call it, it is the view of marriage that is heard most often, and in the context of the debate over gay marriage it is heard almost exclusively. In its most straightforward form it goes as follows (I quote from James Q. Wilson's fine book *The Moral Sense):*

A family is not an association of independent people; it is a human commitment designed to make possible the rearing of moral and healthy children. Governments care—or ought to care—about families for this reason, and scarcely for any other.

Wilson speaks about "family" rather than "marriage" as such, but one may, I think, read him as speaking of marriage without doing any injustice to his meaning.

Secrets of the Temple

At first glance, the recent decision by a council of Reform rabbis to endorse gay and lesbian civil marriage seemed an odd deflection of responsibility: If the government should do it, why not the rabbis themselves? In fact, this is exactly where the debate is heading. And the closer it gets, the more divisive it becomes.

In Berkeley, California, a small, Conservative-movement synagogue has a solution. Netivot Shalom's Rabbi Stuart Kelman is seeking to redraw the boundaries Jewish practice places around sex while still adhering to Jewish law. In a rabbinical *responsa*, or *teshuvah*, Rabbi Kelman proposed an alternate sphere of recognition for gay and lesbian couples. Called a "covenant of love," the soon-to-be-written ceremony would be performed for gay couples wishing to sanctify lifelong, monogamous relationships. The new sphere would be distinct from Jewish marriage, which is based on a transaction of property rather than a mutual promise (brides do not voice their assent in the traditional ritual, and goods are exchanged as part of the contract). But it would offer parallel honors, including the customary week-before joint calling to the Torah complete with a flower-and-candy pelting from well-wishers.

The balance between traditional observance and liberal values addressed by Kelman's *teshuvah* is particularly tricky for the Conservative movement. Orthodox practice allows only slow and painstaking change to biblical and rabbinic law. Reform Jews do not necessarily see the law as binding (though by no means are all ready to honor gay and lesbian relationships). But Conservative Jews try to balance Jewish law and tradition with rabbinical innovation—a perennial juggling act.

The problem begins with Leviticus. "Do not lie with a male as one lies with a woman; it is an abhorrence," the Bible states, and traditional religious denominations have interpreted the passage as a resounding rejection of gay and lesbian relationships. Like the Reform rabbis, a subcommittee of the 1,400-member Rabbinical Assembly of the Conservative Movement is studying gay and lesbian commitment ceremonies. But, for now, the assembly continues to proscribe same-sex unions and does not sanction the ordination of openly gay and lesbian rabbis. The Presbyterian, Episcopalian, Methodist and Lutheran Churches hold similar positions.

Rabbi Kelman's argument for the "covenant of love" is rooted in rabbinical precedent for adapting Jewish law in response to ethical dilemmas, social currents, changing times and technological advancements. And he adopts an alternate reading of Leviticus, questioning the meaning of the Hebrew word *toevah*, traditionally translated as "abhorrence" or "abomination." Kelman argues that, rather than forbidding gay relationships, Leviticus may simply be setting them apart, thus leaving room for a distinct covenant ceremony. "In Judaism," he argues, "boundaries are permeable, not concrete. No less an authority than Rabbi Moshe Isserles [a sixteenth-century Polish scholar known as the *Ramah*] once broke the law against performing marriages on the Sabbath because he believed the standing of the bride in the community was at stake. What that says to me is that, in this case, the principle of human dignity superseded even the strictest of commandments."

But some biblical experts say that Kelman's reading of Leviticus, while well-meaning, does not hold up. "*Toevah* is a general condemnation," says Jacob Milgrom, an emeritus biblical studies professor at the University of California at Berkeley who has written extensively on the passage. "You can't hide behind the fact that the verses are a prohibition against male intercourse for Jews. That is the plain meaning of the text."

A small group of Netivot Shalom members agree. They argue that the synagogue does not honor members who commit adultery or have premarital sex and that Rabbi Kelman's *teshuvah* far oversteps the procedure for altering traditional practice. Respect for Jewish law, not the demands of a few *teshuvah* members, should determine the synagogue's policy, they believe. "Today's social or political issue is tomorrow's trash," says Seymour Kessler, who considered leaving the synagogue over the issue. "*Halakha* [Jewish law] should not be changed unless there is a long-proven need and a carefully regulated, thoughtful procedure for doing so. Is this decision a threat to tradition and to the authority of the Conservative movement? Of course it is."

Still, the Rabbinical Assembly of the Conservative Movement has posed no objection to Kelman's *teshuvah*, unlike some church bodies that have expelled or disciplined congregations for welcoming gay and lesbian members or clergy. Rabbi Joel Meyers, executive vice president of the assembly, does not think the Conservative rabbinate will advocate gay and lesbian commitment ceremonies anytime soon. But he says the movement has room for rabbis like Kelman.

Gay and lesbian members of Netivot Shalom are pleased with Rabbi Kelman's *teshuvah*. Substituting a covenant-based ritual for marriage does not trouble those who believe the traditional liturgy needs to change in any case. "I don't see this as a gay ceremony. I see it as an alternative ceremony that a straight couple might also choose to use," says Deborah, a lesbian congregant who didn't want her full name revealed.

Most important to her, Deborah says, is knowing that her family will stand on equal footing in the congregation. "I was especially concerned about how a *brit milah* [naming ceremony] for our baby might be handled," she says. "I didn't want to be at a synagogue if my family could not feel fully included. Now I feel like we belong here."

Whether or not Kelman's *teshuvah* will gain acceptance in either the Reform or the Conservative movements is an open question. A scattering of rabbis now use the traditional Jewish wedding ceremony to unite gay couples, and some gays and lesbians have formed their own separate congregations.

But at Netivot Shalom most members see Rabbi Kelman's compromise as preferable to either segregated congregations, identical marriage ceremonies or stasis. Jewish tradition holds that rabbis should only make changes their congregants are prepared to follow, and, despite the grumbling of some, many at Netivot seem proud that their synagogue is proving the Jewish tradition's ability to adapt. "I know this is a divisive issue because staying within tradition has historically been the best way to keep the Jewish community together," says Rena Dorph, a Berkeley doctoral student who observes traditional Jewish law. "But the most important thing about these couples is that they are two Jews committed to being part of the Jewish community. We've got to find a way to make room for them."

EMILY BAZELON

EMILY BAZELON is a reporter for the Alameda Newspaper Group in Northern California.

The resulting proposition—government ought to care about marriage almost entirely because of children—seems reasonable. But there are problems. The first, obviously, is that gay couples may have children, whether through adoption, prior marriage or (for lesbians) artificial insemination. Leaving aside the thorny issue of gay adoption, the point is that if the mere presence of children is the test, then homosexual relationships can certainly pass it.

You might note, correctly, that heterosexual marriages are more likely to produce children than homosexual ones. When granting marriage licenses to heterosexuals, however, we do not ask how likely the couple is to have children. We assume that they are entitled to get married whether or not they end up with children. Understanding this, conservatives often make an interesting move. In seeking to justify the state's interest in marriage, they shift from the actual presence of children to the anatomical possibility of making them. Hadley Arkes, a political science professor and prominent opponent of homosexual marriage, makes the case this way:

> The traditional understanding of marriage is grounded in the "natural teleology of the body"—in the inescapable fact that only a man and a woman, and only two people, not three, can generate a child. Once marriage is detached from that natural teleology of the body, what ground of principle would thereafter confine marriage to two people rather than some larger grouping? That is, on what ground of principle would the law reject the claim of a gay couple that their love is not confined to a coupling of two, but that they are woven into a larger ensemble with yet another person or two?

What he seems to be saying is that, where the possibility of natural children is nil, the meaning of marriage is nil. If marriage is allowed between members of the same sex, then the concept of marriage has been emptied of content except to ask whether the parties love each other. Then anything goes, including polygamy. This reasoning presumably is what those opposed to gay marriage have in mind when they claim that, once gay marriage is legal, marriage to pets will follow close behind.

But Arkes and his sympathizers make two mistakes. To see them, break down the claim into two components: (1) Two-person marriage derives its special status from the anatomical possibility that the partners can create natural children; and (2) Apart from (1), two-person marriage has no purpose sufficiently strong to justify its special status. That is, absent justification (1), anything goes.

The first proposition is wholly at odds with the way society actually views marriage. Leave aside the insistence that natural, as opposed to adopted, children define the importance of marriage. The deeper problem, apparent right away, is the issue of sterile heterosexual couples. Here the "anatomical possibility" crowd has a problem, for a homosexual union is, anatomically speaking, nothing but one variety of sterile union and no different even in principle: a woman without a uterus has no more potential for giving birth than a man without a vagina.

It may sound like carping to stress the case of barren heterosexual marriage: the vast majority of newlywed heterosexual couples, after all, can have children and probably will. But the point here is fundamental. There are far more sterile heterosexual unions in America than homosexual ones. The "anatomical possibility" crowd cannot have it both ways. If the possibility of children is what gives meaning to marriage, then a post-menopausal woman who applies for a marriage license should be turned away at the courthouse door. What's more, she should be hooted at and condemned for stretching the meaning of marriage beyond its natural basis and so reducing the institution to frivolity. People at the Family Research Council or Concerned Women for America should point at her and say, "If she can marry, why not polygamy?"

Obviously, the "anatomical" conservatives do not say this, because they are sane. They instead flail around, saying that sterile men and women were at least born with the right-shaped parts for making children, and so on. Their position is really a nonposition. It says that the "natural children" rationale defines marriage when homosexuals are involved but not when heterosexuals are involved. When the parties to union are sterile heterosexuals, the justification for marriage must be something else. But what?

Now arises the oddest part of the "anatomical" argument. Look at proposition (2) above. It says that, absent the anatomical justification for marriage, anything goes. In other words, it dismisses the idea that there might be other good reasons for society to sanctify marriage above other kinds of relationships. Why would anybody make this move? I'll hazard a guess: to exclude homosexuals. Any rationale that justifies sterile heterosexual marriages can also apply to homosexual ones. For instance, marriage makes women more financially secure. Very nice, say the conservatives. But that rationale could be applied to lesbians, so it's definitely out.

The end result of this stratagem is perverse to the point of being funny. The attempt to ground marriage in children (or the anatomical possibility thereof) falls flat. But, having lost that reason for marriage, the anti-gay people can offer no other. In their fixation on excluding homosexuals, they leave themselves no consistent justification for the privileged status of *heterosexual* marriage. They thus tear away any coherent foundation that secular marriage might have, which is precisely the opposite of what they claim they want to do. If they have to undercut marriage to save it from homosexuals, so be it!

For the record, I would be the last to deny that children are one central reason for the privileged status of marriage. When men and women get together, children are a likely outcome; and, as we are learning in ever more unpleasant ways, when children grow up without two parents, trouble ensues. Children are not a trivial reason for marriage; they just cannot be the only reason.

What are the others? It seems to me that the two strongest candidates are these: domesticating men and providing reliable caregivers. Both purposes are critical to the functioning of a humane and stable society, and both are much better served by marriage—that is, by one-to-one lifelong commitment—than by any other institution.

Civilizing young males is one of any society's biggest problems. Wherever unattached males gather in packs, you see no end of trouble: wildings in Central Park, gangs in Los Angeles, soccer hooligans in Britain, skinheads in Germany, fraternity hazings in universities, grope-lines in the military and, in a different but ultimately no less tragic way, the bathhouses and wanton sex of gay San Francisco or New York in the 1970s.

For taming men, marriage is unmatched. "Of all the institutions through which men may pass—schools, factories, the military—marriage has the largest effect," Wilson writes in *The Moral Sense*. (A token of the casualness of current thinking about marriage is that the man who wrote those words could, later in the very same book, say that government should care about fostering families for "scarcely any other" reason than children.) If marriage—that is, the binding of men into couples—did nothing else, its power to settle men, to keep them at home and out of trouble, would be ample justification for its special status.

Of course, women and older men don't generally travel in marauding or orgiastic packs. But in their case the second rationale comes into play. A second enormous problem for society is what to do when someone is beset by some sort of burdensome contingency. It could be cancer, a broken back, unemployment or depression; it could be exhaustion from work or stress under pressure. If marriage has any meaning at all, it is that, when you collapse from a stroke, there will be at least one other person whose "job" is to drop everything and come to your aid; or that when you come home after being fired by the postal service there will be someone to persuade you not to kill the supervisor.

Obviously, both rationales—the need to settle males and the need to have people looked after—apply to sterile people as well as fertile ones, and apply to childless couples as well as to ones with children. The first explains why everybody feels relieved when the town delinquent gets married, and the second explains why everybody feels happy when an aging widow takes a second husband. From a social point of view, it seems to me, both rationales are far more compelling as justifications of marriage's special status than, say, love. And both of them apply to homosexuals as well as to heterosexuals.

Take the matter of settling men. It is probably true that women and children, more than just the fact of marriage, help civilize men. But that hardly means that the settling effect of marriage on homosexual men is negligible. To the contrary, being tied to a committed relationship plainly helps stabilize gay men. Even without marriage, coupled gay men have steady sex partners and relationships that they value and therefore tend to be less wanton. Add marriage, and you bring a further array of stabilizing influences. One of the main benefits of publicly recognized marriage is that it binds couples together not only in their own eyes but also in the eyes of society at large. Around the partners is woven a web of expectations that they will spend nights together, go to parties together, take out mortgages together, buy furniture at Ikea together, and so on—all of which helps tie them together and keep them off the streets and at home. Surely that is a very good thing, especially as compared to the closet-gay culture of furtive sex with innumerable partners in parks and bathhouses.

The other benefit of marriage—caretaking—clearly applies to homosexuals. One of the first things many people worry about when coming to terms with their homosexuality is: Who will take care of me when I'm ailing or old? Society needs to care about this, too, as the AIDS crisis has made horribly clear. If that crisis has shown anything, it is that homosexuals can and will take care of each other, sometimes with breathtaking devotion—and that no institution can begin to match the care of a devoted partner. Legally speaking, marriage creates kin. Surely society's interest in kin-creation is strongest of all for people who are unlikely to be supported by children in old age and who may well be rejected by their own parents in youth.

Gay marriage, then, is far from being a mere exercise in political point-making or rights-mongering. On the contrary, it serves two of the three social purposes that make marriage so indispensable and irreplaceable for heterosexuals. Two out of three may not be the whole ball of wax, but it is more than enough to give society a compelling interest in marrying off homosexuals.

There is no substitute. Marriage is the *only* institution that adequately serves these purposes. The power of marriage is not just legal but social. It seals its promise with the smiles and tears of family, friends and neighbors. It shrewdly exploits ceremony (big, public weddings) and money (expensive gifts, dowries) to deter casual commitment and to make bailing out embarrassing. Stag parties and bridal showers signal that what is beginning is not just a legal arrangement but a whole new stage of life. "Domestic partner" laws do none of these things.

I'll go further: far from being a substitute for the real thing, marriage-lite may undermine it. Marriage is a deal between a couple and society, not just between two people: society recognizes the sanctity and autonomy of the pair-bond, and in exchange each spouse commits to being the other's nurse, social worker and policeman of first resort. Each marriage is its own little society within society. Any step that weakens the deal by granting the legal benefits of marriage without also requiring the public commitment is begging for trouble.

So gay marriage makes sense for several of the same reasons that straight marriage makes sense. That would seem a natural place to stop. But the logic of the argument compels one to go a twist further. If it is good for society to have people attached, then it is not enough just to make marriage available. Marriage should also be *expected*. This, too, is just as true for homosexuals as for heterosexuals. So, if homosexuals are justified in expecting access to marriage, society is equally justified in expecting them to use it. I'm not saying that out-of-wedlock sex should be scandalous or that people should be coerced into marrying. The mechanisms of expectation are more subtle. When grandma cluck-clucks over a still-unmarried young man, or when mom says she wishes her little girl would settle down, she is expressing a strong and well-justified preference: one that is quietly echoed in a thousand ways throughout society and that produces subtle but important pressure to form and sustain unions. This is a good and necessary thing, and it will be as necessary for homosexuals as heterosexuals. If gay marriage is recognized, single gay people over a certain age should not be surprised when they are disapproved of or pitied. That is a vital part of what makes marriage work.

It's stigma as social policy.

If marriage is to work it cannot be merely a "lifestyle option." It must be privileged. That is, it must be understood to be better, on average, than other ways of living. Not mandatory, not good where everything else is bad, but better: a general norm, rather than a personal taste. The biggest worry about gay marriage, I think, is that homosexuals might get it but then mostly not use it. Gay neglect of marriage wouldn't greatly erode the bonding power of heterosexual marriage (remember, homosexuals are only a tiny fraction of the population)—but it would certainly not help. And heterosexual society would rightly feel betrayed if, after legalization, homosexuals treated marriage as a minority taste rather than as a core institution of life. It is not enough, I think, for gay people to say we want the right to marry. If we do not use it, shame on us.

Receipts from

A Marriage

SUMMARY   Married-couple families are America's largest and most powerful consumer segment. These traditional households experience life as a roller coaster of child-rearing and spending. As married couples advance through various lifestages— from childless couples to new parents, prime-time families, mature families, and empty nesters—their spending waxes, wanes, and shifts in important ways.

Margaret K. Ambry

Margaret K. Ambry is director of consulting services at New Strategist Publications & Consulting in Ithaca, New York.

While single parents and alternative lifestyles get a lot of media attention, business's best customers are still "traditional" families. Married-couple families account for 55 percent of all U.S. households, and seven in ten Americans live in them. Married-couple families also account for 70 percent of total consumer spending. The biggest spenders—married couples with children under 18—comprise just 27 percent of all households, but the number of such households is projected to grow 12 percent during the 1990s.

Blame it on the baby boomlet. There is nothing like a child to change a couple's spending priorities, and baby-boomer par-ents have been making a lot of changes since the mid-1980s. Having a child doesn't mean getting an automatic raise, however. When the average young married couple makes the transition from childless couple to new parents (oldest child under age 6), their total expenditures increase less than 1 percent. Yet their spending patterns shift considerably: they spend more than their childless counterparts on health care, clothing, housing, and food, and much less on alcohol, education, and transportation. They also spend more on cigarettes and less on personal care and entertainment.

As parents and children get older, income and spending increase in nearly every category of household products and services. Married couples who make the transition to prime-time families (oldest child aged 6 to 17) spend 11 percent more overall than new parents. They spend more on virtually all products and services, although they spend less on alcohol and housing.

Mature families are couples with children aged 18 or older at home. They spend 9 percent more than prime-time families, and they generally have the highest incomes. But when children finally leave home, household spending falls by almost 30 percent. Empty-nester couples spend less than mature families on everything except health care and cash contributions.

Our analysis of the 1989-90 Consumer Expenditure Survey (CEX) shows how the birth, growth, and departure of children affect a married couple's spending. It shows that a couple's lifestage is at least as important as their ages in determining consumer behavior.

CHILDLESS COUPLES

Childless couples with a householder aged 25 to 34 have an average annual before-tax income of nearly $46,000. Each year, they spend an average of $34,000, 22 percent more than the average for all American households. The biggest chunk of a childless young couple's budget (32 percent) is devoted to housing. One-fifth of their spending (20 percent) goes directly into dwellings, and another 5 percent is spent on furnishings; both are higher-than-average shares. Yet childless couples spend very little on household operations. With fewer people to care for, their average annual tab for housekeeping supplies—about $400—is less than their liquor bill.

Like other households, childless couples devote the second-largest share of their spending to transportation. Although they spend an average amount on used cars, they spend 72 percent more than the average household on new cars. Spending on new cars drops off once there are young children in the household, then bounces back. It peaks among mature families and young empty nesters.

> When children finally leave home, household spending falls by almost 30 percent.

Just 13 percent of a childless couple's spending goes to food, but more than half of those dollars are given to restaurants and carry-out places. In all other lifestages, couples spend the majority of their food dollars on groceries. Childless couples spend an average of $440 a year on alcohol, more than 1 percent of their average annual budget.

Payments to personal insurance, pensions, and Social Security account for nearly 12 percent of a young childless couple's budget, about $4,000 a year. Because most are two-earner households, childless couples spend 70 percent more than average on pensions and Social Security.

Childless couples devote 5 percent of their spending to clothing, a smaller share than other couples. Another 5 percent goes to entertainment, with equal shares devoted to tickets for movies, theater, sports, and other events; TV, radio, and sound equipment; and other entertainment products and services such as sports equipment and boats. Although

they have no children, childless couples also spend more than average on pets and toys.

They're young and don't have children to take to the doctor, so childless couples spend 34 percent less than the average household on out-of-pocket health-care expenses. Health care accounts for only about 3 percent of their budgets. They also spend less than average on tobacco

Doling Out

	ALL HOUSEHOLDS	CHILDLESS COUPLES	
		25 to 34	25 to 34
NUMBER OF HOUSEHOLDS (in thousands)	96,393	3,020	4,038
AVERAGE INCOME BEFORE TAXES	$31,600	$45,835	$37,846
AVERAGE HOUSEHOLD SIZE	2.6	2.0	3.5
AVERAGE TOTAL EXPENDITURES	$28,090	$34,323	$32,793
FOOD	4,224	4,533	4,492
At home	2,438	2,126	2,826
Away from home	1,787	2,407	1,666
ALCOHOLIC BEVERAGES	289	441	288
HOUSING	8,748	11,119	11,589
Shelter	4,934	7,024	6,279
Owned dwellings	2,902	4,132	4,051
Rented dwellings	1,517	2,390	1,933
Utilities, fuels, public services	1,863	1,746	1,960
Household operations	453	178	1,435
Housekeeping supplies	400	407	495
Household furnishings	1,099	1,763	1,420
APPAREL AND SERVICES	1,600	1,725	1,786
Men and boys	395	449	430
Women and girls	665	658	509
Children younger than age 2	71	38	384
Footwear	207	170	214
Other apparel products and services	262	409	249
TRANSPORTATION	5,154	6,989	6,253
Vehicle purchases	2,209	3,095	2,986
Cars and trucks, new	1,188	2,046	1,430
Cars and trucks, used	999	998	1,533
Gas and motor oil	1,016	1,216	1,149
Other vehicle expenses	1,636	2,286	1,934
Public transportation	293	392	184
HEALTH CARE	1,444	970	1,458
ENTERTAINMENT	1,423	1,867	1,591
Fees and admissions	374	485	290
TV, radios, sound equipment	441	525	484
Pets, toys, playground	263	312	392
Other products and services	345	545	425
PERSONAL-CARE PRODUCTS AND SERVICES	365	427	391
READING	155	189	155
EDUCATION	386	284	192
TOBACCO PRODUCTS	68	226	222
CASH CONTRIBUTIONS	858	791	472
PERSONAL INSURANCE, PENSIONS, SOCIAL SECURITY	2,532	4,026	3,343
MISCELLANEOUS	644	737	562

* Cash contributions include alimony, child support, cash gifts to nonhousehold members, and charitable contributions.

products, education, and cash contributions (perhaps because the latter category includes alimony and child support). They spend less than 1 percent of their money on reading materials, although the $190 spent is 22 percent more than average. Young childless couples' trips to the hairdresser, cosmetics, shampoo, and other personal-care products and services take up another 1 percent of their household spending. This share doesn't vary much from lifestage to lifestage.

NEW PARENTS

New parents are couples whose oldest

Dollars

Older families with children have the highest incomes among married couples, but new parents and mature families spend the most.

(average total income before taxes, average household size, and average annual expenditures by expenditure category and by married-couple lifestage and age of householder)

PARENTS	PRIME-TIME FAMILIES			MATURE FAMILIES			EMPTY NESTERS		
35 to 54	25 to 34	35 to 44	45 to 54	35 to 44	45 to 54	55 to 64	45 to 54	55 to 64	65 and older
1,466	3,952	7,334	2,011	1,857	3,455	1,819	2,796	4,718	7,601
$53,270	$35,251	$47,845	$49,374	$49,214	$51,948	$55,216	$52,736	$38,701	$24,477
3.5	4.3	4.2	3.9	4.5	3.9	3.5	2.0	2.0	2.0
$44,839	$31,500	$41,144	$41,816	$43,149	$45,163	$40,730	$40,778	$31,534	$24,136
5,424	4,993	6,403	6,820	6,634	7,015	6,508	5,252	4,685	3,809
3,350	3,175	3,742	3,724	3,993	3,854	3,830	2,674	2,668	2,399
2,074	1,818	2,661	3,096	2,640	3,160	2,677	2,579	2,017	1,411
371	250	295	271	248	343	407	348	291	192
16,539	9,861	12,518	11,986	11,244	12,052	10,264	12,263	9,034	7,407
9,005	5,397	6,946	6,829	6,176	6,584	5,079	7,179	4,496	3,524
7,003	3,296	5,423	4,604	4,803	4,763	3,848	4,939	3,250	2,335
1,029	1,716	858	1,067	728	683	582	881	390	562
2,366	2,075	2,428	2,513	2,703	2,832	2,674	2,242	2,180	1,959
2,357	760	699	638	322	345	334	301	419	512
637	463	593	596	623	574	687	579	508	482
2,174	1,166	1,852	1,411	1,419	1,717	1,490	1,962	1,432	930
2,490	1,726	2,515	2,815	2,844	2,385	2,119	2,300	1,808	1,108
600	447	704	845	846	721	517	561	457	266
882	679	1,041	1,142	1,202	966	852	1,028	887	511
385	123	53	37	41	65	64	57	39	24
225	240	343	397	315	253	293	215	205	171
399	236	373	393	440	380	393	439	220	137
6,737	6,362	7,366	7,469	9,598	9,655	8,251	7,789	5,585	4,188
2,694	3,104	3,516	3,107	4,300	4,261	3,614	3,518	2,151	1,718
1,441	1,512	1,968	1,790	2,099	2,358	2,089	1,802	1,347	1,078
1,253	1,576	1,504	1,283	2,166	1,868	1,443	1,700	788	640
1,249	1,378	1,414	1,503	1,965	1,886	1,615	1,424	1,194	883
2,387	1,769	2,127	2,468	3,070	3,035	2,607	2,424	1,808	1,307
407	111	309	391	263	473	416	423	432	330
1,862	1,262	1,699	1,794	1,518	1,736	2,123	1,705	2,154	2,824
2,478	1,741	2,486	2,216	2,923	2,358	1,974	2,059	1,765	1,069
541	363	745	621	566	588	566	449	437	428
674	610	680	746	675	644	464	534	402	306
550	401	454	425	360	306	367	407	253	199
713	368	607	424	1,322	820	578	668	673	136
453	372	521	583	562	606	592	462	410	374
281	154	209	208	174	209	216	222	198	180
298	314	633	812	1,125	1,437	1,022	573	99	35
253	353	306	300	401	404	384	321	327	163
921	458	880	1,372	1,197	1,509	1,397	1,721	1,265	1,421
5,734	2,961	4,407	4,333	3,877	4,523	4,472	4,877	3,328	882
997	692	908	837	806	931	1,001	887	585	483

Source: 1989-90 Consumer Expenditure Survey

Parents' Progress

As married couples move through life, their spending patterns change. New parents spend less on alcoholic beverages than young childless couples. As children age, couples spend more on education. When children leave, couples reduce their spending on almost everything.

(percent change in average annual expenditures of married couples by lifestage change and expenditure category)

	childless couples to new parents	new parents to prime-time families	prime-time families to mature families	mature families to empty nesters
TOTAL EXPENDITURES	0.3%	11.0%	8.8%	-29.0%
Food	2.4	29.8	8.6	-33.5
Alcoholic beverages	-33.8	-6.2	17.5	-21.8
Housing	9.5	-5.0	-6.2	-18.8
Apparel and services	10.8	20.4	-0.2	-32.7
Transportation	-10.1	12.6	24.7	-40.1
Health care	49.3	9.2	18.9	28.1
Entertainment	-5.6	25.2	1.8	-34.6
Personal-care products	-7.3	21.7	16.6	-28.6
Reading	-7.4	9.7	4.7	-3.8
Education	-28.9	178.7	101.1	-86.4
Tobacco products	12.4	26.0	25.3	-39.3
Cash contributions*	-32.1	62.8	54.6	5.7
Personal insurance, pensions, Social Security ...	-8.3	6.2	4.3	-41.7
Miscellaneous	-13.3	29.7	5.9	-32.9

Cash contributions include alimony, child support, cash gifts to nonhousehold members, and charitable contributions.

Note: A prime-time family may have both preschool and school-aged children, while a mature family may have both adult children and children aged 0 to 17.

Source: Author's calculations based on 1989-90 Consumer Expenditure Survey data

Older new parents also spend more than younger new parents on transportation, although getting around consumes a smaller share of their total spending (15 percent versus 19 percent). Younger new parents outspend their older counterparts on cars, trucks, and other vehicles, while older new parents spend more on operating costs and public transportation.

Because of their higher incomes, older new parents are free to spend more on food and alcohol, although they allocate a smaller share of income to those categories. Food accounts for nearly 14 percent of young new parents' budgets, compared with 12 percent for older new parents. But older parents channel a larger share of funds to personal insurance, pensions, Social Security, entertainment, and cash contributions.

Older new parents outspend younger ones on all other major products and service categories, but the share they spend is similar. For example, both kinds of couples devote about 0.5 percent of their spending to reading materials. But younger couples spend an average amount, while older couples spend 81 percent more than the average household.

PRIME-TIME FAMILIES

Once the oldest child reaches school age, a family's lifestyles and spending patterns shift again. Like Ozzie and Harriet's family, the average household in the prime-time lifestage has two parents and two children, the oldest of whom is aged 6 to 17. Yet householders in this stage range in age from 25 to 54, and their average before-tax household income ranges from $35,000 for households with a head aged 25 to 34 to just over $49,000 for households with a head aged 45 to 54. Their total spending ranges from 12 percent above average for prime-time families headed by 25-to-34-year-olds to 49 percent above average for those headed by 45-to-54-year-olds.

Housing accounts for a smaller share of spending for prime-time families than for

child is under the age of 6. They break down into two groups—younger parents (householders aged 25 to 34) and older new parents (householders aged 35 to 54). Although both types of households average 3.5 people, the older group's average income is just over $15,000 higher. Consequently, older new parents spend more on all major categories of products and services. They also allocate their funds differently than younger new parents do.

Both younger and older new parents devote a larger-than-average share of spending to housing—35 percent and 37 percent, respectively. Younger parents' housing expenditures are boosted by the 4 percent share that goes to household opera-

tions, mostly child care. But older parents of preschoolers outspend all other households on child care, mortgage payments, home maintenance, and other household

> The average childless couple spends more than 1 percent of their entire budget on alcoholic beverages.

services such as housekeeping, lawn-and-garden work, and household furnishings.

childless couples or new parents. Prime-time households headed by 45-to-54-year-olds spend just 29 percent of their budget on housing, compared with the 35 to 37 percent allocated by younger householders. With larger households and older children, however, prime-timers devote 16 percent of their budgets to food. They don't allocate more than half of their food budget to restaurants and carry-out food as childless couples do, but they tend to outspend new parents on food away from home.

Transportation claims 18 to 20 percent of a prime-time family's spending. This group outspends new parents on new ve-hicles, and they drive a lot more. Their tab for gas and oil is 36 percent more than the average household's.

Prime-time families have a lot to pro-tect. That's why they spend 74 percent more than the average household on per-sonal insurance and pensions, allocating 9 to 11 percent of their budgets to this

---

CINCINNATI, OHIO

DEMOGRAM

Tom Parker

Giving birth to twins in America isn't a big deal—it happens about 1,600 times a week. Quadruplet births, on the other hand, only hap-pen four times a week. Quads make the eve-ning news. But what about the 40 mothers a week who give birth to triplets? They get big guts, but what about the glory?

Janet Davis, 25, didn't even think she was pregnant. She went to the doctor for a routine exam. Later, when she gained weight faster than expected, her doctors thought her due date was wrong. So they scheduled a sono-gram. "There's a very good reason you're get-ting so big," said the sonogram technician. "You have three babies in there." Janet, al-ready the mother of two kids, ages 8 and 6, just sat in shock. Her mother said, "Oh, my God! I'm leaving town!" Her husband Pat got the news while at his job moving office furniture. He said he would have fainted if he hadn't been wedged into a phone booth.

That's where the fireworks ended. Janet didn't even discuss the triplets with her doctor until her next appointment a week later. Luckily, she stopped at a garage sale to look at a carseat. When she mentioned needing two more seats, the lady at the sale told her about a woman who lived just up the street with three newborn baby boys. Janet stopped and left a note on the woman's door. That's how she found The Triplet Connection.

The Triplet Connection is a nonprofit informa-tion clearinghouse and network for multiple-birth families based in Stockton, California. It was founded by Janet Bleyl, mother of ten, after a particularly difficult triplet pregnancy in 1982. According to Bleyl, the organization now has the largest database of multiple-birth informa-tion in the world. "We are in contact with more than 7,000 families of triplets and larger multi-ple births," she says. "And we currently work with over 1,250 expectant mothers per year."

Bleyl says that because triplets are not very common, most doctors have little experience in the special problems of large multiple pregnan-cies. And she adds that many doctors lack the nutritional training that is critical for these births. "We've found that the most important factor in large multiple pregnancies is keeping close track of nutrition and weight gain," says Bleyl. "As a rule, a mother hoping to walk out of the hospital with healthy triplets should plan on walking in with a weight gain of 50 to 70 pounds.

"We are also very concerned with the insid-ious nature of early contractions and preterm labor. In large multiple pregnancies, the uterus becomes so distended that it doesn't behave normally. Unless you take some extraordinary measures, it is often quite difficult to know if you are in premature labor. I had six kids before my triplets, but I didn't know!"

Bleyl's organization relies on two sources: a panel of medical advisors, and what she calls the "fabulous networking abilities of mothers" to help expectant parents and inexperienced physicians.

The Triplet Connection sent Janet Davis a packet of information, a medical questionnaire, an audiotape, and a quarterly newsletter. She says the material helped her check the quality of her doctor's advice. Janet's pregnancy was far from easy. Twice, she went to the hospital with premature contractions. Her doctors sent her home hooked to a Terbutaline pump to help prevent early labor. They kept track of Janet's progress with a fetal monitor hooked to a mo-dem. The identical boys, Andrew, Adam, and Anthony, were delivered at 31 weeks—6 weeks early—by emergency C-section. Pat spent the last hour waiting at the hospital while Janet and her dad sat stuck in Cincinnati traffic.

I met the triplets at age 10 weeks. All three seemed healthy and as hard to tell apart as matching spoons. "Thanks to the good medical care, the boys were in the hospital for less than three weeks," Janet says. "The bill came to $90,000. Luckily, Pat's insurance paid most of it. Since then, Andrew and Anthony have had bouts with viral meningitis, we've moved to a different house, our car died, and our plumbing went out.

"Other than that, my biggest problem is sim-ply getting the babies from one place to the next. Just to get into the doctor's office, I have to call ahead and ask the nurse to watch the parking lot for my arrival. Believe it or not, some mothers have figured out how to nurse triplets. Nursing is one thing, but lifting three babies is a different story. When your babies outnumber your arms, you've got problems."

If life's changes didn't throw us for a few loops, they wouldn't be changes at all. At first, most people respond with their own versions of, "Oh my God! I'm leaving town." But few of us ever really leave. We just gather our wits and do the best we can. And that's what Janet Davis is doing. She's got three bedrooms, one bath, two arms—and she's doing her best to hold seven people together. For more information: The Triplet Connection, P.O. Box 99571, Stockton, CA 95209; telephone (209) 474-0885.

> **Mature families have consistently above-average spending levels for food, transportation, entertainment, personal-care products and services, and education.**

spending category. Clothing and entertainment account for another 5 to 7 percent of their total spending. The amount spent on clothing is highest among prime-timers with householders aged 45 to 54. Households headed by 35-to-44-year-olds spend more on entertainment than others in this lifestage. Prime-time families are also among the biggest spenders on pets and toys.

MATURE FAMILIES

Mature families are couples whose oldest child at home is aged 18 or older. They have consistently above-average spending levels for food, transportation, entertainment, personal-care products and services, and education. Parents in mature families tend to be in their peak earning years, and many adult children also contribute to the family income. Average incomes in this lifestage range from a high of $55,000 for households headed by someone aged 55 to 64 to a low of $49,000 for those headed by someone aged 35 to 44. Mature families also shrink as householders age, from an average of 4.5 persons in families headed by 35-to-44-year-olds to 3.5 persons among those headed by 55-to-64-year-olds.

Compared with families in other lifestages, mature families allocate the smallest share of their budgets (25 to 27 percent) to housing, although they spend more than average on everything except rent, personal services, clothing for children younger than age 2, and household operations. What they save on housing prob-

ably goes to automobiles. Mature families spend 64 to 95 percent more than the average household on vehicles. They also spend above-average amounts on related items such as fuel and maintenance.

Because mature families support ravenous college-age youths, they spend more than other households on food and education. Their expenditures on food are at least 54 percent greater than average, and they allocate 15 to 16 percent of their budgets to food. Education eats up about 3 percent of the average mature family's spending dollar, triple the average amount.

EMPTY NESTERS

Couples' spending doesn't necessarily drop off as soon as the children leave the nest, especially if both spouses are still working. The average before-tax income of empty-nest households headed by people aged 45 to 54 is 67 percent greater than average, and their spending is 45 percent higher than average.

Income and spending do fall off among older couples. But the average income for empty nesters aged 55 to 64 is still 22 percent above the average for all households, and their spending is 12 percent above average. Among empty nesters aged 65 and older, both income and spending are below average (by 23 percent and 14 percent, respectively).

Not surprisingly, empty nesters spend more than younger couples on health care. Young empty nesters spend 18 percent more than average on health care, and their counterparts aged 65 or older spend almost twice as much as the average U.S. household. The share of spending devoted to health care by empty nesters climbs from 4 percent for pre-retirees to 12 percent among the elderly. As empty nesters age and their incomes decline, they also spend higher shares of income on food, personal-care products and services, reading, and cash contributions.

> **Children born to baby boomers will determine household spending for the rest of the decade.**

Young empty nesters spend nearly 60 percent more than the average household on vehicles, while the oldest empty nesters spend 22 percent less than average. Aging empty nesters also spend increasingly smaller budget shares on clothing, education, personal insurance, pensions, and Social Security.

Spending patterns change as children arrive and grow up. Children born to baby boomers during the 1980s and early 1990s will determine the lion's share of household spending for the rest of the decade. As they grow, their family's budget will almost certainly expand. For businesses that have struggled through the recession, this is something to look forward to.

Behind the Numbers This analysis is derived from the Bureau of Labor Statistics' annual Consumer Expenditure Survey (CEX). The unit of analysis in the CEX is a consumer unit, referred to in this article as a household. The analysis is based on a cross-tabulation of age of consumer unit head by composition of consumer unit. In order to obtain a large enough sample, data for the survey years 1989 and 1990 were combined. Because of low frequency counts, spending data could not be tabulated for all types of consumer units for all age groups. The lifestage called childless couples, for example, includes only those headed by someone aged 25 to 34 because there are so few couples headed by a person under age 25. Likewise, most couples aged 35 to 44 have children; the small number who do not are also excluded from the analysis. For more information about the CEX, contact the Bureau of Labor Statistics at (202) 272-5060. Margaret Ambry is co-author of *The Official Guide to American Incomes* and *The Official Guide to Household Spending*, to be published by New Strategist in spring 1993. Some of the data in this article come from these books.

The Work of Oneness

How to make marriage a sacred union

 Interview with Bo Lozoff

By W. Bradford Swift

In this era of staggering divorce rates, it is increasingly rare to meet a couple who married in the '60s and are still profoundly in love. Bo and Sita Lozoff are living testimony to this possibility.

You don't have to be around them long before you realize that there is something intriguing about this couple. Bo explains that he and Sita don't see themselves as being in a relationship at all; instead, they view the sacred institution of marriage as a merging of two people into one entity. They represent one force in the world, not two. In short, their concept of marriage flies in the face of society's obsession with individualism.

Bo and Sita also operate as one in the business of running the Human Kindness Foundation, a nonprofit organization dedicated to promoting simple living and compassion for others. Bo, 49, is the author and spokesperson, and Sita, 52, makes everything run smoothly. Does this mean she has settled for a subservient role? "The thought is absurd," says Sita. Besides, she adds, "Who says writing books and being better known is more important or more fulfilling than working in the background? We each do what we do best."

The Lozoffs, who live at the Kindness House in Mebane, North Carolina, with their 25-year-old son, Josh, and a small community of foundation workers, have devoted their marriage to the service of others, which Bo claims has allowed them to move beyond romance and sentimentality. Sita agrees. "I think the whole notion of romance is based on not really knowing each other," she says. "That's why it's one of the first things that goes. But I feel we love each other more and are more affectionate than we have ever been."

Since the following interview is with Bo, it's worth noting that Sita likes it that way. As she puts it, "We are both speaking, but Bo has the mouth."

For every two marriages in this country there is one divorce. What do you think has led to this staggering statistic?

Divorce is symptomatic of a profound loss of vision about life—what we're doing here in the first place, whether there is any purpose to being here other than just "me and mine." Like the bumper sticker "He who dies with the most toys wins" indicates, a lot of people feel that life really isn't about anything. The superficial way many people view marriage and the relative frequency with which they break their vows reflect this.

Marriage is one of the core institutions in our civilization. Wedding ceremonies have always involved the sacred, but these days our marriages are not being lived as though the union were sacred. Marriage seems to be about nothing beyond the two people who are joining together in matrimony. The bride's and groom's families or communities have little to do with it, for example. The process resembles a business deal rather than a sacred ritual.

Marriage is a tool in the service of the spiritual journey, a way of combining forces and helping each other become enlightened. Yet we're using marriage to help us make it through various career moves, and to provide solace in a purposeless and nasty world. We only have to look at the consequences of this attitude—the divorce rate, the fatalistic view we have toward married life and life in general—to see that something is wrong. It may be that something is wrong with our basic view of marriage.

Are you saying that part of what has led to the high divorce rate is that we are not using marriage in the way it was intended?

That's right. Two people fall in love and get married. For whatever reason—karma, fate, destiny—they looked at each other and saw something sparkling, divine. But if you're together long enough your spouse is going to be privy to the worst, ugliest, and pettiest in you. That's why the wedding vow is traditionally "till death do us part, through richer or poorer, through thick or thin, sickness or health." Strong wedding vows were meant to help us stick around long enough to come out on the other side.

If you do stick it out, eventually it begins to dawn on you that marriage can be a sacred tool for helping you transcend conditional love. Your partner has seen not only the best that she fell in love with but also the worst, and she still loves you. And the same is true for you. This is whole love, which allows us to say "I love you because you are, not because you are good to me. I've seen all of you and I love you." Through our spouse, then, we can seek to touch divine love.

What does one do to stay true to this deeper view?

Most of us are going to grow up, get married, have kids, and be householders. Marriage and family life is our way to contribute something wholesome to our culture. Through our relationships with our spouse and our kids, we must try to live in a way that personifies everything that is good about connectedness and caring for others. This view is more in tune with the great cultural traditions, which emphasize compassion and sharing over accumulation and personal achievement.

One of the best-selling New Age authors says in his book on creating affluence, "Fulfill every material and nonmaterial desire. Make and spend money lavishly." This is not atypical. Most books of this kind acknowledge the spiritual powers of mind and body but still bundle them all in the service of the small self. Yet the small self can never be satisfied. There is no amount of material well-being that will give us a sense of connectedness; in fact, it seems that the more we have the harder it is to maintain a sense of connectedness with others. In Joseph Campbell's words, it's the small separate self that is the dragon, the enemy of the hero's journey.

What has been available for you and Sita by staying married for 30 years that isn't available to somebody else who has been married and divorced two or three times over that length of time?

We were talking about the sacred journey and the point in marriage at which you've seen the other in every possible light, the very ugliest and worst and the most evil, as well as the most divine and compassionate. There's no way to do that in a short time.

People who have been married for five years sometimes say, "We know exactly what it's like between you and Sita because it's already like that with us." But there's no way in five years that you can know what it's like to be with somebody for 30 years. There is a gradual deepening and an enlightenment that come over time. The rea-

son that yoga was developed, thousands of years ago, was so that those holy men and women could stay healthy long enough to reach enlightenment. If you consider marriage a path toward enlightenment, then obviously the longer we are married the better our shot at enlightenment—at understanding the meaning of the saying "When one cries, the other tastes salt."

I understand that you are planning to call the introduction of your forthcoming book on marriage This Is Not a Book on Relationships. *Why?*

Marriage is a union, a single entity, while a relationship exists between two separate individuals. The great problem in our culture is that the idea of getting married and maintaining separate identities is considered a healthy view. Yet the only way marriage can really work is if we realize that the act of getting married fundamentally and forever changes us. We are one part of a committed couple. That's the reason we wear a ring, so that everywhere we go people can recognize at a glance that we are not representing only ourselves. In the ancient Hindu tradition, the bride and groom poured their "birth fires" into one clay vessel. The resulting fire is a new, inseparable entity.

Lots of other things can be defined as relationships, but marriage is a merging of two fires into one, a mystical union. We don't know exactly what we're going to be like on the other side, but we have to be open to never being the same as we were when we were single. You can love your home, you can love the area of the world that you live in, but by putting the ring on your finger you are saying "This above all else is my reference point, this union."

As long as I'm married to Sita, I don't care where I am. I could be in Alaska flipping burgers—it wouldn't matter. The same goes for our son, Josh. In fact, early on we were living in California, but Josh decided that he hated school there, so we moved back to North Carolina.

There is a biblical passage that states "No greater love hath man than laying down his life for his fellow man." The cult of individualism that we have fallen into in America is so strong at this point that we can't seem to fathom the meaning of this passage. We seem to think that the only important thing is individual success. If your kids stand in the way, too bad. If your husband stands in the way, leave him. Your personal success is all that's important. If it breaks the heart of your whole family, hey, they've got to understand. Let them get counseling.

I don't mean to imply that those who get divorced are failures. My point is that divorce is part of a widespread cultural phenomenon that's very much supported and rarely questioned in our society.

People often speak about "healthy divorce." But the truth is, divorce is tough on everyone involved. Divorce distorts children's perceptions of love, loyalty, and even the sacred language of the marriage vows. But perhaps worst of all, it fuels our obsession with individualism by affirming that neither wife nor husband nor children nor family life should stand in the way of what we like to call our "personal happiness."

When His Holiness the Dalai Lama says "Perhaps in some cases a marriage must end, but when there are children involved divorce should be unthinkable," he, too, is speaking in favor of personal happiness, not against it. He is not asking us to stay together in loveless marriages. He is reminding us of a deeper kind of happiness that comes from honoring one's commitments. He is exhorting us to devote ourselves to each other once again, to rediscover whatever wonderful qualities we once saw in our beloved "other," to sacrifice our self-centered conflicts and ambitions in order to create that most essential component of civilization: family life. What greater achievement is there than raising happy, secure children?

In your view, what is love?

Love is the ground of all reality.

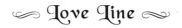
Love Line

Prehistory
The wedding ring as we know it stems from the ancient German practice of offering a ring to a bride on the tip of a sword—a pledge of union.

5th Century BC
Socrates writes, "By all means marry; if you get a good wife, you'll become happy, if you get a bad one, you'll become a philosopher."

323 BC
The Egyptian wife has plenty of power over her husband: He must pay a fine to his first wife, for example, if he wishes to marry a second one.

1st Century AD
With the emergence of Christianity, Roman marriage changes from a procreative duty into a choice. Marriage requires female consent, and the role of "wife" takes on as much dignity as that of "friend." But "love" isn't necessary for marriage. In Greece, Plutarch calls love a "frenzy" and says that "those who are in love must be forgiven as though ill." Meanwhile, virginity is glorified, sexual connection is deemed foul and homosexuality is punishable by death.

c. 270
St. Valentine is martyred on Feb. 14. The association of this chaste, holy man with the ancient pagan fertility festival of the Lupercalia, an ancestor of Valentine's Day, is believed to be pure accident.

2nd–3rd Centuries
Christians stress morality in love. Intercourse is to be passionless and, as Clement of Alexandria stresses, should occur only after supper so that daylight hours could be devoted to studies or prayer. "He who too ardently loves his own wife," he writes, "is an adulterer."

3rd–4th Centuries
In India, Brahmin priest Vatsyayana, believed to be a lifelong celibate and ascetic, writes the erotic classic, the *Kama Sutra*. In Europe, Jovian, a maverick monk, is excommunicated in 385 A.D. on the grounds of heresy and blasphemy for calling marriage superior to celibacy.

5th Century
Religion governs marriage. Almost all weddings in the Roman Empire now include an ecclesiastical benediction, and marriage is considered a sacrament. In the centuries to come, Emperor Justinian will make adultery a capital offense and divorce nearly impossible.

6th Century
Buddhists and Hindus in India begin to practice Tantrism in an attempt to transform the human body into a mystical one. Through maithuna (ceremonial sex), human union becomes a sacred act.

959
In one of the first known attempts to suppress the ancient Japanese practice of phallic worship, a large phallic image that had been displayed and worshipped in Kyoto is moved to a less prominent place.

11th Century
Chinese philosophers begin to interpret the ancient yin and yang symbols as interdependent—like man and woman. The undivided circle becomes known as t'ai chi t'u: "the supreme ultimate." Around the same time, a few wags in southern France concoct a little game of flattery called "cortezia, courtesie." Soon their little amusement blossoms into the social philosophy of courtly love.

1244
Sufi teacher and poet Rumi meets Shams of Tabriz and abandons himself to divine and earthly love.

1477
Margery Brews of England writes the earliest known valentine to her "Right Worshipful and well-beloved Valentine," hoping that he'll make her "the merriest maiden on the ground" despite a meager dowry.

16th Century
Some 400 years before *The Joy of Sex* comes India's *Ananga Ranga*, which shows husband and wife how to keep a marriage lively with 32 sexual positions. Meanwhile, in Germany, religious reformer Martin Luther, believing that the sexual impulse is natural and irrepressible, persuades a group of nuns to leave the convent and helps them find husbands. When one of them, Katharina von Bora, remains unwed, Luther marries her. Later he writes, "My wife is more precious to me than the Kingdom of France and all the treasures of Venice."

1536
John Calvin, head of Geneva's religious government, creates a code of morals that limits engagements to six weeks and prohibits revelry at weddings. If the bride or groom arrives late, the wedding is canceled.

c. 1613
Don Juan comes to life in Tirso de Molina's play *The Joker of Seville*.

c. 1625
While Puritan author William Gouge is advising wives to address their mates only as "Husband" and never as "sweet, sweeting, heart, sweetheart, love, joy, dear, duck, chick, or pigsnie," English adventurer Thomas Morton establishes "Merry Mount," a plantation in the Massachusetts Bay colony where whites and Native Americans openly engage in sexual relations. The Pilgrims later deport him for reviving the erotic pagan May Day festival. During this period, Massachusetts demands that every town "dispose of all single persons," and Connecticut taxes bachelors 20 shillings a week.

1691
In Virginia, whites who marry or have sex with a "Negro, mulatto or Indian" are banished from the colony. By 1705 the ante has been upped to six months imprisonment and a 10 pound fine.

1725
Giacomo Casanova, lover of life, is born in Venice. In his memoirs he will write of hundreds of mistresses—116 of them by name.

c. 1750
As out-of-wedlock pregnancies increase, some New England towns attempt to prohibit "bundling"—a practice wherein courting couples are allowed to sleep together so long as they remain fully dressed or have a "bundling board" between them.

1870
One hundred years before the much-discussed divorce boom of the disco years, the women's rights movement in the United States is already influencing women to choose self-sufficiency over unhappy marriages. The divorce rate grows sixfold between 1870 and 1900.

1896
John Rice gives May Irwin the first movie kiss—which looks more like a peck. But the press harrumphs that the "unbridled kissing, magnified to gargantuan proportions and repeated thrice, is absolutely loathsome."

1901
Japanese poet Akiko Yosano publishes *Tangled Hair*, a book of poetry that replaces the traditional Japanese poetic approach to love—all emotions, no body contact—with a frank sensuality that is immediately popular among young lovers in the rapidly Westernizing nation.

1910
The company that makes Hallmark Cards is established in Kansas City, Missouri.

1910s–1920s
Margaret Sanger publishes birth control information in a New York newspaper. Marie Stopes of England salutes the female orgasm in her book *Married Love*. With flappers frequenting speakeasies and petting parties, the Twenties roar.

1931
Anaïs Nin meets Henry Miller.

1960s
Scenes from a sexual revolution: On May 9, 1960, the FDA approves the first birth control pill. Matchmaking hits prime time with *The Dating Game* in 1965. The U.S. Supreme Court voids all laws against miscegenation in 1967. In the fall following the Summer of Love, feminists crash the 1968 Miss America pageant, proclaiming "women's liberation" and urging women to throw fake eyelashes, dishcloths, *Playboy*, *Vogue*, and their bras into "freedom trashcans."

1975
Unable to find any law prohibiting same-sex marriage, Clela Rorex, a county clerk in Boulder, Colorado, marries Dave Zamora and Ave McCord. Five more same-sex couples come to Rorex to be wed. When an angry cowboy walks in with his fiancée, an 8-year-old mare, Rorex refuses to grant the marriage—noting that the horse is underage.

1980–1981
Doctors begin to notice rare forms of pneumonia and cancer killing young gay men. Soon it becomes clear that this infectious disease, AIDS, is not exclusive to homosexual males.

1996
The U.S. Congress passes the Defense of Marriage Act, defining marriage narrowly as the official link between a man and a woman.

—Libby Stephens

Love is what enlightenment feels like. Enlightenment is not an accomplishment; it's better described by the word *realization*. If I say I am self-realized, I have realized a truth. That doesn't mean I have accomplished or attained something that you haven't. It's more like this: You and I are both wearing blue shirts, but I've just realized I'm wearing one and you haven't yet.

In all the traditions, the overwhelming description of the enlightened or realized state is love, devotion, gratitude. Marriage and family life help us touch love. Not to touch just the romantic love for our spouse, nor just the parental love, for our kids, but through romantic and parental love to touch the unconditional love that includes everything and everybody, the love that's universal.

Let me explain by using the example of my son. Every day I say a prayer and offer a blessing of goodwill to him—wherever he may be. When I feel all of my love for him, then I'll say a little prayer along the lines of "May I love all beings and my son equally." I use this love for my son to trigger that infinitely greater love, not only for him but for all beings. Ultimately that is the only way that it is really love. It's an impossibility to truly love my son more than I love Charles Manson. I'm either in the state of love or I'm not. True love is a profound, revolutionary force.

You've said you think people should choose carefully before getting married, but how do you know when you've met the right person?

When I talk about being more cautious, I mean reflecting first on your view of marriage. It's good to have a clear idea beforehand and discuss it openly with the one you've fallen in love with. Does love have to be this passionate, chemical *Beverly Hills 90210* kind of thing? Or does it have more to do with deep trusting and friendship?

So many marriage books focus on how to keep the passion and romance alive. They are filled with all kinds of degrading techniques for deluding your partner. That's silly, because it assumes that your initial passionate infatuation is extremely important. With this orientation, we become afraid that we are failing if we feel the romance sliding. Instead we must ask "What had meaning for us in this union?" And then "Is our partnership deeply connected in this meaning?" Also, we must not be afraid to go in the direction opposite that of the culture. When it comes to marriage we should be able to say "We don't have much romance in our life and that's fine."

Sita and I have less and less romance and sentimentality in our marriage, and that's great. What a relief! In this way we will eventually reach a point where there is no difference between Sita and me as husband and wife, brother and sister, or best friends. Where we're going is way beyond groping each other's bodies for a few minutes, a few times a week. It's living together as life partners and pursuing truth together.

Are there certain practices you recommend to build and maintain intimacy in marriage and family life?

The most powerful is to forge a simple lifestyle so that both partners are not working their tails off to pay elaborate mortgages, car payments, and so on. Create a life that puts a premium on family time rather than on how the family lives. This allows us to spend a maximum of time being a parent, enjoying life, enjoying music, watching the sun come up and go down. That's a practice whose mantra is "The best things in life are free."

I believe our task is to rediscover our personal responsibility toward the greater world rather than merely toward our private lives. Each of us has a mission to contribute something positive to the world, and we cannot become truly happy if we don't fulfill that mission. In any society, marriage and family life are the most basic units of that mission. A family has the capacity to bring new human beings into the world and raise them in a loving, calm, unselfish environment, and the equally awesome responsibility of helping spouses, parents, and family members die in a loving, calm, unselfish environment. Cherishing each other from birth to death is what taps us into the sacredness of life. It's such a tragedy when the members of a family hardly even eat meals together, let alone face life's deepest challenges and mysteries together.

Simply living, dedication to service, and daily spiritual practice are my own family recipe. It's really very simple.

W. Bradford Swift is a North Carolina-based freelance writer and co-director of The Life on Purpose Foundation, an organization dedicated to people clarifying their life purpose and living true to it. Part of his work with the foundation involves writing articles about people whose lives are dedicated to a bold and inspired purpose or vision. If you would like to nominate someone for such an article, contact the foundation at 1160 W. Blue Ridge Rd., Flat Rock, NC 28731; e-mail: LifeOnPurpose@a-o.com.

THE HEALING POWER
of Intimacy

Healthy long-term relationships offer big rewards—better health, longer life, even more sex than the single life offers. But less than 50 percent of couples stick together for the long haul. Here's how some therapists are teaching couples to use their relationship "hot spots" for greater intimacy and lasting love.

BILL THOMSON

Bill Thomson is Senior Features Editor of Natural Health.

Joe and Martha came to see couples therapist Seymour Boorstein when their relationship was in crisis. They'd been married many years but were locked in a terrible battle over the renovations of their guest cottage. Martha wanted a much bigger refrigerator and stove than Joe wanted. He was interested in aesthetics and insisted on less intrusive appliances. She became outraged at his refusal to go along with her plan. Caught in a deadlock, they went to Boorstein.

A psychiatrist and editor of a textbook on transpersonal psychology, Boorstein looks at marriage from a mind/body perspective. His wife and co-teacher, Sylvia, teaches meditation and has a new book out, *IT'S EASIER THAN YOU THINK: THE BUDDHIST WAY TO HAPPINESS* (HarperSanFrancisco, 1995). They've been together forty-three years.

In his work, Seymour has found that the majority of problems in couple relationships are caused when our primitive instinct for survival is triggered. When you or your partner get angry—whether you're peeved at him for burning the toast or outraged at her for wrecking the car—it is because the mind has perceived a threat and sent the body into a fight-or-flight mode.

"It's important for the couple to see that although they are disagreeing about

the size of a stove, they really aren't," says Boorstein. "It's an issue of survival. What's upsetting Martha is not so much the now, but what she's projected from the past into the now."

In therapy sessions with Boorstein, Martha learned that as a child she had not been fed regularly and needed to scream for food. As a woman, she had always been more comfortable with a well-stocked, large refrigerator.

"The instant she got that awareness," Boorstein says, "her rage disappeared." She saw the unreasonableness of her demand and was more comfortable with smaller appliances. Joe felt compassion for his wife. He sincerely told her to renovate the cottage and install appliances in a way that made her comfortable.

Because the parts of the brain that perceive threats, the limbic and reptilian brains, are the more "primitive" ones, which respond as if survival were at stake, our automatic tendency when we perceive a threat is to fight or flee—the two classic reactions during relationship struggles. A third part of the human brain, the neocortex, is the relational part of the brain which Boorstein believes is where our lovingness originates. The neocortex is able to distinguish between true threats to our survival and imposters, while the primitive parts of the brain (which develop in children before the relational part does) respond swiftly to anything even resembling a threat.

"When we get frightened on any primitive level," Boorstein explains, "the primitive brain overrides the neocortex and does what's necessary for survival. These are very different from the strategies we need to make a relationship work."

When two people—whether married, long-term heterosexual, or same-sex couples—begin to understand one another in this way, it becomes easier to override the primitive brain. As a couple learns to examine what's triggering their feelings, they slowly pull away from living in survival mode. Not only does this enable them to get along, they stop subjecting their bodies to the chronic stress that accompanies repeated fight-or-flight reactions.

Numerous studies have confirmed the effects of chronic stress, from high blood pressure to immune disorders to depression. From a health standpoint, in other words, the brain that's loving wins out over the brain that's stressing, every time. This explains, in part, why couples who work out their problems are likely to be healthier (*see* box "Marriage Will Make You Healthier, Wealthier, and Sexier").

Couples can learn strategies to understand their "hot spots"—the areas of conflict within their marriage or long-term relationship—and use them to strengthen bonds and build trust.

Indeed, the Boorsteins and other innovative therapists are now helping couples access issues from the past that set off the primitive brain and cause ranting and raving or splitting. Their work is

MARRIAGE WILL MAKE YOU HEALTHIER, WEALTHIER, AND SEXIER

While our national divorce rate—50 percent—might make you think marriage doesn't have much to offer, Linda J. Waite, Ph.D., a researcher at the University of Chicago, recently assembled some impressive data on the fate of unmarried versus married people. Consider the following evidence:

■ **Being single lowers life expectancy more than cancer.** For both men and women, being unmarried eats into life expectancy more than the risks of being overweight and getting cancer. For single men, bachelorhood is a greater risk factor than heart disease. They pay for their freedom with 3,500 days of their life (almost ten years) while heart disease, on average, takes only 2,100 days off their life. On average, the single life takes 1,600 days off a woman's life while cancer takes 980 days.

■ **Married men have fewer alcohol problems.** Married men have about half the alcohol-related troubles as their party-going single counterparts. In other words, the wedded average one-half incident per month while singles are getting into pickles one time a month. (Regardless of marital status, women have one-tenth the booze problems of men.)

■ **Married families save more money.** The median household wealth of marrieds is $132,000. It's less than one-third that for divorced, widowed, and the never married—around $40,000.

■ **Marriage reduces risk-taking behavior.** Both divorced men and women take risks—driving too fast, getting into fights, and practicing unhealthy lifestyle habits—at a higher rate than marrieds do (about 30 percent higher for men and 45 percent for women).

■ **Married people have sex twice as often.** If you're an average married man, you're having sex 6.84 times a month; if you're a woman, you're having sex 6.11 times a month. (These different figures raise questions about where men are getting the additional sex that the women aren't getting. But rest assured, this is a "statistical anomaly.") Single people have sex only about half as much—women, 3.23 times a month, and men, 3.63 times.

■ **Married men get more physical pleasure from sex.** Fifty-four percent of married men report being physically satisfied from sex with their wives while 43 percent of single men say they're satisfied with their sex. Married women, however, are only barely "statistically" happier than unmarried women.

■ **Married men and women are more emotionally pleased with sex.** Fifty-one percent of married men report emotional satisfaction from sex versus 36 percent of single men. For women, 44 percent of the marrieds are emotionally gratified with their lovemaking versus 33 percent of the single women.

Gray recalls, "I had one woman yelling at me on a radio show recently, 'I don't need a man. I've got a sperm bank!'

"Women are having careers to support themselves and be independent. They're feeling the same responsibilities their fathers felt, but they also want to create a beautiful relationship and have children and a home. Women are carrying a weight that is heavier than any woman in history has ever carried. Naturally, they are going to be unhappy."

Men, for their part, don't know what women want to make them happy. "After listening to couples again and again," Gray says, "right before they're about to get a divorce, the message I hear from men is 'I've given and I've given and I've given and no matter how much I give, it's not enough to maker her happy.'

"Women, when they're ready to give up say the same thing—'I've given and I've given and I've given, and no matter how much I give, I don't get back. I feel empty. I have nothing left to give.' "

"TILL DISSATISFACTION DO US PART"

"We are at a turning point in the history of couple consciousness," says John Welwood, Ph.D., a psychologist from Mill Valley, California, and author of several books on intimacy, including *JOURNEY OF THE HEART* (HarperCollins, 1990) and one to be released in January, *LOVE AND AWAKENING* (HarperCollins).

---

proving to help couples not only stick it out, but in the long run, make each of the partners stronger and healthier.

MARRIED, AMERICAN STYLE

Every fifteen minutes in America, sixty married couples untie the knot and opt for life alone, and untold others in relationships walk away from them. At the turn of the century, one out of fourteen marriages ended in divorce; today, every other one does. According to Census Bureau data, since 1970, the percentage of married Americans (among all adults eighteen and over) has declined 15 per-

cent, while the number of divorced has risen 300 percent.

Why aren't people staying together? John Gray, Ph.D, couples therapist and author of *MEN ARE FROM MARS, WOMEN ARE FROM VENUS* (HarperCollins, 1992), offers at least some insight.

Marital malcontent, he says, stems from a colossal shake-up in men's and women's roles. "Women don't need men the way they once did," says Gray, a forty-four-year-old former celibate monk who is now married with three kids. "A woman today doesn't need a protector—she can carry her Mace; she's got police forces; she's got lawyers; what does she need a guy for?"

The problem with basing marriage purely on pleasure and having your needs met is that those things come and go.

"In the past, marriage was a functional business that maintained the family and society," states Welwood. "During the last half century, people in the West have begun to look to marriage simply as a source of personal pleasure and need gratification. That's very new and we're seeing the limits of it."

Indeed, instead of "till death do us part," couples often stay together only "till dissatisfaction do us part." Also, divorce laws in the last several decades have been relaxed. Couples don't need to claim grounds of cruelty or abuse to get out of marriage. They can end it due to "irretrievable breakdown of the marriage," which can mean your spouse's sloppiness drives you crazy, or else you're just bored.

"The problem with basing marriage purely on pleasure and having your needs met is that those things come and go," Welwood says.

And when they go, disappointed partners look for insights on magazine racks and in bookstores—making books such as Gray's and Thomas Moore's SOUL MATES behemoth best-sellers. Alas, the popular newsstand solutions (often running along the lines of how to have "hotter, happier sex") are less than satisfying. Even Gray sometimes offers questionable cures. His advise that men must make women feel they're being heard (even if the guy has to *pretend* that he hears her) and that women must make men feel appreciated (however hard it is for her to imagine *why*) may win temporary peace in a relationship, but lasting love?

Welwood believes we need a new vision of intimate relationships if we are going to find lasting love. "There is a much deeper kind of happiness—which goes far beyond immediate gratification—that comes from realizing who you are and sharing that with someone you love," says Welwood. "*This* is the basis for healthy and satisfying relationships."

Welwood's definition of a healthy relationship involves working with the obstacles that arise when the going gets rough between partners. Indeed, hard times are the catalyst for healing emotional wounds that go back to childhood and that threaten not only our marriages but other arenas of our lives as well. In fact, recognizing and dealing with each partner's psychological wounds is necessary for a successful relationship.

As these wounds heal, instead of putting the blame for our marital difficulties on our partners, we learn to take responsibility for them, to "own them," the psychoanalyst would say. When we work to make this happen, we become

less stressed and the relationship—instead of dying out—grows into a trusting intimacy that we value both in spite of its troubles, and because of them.

FINDING A SOUL CONNECTION

Welwood's explanation of how relationship conflicts arise is different than Boorstein's, though he, like Boorstein, looks to the couple's past. Often as children Welwood explains, we build a psychological shell around us to protect ourselves from feeling pain. Born open and loving, as children we are often taught that some aspect of ourself is unacceptable. Maybe our exuberance wa squelched or our creativity was dampened. Or, maybe we were taught we had to behave a certain way in order to be good.

"No matter how much our parents love us," Welwood writes in LOVE AND AWAKENING, "they generally see their version of who we are, reflecting their own hopes, fears, expectations, and unmet needs." Instead of suffering the pain of rejection by our parents, we often develop a personality that will win their acceptance.

This adaptation, which is necessary for a child's psychic survival and integration into the family, forces children to build a false personality that they struggle to maintain throughout their lives. "The young child is like an open hand that gradually contracts and closes," says Welwood. "Eventually, we learn to shut ourselves down."

This protective tightening gets installed in our body and mind as a rigid set of defenses. "In this way," he says, "we inflict on ourselves the core wound that will haunt us the rest of our lives— we separate from our deeper spiritual nature, which is an openness to life."

Falling in love provides a glimpse of this spiritual nature. As Welwood details in LOVE AND AWAKENING, in love's early stages, feelings such as openness, peace, and expansiveness simply emerge, unbidden. We become inspired to commit ourselves to a new partner who is able to generate such feelings in us. When people are truly in love, which Welwood calls a "soul connection," they see behind the false facade of one another and connect on a deeper level. They connect with one another's "essential nature," which brings out the feelings of open-

ness and peace. One of the most complimentary things you can say about a partner is "I feel I can be myself with him." Or, simply, "He understands me. He gets who I am." This, says Welwood, is because when someone loves you in this way, they see through your facade and see who you really are. Being seen in this manner, however, can also bring about conflicts.

"If, for example, we harbor an image of ourselves as unlovable, then when the opportunity arises to be loved for who we really are, we won't know how to handle it," Welwood says. "Even though this is what we truly long for, it will also frighten us to death—because it threatens our whole identify." To let love enter, we have to give up who we think we are.

"I don't know any couples who have not suffered this fall from grace at some point, losing touch with the original bright presence that first drew them together," says Welwood. The longer we avoid these old psychological wounds and our rigid set of defenses, the greater becomes their hold on us. If left unresolved, we wind up living an exhausting charade, as Welwood calls it.

We resist our partner's confrontations because they threaten to blow our cover. But actually they're doing us a favor.

The antidote, Welwood says, is to let ourselves open to the feelings we fear the most. When people learn to open to their pain—within the context of an intimate relationship—there results a softening, a relaxation, and greater self-acceptance; it also deepens their connection with themselves and with each other, and can provide them a lifelong mutual path and direction.

"That's the real work of the relationship—and the real opportunity to develop deeper, lasting intimacy," says Welwood.

Of course, facing the challenges on this path takes great courage. As Welwood discusses in LOVE AND AWAKENING, in many ways, having a soul connection is like finding a worthy opponent. We have met our match, someone who won't let us get away with anything that is false or diminishes our being. This is often apparent in the first few years of a relationship, as the partners challenge each other, saying, in effect, "Why are you so stuck in your ways?"

If two partners confront each other like this in order to prove something or to get their own way, it will only result in a power struggle between two egos. Often we resist our partner's confrontations because they threaten to blow our cover, exposing parts of us we have a hard time acknowledging. Yet in blowing our cover, our partner is actually doing us a favor. This is what happened to Keith and Melissa, whose relationship Welwood describes in LOVE AND AWAKENING.

SACRED COMBAT

Keith was first attracted to Melissa because of her generosity of spirit. Everything about her—her warmth, her smile, her capacity to lavish affection, her emotional expressiveness—expressed this abundance. Although Keith loved these qualities in her, he felt threatened by them since he felt that these qualities were lacking in himself. In truth, Keith was very unexpressive because he had closed down his feelings as a child in order not to be overwhelmed by his emotionally intrusive mother.

In their typical conflict, Melissa would be unhappy about Keith's austerity and constrictedness while he became defensive, reacting in an angry, controlling manner. He would try to tone her down, while she remained intent on loosening him up. As the conflict between their different strategies escalated, their fights grew more fierce.

In examining the deeper source of their conflict, Keith eventually saw that Melissa was forcing him—by her very presence in his life—to confront ways in which he remained constricted. Melissa also saw that because she had grown up in a repressive family, she had come to believe that any self-restraint or detachment was a form of death. However, her emotional extravagance often veered into self-indulgence. When she was swept up in her feelings, she would exaggerate their significance, and this often left both of them feeling hurt and confused. Melissa had something impor-

IN A LOVE CRISIS?

That's good! Use your relationship's "hot spots" to learn more about yourself and your partner. Here are nine ideas for dealing with love's day-to-day trials, taken from talks and writings by psychotherapists who specialize in working with couples: Seymour and Sylvia Boorstein, John Gray, and John and Jennifer Welwood.

1. Shut up. One thing that makes Gray's MEN ARE FROM MARS, WOMEN ARE FROM VENUS so popular is that he tells men a hundred different ways, LISTEN! This happens to be the single most powerful tool either sex has for averting trouble. If your partner wants to talk, let him or her talk. Don't interrupt. Don't vaccum. Don't answer the phone. Don't look to see what's on TV later. Listen.

2. Good happens. Students of Buddhism learn to observe that *everything* arises and passes. If you are angry or lonely or hurt and are distraught over your feelings and can't seem to get them resolved, allow them to pass before you act on them. They usually will pass. Your anger will somehow get soothed. Bad stuff happens. So does good.

3. Avoid the "67th argument." Every couple has had some particular discussion about sixty-seven times a year that *always* leads to an argument. You can see it coming. He says this, you say that, he says this again, and you know what's coming after you say that again: Mount Saint Helens erupts. So, change the script. It doesn't work. Do something else. Order a pizza, walk to the mail box, or watch the squirrels outside.

4. What are you afraid of? Beneath all anger is fear. If you understand this, then the next time you're so angry that you're ready to throw your plate of spaghetti at your lover's face, stop for a minute. Ask yourself, what am I so afraid of that I've gotten this mad? Or, if it's your partner who is brewing up a storm, try to feel empathy for the fear. What's he or she so afraid of? Compassion melts anger.

5. Feel lust, don't feed it. President Jimmy Carter made news when he confessed in *PLAYBOY* magazine that he had lusted in his heart. As he described his lusting, he had responded as a true Buddhist. He didn't act on his lust. He just felt it. Lust, like any powerful appetite, can never be fed enough. If you feed your lustful feelings in inappropriate ways, they will just want to be refed. Don't feed lust, feel it.

6. "Don't feed your lover a 150-pound burger." Boorstein says when you want to get a point across to your partner, you have to watch both the timing and the dosage of your efforts. Harping becomes nagging, which is counterproductive. Boorstein says, "You can't take a 150-pound hamburger and stuff it into a baby and get an adult. You have to put a little bit in. They chew a while, spit some out, swallow some. After a while, they grow a little."

7. The cure is in the poison. If your jealousy—or any strong emotion—is too much to bear, the most potent way of dealing with it is to walk right up to it and look it right in the eye. Say to yourself, "That's me. I am jealous." You feel the part of your body where it hurts. Your belly? Your neck? Your chest? Wherever it is, feel it and acknowledge it. Welwood and others say this is the entry point to meeting painful emotions head-on. If you confront them like this, they often back down.

8. It's up to you. One of the hardest things for people to accept and understand is that even in love, they're on their own when it comes to finding happiness. "Being responsible" means that you have to look at *your* issues and work them out with yourself. You may think the other person is the cause of the, or can be the answer. But that's generally not the case. What partners can do is *support* one another's struggles.

9. Pretty good is perfect. A woman in her late seventies, married for fifty years, heard another woman say, "My relationship is pretty good, but it isn't perfect." The older woman said, "Listen, when you're talking about relationships, 'pretty good' is perfect.

tant to learn from Keith in this regard— about not always acting out her feelings. By confronting Melissa's emotional

tyrannies, Keith had a grounding effect on her; in learning to reflect on her feelings before rushing into action, she was able to settle into herself in a new way.

As Keith and Melissa come to appreciate how they were each other's teachers, this helped them see their conflict in a new light—as part of a creative and fruitful "sacred combat"—rather than just a divisive struggle. This, says Welwood, is what a soul connection is about—two people joining together to nurture, stimulate, and provoke important steps in each other's unfolding.

RECOGNIZE YOUR SHADOW

Psychotherapists Kathleen Hendricks, Ph.D., ADTR, and Gay Hendricks, Ph.D., have counselled thousands of people with relationships problems over a fifteen-year period. One thing they say you can count on a relationship to do is to pull this kind of "unconscious stuff"—what psychoanalysts call your shadow—to the surface.

Robert A. Johnson, the author of many books on Jungian analysis, explains the shadow concept in *OWNING YOUR OWN SHADOW*. He writes, "We are born whole, but early on our way, we begin the shadow-making process; we divide our lives. We sort out our God-given characteristics into those that are acceptable to our society and those that we have to put away."

Johnson says we can hide these parts of ourselves, but they do not go away. "They only collect in the dark corners of our personality," he says. "When they have hidden long enough, they take on a life of their own." Our shadow can gain power over years. "If it accumulates more energy than our ego, it erupts as an overpowering rage or some indiscretion," says Johnson.

To remedy the problem, Hendricks explains, we teach couples to tell the "microscopic truth." Say, "my stomach is tight," or "I'm scared. I'm afraid of losing you when you do that." This is what psychoanalysts call "owning your shadow."

Johnson says, "The shadow is very important in marriage, and we can make or break a relationship depending on how conscious we are of this. We must come to terms with what we find annoying and distasteful—even downright intolerable—in the other and also in ourselves. Yet, it is precisely this confrontation that leads to our greatest growth."

Owning your shadow, say the Hendrickses, is about being truthful, with your partner and yourself. "It takes actual physical energy," says Kathleen, "to keep yourself from telling the truth. It can happen in a split second. You can suddenly be defensive without realizing that a fear has come up. You can withdraw, withhold, and project in an instant and suddenly it looks like the other person's fault."

Psychotherapists such as the Hendrickses and John Welwood, and his wife of ten years, Jennifer—also a psychotherapist who counsels couples—agree that the intimate partnership is the ideal setting where two people can support one another's inquiry into the recesses of the shadow. In an honest, open relationship, each partner summons the shadow—the anger, the hurt, the pain—and owns it, takes responsibility for it as his or her own, instead of "projecting" it onto others. When we project it, we're basically trying to dish it off to someone else, to disown it. All that this accomplishes, of course, is to arouse anger and reaction from the other person.

"What we found in the early years of our relationship," says Gay, "was that we had awesome barriers to overcome in learning to tell each other the truth, even the simplest truth, like 'I was angry when you wrecked my car.' That was hard for me to say because my programming was to be Mr. Reasonable. I was angry, but it took me weeks to get past being Mr. Reasonable. It was a big breakthrough for me, to say, 'I'm angry.' "

And this process is ongoing, says Kathleen, "In relationships, taking healthy responsibility is something you will have opportunity to do over and over."

COMPASSION FOR BUGABOOS

It's much easier for partners to take responsibility for their shadows when they're extending empathy—compassion—to one another. The Boorsteins learned this lesson in their own marriage.

"If we were criticized a lot early in life," Seymour says, "as I was by my mother, we tend to project onto people around us the image of the person who was critical of us. Even though she died ten years ago, my mother still follows me." Seymour often speaks in public, but he says if he sees disapproving looks in the audience, he gets nervous. The biggest problem he's had in marriage,

he says, is convincing his conscious mind that Sylvia is not his mother.

"Sylvia's not like my mother at all, but I've been sure at times that she was," he says. "It's gotten much better over the years, but I still slip up on occasion. I say to myself 'Ah-ha! I've been waiting forty-three years. I *knew* she would get like that.' "

Sylvia says she sees her mother too. But hers was approving, so she's not uncomfortable in front of audiences, she doesn't easily read criticism into innocent looks or comments, as Seymour might. Sylvia's bugaboo, however, is that she easily becomes fretful. Fifteen years ago, when their youngest daughter was studying theater dance in San Francisco, which required her commuting into the city, Sylvia could not sleep at night while worrying about the girl's safety.

"Seymour and I would be in bed and he'd fall asleep, and I'd get up at 10:45 when our daughter was to be home at 10:30 and I'd say to him, 'Get up. Worry.' He'd say, 'I have to work in the morning. I can't get up now.' He'd go back to sleep while I worried."

Couples seldom look for reasons *why* they're fretful or fearful. But doing so, says Sylvia, builds empathy, a foundation of successful relationships.

THE REASON FOR INTIMACY

Not a few people today wonder whether the struggles of a committed relationship are worth the troubles they seem to bring about. Jennifer and John Welwood have been together for ten years, and they've asked themselves what they give one another that they couldn't get on their own.

Jennifer says, "John creates an environment for me to develop as a human being. I'm very aware of needing him in my life to help me in this way. And it's mutual. That is what our relationship gives to both of us."

John adds, "When you find a larger purpose for your relationship—such as stimulating and supporting one another's deepest unfolding—that provides a bond that can hold two people together for a very long time. Then, whether things are going well this week or not, whether we're happy or not at any give moment, is secondary."

PARENTAL RIGHTS

An Overview

Colby M. May

The issue of parental rights in the face of government intervention is not a new one in this country[1]; it has simply become a more burning issue as the intrusions have become more pronounced. As long ago as 1923, in a case called *Meyer v. Nebraska*,[2] the United States Supreme Court rejected the argument that the government's view of what led children to become patriotic and good citizens should prevail over the parents' view. The Court noted that in Plato's *Republic* the state was to rear children, and "no parent is to know his own child, nor any child his parent."[3] The Court concluded, however, that the U.S. Constitution was founded upon precisely the opposite principle—that parents and not the government should bear responsibility for raising children:

> Although such measures have been deliberately approved by men of great genius, their ideas touching the relation between individual and State were wholly different from those upon which our institutions rest; and it hardly will be affirmed that any legislature could impose such restrictions upon the people of a state without doing violence to both let-

Colby M. May is senior counsel, heading the Office of Government Affairs, American Center for Law and Justice, Washington, D.C.

1. As early as 1901, the Indiana State Supreme Court, in a ruling upholding the state's compulsory education law, stated, "[t]he natural rights of a parent to the custody and control of his children are subordinate to the power of the state." *State v. Indiana v. Bailey*, 157 Ind. 324 (1901).
2. *Meyer v. Nebraska*, 262 U.S. 390 (1923).
3. *Meyer*, 262 at 401–402.

ter and spirit of the Constitution.[4]

Time and again, the Supreme Court has recognized the rights of parents to control the upbringing of their children—rights founded upon the First, Fifth, Ninth, and Fourteenth Amendments to the Constitution. As recently as 1990, the Supreme Court observed that, under the Fourteenth Amendment, the fundamental liberty interest of the parent to direct the education of the child is subject to strict scrutiny and cannot be overridden without showing a compelling state interest.[5]

On the local level, however, the culture wars are raging around the rights of parents in the health, education, and moral upbringing of their children. Local government encroachment into areas traditionally the province of parents has resulted in a populist outcry and possible congressional intervention. Some relatively recent examples of current case law serve to illustrate trends in the ongoing battle between parents and the government.

UPBRINGING

In the 1970s and early '80s the "children's rights" movement was in vogue. That line of sociological thinking led to the idea that children should have an equal say in their own upbringing. It was, perhaps, this underlying notion of childhood independence from parental authority and supervision that led the Washington State Supreme Court to find that parents could not punish a minor for involvement with sex and drugs.[6] Parents had grounded their eighth-grade daughter because she engaged in premarital sexual activity and smoked marijuana. When the parents continued to have difficulty getting their daughter to obey, they asked for state assistance. While recognizing that the parents had imposed "reasonable rules which were reasonably enforced" upon their daugh-

ter, the court nonetheless removed her from the home.

Social mores have guided much of the jurisprudence in the area of parental rights. In the 1960s the U.S. Supreme Court upheld a law banning the sale of pornographic magazines to children under seventeen years of age. In so doing the Court acknowledged that "[c]onstitutional interpretation has consistently recognized that the parents' claim to authority in their own household to direct the rearing of their children is basic in the structure of our society."[7]

Thirty years later, Texas parents were denied the opportunity to see a mandatory assessment test that asked students personal questions concerning their family life, moral values, and religious beliefs. The parents sued and won, alleging that their responsibility for the upbringing and education of their children had been infringed. The Texas Education Agency on appeal asserted that "the right to direct the education and upbringing of your child is *not* a fundamental right."[8] This position by the Texas Education Agency is not unique, but it is consistent with the view of many public educators that parental rights end at the schoolhouse gate.

EDUCATION

The battle concerning parental authority is most pronounced in the area of education. In the public school arena, recent state court rulings prevent parents from opting their children out of sexually explicit presentations that they find religiously or morally offensive. In a Massachusetts case, a presentation was given in which the instructor:

1) told the students that they were going to have a "group sexual experience with audience participation"; 2) used profane, lewd, and lascivious language to describe body parts and excretory functions; 3) advocated and approved oral sex, masturbation, homosexual sexual activ-

---

4. *Meyer*, 262 at 402.
5. *Employment Division v. Smith*, 110 S.Ct. 1595, 1617–18 (1990).
6. *In re Sumey*, 94 Wash. 2d 757, 621 P.2d 108 (1980).

7. *Ginsberg v. New York*, 390 U.S. 629, 639 (1968).
8. *Texas Education Agency v. Maxwell*, No. 14–95–00474–CV (5th Cir.), Appellants' Brief at 11.

The Massachusetts State Supreme Court found no constitutionally protected right for parents to object to public school condom distribution to their children.

ity, and condom use during promiscuous premarital sex; 4) simulated masturbation; 5) characterized loose pants worn by one minor as "erection wear"; 6) referred to being in "deep sh—" after anal sex; 7) had a minor lick an oversized condom, after which the instructor had a female minor pull it over the male minor's entire head and blow it up; 8) encouraged a male minor to display his "orgasm face" for the camera; 9) informed a male minor that he was not having enough orgasms; 10) closely inspected a minor and told him he had a "nice butt"; and 11) made eighteen references to orgasms, six references to male genitals, and eight references to female genitals.[9]

The 1st U.S. Circuit Court of Appeals found that no conscience-shocking activity had occurred at the public school assembly, because no physical intrusive contact had transpired.[10] The court also found no constitutionally protected right for parents to opt their children out of the program.[11] In a similar decision, the Massachusetts State Supreme Court found no constitutionally protected right for parents to object to public school condom distribution to their children.[12] A contrary decision in New York found such a protected parental right.[13]

The issue of character development, which has come to the fore in recent years, has engendered community service requirements as an integral part of public school education. A North Carolina school board recently required community service for graduation and told parents which specific extracurricular activities their children could engage in to meet the requirement. An Eagle Scout,

however, in pursuit of his scouting achievements was not considered to be fulfilling a "true and selfless" community service, according to the school board.[14]

One of the most hotly contested areas of education is home schooling and the question of how much oversight public authorities can have over parents teaching their children. In 1993, the Supreme Court of Michigan considered two home-schooling cases that were consolidated for oral arguments. At issue in the case was Michigan's requirement that all teachers be certified to teach, thus including home-schooling parents. In both cases, the children tested well within the state-specified boundaries for their educational peer groups.

In the case involving a family that home-schooled because of religious convictions, the court found that the statute was unconstitutional because it violated the principles of religious freedom when combined with parental rights.[15] In the second case, involving a family home schooling for nonreligious reasons, the parents lost. The rationale of the court was that the fundamental-rights analysis did not apply to a pure parental-rights claim without a religious component.[16]

MEDICAL

It is axiomatic that parents have a duty to their children for their health and medical upkeep. The government, acting in its *parens patriae* (the country as parent) authority, can override a parent's wishes concerning his child's medical treatment. Most notable are those situ-

9. *Brown v. Hot, Sexy and Safer Productions, Inc.*, 68 F.3d 525, 529 (1st Cir. 1995).
10. *Brown*, 68 F.3d at 531.
11. *Brown*, 68 F.3d at 532–33.
12. *Curtis v. Falmouth*, 420 Mass. 749, 652 N.E.2d 580 (1995).
13. *Alfonso v. Fernandez*, 195 A.D.2d 46, 606 N.Y.S.2d 259 (2 Dept. 1993).

14. *Herndon v. Chapel Hill–Carrboro City Board of Education*, No. 1:94–CV–00196.
15. *People of the State of Michigan v. Dejonge*, 501 N.W.2d 127 (Mich. 1993).
16. *People of the State of Michigan v. Bennett*, 501 N.W. 2d 106 (Mich. 1993).

ations where the government has prevailed over parents' religiously based objections to such treatment as blood transfusions.[17]

The issue of greatest concern for many parents has been their children's sexual education and involvement. A particularly contentious area has been parents' desire to intervene in a daughter's decision to have an abortion. The confluence of minors obtaining abortions and parental rights and responsibilities for medical care has led to a patchwork quilt of laws concerning medical procedures and parental authority. For example, in most states it is illegal for minors to get their ears pierced without parental consent. However, in many states government officials take the position that chil-

dren's rights to serious medical procedures outweigh parental authority.

Beginning with *Carey v. Population Services*, 431 U.S. 678 (1977), the U.S. Supreme Court reviewed a New Jersey statute that made it a criminal offense to sell or distribute contraceptives to minors under the age of sixteen. The Court found this total prohibition to be in violation of the privacy right of minors who made the personal decision to use such devices. There was no majority opinion, however, on this particular issue. At that time, the justices declined to indicate a belief that parents have a constitutional right to be notified by a public facility when it distributes contraceptives.

Later cases wrestled with the issue of a minor's right to receive contraceptives without parental notification or consent. Generally, courts applying *Carey* found that there was no independent fundamental "right of access to contraceptives," but access to contraceptives was essential to exercise the constitutional right of decision in matters of childbearing.[18] The underpinnings for the minor's right of private access to contraceptives remained grounded in the concept that the minor's right of privacy superseded the parents' right to direct their child's moral education.

In 1990, the Supreme Court began applying a different rationale to the issue of a minor's right of privacy in matters of childbearing, expressly overruling prior decisions on this point. In *Hodgson v. Minnesota*, 497 U.S. 417 (1990), and *Ohio v. Akron Center for Reproductive Health* (Akron II), 497 U.S. 502 (1990), the Court upheld a statutory requirement of parental notification and/or consent prior to abortion if certain safeguards were met. The Court reiterated the basis for its transition on this issue in *Planned Parenthood v. Casey*:

> We have been over most of this ground before. Our cases establish, and we reaffirm today, that a State may require a minor seeking an abortion to obtain the consent of a parent or guardian, provided there is an adequate judicial bypass procedure. . . .

---

17. *People ex rel Wallace v. Labrenz*, 411 Ill. 618, 104 N.E.2d 769, *cert. den.* 344 U.S. 824; *Custody of Minor*, 378 Mass. 732, 393 N.E.2d 836; *Morrison v. State*, 252 S.W.2d (Mo. app.); *Re Vasko*, 238 App. Div. 128, 263 N.Y.S. 552; *Mitchell v. Davis*, 205 S.W.2d 812 (Tex. Civ. App.).

18. *Roe v. Wade*, 410 U.S. 113 (1973); *Planned Parenthood of Central Missouri v. Danforth*, 428 U.S. 52, 74–75 (1976); *Bellotti v. Baird*, 443 U.S. 622 (1979).

This idea that parents have a right in counseling and being involved with their children's sexual decisions and upbringing has often not been embraced by government authorities.

Indeed, some of these provisions regarding informed consent have particular force with respect to minors: the waiting period for example may provide the parent or parents of a pregnant young woman the opportunity to consult with her in private, and to discuss the consequences of her decision in the context of the values and moral or religious principles of their family.[19]

This idea that parents have a right in counseling and being involved with their children's sexual decisions and upbringing has often not been embraced by government authorities. For example, some Georgia parents found condoms in their daughters' room and subsequently discovered that their two teenage daughters had been driven to a county health facility during school hours where they received Pap smears, AIDS tests, condoms, and birth control pills. The parents were not informed of these medical procedures and did not consent to these activities. Moreover, when contacted by the parents for the results of their daughters' Pap smears and AIDS tests, both the school district and the county health facility refused to release the information, claiming patient confidentiality.[20]

In 1944, the U.S. Supreme Court held that "[i]t is cardinal with us that the custody, care and nurture of the child reside first in the parents, whose primary function and freedom include preparation for obligations the state can neither supply nor hinder. And it is in recognition of this that these decisions have respected the private realm of family life which the state cannot enter."[21] The Massachusetts Supreme Court recently disagreed with this standard, however, ruling that par-

ents had no claim in regulating or prohibiting the distribution of condoms within the Falmouth County public schools. The court found that a parental rights claim could not be made unless the schools coerced students in the distribution of condoms.[22]

In the same vein, the 6th U.S. Circuit Court of Appeals affirmed a district court ruling that a Michigan couple did not have a fundamental parental right to prevent public school officials from forcing their third-grade son to undergo psychological counseling. The court held that the parents had no constitutionally protected right to object to the mental health treatments, or to even view the child's counseling records.[23] The parents' solution to this dilemma of unwanted public school psychological counseling was to remove their son from the public school system and place him in a private school.

CURRENT LEGISLATIVE TRENDS

In 1995 companion legislation was introduced by Sen. Charles Grassley (R-Iowa) and Rep. Steve Largent (R-Oklahoma) called the Parental Rights and Responsibilities Act (PRRA).[24] The purpose of the act was to place the burden upon government officials, rather than parents, to prove the necessity of a governmental intrusion upon parental rights. Largent testified before a Senate subcommittee that

[t]his protection is needed because the government is using its coercive force to dictate values, offend the religious and moral beliefs of families, and restrict the freedoms of families to live as they choose. State and lower Federal Court cases

19. *Planned Parenthood v. Casey*, 120 L.Ed.2d 674, 729 (1992).
20. *Earls v. Stephens County School District*, No. 2:95–CV–0097 (N.D. Ga. Gainesville Division, 1995).
21. *Prince v. Massachusetts*, 321 U.S. 158, 166 (1944).
22. *Curtis v. Falmouth*, 420 Mass. 749, 652 N.E.2d 580 (1995).
23. *Newkirk v. Fink*, 1995 WL 355664 (6th Cir. 1995) (unpublished decision).
24. *Parental Rights and Responsibilities Act of 1995*, S. 984.

While the "Parents Movement" may be just beginning, parental rights, like all personal liberty issues, have been with us as a society from our country's founding.

across the country illustrate that often times courts are using an inappropriate and unconstitutional standard in their consideration of parental rights claims.[25]

The ACLU, the National Education Association, and a host of other groups opposed this legislation, which expired with the end of the 104th Congress. Generally, the argument in opposition to the PRRA (and similar state proposals) is that it would unduly burden state and local authorities by forcing them to prove the necessity of decisions that impact families. In addition, they argue that the legislation would limit literature choices for youth, as well as have a negative impact on state child-abuse laws.[26]

On the state level, efforts to strengthen parental rights have been made as proposals to amend state constitutions, as was the case in the November 1996 Colorado elections. While the measure was defeated, supporters have vowed to bring the measure up again, along with a more sophisticated "get out the message" effort to offset opposition by the large educational administrator and teacher unions. State laws codifying parental rights have also been proposed and are currently under consideration.

---

25. Testimony of Rep. Steve Largent before the Senate Subcommittee on the Courts, of the Judiciary Committee (December 5, 1995) at 1.

26. Daniel Katz, "Parental Rights without Responsibility," *Federal Lawyer* (September 1996), 39.

CONCLUSION

At a time when more and more Americans believe the family is under severe pressure from government activities—from court rulings in Hawaii that hold denial of a marriage license to members of the same sex to be illegal discrimination, to programs that distribute condoms to eleven-year-old students but forbid the teaching of abstinence—is it any wonder the issue of parental rights has become so serious? While the "Parents Movement" may be just beginning, parental rights, like all personal liberty issues, have been with us as a society from our country's founding. As James Madison so compellingly wrote in *Federalist* 51:

> What is government itself but the greatest reflections on human nature? If men were angeles, no government would be necessary. If angeles were to govern men, neither external nor internal government would be necessary. In framing a government which is to be administered by men, over men, the great difficulty lies in this: You must first enable the government to control the governed; and in the next place oblige it to control itself.

The right of parents to direct the upbringing and education of their children is a profound right indeed. In today's America, with its numbing array of challenges, it seems sure this issue will be forced evermore to the front.

The Myth of Quality Time

Kids don't do meetings. You can't raise them in short, scheduled bursts. They need lots of attention, and experts warn that working parents may be shortchanging them. BY LAURA SHAPIRO

FOR THE NEW YORK LAWYER, IT ALL HIT HOME in the grocery store. She had stopped in with her 6-year-old to pick up a few things, but since the babysitter normally did the shopping, she was unprepared for what was about to happen. Suddenly there was her son, whooping and tearing around the store, skidding the length of the aisles on his knees. "This *can't* be my child," she thought in horror. Then the cashier gave a final twist to the knife. "Oh," she remarked. "So *you're* the mother." That was the moment when the lawyer was forced to admit that spending "quality time" with the kids didn't seem to be working. She and her husband, a journalist, had subscribed in good faith to the careerists' most treasured rule of parenting: it isn't how much time you spend with your kids, it's how you spend the time. But despite those carefully scheduled hours of parental attention between dinner and bed, their two kids were in danger of turning into little brats. "I don't want to come home and find my kids watching cartoons and demanding every new product Disney put out this week," she says. "It's not that sitters do a bad job, but sitters don't raise kids. Parents do." Next month the family is moving to a suburb, and she'll go to work part-time.

Not every family can, or wants to, make a life change on that scale. But many are starting to question whether time devoted to their children really can be efficiently penciled into the day's calendar, like a business appointment with a couple of short, excitable clients. No wonder a growing number of psychologists and educators who work with children would like to get rid of the whole idea of quality time. "I think quality time is just a way of deluding ourselves into shortchanging our children," says Ronald Levant, a psychologist at Harvard Medical School. "Children need vast amounts of parental time and attention. It's an illusion to think they're going to be on your timetable, and that you can say 'OK, we've got a half hour, let's get on with it'." For parents who love their kids and also love their work, there's no more insistent wake-up call than Arlie Hochschild's new book, "The Time Bind," just published and already hovering in the nightmares of anyone who has ever sung a lullaby over the phone. Hochschild's most chilling insight is our complicity in depriving our children. "Many working families," she writes, "are both prisoners and architects of the time bind in which they find themselves."

Quality time arrived on the scene in the early '70s, featured in a wave of research including a now famous study by Alison Clarke-Stewart of the University of California, Irvine. She found (and recent brain research backs her up) that the more actively mothers were involved with their babies, talking and cooing and so forth, the better it was for the babies' cognitive and social development. Babies who spent time with their mothers but didn't get as much of the goo-gooing and eye contact did less well. "But to be able to have that high-quality time, you have to invest a certain amount of pure time," says Clarke-Stewart. "It's not just 10 minutes a week." Such nuances quickly dropped away as baby-boomer couples found quality time an immense help in juggling two careers and a potty chair. Today it's not even clear what most people mean when they use the term—is playing patty-cake supposed to be a higher-quality activity than driving to ballet lessons? Does family dinner count if the TV is on? Very softly? All we reliably know is that whenever time with kids is in short supply, calling it "quality time" makes parents feel better.

Experts say that many of the most important elements in children's lives—regular routines and domestic rituals, consistency, the sense that their parents know and care about them—are exactly what's jettisoned

 From *Newsweek*, May 12, 1997, pp. 62-65, 67-69. © 1997 by Newsweek, Inc. All rights reserved. Reprinted by permission.

when quality time substitutes for quantity time. "Mom is working until 4:30 and has to get the groceries and do the laundry and the chores and pick somebody up from soccer and drop somebody off at ice skating," says Chicago psychologist Vicki Curran. "The structure of the day disappears. But the structure, and the availability to one another, provide the safe arena we know as home." Nor do kids shed their need for parental time when they get to be teenagers. "One of the functions of parents is monitoring—you monitor their homework, their friends, what they're really doing in their spare time," says Jeanne Brooks-Gunn, a developmental psychologist at Columbia University. "I don't think we've said enough to parents about how the demands on them change when early adolescence hits, and kids may start to engage in drugs or sex. Monitoring is critical."

> ## "On weekends, I feel like a taxi service. It's as bad as work can be some days. You're just torn in so many directions."
> —EILEEN O'DONNELL of Lynnfield, Mass., with husband Michael, son John Ryan, 7, and daughter Kelsey, 5

Parents who race in the door at 7:30 p.m. and head straight for the fax machine are making it perfectly clear where their loyalties lie, and the kids are showing the scars. "I see apathy, depression—a lack of the spunkiness I associate with being a kid," says Levant. "These kids don't have the self-esteem that comes from knowing your parents are really interested in you, really behind you." Kevin Dwyer, assistant executive director of the National Association of School Psychologists, says teachers are reporting increases in discipline problems and classroom disruptions. "One of our concerns is that parents are not spending enough time with their kids," he says. "Most of the parents we see are really drained at the end of the day." The result is inconsistent discipline and all the problems it spawns. "There's a tremendous amount of research showing that inconsistency leads to kids' being more aggressive, more deviant and more oppositional," says Dwyer.

In "The Time Bind," Hochschild analyzes in depth a large corporation she calls "Amerco." She spent months interviewing employees, from the CEO to the factory shift

workers, and found many who complained about long workdays and hectic home lives. But few of the employees were taking any steps to carve out more time with their families—they weren't taking unpaid family leave even if they could afford it, and they weren't applying for flextime or job sharing. Hochschild's startling conclusion was that for many workers, home and office have changed places. Home is a frantic exercise in beat-the-clock, while work, by comparison, seems a haven of grown-up sociability, competence and relative freedom. Quality time has been a crucial component of this transformation. "Instead of nine hours a day with a child, we declare ourselves capable of getting the 'same result' with one, more intensely focused, total quality hour," she writes. Hochschild describes some of the Amerco kids as essentially on strike against their assembly-line lives. "They sulk. They ask for gifts. They tell their parents by action or word, 'I don't like this'."

Not all researchers agree with Hochschild's analysis or her view of its consequences for kids. "What she's describing is a class phenomenon," says Rosalind Barnett, a psychologist and senior scholar at Radcliffe College. "I don't think most ordinary Joes confuse work with family. Work is work." Barnett and journalist Caryl Rivers are the authors of "She Works/He Works," which describes the results of a four-year, $1 million study of 300 two-earner couples in the Boston area. The authors and their team of interviewers found that both men and women in this random sample reported high levels of satisfaction with their lives, despite the stress, and warm, close relationships with their children. "Most see their families as the center of their emotional lives," they write. Barnett says their study jibes with many others—for instance, a 1995 survey of more than 6,000 employees at DuPont, showing that nearly half the women, and almost as many men, had traded career advancement to remain in jobs that gave them more family time. Fran Rodgers, CEO of Work/Family Directions in Boston, agrees that national surveys give results different from Hochschild's focus on one company. "What peo-

ple really want is both to be good parents and good at work," she says.

Underlying at least some of the criticism of Hochschild's work is the fear that to acknowledge problems with our kids is to invite a backlash against women's working. That's mighty unlikely to change. Not only do women work for the same reason men do—they need the money—but surveys have also consistently shown that employed women are happier, healthier and feel more valued, even at home, than women who are full-time homemakers. "Even if women *did* go home, it wouldn't be the best solution," says Stephanie Coontz, author of "The Way We Never Were," an examination of the real, as opposed to the mythic, world of the

> ## "I think she's doing OK. If it were up to me, I'd spend more time with her. I wish I were able to stay home. But that's just not possible."
> —ZEFONIC DOBYNES of Calumet City, Ill., with husband Calvin Stringer and daughter Lauren Ashley, 3

'50s. Her new book, "The Way We Really Are," takes a similarly unblinkered look at the present. "Suppose the wife quits work for a year when the kids are little," she says. "She becomes the specialist in child nurturing, and the man never catches up. He doesn't have the initial skills, and she's got a year's head start. Research shows that men do more and better child care when their wives aren't home." Studies also clearly indicate that children whose fathers are thoroughly involved in their care do better socially and cognitively than kids whose fathers play a more marginal role. What's more, the involved fathers are happier than the marginal ones—you know, the daddies talking intently into cell phones during the entire Little League game.

In light of this data, one way to start solving the problems posed by quality time seems obvious: guys, go home. It's 5 p.m. Women may feel guiltier than men about working, women may choose to cut back their careers, but if our kids are hurting for lack of family time, it's not a women's issue, it's a family issue. And studies overwhelmingly show that men's contribution

Attention Deficit

Even for the most essential child-care responsibilities—bathing, feeding, reading and playing—parents' time is scarce.

AVERAGE HOURS PER WEEK PARENTS DEVOTE TO UNDIVIDED CHILD CARE*

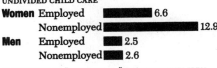

		Hours
Women	Employed	6.6
	Nonemployed	12.9
Men	Employed	2.5
	Nonemployed	2.6

*1995 ESTIMATES. "TIME FOR LIFE," PENN STATE UNIV. PRESS

to housework and child care ranges from a third to a half of what women do (chart), though the numbers have been inching closer in recent years. Then there was the 1993 survey by the Families and Work Institute that asked dual-earner couples how they divided responsibility for child care. "We share it 50-50" was the response of 43 percent of the men—and 19 percent of the women.

James Levine, director of the Fatherhood Project at the Families and Work Institute, says change is happening slowly, but it's happening. Time with their children is increasingly important to men, he says, but some are unwilling to confront a corporate culture that values long hours and face time above all. "I find guys doing all kinds of strange things to avoid publicly acknowledging that they have parental responsibilities," says Levine. "They'll sneak out to pick up their kids at day care, or wait just a few minutes after their boss leaves to go themselves. People need to break this pattern and start taking responsibility."

"I've curtailed my business to be with them more, but I hope as they get older and our lives slow down a little I'll get to spend more time at the office."

— PAUL BONAPART *of Mill Valley, Calif., with wife Barri, son Adin, 4, and daughter Mayana, 2*

Some men do break the pattern, though it's easier at the high end of the pay scale. New York Attorney Franz Paasche tried hard to keep weekends with his family sacrosanct. But he found that work was lasting later and later on Fridays, and starting up earlier on Sundays. So he changed to a new job with more flexible hours. Now, he says, he never misses walking his daughter to the school bus and buckling her seat belt; and even if he has to work at night, he has dinner with the family and reads bedtime stories first. "These days are not replaceable," he says. "My children are different every day. That may be the myth of quality time—that time is interchangeable."

The family-friendly policies introduced by some companies with much fanfare— job sharing, flexible hours and the like—often don't hold up in practice. "The easiest thing for the corporate world to do is fall back on family-friendly benefits," says Lotte Bailyn, a professor at MIT's Sloan School of Management. "They're wonderful, but they're underutilized. Men hardly ask for them, and if they do they're seen as wimps. If women take them, they're put on the mommy track." Bailyn heads a research team that develops new organizational structures designed to help companies become more productive while eating up less of their employees' time. "We're reversing the idea of quality time," she says. "Quality time belongs at work. Quantity time belongs with the family."

Unfortunately, there's little in the current business climate that encourages most employees to do anything about their long hours except cling desperately to their jobs as colleagues disappear around them. Now more than ever, people have powerful financial incentives to resist making more time for families. And men, who still tend to make more money than their wives—and work about eight more hours per week—are caught in a special time bind: if they do cut back for the family's sake, the family suffers financially. But Elizabeth Perle McKenna, whose book "When Work Doesn't Work Anymore" will be published in September, says corporate downsizing might well prompt some men to look harder at their values. "When motherhood hit the babyboomer women, we were forced to stop and really look at work for the first time, and ask, 'Is this worth it to me?'" she says. "I think all the downsizing in business, and its effect on men's lives, could make them do the same thing." She also believes that younger workers, men and women starting their careers now, will have a major impact on how corporations treat families. "I interviewed young women who have no intention of sacrificing their lives for their jobs," she says.

"If you're company X and you're trolling for the best people, you won't be able to ignore those issues anymore."

Corporate utopia may be a long way off, but men and women can change their own lives right now. Cutting back on work hours—and income—might seem an impossible dream; but Seattle psychologist Laura Kastner often reminds her clients that they do have choices. Maybe they can move to a cheaper neighborhood; maybe they can move closer to work and cut their commuting time. Marlene and Keith Winsten, who live outside Providence, R.I., with their two kids, are up and running by 5:30 a.m.; most of their family time is on the weekend. So they're cutting back on the hikes and museums that used to jam Saturday and Sunday; sometimes they all just hang out. "We've been trying hard to calm things down," says Marlene. "Quality time is going at their pace."

Want to hear about some people who don't have to "juggle" work and family because it's so easy for them to carry both? They work in the state attorney general's office in Bismarck, N.D. "Most of the workers go home at noon—they get in their cars and drive home and have lunch with their kids," says Jean Mullen, who moved to Bismarck after working in Washington, D.C., for two decades. "If you look at the computer bulletin board, where the attorneys sign out when they're going someplace, you'll see people have written down things like 'car pool.' They leave at 3 p.m. to pick up their kids from school and take them home. The building generally empties out at 5.

"The men are eligible for the same family leave as the women, and they take it. They take flextime as much as the women. There's total acceptance of the fact that

Taking Care of Family Business

Child care is the biggest job at home for both men and women, but women spend more than three times as many hours tending the kids. Though men cook and shop more than they did a decade ago, they still lag behind in those chores, too.

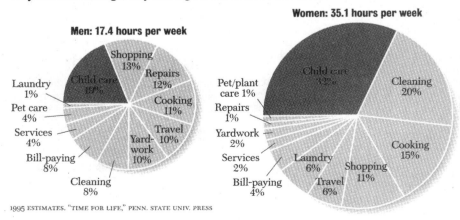

Men: 17.4 hours per week
Shopping 13%
Repairs 12%
Cooking 11%
Child care 19%
Laundry 1%
Pet care 4%
Services 4%
Bill-paying 8%
Travel 10%
Yard-work 10%
Cleaning 8%

Women: 35.1 hours per week
Child care 32%
Cleaning 20%
Cooking 15%
Pet/plant care 1%
Repairs 1%
Yardwork 2%
Services 2%
Bill-paying 4%
Laundry 6%
Travel 6%
Shopping 11%

1995 ESTIMATES. "TIME FOR LIFE," PENN. STATE UNIV. PRESS

Time Bind? What Time Bind?

If you're feeling stressed out and exhausted—get over it. A provocative new book argues that we actually have *more* free time now than ever.

SO YOU THINK YOU HAVE NO TIME FOR YOUR KIDS, NO time to sleep, read, cook exercise, socialize—in short, no time to live? Well, wait a minute (if you can spare one), and get a load of this: a surprising book being published next month by two renowned time–study experts concludes Americans have *more* free time now than at any point in the past 30 years—an average of 40 free hours a week. John Robinson and Geoffrey Godbey, the authors of "Time for Life" (Penn State Press), acknowledge that Americans have more leisure in the aggregate partly because many of us are retiring younger and having fewer time-devouring children than we did in the 1960s. Yet they find that trend holds in almost every demographic, including working parents. Just about the only groups that don't have at least one more hour of free time a week than they did in 1965 are parents of very young children and those with more than four kids under 18. Everyone else—stopwhining.

Needless to say, this is controversial stuff. Robinson and Godbey spent five years trying to find a publisher. One female editor rejected the book immediately—and angrily—when she got to the statistics showing that women have almost the same amount of free time (39.3 hours per week) as men (41.6). "She said, 'I know this can't be right. I know women work longer than men'," says Godbey, a professor of leisure studies at Penn State. "She didn't say we're chauvinist pigs, but almost." The authors weren't entirely surprised by that reaction. The most trenchant aspect of their work is its ability to separate faulty perceptions of time use from reality. Instead of just asking people how many hours they work, eat, tend to the children, etc.— which is how most government data is collected—the 10,000 survey participants kept minute-by-minute diaries. Robinson, who has taken these surveys every 10 years since 1965 as part of the Americans' Use of Time Project,

found that when people are simply asked how much time they work, they exaggerate (chart). "Being busy has become a status symbol," says Robinson, a sociologist at the University of Maryland. "As you say time is more important to you, you become more important yourself." In fact, Americans are working fewer hours than they did in 1965: about five fewer hours per week for working women, six fewer for men.

So where is all this alleged free time going? Not surprisingly, into the greatest time sinkhole of all: television. On average, Americans squander 15 of their 40 hours of free time every week on the boob tube, more than the time spent socializing (6.7 hours), reading (2.8 hours) and in outdoor recreation (2.2 hours) combined. It's not so much that we're lazy. Godbey and Robinson have also found that an increasing amount of free time now comes in tiny portions: a half hour here, an hour there. It's much easier to fit a "M*A*S*H* rerun into that fractured space than a mountain hike.

At least some of our time is well spent. The amount of time parents spend on the most essential child-care activities, such as reading, bathing, talking and playing with kids, has remained fairly static since 1965 for everyone but stay-at-home moms (who average 13 hours a week, compared with 2.5 for working dads). But Robinson and Godbey argue that because families have fewer children now, each child receives more parental attention than kids did in the '60s. And wives are getting more help from their husbands. While women still spend about twice as much time doing housework as men, the gap has closed considerably since 1965, when women spent more than five times the hours cleaning. Whether the guys have one eye on the TV while they're vacuuming is another question.

Perception vs. Reality

People tend to exaggerate the number of hours they work each week. A different picture emerges when they keep detailed, 24-hour diaries of their days.

AVERAGE HOURS PER WEEK SPENT AT PAID WORK*

Women	Actual	32.0
	Perceived	40.4
Men	Actual	40.2
	Perceived	46.2

*1995 ESTIMATES. "TIME FOR LIFE," PENN. STATE UNIV. PRESS

MARC PEYSER

you'll take off time to go to your child's school conference. It's not free time—they expect you to make it up—but you can openly say that's where you're going." Mullen talks on and on—about taking her kids to the dentist, about receiving phone calls from them during a staff meeting, about being taken seriously as a professional woman, family and all. Maybe utopia does exist. Or maybe the attorney general's office in Bismarck, N.D., is just the way real life runs, when people acknowledge what's important to them—and live that way.

With CLAUDIA KALB *in Boston,* PAT WINGERT *in Washington, D.C.,* ROBINA RICCITIELLO *in Chicago,* PATRICIA KING *in San Francisco and* ANNE UNDERWOOD *in New York*

EFFECTIVE FATHERS

WHY ARE SOME DADS MORE SUCCESSFUL THAN OTHERS?

Ken R. Canfield

Ken R. Canfield is the author of The Seven Secrets of Effective Fathers *and* Beside Every Great Dad. *His articles have appeared in* Psychological Reports, Educational and Psychological Measurement, Parents, *and other publications. He is the founder of the National Center for Fathering in Shawnee Mission, Kansas, which seeks to inspire and train men to be responsible fathers.*

Fathers win when they actively father. There is a deep sense of satisfaction that pervades a father's life when he becomes an involved dad. Vice President Al Gore spoke to this point recently when he said, "There is nothing more noble than to see a father succeed." Bravo! I couldn't agree more. As a researcher over the past seven years, I have tapped into the experiences of some seven thousand fathers across the nation. These dads come from a range of experiences: fathers in prison, fathers in the military, stepfathers, divorced dads, inner-city fathers, suburban fa-

thers, and fathers from different ethnic backgrounds. Each group faces some unique challanges.

AN EFFECTIVE FATHER CAN REMAIN LEVELHEADED BOTH IN A CRISIS LIKE AN AUTO ACCIDENT AND IN THE MIDST OF MEDIA MESSAGES THAT ARE HOSTILE TO TRAINING RESPONSIBLE CHILDREN.

Still, in order to systematize and understand the role of fathers as such, a survey inventory was developed, and the differ-

ent dads I have just mentioned were surveyed on their practices as fathers. A national Gallup poll was conducted. The sample used for this poll differed from the national average, however, in that only 7 percent of the men who were surveyed were noncustodial fathers—all the rest were living with their families. Thus, our sample was above the national average in terms of commitment to fatherhood.

Then, in the course of this research, my colleagues and I identified a group of effective fathers within the larger group. These "effective fathers" had raised at least one child to adulthood and were nominated by peers and/or professionals who knew them. Then, in combing through the survey responses, I found seven aspects of fathering that these fathers demonstrated to a significantly greater degree than did other fathers. Here is the essence of the study.

The seven aspects of effective fathering identified are:
- Commitment
- Awareness
- Consistency

- Protecting and providing
- Loving the children's mother
- Active listening
- Spiritual equipping

1. COMMITMENT

Commitment is being both eager to be with your children and willing to be with them when you are not so eager.

The strong fathers identified by their peers scored 77 percent on the commitment scale on the questionnaire, compared with 59 percent for other fathers. The difference—18 percentage points—was greatest in this area of the survey.

How does a father strengthen commitment? One way is by verbalizing to his children that he is committed to them and available for them. Giving his school-age children his work phone number is one way of emphasizing the point.

Telling others about your commitment to your children is another way of holding yourself accountable. Don't be embarrassed to tell an office mate that you are taking an afternoon off because of a son's ball game. What you're demonstrating is that you are committed to that child.

Symbols can help, too. When the president of the United States looks up from his desk, he can see the seal of his authority. When you look around you, what have you placed within your view that reminds you "I'm a dad!"?

2. AWARENESS

Effective fathers answered that it was "somewhat true" that they knew their children. Other fathers were "undecided" or "unsure" on questions measuring awareness.

Awareness has a couple of aspects. One is knowing your child's specific moods, temperament, abilities, situation at school, friends, dreams, and so on. The other is knowing the general developmental phases in a child's life.

Another secret within the secret of being aware of your children is being aware of the ways that their mom is in tune with them and paying attention to what she notices.

Knowing your children and their situation requires that you heavily invest yourself in digesting what your children tell you. Once I was trying to understand why my son was having trouble with his teacher. By listening hard and forcing myself to pay attention over a period of time, it suddenly clicked. This teacher didn't like my son because he reminded her of someone else. That problem didn't need a father's lecture or discipline—it called for a change in schools.

3. CONSISTENCY

Ahhh, consistency. Remember the often-misquoted phrase: "*Foolish* consistency is the hobgoblin of little minds." We need consistency that isn't stifling, or boring but that communicates love to our children.

When assessed on their stability in such things as their treatment of their children, their emotions, and even their schedule for coming home, effective fathers scored 80 percent, while the others got 68 percent.

Consistency is, first of all, being there. Far too many fathers live apart from their children. But don't let that definition of fatherlessness mislead you. Fathers can be emotionally absent as well. In the movie *Hook*, the successful Wall Street lawyer (played by Robin Williams), says to his son: "When we get back, I'll go to all

the rest of your games. I promise. My word is my bond." His son, the victim of numerous broken promises, replies, "Oh, yeah. Junk bonds."

At the same time, let me offer hope to those dads who aren't living with their children: Consistency still makes a difference. Consistency in regular communication, being predictable down to the day and even the minute, speaks volumes. Consistency in financial support is crucial. And what you do during the time you spend with your children makes an enormous difference in your children's lives.

4. PROTECTING AND PROVIDING

One of the most accepted attributes of fatherhood is providing for and protecting children. That could be why the two groups of fathers we surveyed were closest in this area. Effective fathers rated 93 percent, while the others got 82 percent. These high scores are, of course, importantly a result of our sample being disproportionately made up of at-home dads.

An effective father can remain levelheaded both in a crisis like an auto accident and in the midst of media messages that are hostile to training responsible children.

I view the first formal talk I had with my son about sex as a form of protecting him. He was only seven years old, and this was not a full-blown "birds and bees" talk; it was simply a discussion about human anatomy that I undertook because my wife had noticed our son's curiosity about his older sisters. I wanted to protect my son from learning about anatomical differences in a locker-room-type situation. I wanted him to hear about these things firsthand from his dad, so that he would have a family-dom-

THE FATHERHOOD MOVEMENT

One definition of a movement includes the following three parts: A movement has (1) a group of people who identify themselves as members of the movement, (2) literature that advances their cause, and (3) opposition from other forces.

Defined this way, the "fatherhood movement" is embryonic. By and large, public advocates of responsible fatherhood do not see themselves as a coherent group but as lone prophets shouting in a wilderness of neglect. And opposition to responsible fatherhood is difficult to find.

Still, there are some developments that have the feel of a movement:

The National Fatherhood Initiative has been formed to raise public awareness of the need for responsible fatherhood. The National Fatherhood Initiative is led by Don Eberly (president), who once served as a key aide to Jack Kemp; Wade Horn (director), commissioner of Children, Youth, and Families under President Bush; and David Blankenhorn (chairman), who was a civil-rights activist and community organizer before becoming involved in research on the need for fathers to be present and involved with their families. The group hosted a National Fatherhood Summit in October 1994 to educate civic leaders. After a tour this spring and summer featuring talks by David Blankenhorn, it will be aiming to spearhead an Ad Council campaign on the need for responsible fathers.

Another effort is that of Vice President Al Gore under the name "Father-to-Father." Through meetings of researchers and social-work practitioners (which have been deliberately low-key to ensure that this cause is not seen as partisan), the group is working to develop a private-sector mentoring program matching experienced fathers with newer dads. Gore personally signs on to Father-Net, a computer bulletin board sponsored by the Children, Youth, and Family Consortium of the University of Minnesota. Gore has brought together pioneers in the area of fathering such as Jim Levine and Ed Pitt of the Fatherhood Project and Ralph Smith of the Philadelphia Children's Network.

Levine's Fatherhood Project is sponsored by the Family and Work Institute in New York City. He champions "father-friendly" policies in the workplace and has developed practical materials on how to get men involved in early childhood development programs such as Head Start.

During his years as founder and president of the Philadelphia Children's Network, Ralph Smith promoted "father reengagement," refusing to accept the assumption of many social-welfare bureaucrats that fathers are unwilling or unable to support their children. Smith, now of the Annie E. Casey Foundation, recently helped found the National Center on Fathers and Families at the Graduate School of Education at the University of Pennsylvania. This center aims at closing the research gap in the social sciences on knowledge about fathers.

Meanwhile, a grass-roots group that makes no effort at changing public opinion, Promise Keepers, has motivated a stratum of men from the churches to take up the cause of fatherhood. The Christian group, headquartered in Denver, Colorado, is impressive through raw numbers: It attracted a total of more than 280,000 men for seven day-long events in stadiums across the nation last year and aims to conduct thirteen similar events this year.

While their speakers are a cross-section of evangelical Christians, the message is consistent: Men need to be servant-leaders of their families, get together with a few other men to encourage and support one another, and cross ethnic barriers to reach toward racial harmony. This group attracted some incidental opposition, as homosexual and feminist activists rallied outside one site last year, attacking and misinterpreting the group's motives.

Other developments, spontaneous and unconnected but portending bigger changes, include the following:

• Community colleges offering parent-education classes are starting to aim not just at mother-oriented preschool classes but at classes for fathers as well. Susanne Spandau, an instructor at Pasadena City College in California, went so far as to offer a fathers-only class,

"Being A Father and Loving It." Her class was well attended.

• Corporations are beginning to see resolving work-family tensions in a new light. IDS in Minneapolis recently hosted a fathering seminar taught by professional trainers that drew an overflow crowd, exceeding management's expectations. *Personnel Journal* reported in October 1994 that currently 60 percent of *Fortune* 500 companies offer parenting education programs. Those programs do not consistently take the fathers' needs and desires into account, but they may start to.

• A quasi-corporate municipal agency has gone one better than simply offering parenting education. The Los Angeles Department of Water and Power has an actual "Fathering Program" as part of its Work and Family Life Services office. The program coordinator arranges "Daddy-n-Me" recreation outings once a quarter for employees, lends beepers to dads with expectant wives, and sponsors noontime "information groups" for dads who get together monthly to talk and share ideas.

There may be a place for this kind of "affirmative action" for dads. Work and Family Life coordinator Ray Castro puts it this way, "Every time we hung out a sign 'Family Life Workshop' moms came, so the idea was to target men." No doubt part of the appeal of their offerings is that other men identify with Castro, who told me, "As a 22-year-old with all my degrees nobody had prepared me for the toughest job I would ever have: fatherhood."

• Programs to encourage unwed urban dads to form families are springing up as well. Charles Ballard's work in Cleveland, Ohio, has been so successful that he has been funded to replicate his program in five other cities. His program, the National Institute for Responsible Fatherhood, helps unwed young men acknowledge paternity, get regular jobs so they can support their kids, and develop stable relationships with their child's mother. Many formerly unwed couples have married as a result of participating in the program. Uncovering a man's paternal instinct is actually the first step in Ballard's program— and a much-neglected one.

• Fathers' Education Network in downtown Detroit, with Don Burwell, is taking fifty-two men through weekly gatherings aimed at instilling purpose in their lives and commitment to their children.

• MAD DADS in Omaha, Nebraska, was an "emergency response" when Eddie Staton and two other fathers founded it some five years ago. Dads were needed to take responsibility not just for their own children but for those wandering the streets at night. The group, which has thirty-two chapters nationally, has as its main focus patrolling the streets and talking with young people, especially those who are out after ten at night. The group confronts drug pushers with the consequences of their actions and brings together warring gangs simply to talk. MAD DADS is now taking the step of equipping both young and old fathers so that they may be more effective in rearing their children.

—*K.R.C.*

MORE INFORMATION

NATIONAL FATHERHOOD INITIATIVE:
800-790-DADS.

FATHERNET:
612-625-7251
email address:
cyfcec@maroon.tc.umn.edu

THE FATHERHOOD PROJECT:
212-465-2044

NATIONAL CENTER ON FATHERS AND FAMILIES:
215-686-3910

PROMISE KEEPERS:
800-888-PK95.

LOS ANGELES DEPARTMENT OF Water and Power,
WORK AND FAMILY LIFE SERVICES:
213-367-3546.

NATIONAL INSTITUTE FOR RESPONSIBLE FATHERHOOD:
216-791-8336

FATHERS' EDUCATION NETWORK:
313-831-5838

MAD DADS:
402-451-3500.

—K.R.C.

inated environment within which to assimilate them.

5. LOVING YOUR WIFE

The National Center for Fathering has sponsored essay contests for children about their dads. One fourth-grader, Tasha, wrote: "He treats my mom very nicely, which makes me feel wanted." That is saying that her father's love for her mother indirectly supplies that love to her, too.

Effective fathers on the average reported their marriages were "good," while the average for typical fathers was "fair."

Fathers who are aware of the interplay between their lives and their children's lives know they need to consciously work on loving their wives. It's easy in the aftermath of birth and young children to let your own relationship slide. In fact, our research found that satisfaction with marriage typically drops off as the children grow up and then climbs back up when they leave the nest.

6. ACTIVE LISTENING

Fathering satisfaction goes down when children hit adolescence. But one trait that distinguishes the fathers who are more satisfied during those years from those who aren't is active listening.

Fathers who engage their children verbally are the most satisfied. Effective fathers scored 82 percent on items such as allowing children to disagree, creating an atmosphere of caring

and acceptance that encourages children to share their ideas, and listening closely to their concerns. Other fathers averaged 68 percent.

Active listening is part skill and part motivation. Listening skills include:

- Eye contact. Getting on the same level with your child helps the two of you have a heart-to-heart talk.
- Asking questions or paraphrasing back your child's words. This provides you with a check to make sure that you understand what he or she is saying.
- Nodding or signaling that you are listening helps, too.

Staying relaxed and stopping any "mental overtime" from your job or other interests is largely a question of motivation. So is turning off the television or other distractions.

But, ohhh, the rewards of active listening! Ron Levant and John Kelly give a wonderful example in their book *Between Father and Child*:

Twice in the course of a ten-minute soliloquy on Batman, five-year-old Harry McCann interrupted himself to ask his father, "Dad, how far away is the movie you and Mom are going to tonight?" Harry's question didn't have much to do with Batman; it had a great deal to do with his hidden message, which was "Dad, I'm anxious about the new baby-sitter who's coming tonight."

His dad was able to draw him out on the subject of his worries about the new baby-sitter and reassure him. That's active listening.

7. SPIRITUAL EQUIPPING

Here I am talking about both serving as a moral guide for your family and introducing your children to the transcendent. Children have questions—will we as dads serve as their guides and help them discover answers?

Although this is one area that has been frozen out of much public discussion (and is sometimes ignored when our research is reported in the press), it is significant that this area revealed the second-largest difference between effective dads and the others: Effective fathers averaged 72 percent here, while others averaged 56 percent.

Responding to the Gallup poll we commissioned, only 48.5 percent of Americans agreed that "fathers feel comfortable discussing spiritual matters with their children." Spiritual equipping comes as much by an exemplary life lived as by the conscious education of our families in scriptures or habits of prayer.

David Blankenhorn of the Institute for American Values addresses the issue of living exemplary lives when summing up discussions he has had with groups of dads in his book *Fatherless America*:

All the pieces of the puzzle fit together, adding up to one man: the good father. Their ideals are public as well as private. For this reason a good father is not simply a man who performs certain tasks for his children. He is a man who lives a certain kind of life.

The Great Ages of Discovery

THE WORLD

They start swaddled and protected; Mom is just an appendage. Then everybody else starts showing up: grandparents, siblings, babysitters, friends and eventually salesmen. They're a little taste of the world to come. Children can learn lessons from them that, for better or worse, will stay with them for the rest of their lives.

AS SOON AS THEY START MOVING, they start moving away. Surely it's hard to imagine while you're beaming down at your fuzzy little newborn, but you've already launched him on a life that will inevitably take him out of your arms, if never out of your heart.

You're not in this alone, and therein lies both the opportunity and the challenge. You will be the child's first guardian, teacher and moral compass. But you can't shield your baby from the world. Nor would you want to. Grandma wants to hold her; Sister wants to see if she'll bounce; babysitters are ready to rock the cradle. With any luck, you'll be able to look to your parents—whom, in a blizzard of energy and rebellion, you may have left behind years ago—for help and guidance, and love for their newest family member. (Amazing, isn't it, how the same people who were so seemingly flawed as parents can turn out to be such insightful grandparents?) It does take a family to raise a family.

It's all perfectly natural, the slow but steady transition of a little baby into the big, wider world. It starts with other family members, then moves outward as day care, then friends, then television and marketers begin to exercise their influence. This is a journey babies are built for. They're born scientists, eager to test and taste and learn. You're there to be dazzled at their discoveries. Ride with them as long as you can.

A Grandparent's Role

BY KENNETH L. WOODWARD

AT BIRTH, A CHILD ENTERS THE mysterious world of its parents. At the same time, the child also enters the wider, even more mysterious world of its grandparents. Grandparents can, if they choose, remain aloof, becoming merely titular family figures in a grandchild's life, like the wooden image on the top of a totem. Or they can enrich that child's life—and their own—as a powerful and irreplaceable presence.

Unfortunately, some experts on the family dismiss the role of grandparents as old-fashioned, inadequate and even unnecessary in an age of new family patterns and government programs. In her best-selling book, for example, Hillary Rodham Clinton misconstrues the old African proverb "It takes a village"—her title—"to raise a single child." Those African villages were not at all like small-town America in the 1950s. They were tribal clans, extended-family networks of grandparents and aunts and uncles with strong spiritual, emotional and biological ties. A more apt proverb for today's truncated nuclear family would be "It takes a whole village to replace a single grandparent." Indeed, in terms of nurture and emotional commitment, grandparents are infinitely more precious to grandchildren than a whole villageful of babysitters, child-development specialists, day-care centers and after-school programs. And when it comes to support for working single mothers, close grandparents can be indispensable.

Research by Arthur Kornhaber, a child psychiatrist with whom I wrote a book, "Grandparents/Grandchildren: The Vital Connection" *(280 pages. Transaction Press. $24.95)*, shows that "the attachment between grandparent and grandchild is second in emotional power and influence only to the relationship between parents and children." But there is an important psychological difference between the two. The normal tensions between parent and child simply do not exist between grandparent and grandchild.

Bonding between grandparents and grandchildren begins with the first viewing of the baby. For grandparents, the experience is usually love at first sight. (Some women have even been known to lactate when a daughter delivers her first child.) Infants need a few years before they can reciprocate that love. But gradually, children come to realize that, like themselves, their parents have parents—"great parents" who seem to have existed since the creation of the world. In the same way,

59% of all those polled say grandparents are very involved in their child's life; 37% say other relatives are very involved

they eventually learn to recognize close aunts and uncles as "elders" of the family "tribe."

Attentive grandparents play a number of vital roles in the life of a developing child. One is oral historian. Grandparents are inherently interesting for having lived in "olden" days. Children are especially intrigued by stories about what their parents did when they were children themselves. To know that their parents were mischievous and made mistakes reassures children that they are just like Mom and Dad. In matters of family history, grandparents—not parents—are the ultimate authorities. A kindred role is family archivist. Children love exploring the grandparental attic, discovering old pictures, clothing, knickknacks and, in the process, their own roots. In these and other ways, grandparents supply grandchildren with a "we" as well as an "I."

Regardless of their education or experience, grandparents are natural-born mentors if they take the time and trouble. When the emotional attachment is strong, learning is playing in the presence of a grandparent. Whatever the "curriculum," young children readily absorb what a loving grandparent has to teach. Many years later, grown children often cannot remember when or how they learned to build or bake, fix or make, the way a grandparent taught them. It has long since become instinct.

In religious matters, it is often a grandparent who provides spiritual sustenance to children of indifferent parents. Children always ask the big questions, like "Where does God live?" and "What does he look like?" Regardless of their grandparents' actual age, grandchildren always see them as old and "closer to God"—and therefore in a position to know. As history has shown, Christianity survived in Russia largely because the grandmothers—the *babushkas*—kept the flame of faith alive during more than seven decades of communist rule.

With the emergence of two-worker families, some grandparents are taking on more practical roles, as part- or full-time parents to their own grandchildren. And with the increase in the numbers of divorced and never-married parents, aunts and uncles, often single, are rediscovering their importance to nieces and nephews. Like grandparents, aunts and uncles are family, but their nurture is delightfully different from that of parents. In short, Americans are gradually relearning an ancient truth: that the natural family is the extended family. In that widened womb, every child thrives with aunts and uncles and—as the family's foundation—those mysterious figures called grandparents.

The Sibling Link

BY TOM MORGANTHAU

JASON IS 4 YEARS OLD AND ALL boy—a dynamo, bursting with energy and curiosity, part Luke Skywalker, part Dennis the Menace, part comedian. It wasn't always that way, for Jason was adopted at 14 months, old enough to feel the loss of his biological family and the home he had known. But Jason was lucky. His adoptive parents, Tim and Ginny, already had two sons—Billy, 8, and David, 10—who took to Jason as if he were their own. "His eyes lit up the minute he walked in the door and saw the big guys," Ginny says. "They're everything to him now—he wants to do exactly what they do. He swam at 2 and rode a two-wheeled bike at 3. When they do their homework, he has to do 'homework' too. He'll do anything to get their attention—sometimes he's so aggressive I have to intervene to protect *them*. But they're great with Jason, and they helped a lot when he was settling in. There's just something terrific about raising kids with other kids."

None of this happened by accident. Ginny and Tim spent a lot of time explaining their decision to adopt Jason to Billy and David, and they reacted quickly to any sign of sibling rivalry. Ginny says David, as the oldest, was "fine" about Jason's arrival, but Billy, who was used to being the center of attention, was "freaked." That called for quality time, reassurance and firm rules. Billy and Jason are now very close, Ginny says, but when they begin to squabble, she reminds them there will be no hitting and no mean talk. "My kids aren't perfect, and I don't want them to be," she says. "But they're very loyal to each other. When they get into a squall, I say, 'Just remember, your brother's going to be your friend for life'."

All of which says sibling relationships are powerfully important in a young child's life—and that they are far more complex than the traditional psychiatric view, with its heavy emphasis on the inevitability of sibling rivalry, allows. This is something wise parents have always known. But psychologists have only recently begun to see sibling relationships in the round—to see that infants bond with their siblings during the first year of life, and to understand that even very young children know the difference between parents and other children in the family. Parents are godlike beings, the Source of All. Siblings are fascinating simply because they're kids. "Do they know the difference? I'm sure they do," says Judy Dunn, a developmental psychologist at the Psychiatric Institute in London. "They start enjoying their brothers and sisters pretty early on, even by the age of 6 months if the older sibs try to entertain them. It's very obvious in the ways babies behave toward their sibs. Often they're much more amused by their brothers and sisters than they are by their parents. There are shared interests and shared sources of what kids find funny, even in the second year."

Dunn, who is the mother of three (now adult) children, is the author of four books, including a common-sensical parent's guide called "From One Child to Two" *(Fawcett Columbine. 1995)*. She is also one of the world's ranking authorities on the developmental significance of sibling relationships. Her research, typically based

30% of all parents say finding good day care has been a problem; 32% say they've had trouble finding a job with flexible-time options

on extensive observation of the children in the home, suggests that sibling relationships can give a very young child a developmental head start—particularly if, like Jason's adoring bond with Billy and David, the relationship is warm and affectionate. Dunn and other psychologists are particularly interested in "pretend play," games in which children consciously share a fantasy ("You be Darth Vader—I'll be

Han Solo"). This apparently simple act may be a critical step toward understanding the mental states of others—and, conversely, a major step toward a child's definition of self. Dunn's research shows that children with siblings begin such play six months to a year earlier than only children. More generally, she says, kids with sibs have a much richer experience with the whole range of human relations, including competition, rivalry, negotiation and just getting along. "It may mean that their whole way of understanding other people is different," she says.

Dunn does not argue that sibling relationships lead to higher IQ scores, or that the developmental advantage they seem to confer carries over into later childhood. No one has studied that yet. But her findings, taken as a whole, make a powerful case for revising the traditionally bleak view of sibling rivalry—of childhood hostilities that stereotypically lead toward neurosis. Siblings can get along, and benefit when they do.

Caring and Giving

By Sarah Van Boven

ALICIA BOND KNOWS THAT she is lucky to have found a nanny like Aimee. The Minneapolis mother can't say enough good things about the woman who has cared for her 4-year-old twin sons since they were 6 weeks old. "Aimee taught them to appreciate music by playing the piano, and she's teaching them how to grow vegetables in the garden," says Bond. Lowering her voice so Aimee won't hear, Bond adds, "I just hope the boys are learning as much from me." Like many parents who spend the workday far from their children, Bond can't help but worry that her sons will love their nanny "more." Fortunately, kids are capable of loving more than one caring adult—and these adults can teach a child a lot about the world.

Beginning at birth, babies form strong bonds with the caregivers in their lives—be they parents, grandparents or babysitters. According to Jay Belsky, Distinguished Professor of Human Development at Penn State University, not only can children

form multiple attachments; they can benefit from them. "If you're secure to Mom and Dad, that's better than being secure to just Mom. If you're secure to Mom, Dad and the babysitter, even better."

Parents would do well to worry less about kids' getting overly attached to a caregiver and more about finding the best possible care. According to a study by the National Institute of Child Health and Human Development, scheduled for release in April, high-quality care is extremely important. The NICHD tracked 800 children to see how nonparental care affects mental and linguistic growth at 15, 24 and 36 months. The researchers found that "whether a baby spent zero hours or 60 hours a week in care, *quantity* of care did not influence cognitive and linguistic development," says Sarah L. Friedman, scientific coordinator for the study. Children in "extensive care," defined as more than 30 hours a week, did not score lower on tests of either cognition (problem solving, reasoning and attention) or language (vocabulary and sentence complexity).

More critical was *quality* of care. The NICHD researchers looked for "positive caregiving"—hugs, responsiveness to the child's needs and, especially, verbal stimulation. The better the care, the better kids tended to score on cognitive and language tests. This doesn't surprise Ellen Galinsky, president of the Families and Work Institute. "Children need warmth and responsiveness," she says. "If a 2-year-old comes to day care excited about seeing a fire truck, I want to hear the provider say, 'We've got a book about fire trucks. Let's look at the pictures'."

If parents can find a caregiver who does that, their children reap the benefits. "A warm, loving care provider can give children a broader social horizon and teach them how to get along with adults who have different temperaments, different strengths and weaknesses, different skills," says psychologist Alicia Lieberman of the University of California, San Francisco. Aimee, the Bond family's nanny, gets a little embarrassed by her employer's praise about how she has enriched the boys' days. "I try to teach them as much as I can and to make it fun, because they are just as important to me as I am to them," Aimee says. "I'm really just doing my job."

Grandparent Development and Influence

Robert Strom and
Shirley Strom

Robert Strom is Professor of Lifespan Developmental Psychology, Division of Psychology in Education, Arizona State University, Tempe, Arizona 85287-0611. Shirley Strom is Research Coordinator, Office of Parent Development International Division of Psychology in Education, Arizona State University, Tempe, Arizona 85287-0611.

ABSTRACT

The educational needs of grandparents have been overlooked. They deserve access to a curriculum that can help them adjust to their changing role and illustrates how to build satisfying family relationships. The nation's first educational program developed for grandparents is described in terms of underlying assumptions, measures to assess learning needs, elements of curriculum, and procedures for instruction. Fieldtest evidence regarding the effectiveness of this approach to strengthening families is presented along with implications for the future.

A strong family is one that includes mutually satisfying relationships and the capacity of members to meet each other's needs (Stinnett & DeFrain, 1985). Most efforts to strengthen families involve classes which help parents acquire effective methods of guidance and set reasonable expectations for children. A similar approach could provide greater success for 55 million grandparents in the United States. Observers agree that grandparents have the potential to make a more significant contribution to their families and society should do whatever is necessary to ensure this possibility (Bengston & Robertson, 1985; Elkind, 1990; Kornhaber, 1986). The status of grandparents can be enhanced by (1) better understanding of how family relationships are influenced by technological change, (2) widespread recognition of the need to establish educational expectations for

This paper was presented to the Japan Society for the Promotion of Science in Tokyo, Japan on July 1, 1991.

grandparents, and (3) the development of practical curriculum to help them adjust to their emerging role.

FAMILY RELATIONSHIPS AND TECHNOLOGICAL CHANGE

Learning in a past-oriented society. When the older people of today were children, the world was changing less rapidly. Because there was a slower rate of progress, the past dominated the present. Consequently, youngsters learned mostly from adults. In those days a father might reasonably say to his son: "Let me tell you about life and what to expect. I will give you the benefit of my experience. Now, when I was your age . . ." In this type of society the father's advice would be relevant since he had already confronted most of the situations his son would face. Given the slow pace of change, children could see their future as they observed the day-to-day activities of parents and grandparents.

There are still some past-oriented societies in the world today, places where adults remain the only important source of a child's education. On the island of Bali in Indonesia, parents can be observed passing on their woodcarving and painting skills to sons and daughters who expect to earn a living in much the same way. Similarly, aboriginal tribes in Australia are determined to perpetuate their traditional community. Amish people in the United States maintain a pattern of living that closely resembles the priorities and routine of their forefathers. For children growing up in each of these static environments, the future seems essentially a repetition of the past. When life is so free of uncertainty, so predictable, it appears justified to teach boys and girls that they should adopt the lifestyle of their elders. Therefore, in every slow-changing culture, grandparents are viewed as experts, as authorities, as models for all age groups. The role expected of children is to be listeners and observers, to be seen but not heard (Strom & Strom, 1987).

Learning in a present-oriented society. When technology is introduced and accelerated in a society, there is a corresponding increase in the pace of social change. Long-standing customs and traditions are permanently modified. Successive generations of grandparents, parents and children come to have less in common. Children today have many experiences that were not part of their parents' upbringing. This means there are some things adults are too old to know simply because we are not growing up at the present time. It is a reversal of the traditional comment to children that "You're too young to understand." Boys and girls now encounter certain conditions which are unique in history to their age group. Access to drugs, life in a single parent family, computer involvement and global awareness are common among children. They are exposed to day care, racially integrated schools, and the fear of life-threatening sexually-transmitted diseases. Adults cannot remember most of these situations because we never experienced them.

The memory of childhood as a basis for offering advice ("When I was your age . . .") becomes less credible as the pace of social change quickens. Because of the gap between experiences of adults and children, there is a tendency to seek advice mostly from peers. An increasing number of people feel that the only persons who can understand them are those at the same stage of life as themselves or who share similar challenges. Unfortunately, when people are limited to their peers for extended conversations, they are less inclined to develop the communication skills needed for successful interaction with other generations.

A peer orientation undermines cultural continuity as it divides the population into special interest groups. Because a rapidly changing society assigns greater importance to the present than the past, older people cease to be seen as models for everyone. Each generation chooses to identify with famous people of their own or next higher age group. Therefore, respect for the elderly declines. Older adults are no longer regarded as experts about much of anything except aging (Strom, Bernard & Strom, 1989).

Learning in a future-oriented society. The phase of civilization we are entering is referred to as the Information Age. Within this context schooling for children begins earlier, continues longer, and includes a vast amount of knowledge which was unavailable to previous generations of students. Given these conditions, children are bound to view the world from a different vantage and therefore should be seen by adults as an important source of learning. Certainly intergenerational dialogue is necessary to shape the future in a democratic society. Unless such contacts are sustained and mutually beneficial, the future could bring conflict as low birth rates provide fewer working age taxpayers to meet the needs of a growing elderly population. Some social scientists expect relationships between the young and older populations to replace the relationship between races as the dominant domestic conflict in the next half century (Toffler, 1990).

Intergenerational relationships are valuable because they offer a broader orientation than can be gained from any peer group. Until recently, it was supposed that aging is accompanied by a sense of perspective. This assumption still makes sense in slow-changing cultures. But, in technological societies the attainment of perspective requires something more than getting older. Becoming aware of how age groups other than our own see things and feel about the world is necessary for a broad perspective and responding to the needs of others. Unless the viewpoints of younger generations are taken into account, perspective tends to diminish rather than grow as people age (Strom & Strom, 1985, 1991).

ESTABLISHING EDUCATIONAL EXPECTATIONS FOR GRANDPARENTS

Our efforts to help grandparents began by offering a free course for them at senior citizen centers and churches in metropolitan Phoenix. The 400 people who enrolled in these classes were told they would learn something of what it is like for children to be growing up in the contemporary society and how parents view their task of raising children at the present time. In return, the participants agreed to share their experience as grandparents. This format was chosen because the literature on family relations revealed a patronizing attitude toward grandparents instead of educational programs to help them grow. Previous investigators had not made an effort to identify grandparent learning needs so there were no educational solutions. The following assumptions emerged from our preliminary research and guide the continuing project (Strom & Strom, 1989).

Grandparent responsibilities can be more clearly defined. Mothers and fathers have access to parenting courses that help them maintain competence in their changing role but similar opportunities are unavailable to grandparents. Instead, they are left alone to wonder: What are my rights and my responsibilities as a grandparent? How can I continue to be a favorable influence as my grandchild gets older? How well am I doing as a grandparent? These kinds of questions are likely to persist until there are commonly known guidelines for setting goals and self-evaluation. Many grandparents have difficulty defining their role and understanding how they could make a greater contribution. As a result the responsibility for raising youngsters has become disproportionate in many families with grandparents assuming less obligation than is in everyone's best interest.

Grandparents can learn to improve their influence. Mothers and fathers who can count on grandparents to share the load for caregiving and guidance less often seek support outside the family. The success of grandparents requires being aware of the parenting goals of sons and daughters and acting as a partner in reinforcing these goals. However, even though research indicates that people remain capable of adopting new attitudes and skills during middle and later life, grandparent development has not received priority in adult education. This missing element lessens the possibility of a meaningful life for many grandmothers and grandfathers.

The concept of life-long learning should include a concern for curriculum development. This means society has to reconsider its view that continuous learning is essential only for young people. The myth that aging is accompanied by wisdom has misled many older adults to underestimate their need for further education. When grandparents are mentally active, they remain a source of advice. Everyone at every age has a responsibility to keep growing in order to achieve their potential.

A practical grandparent program should be widely available. Older men and women have been led to believe that learning in later life should consist of whatever topics they find interesting without any societal expectations as there are for younger learners. But as people continue to age, they should also continue to grow—and not just in terms of acquiring leisure-oriented skills. Some of education in later life should emphasize obligations and roles, just as curriculum does for younger age groups. Senior citizens are the only population without any defined educational needs or cooperatively planned curricula. Since the size of this group is expected to grow faster than any other age segment, it seems reasonable to provide them educational opportunities which can help strengthen their families.

Society should set higher expectations for grandparents. By themselves grandparents may be unable to generate the motivation necessary to stimulate educational commitment within their peer group. This is a difficult task because so many people think of retirement as a time when they can withdraw from active community responsibility. Peers reinforce the perception that being carefree and without obligation is an acceptable goal in later life. The problem is compounded by age segregation. When older adults are limited to one another for most of their interaction, they establish standards which may not be in accord with what the society as a whole believes is best.

In order to favorably revise existing norms for older adults in terms of greater learning and more significant contributions to the family, younger age groups must raise their expectations and make these known. The talent and potential contribution of seniors could enrich the lives of everyone. Accordingly, we should expect them to demonstrate a commitment to personal growth, concern themselves about others through volunteering, and support the schools to ensure a better future for children. If educational expectations are not established for older adults, they will experience less influence and lower self-esteem.

The benefits of grandparent education can be assessed. Popular support can be expected for programs that help grandparents enlarge the scope of their influence, improve their ability to communicate with loved ones, become more self confident, and experience greater respect in the family. These benefits would be even more credible if the sources confirming them included other persons than just the participating grandparents. By comparing the results from three generational versions of the authors' Grandparent Strengths and Needs Inventory, the merits of various educational approaches to family development can be determined. This inventory also enables educators to adapt curriculum in a way that honors group and individual differences (Strom & Strom, 1990; Strom, Strom, & Collinsworth, 1991).

GOALS FOR GRANDPARENT DEVELOPMENT

There are six fundamental aspects of the grandparent experience that we try to influence in our program. Each of them have implications for child and adult development. The goals we pursue are to:

Increase the satisfaction of being a grandparent. It would seem that the longer lifespan today gives grandparents more years to influence their grandchildren. But the actual consequence depends on whether or not a relationship is mutually satisfying. When family members avoid sharing their feelings, or they experience insufficient satisfaction with one another, the relationship is in jeopardy. Grandmothers and grandfathers who enjoy their role are more able to cope with difficulties.

Improve how well grandparents perform their role. The efforts of grandparents to guide grandchildren depend on how self-confident they feel in their family role. Those who seek to support the parenting goals of their sons and daughters will continue to teach grandchildren. These persons realize that it is unreasonable to expect parents to be exclusively responsible for the care and guidance of grandchildren. By being active contributors in the family, they are seen as a valuable and long-term source of influence.

Enlarge the scope of guidance expected of grandparents. There is abundant evidence that, by itself, academic learning is an insufficient preparation for success in life. It follows that grandparents should help grandchildren acquire some of the out of school lessons they need. By defining the aspects of growth that should be obtained at home, it is possible to improve a child's total education and establish a helpful role for grandparents.

Decrease the difficulties of being a grandparent. Grandparents encounter some difficulty in getting along with sons, daughters, in-laws, and grandchildren. The manner in which these problems are handled is a sign of personal effectiveness. Every grandmother and grandfather should have access to education which focuses on their changing role. When grandparents are aware of the childrearing strategies of their sons and daughters and they know the predictable difficulties to expect as grandchildren get older, they can prepare themselves by obtaining the skills necessary for continued success.

Reduce the frustrations experienced by grandparents. Some frustration is to be expected. But grandparents vary in the frequency with which they sense frustration. One way to reduce their discontent is by understanding why certain child behaviors occur and why some of them should be allowed to continue. When the expectations of grandparents are consistent with a child's developmental needs, the tendency is to encourage normative behavior and offer support for a favorable self concept.

Reduce the family information needs of grandparents. Grandparents need accurate perceptions about their grandchild's abilities and their social relationships. Besides the information which teachers and parents provide for them, grandparents should listen to grandchildren themselves to learn about their hopes, fears, goals and concerns. If educational programs for grandparents can regularly include access to the views of people who are the same age as grandchildren, it is easier to understand how family members resemble and differ from their peers.

ELEMENTS OF CURRICULUM AND INSTRUCTION

The learning activities that grandparents consider appealing deserve priority in planning educational programs for them. Just as young students need a variety of teaching methods, older men and women can also benefit from a wide range of instructional techniques. The two courses we have developed on "Becoming A Better Grandparent" and "Achieving Grandparent Potential" follow the same format of focusing on all three generations. Some of the lessons concerning grandparents involve keeping up with the times, giving and seeking advice, communicating from a distance, growing as a couple, and learning in later life. Lessons about the middle generation call for recognizing indicators of parental success, helping single and blended families, developing values and morals, building child self-esteem, and watching television together. The lessons on grandchildren emphasize getting along with others, sharing fears and worries, understanding children's thinking, deciding about sex and drugs, and encouraging the college student. All twenty-four lessons consist of the same instructional elements. In turn, each of these elements deserve a brief explanation.

Discussion and brainstorming. Grandparents meet in small groups to consider agenda from their guidebook that encourages their expression of ideas, concerns, mistakes, goals and solutions (Strom & Strom, 1991a, 1991c). During these discussions the participants inform, challenge, and reassure each other. They quickly discover there is much to gain from sharing feelings and thoughts. Conversations with emotionally supportive peers cause men and women to feel less alone, help them organize their thinking, and increase awareness of the possibilities for becoming a better grandparent. Creative thinking is practiced during each discussion when the group shifts to consideration of a brainstorming task.

Problem solving. The next activity invites grandparents to consider how they might handle a particular problem if they had to cope with it. A family incident is described which offers everyone the same information including several possible solutions. Grandparents like to reflect and then discuss pros and cons they see for each of the given choices. It is stimulating to think of additional options and to identify relevant information that may be missing. Everyone has an opportunity to share their reasoning about the advice they consider to be best. This scenario approach broadens the range of solutions individuals see and discourages premature judgment. Later, in their home, grandparents present the scenarios to relatives and find out their viewpoint.

Grandparent principles. Several written principles accompany each unit. Grandparents rely on these practical guidelines for review, reflection, and personal application. Participants benefit from reading the companion volume of viewpoints which match each lesson in the guidebook (Strom & Strom, 1991b, 1991d). These essays, from which the principles are drawn, offer insights, observations and suggestions for making the grandparent experience more satisfying. In addition, local resource persons can enrich the learning by acquainting grandparents with the way problems are handled in their own community. Because each individual represents a unique family, grandparents must decide for themselves which principles are most appropriate in their present situation, the ones to apply immediately, and those that can be deferred until a later time.

Self-evaluation and observation. Personal growth requires self-examination. Grandparents are encouraged to practice this important skill as part of their homework. Each homework assignment consists of several multiple-choice questions that give participants a chance to state their feelings about issues such as family relationships, communication problems, and expectations of children. The anonymous homework is submitted at the beginning of each class. After responses are tallied for each item, the previously unknown norms of perception and behavior are announced to the class. This helps individuals know how their experience as grandparents resemble and differ from peers.

Intergenerational conversations. Grandparents should strive to know each grandchild as an individual. The way to achieve this goal is through interaction with the particular grandchild. However, most grandmothers and grandfathers admit that they sometimes have difficulty keeping a conversation going with youngsters. This is why they appreciate questions focusing on realms of experience that the generations commonly encounter, topics that transcend age. Every lesson includes a set of questions dealing with topics of mutual concern such as music, health, school, money, fears, friends, and careers. These questions facilitate the dialogue that we expect grandparents to initiate face to face or by phone. Most of the inquiries fit all grandchildren while some are more appropriate for teenagers. A portion of each class session is devoted to hearing grandparents comment about the insights they have acquired through intergenerational interviews.

Grandparents also need to know something about the norms of their grandchild's age group. It is unreasonable to suppose that all the information we need about the orientation of relatives will be provided by them alone. In a society where peers have considerable influence it is wise to find out how people in a grandchild's age group think and feel. This improves our understanding of how loved ones resemble and differ from their peers. One approach we use is to videotape interviews with children and parents who express their views on topics like peer pressure, school stress, and family conflict. This method reflects our belief that the broad perspective of life each of us ought to acquire emerges only when the thoughts and feelings of other age groups are taken into account.

EVALUATING GRANDPARENT SUCCESS

The effectiveness of grandparent education has been confirmed by research. In one study 800 people representing three generations evaluated the attitudes and behavior of grandparents before and after their participation in the "Becoming A Better Grandparent" course. At the end of the program grandparents reported that they had made significant improvements. This progress was corroborated by inventory scores of the parents and grandchildren (Strom & Strom, 1990). Specifically, grandparents benefit from the mentally stimulating experience by understanding how their role is changing, acquiring a broader perspective, learning new attitudes, gaining greater confidence and self-esteem, improving communication skills, and strengthening family relationships (Strom & Strom, 1985, 1989; Strom, Strom & Collinsworth, 1990).

These feelings expressed by the grandparents show the importance of the program for them: "I realized that I must keep on growing in order to understand other family members and be seen by them as a positive influence." "Now I understand my privileges as a grandparent as well as the duties I owe my grandchildren." "I found that helping my son and daughter achieve their parenting goals has upgraded my status to that of a valued partner." "I feel so much better about myself as a grandmother and more optimistic about my grandchildren."

Sons and daughters also identified some important benefits of grandparent education: "My parents seem more willing to share their feelings with us and they are more supportive of the way we are bringing up our children." "Taking this class has really helped my mom think about her role in my child's life. She is working hard to get to know my children as individuals." "My Dad has realized that listening and learning from his grandchildren is the key to being respected by them." "My mother has always been kind and loving to all of us but now she is more interesting to be around. It's fun to hear what she is learning."

It would be pleasing to report a balance in the proportion of men and women who seek to improve themselves through grandparent education. However, just as mothers significantly outnumber fathers in parenting classes, grandmothers are over represented in classes for grandparent development. Usually three out of four students in our courses are grandmothers. Does this ratio indicate that grandmothers need more guidance than grandfathers? On the contrary, it suggests grandmothers are more motivated to keep growing in this aspect of life. This conclusion was reached after comparing the influence of 155 grandmothers and 55 grandfathers who had just completed the program. Assessments were made to determine how each gender was perceived by themselves, their sons, daughters and grandchildren. Although the grandmothers reported having less formal education than grandfathers, they were seen as more successful grandparents in the estimate of all three generations (Strom & Strom, 1989).

In this study grandparents, parents and grandchildren portrayed grandmothers as emotionally closer to grandchildren, better informed about family affairs, and more willing to commit themselves to helping others. They were better at seeing the positive side of situations, learning from other family members, and making their feelings known. Grandmothers were credited with knowing more than grandfathers about the fears and concerns of grandchildren and spending more time with them. They were regarded as more effective in teaching grandchildren how to show trust, get along with others, and handle arguments. Grandmothers were viewed as better at passing on family history and cultural traditions, and more willing to accept help from grandchildren.

Strengths of grandfathers were recognized too. They saw themselves as having less difficulty than grandmothers in giving advice to sons and daughters, and were less frustrated by televiewing and listening habits of grandchildren. Parents observed grandfathers as being more satisfied than grandmothers when grandchildren asked for advice. Grandchildren felt their outlook on life was appreciated more by grandfathers.

Perhaps it is unfair to compare grandfathers with grandmothers. Consider the more positive results that emerge when the emphasis is on identifying change in grandfather attitudes and behaviors after instruction. The grandfathers in this study felt they made improvement in terms of satisfaction with their role, success in carrying out their obligations, effectiveness in teaching, overcoming difficulties, coping with frustrations, and

becoming more informed. Parents and grandchildren confirmed these gains had occurred. By joining grandmothers as participants in family-oriented education, grandfathers have proven they can learn to build more successful relationships with their spouse, children and grandchildren. Toward this goal grandfathers are urged to grow along with their partner and be actively involved in strengthening the family (Strom & Strom, 1989).

CONCLUSION

As we contemplate the future it is important to bear in mind that the baby-boomers, those persons born between 1946–1964, will become the largest group of older adults in history. This population of 77 million people is going to be better educated, healthier, and live longer than preceding generations. If the preparation they receive for retirement focuses only on financial and leisure readiness, a lifestyle of strictly recreation could become the norm. On the other hand, if getting ready for leisure activities is joined by an emphasis on continued responsibility as family members, then baby-boomers can make an enormous contribution to society. This possibility is supported by the emerging concept of grandparent education (Strom & Strom, 1991e).

REFERENCES

Bengston, V., & Robertson, J. (1985). *Grandparenthood.* Beverly Hills, CA: Sage Publications.

Elkind, D. (1990). *Grandparenting.* Glenview, IL: Scott, Foresman.

Kornhaber, A. (1986). *Between parents and grandparents.* New York: St. Martin's Press.

Stinnet, N., & DeFrain, J. (1985). *Secrets of strong families.* Boston: Little, Brown.

Strom, R., Bernard, H., & Strom, S. (1989). *Human development and learning.* New York: Human Sciences Press.

Strom, R., & Strom, S. (1985). Becoming a better grandparent. In *Growing together: An intergenerational sourcebook,* K. Struntz & S. Reville (eds.). Washington, DC: American Association of Retired Persons and Elvirita Lewis Foundation, pp. 57–60.

Strom, R., & Strom, S. (1987). Preparing grandparents for a new role. *The Journal of Applied Gerontology,* 6(4), 476–486.

Strom, R., & Strom, S. (1989). *Grandparent development.* Washington, DC: American Association of Retired Persons Andrus Foundation.

Strom, R., & Strom, S. (1990). Raising expectations for grandparents: A three-generational study. *International Journal of Aging and Human Development,* 31(3), 161–167.

Strom, R., & Strom, S. (1991a). *Achieving grandparent potential: A guidebook for building intergenerational relationships.* Newbury Park, CA: Sage Publications.

Strom, R., & Strom, S. (1991b). *Achieving grandparent potential: Viewpoints on building intergenerational relationships.* Newbury Park, CA: Sage Publications.

Strom, R., & Strom, S. (1991c). *Becoming a better grandparent: A guidebook for strengthening the family.* Newbury Park, CA: Sage Publications.

Strom, R., & Strom, S. (1991d). *Becoming a better grandparent: Viewpoints on strengthening the family.* Newbury Park, CA: Sage Publications.

Strom, R., & Strom, S. (1991e). *Grandparent education: A guide for leaders.* Newbury Park, CA: Sage Publications.

Strom, R., Strom, S., & Collinsworth, P. (1990). Improving grandparent success. *The Journal of Applied Gerontology,* 9(4), 480–492.

Strom, R., Strom, S., & Collinsworth, P. (1991). The Grandparent Strengths and Needs Inventory: Development and factorial validation. *Educational and Psychological Measurement,* 51(4).

Toffler, A. (1990). *Powershift.* New York: Bantam Books.

Sibling connections

That most vital but overlooked of relationships

Laura M. Markowitz

The Family Therapy Networker

We agonize over ups and downs with our parents, spouses, and children, but mostly ignore one of our first and most primal bonds—our relationships with our brothers and sisters.

Whether as adults we find those relationships harmonious, acrimonious, or somewhere in between, we discount them at our peril. For the sibling bond is powerful, providing us with connection, validation, and belonging like no other.

Brothers and sisters push buttons you'd forgotten you had, never forget old humiliations and painful nicknames, never let you grow up. They share your obscure, ancient memories of car trips and long-dead pets, know just what you mean about Mom and Dad, and can make you laugh so hard you cry.

To understand the potent cocktail of anger, love, competitiveness, and protectiveness that is the sibling bond is ultimately to come closer to understanding ourselves. Not that understanding always leads to trouble-free friendship. Indeed, achieving tension-free kinship with a sibling is probably impossible, since ambivalence seems to be the most natural state of the relationship. But coming to know why no one else can make you feel more empathy, anger, or delight than those earliest companions provides a useful insight. May it also lead to a closer bond.

At first, the case appeared to have nothing at all to do with siblings. Alice, a 40-year-old journalist and single mother, came in with her only child, 18-year-old Becky, who had threatened to run away form home because "my mom is like a prison warden." Becky told the therapist, Syracuse University doctoral student Tracy Laszloffy, that she would go live with her Aunt Tess, who had told her she was always welcome. This was her trump card, and it had the desired effect: Her mother's eyes narrowed in anger. "I always knew she'd do something like this to get even with me," said Alice.

"Why do you think Becky wants to get even with you?" the therapist asked.

"Not Becky," explained Alice. "Tess! My older sister always hated me and has never let me forget that when I was born, she had to take care of me.

For there is
no friend like a
sister
In calm or
stormy weather;
To cheer one on
the tedious way,
To fetch one if
one goes astray,
To lift one if one
totters down,
To strengthen
whilst one
stands.
—Christina
Rossetti

She's always making me pay for that. Now she wants to steal my daughter away!"

Laszloffy helped Alice and Becky find a compromise for their most pressing problems—Becky's demand to be allowed to go to unsupervised parties and Alice's insistence that Becky get better grades. Despite Becky's description of her mother as harsh, it became evident that Alice vacillated between the conflicting roles of parent and peer. Laszloffy felt that the real work for this family needed to happen elsewhere. She decided that including Tess in a session might be the key, and her hunch was confirmed when Alice flinched at the suggestion. "Why her? She already knows I'm a screwup." She agreed, however, for Becky's sake.

From the first moment the sisters walked in—Tess a matronly 50-year-old woman in sensible shoes, and Alice looking fashionable in a mini-skirt—it was clear their relationship organized the way they thought about themselves. The sisters immediately began to compare themselves to each other: "She was always the creative one," said Tess. "I never had any real talent, except for making pot roast."

"Yeah, but you were also the good daughter, the one everyone approved of," countered Alice. Tess bristled. Was Alice mocking her for being a stay-at-home mom and housewife?

"I feel judged by Alice constantly," Tess said. "I have arguments with her in my head while I'm vacuuming about who has it better, me or her." She admitted that she did sometimes have regrets about her life, but said she never felt comfortable letting down her guard with her sister.

"I guess I feel threatened when Tess isn't her usual confident and bossy self," Alice said. "It's like a balance we have. One of us is the caretaker, one of us is the. . . . Well, I'm used to being the one who needs taking care of. I'm not sure I'd know what to do if she needed my advice, or help."

The next session began with the sisters reporting on a lunch that week that had ended with a big fight over their memories of their mother. Tess had recalled her as a cold, disengaged woman wrapped up in her own problems; Alice remembered her as being affectionate to the point of being stifling. Laszloffy

Only children

Is it really so bad to grow up without sibs?

AT 14 I LEARNED A LESSON THAT MOST KIDS master well before their age hits double digits. When a boy who'd taunted me all through junior high asked me to sign his yearbook, I thought it was a trick—I knew he hated me; he'd been my tormentor for years. So of course I refused. To my surprise, his genuinely quizzical look told me that the request had been sincere.

It was an understandable mistake on my part, though. Most of the kids I knew had learned how to tease and be teased much earlier in life than I finally did. That's because they all had something I lacked: siblings.

As the only child in my family, I grew up with no one to make faces at me, slam me against the wall, steal my hair ribbon, or frighten me with rubber bugs. My parents may have had a bad day now and then, but hey, they never hid

my math book or called me "bunnyface." How was I to know that most kids deal with such treatment every day of their lives?

This lack of sibling savvy made me more sensitive than most of my peers, and maybe I didn't roll with the punches as easily as they did. But those appear to be about the worst effects the absence of brothers and sisters had on me. Otherwise, I grew up happy, made friends, did well in college, and married a great guy (who also happens to be an only child).

So what about the pervasive idea that all children without siblings are selfish, lonely, and spoiled? Well, according to nearly everyone who studies these things, the stereotypical attention-grabbing, foot-stamping, tantrum-throwing only child resides mainly in our collective imagination.

"Being an only child accounts

for no more than about 2 percent of the variants affecting personality and behavior," says Toni Falbo, a professor of sociology and educational psychology at the University of Texas at Austin. "The other 98 percent are determined by a host of more important factors: social class, gender, education, quality of parenting, and family members' physical and psychological health."

After reviewing almost 150 published studies and conducting her own research on the subject, Falbo—who's the country's leading authority on only children—has concluded that onlies are generally just as happy and well-adjusted as kids with siblings. What's more, the differences that do exist are frequently to the onlies' advantage. Only children tend to get slightly better grades, be more ambitious, earn more advanced ac-

explained that no siblings grow up in the same family—the emotional, economic, and even physical circumstances of the family are distinct for each child, and the parents often respond differently to each. Tess looked irritated, unused to relinquishing her right, as eldest, to define the way things were. Alice said she felt guilty that she had gotten the "nice" mother while Tess had gotten the "mean" one.

"So why did you run away from home, if Mom was so loving and caring?" Tess asked her sister, referring to the year when 18-year-old Alice dropped out of high school three weeks before graduation and moved to California.

"To get away from her! She was *too* loving; it was suffocating me!" Alice said, frustrated that her sister needed to be told the obvious.

Tess's mouth dropped open. "I thought you ran away because you were mad at me for leaving you at home with Mom when I got married and had kids of my own."

"No! In fact, I was trying to get out of your hair so you wouldn't have to keep taking care of me, because I knew you hated that—and hated me because of it," Alice choked on the last words, tears welling up.

"I never hated you," Tess said softly. "What ever gave you that idea?"

Alice blew her nose. "I'll never forget the time when I was 5, you were 15, and you were supposed to take me to the playground. You yelled at Mom that you hated me and wanted to go out with your friends. Then you left." Alice, with her tear-streaked face and forlorn expression, looked like the abandoned little girl she was describing.

Tess had no memory of the incident Alice was talking about. Of course there had been moments she resented having to take care of her baby sister, but most of the time she loved and cherished Alice. "Why do you think I rushed ahead to have babies of my own?" Tess asked her. "Because you had been the best thing in my life, and I wanted to have kids just like you." For the first time in 35 years, Alice could hear the love in her sister's voice.

"I've wanted to be close to you for a long time, but you kept pushing me away," said Tess. "I could never figure out what I had done to make you hate me—hate me so much that you don't even want Becky to visit me." Now Tess was crying too.

> Big sisters are the crab grass in the lawn of life.
> —Charles Schulz

> We are family—I got all my sisters with me.
> —Sister Sledge

---

ademic degrees, and display greater self-esteem.

Then why the negative stereotype? Perhaps it's because most people don't have much firsthand experience with only children, who have traditionally been in short supply. A decade ago, just 10 percent of American women had had a single child by the end of their childbearing years. These days, however, that number has jumped to an all-time high of 17 percent—which means that one in six women will be the mother of an only child.

Despite their increasing numbers, Falbo notes that typecasting of only children persists. "The truth," she says, laughing, "is that last-born kids often act more spoiled than onlies do."

Perhaps the sharpest concern many one-child parents feel is that their kids will be lonely. "I did worry at first," admits Anita Daucunas of Boulder, Colorado, who has a 5-year-old daugher. "But Jennifer is in school all day with other kids, and when she gets home she goes right out to play with the neighborhood children."

At the same time, onlies are often more comfortable playing by themselves. Sandra Lee Steadham of Dallas says that her daughter, 9-year-old Zoe, is outgoing but also enjoys spending time on her own. "For Zoe," she explains, "being alone isn't the same as being lonely."

Like any other type of family, single-child households do have trouble spots. For one thing, the parents of an only child have a tendency to be overly attentive, says Murray Kappelman, a professor of pediatrics and psychiatry at the University of Maryland. Too much concern about the child's health, for example, can encourage hypochondria. Performance expectations that are too rigorous can create a heightened need for approval, and an overabundance of material rewards can give the child a bad case of the I wants.

"But those tendencies exist with most firstborns," Kappelman emphasizes, "not just with onlies." The fact is that *any* family size creates its own set of problems. There is no perfect number of children.

—*Katy Koontz*
Special Report

Excerpted with permission from Special Report *(March/April 1993). Subscriptions: $15/yr. (6 issues) from Special Report, Box 2191, Knoxville, TN 37901.*

"Why didn't we ever talk about this stuff before?" Alice wondered. "We've wasted so much time being mad at things that never really happened the way we thought they did."

They also had spent a lot of time frozen in roles that no longer fit them as adults. In therapy, Alice learned that she could be more of an adult with and parent to Becky without turning into her sister. Tess began to accept that she wasn't as stuck in her life as she imagined. As if they were unfolding a map and seeing a multitude of possible roads to take, each of the sisters could now see herself as more than simply the other's road not taken.

Clearly, the sibling relationship was the pivotal factor in this case, yet there was little in her training to lead Laszloffy—or most family therapists—to consider siblings as a point of leverage. Mental health practitioners have spent a century putting the parent-child bond and marital relationship under the microscope, yet sibling connections have been largely ignored. "My pet peeve with the field is that when we say 'family of origin,' most of us really mean parent-child relationships, which is a very limited and linear view of family that derives from our rigidly hierarchical way of seeing the world," says Ken Hardy, professor of family therapy at Syracuse University.

Laszloffy's case is striking because the intensity between the siblings lay close to the surface. Most of us respond to our brothers and sisters with subtler rumblings, having long ago learned to bury powerful emotions in order to survive years of living with them—resentment at having been an easy target of a sibling's anger; longing for closeness masked by habitual guardedness; hidden desires for attention, approval, vindication. As adults, we still may wish our siblings would apologize for past hurts, abandonments, humiliations; we still may feel responsible for them, afraid for them, stuck with them.

Normally articulate and insightful people grow tongue-tied when it comes to describing their relationships with their siblings. Writers of books about siblings struggle to manufacture encompassing theories about our connection to these people after we no longer have to wear their hand-me-downs, share a bedroom, or put up with their teasing. But there are no givens for what kind of relationships emerge between adult siblings. Some grow up to be one another's closest friends; others become like distant acquaintances, sharing nothing of their adult lives. Some continue to use their siblings as a compass point for measuring who they have become. Some consider each other ancient enemies to avoid, while others casually drift apart without concern. For every "truth" about siblings, the exact opposite also may be correct. Most of us are still trying to figure out who these familiar strangers are to us.

In the beginning we orbit our parents like planets vying for the position closest to the sun. They are the primary source of light, warmth, and love, but we have to compete with omnipresent siblings who at times eclipse us, collide with us, and even, at odd moments, awkwardly love us. In myth and literature, the bond between siblings is portrayed as far more ambivalent than the attachment between parents and children, dramatized in extremes of enmity and loyalty. In the Bible, the relationship between the first brothers, Cain and Abel, ended in fratricide. Joseph's brothers sold him into slavery in Egypt. In *King Lear,* Cordelia's older sisters outmaneuvered her to get their father's kingdom and delighted in her banishment. Still, Hansel took hold of Gretel's hand in the forest and promised to protect her; Joseph forgave his brothers and saved them during a deadly famine.

The seeds of enmity between siblings may be planted early: The introduction of a new child into the family is often experienced as an irretrievable loss by the older child. The trauma of being displaced by a younger sibling can turn into rage, envy, even hatred of the usurper. The earliest impulses to commit murder are felt in the young child who has been dethroned as centerpiece of the family. Therapists report cases in which older siblings tried to drown their younger brothers and sisters, or "helped" them have accidents near sharp objects or open windows.

Freud codified the notion of sibling rivalry, which was already widely accepted, saying it was natural that the introduction of a new sibling into a family would stir up envy, aggression, and competitiveness in the other siblings. But normalizing sibling rivalry created an expectation that brothers and sisters were destined to feel lifelong antagonism, resent one another's accomplishments, and envy one another's talents and privileges. Until recently, the phenomenon was believed to be so self-evident that no one bothered to challenge it. But are aggression and envy really the overarching emotions siblings have for one another? Recent feminist theorists suggest that Freud's theory was tainted by male bias. Siblings may not always be locked in mortal combat; interdependence and companionship are as much a part of siblinghood as competition and antagonism, says Laura Roberto, family therapy professor at Eastern Virginia Medical School. "Until we began to see how female development is also forged in affiliation and relationship, we tended to ignore these facets of the sibling bond." Feminists point to the lifelong friendship between many sisters who, increasingly outliving their male relations, may spend the last years of their lives together. This feminist challenge has given us a new lens for regarding both female and male sibling relationships, suggests family therapist Michael Kahn,

Lord, confound this surly sister, Blight her brow with blotch and blister, Cramp her larynx, lung and liver, In her guts a galling give her.
—John Millington Synge

I was the older brother. And when I was growing up I didn't like all those brothers and sisters. No kid likes to be the oldest.... But when they turn to you for help—what can you do? They kept me so busy caring for them that I had no time to become a junkie or an alcoholic.
—James Baldwin

co-author of *The Sibling Bond.* "Women are more interested in horizontal ties," says Kahn, "and are asking new kinds of questions like, 'What is lost when one sibling wins at another's expense?'"

Other critics point out that sibling rivalry isn't a primary force among siblings in other cultures; in some African societies, for example, one's greatest support, both material and emotional, comes not from one's parents but from one's siblings. Not all families in our society operate exclusively from Eurocentric values of individualism, points out Ken Hardy. For example, as a response to racism, African-American parents, brothers, and sisters often pour all their resources and energy into one child, who carries the family torch like a bright beacon into the institutions of mainstream success. "It is not uncommon to see an African-American family in which one brother is a surgeon or lawyer while the other siblings are locked into menial jobs or struggling with unemployment," he says. "The one who made it sends back money and helps the others, repays the debt."

To look only at the negative feelings of siblinghood is to forget how important we are to one another, how in a sense our siblings are as responsible for creating us as our parents are. All planets, though drawn to the sun, exert a pull on one another, shaping one another's course. "I was the coddled one; he the witness of coddling," wrote novelist Vladimir Nabokov about his older brother, describing the natural complementarity that exists among siblings.

Our siblings are peers who share not only the same family, but also the same history and culture, not to mention a sizable chunk of our genetic material. Even among those with a significant age difference, siblings' personal histories intertwine so that there is no escaping a mutual influence. During a family therapy session, two adult sisters and their brother talk about how they were influenced by one another. "I learned to be the family entertainer because you and Mom were always fighting," says the brother to his older sister. "I hated the yelling, so I would try to make you both laugh. I still do that whenever I'm around conflict—try to defuse it."

"I think I wouldn't have been such a rebel if you two hadn't been such goody-goodies," says the younger sister. "You still compete with each other, like who's more successful or whose kids are the smartest. Since I was never in the running, I tried to do things neither of you did. Using a lot of drugs was a way to feel like I had something over both of you, like I was more mature or cool."

"I always felt so responsible for you two," says the older sister. "Mom would yell at me if you guys made a mess or got in a fight. I grew up believing that everyone else's problems come first, because other people are younger, smaller, more needy, or whatever. In my marriage, I kept

on doing the same thing, putting his needs first because it was what I knew. And having kids just replicated what it was like to be the oldest sister. Since the divorce, I've been trying to figure out who takes care of me."

What exactly does it mean to be the product not only of one's parents, but also of one's siblings? How does it happen? The most elaborate theory of siblinghood concerns birth order. Although Freud said that "a child's position in the sequence of brothers and sisters is of very great significance for the course of his later life," the main work in the area of birth order has been done by Austrian-born family therapist Walter Toman, author of *Family Constellation: Its Effects on Personality and Social Behaviour.* Toman's basic assertion is that the order of one's birth determines certain personality characteristics that shape the choices we make and the likelihood of our success and even how we think about ourselves. Toman developed profiles of sibling positions, including only children, saying, for example, that older siblings tend to take on more responsibility and to be somewhat overcontrolling while only children are inclined to be loners, and women who are not fond of children tend to be youngest siblings.

But even without a highly schematized birth order theory about siblings, practitioners have described siblinghood as the first social laboratory, where we learn how to be a peer. Even when the fights make us cry, we are growing a thicker skin, which we need later on as adults; we learn that life doesn't always seem fair; we learn how to forgive. "After listening to my brother and sister hurl insults at each other one day, I was surprised to see them playing together the next morning as if nothing had happened," says a 40-year-old man. "It was a revelation to me that you could hate someone one day and forget about it the next."

It is possible that in siblinghood we experience more intensity of emotion than in any other relationship that follows. Our worlds are shoulder to shoulder, and our vulnerabilities are laid bare. "I've never loved or hated as intensely as I love and hate my brothers," says a 36-year-old youngest brother of six boys. With our siblings, we test the limits of tolerance and forgiveness more than we do in any other relationship. As long as the family provides an appropriate container for the intensity, siblings can benefit from the lessons.

Unless something goes dramatically wrong, as in sibling incest or sibling illness or death, our relationships with our brothers and sisters rarely take center stage in the therapy room. But increasingly, family therapists are discovering what a gold mine of information and support siblings can be. As inheritors of the same multigenerational legacy,

The younger brother hath the more wit.
—English proverb

All happy families resemble one another, but each unhappy family is unhappy in its own way.
—Leo Tolstoy

albeit with different views of the family stories, they can often make a unique contribution to therapy. One family therapist was having a hard time with an 8-year-old boy who had set himself on fire twice because he believed his father hated him. The father was a large, impassive man who never looked at his son and spoke to him only when he had to. Hoping for some clue about why the father was so inaccessible, the therapist invited the father's younger brother to a session.

After the therapist outlined the situation, the younger brother turned to his nephew and asked him to wait in the next room. Then he said to his brother, the boy's father, "I remember right before Mom left him, Dad used to tell everyone you were someone else's bastard." The older brother looked numb, but the therapist sighed with relief. He finally understood what was going on under the surface of this family. His own father's rejection of him had left this father feeling confused about what fathers were supposed to say to sons. "He loved his child, but regarded his own silence as a way of protecting his son from the possibly abusive things that might come out of his mouth in anger," says the therapist. What the man was only dimly aware of himself, his brother had been able to put his finger on immediately.

Family therapy also can help people get out of constraining roles with their siblings. Family-of-origin specialist Murray Bowen years ago described how he dramatically disentangled himself from a lifetime of emotional triangles with his siblings. He believed the family's ongoing emotional process was responsible for the legacy that Walter Toman attributed to birth order. Accordingly, Bowen reasoned that one ought to be able to go back and change the family's emotional process, which created and sustained sibling roles.

One Bowen-trained therapist treated a couple who were fighting about the husband's intrusive family. Lisa was fed up with hearing about her in-laws' problems and wanted Henry to separate himself from their incessant dramas. She was upset that he had loaned his irresponsible younger sister money and had become caught up in the ongoing fight between his older brother and their father. The constant phone calls from Henry's family were driving her crazy. When she drew their family diagram, the therapist says, "a million things seemed to jump out at me," particularly the multigenerational patterns of enmeshment in Henry's family and cutoffs in Lisa's, but the overwhelming fact was the contrast in the couple's birth positions: Henry was a middle child, Lisa an only child.

As an only child, Lisa was used to being the center of attention and didn't like competing with her brother- and sister-in-law. As a middle child, Henry was the family caretaker and peace-

keeper, but he wasn't sure he wanted to keep the role. "If I wasn't in the middle of their lives, maybe I'd have more of a life of my own," he said.

The therapist coached Henry on how to develop more independence from his family. "The next time my brother called to complain about Dad, I told him I was sure he could work it out and changed the subject to football," says Henry. His sister called to cry over her latest investment flop, hinting that she needed another loan. "I told her she had a lot of experience pulling herself out of holes, and I was sure she would find a way to do it again," Henry recalls.

The therapist suggested that Lisa could help Henry remember that he was entitled to be the center of attention sometimes, too. During the next family gathering, Henry and Lisa both deliberately steered the conversation to Henry's latest project at work. "It was a surprise to realize that no one in my family knew much about me," says Henry. Changing his behavior shifted his relationship with his siblings, who became "much more respectful of my boundaries," almost timidly asking if it was all right to call, spending more time listening to Henry instead of talking at him.

One of the most wrenching issues that brings siblings to family therapy occurs at midlife, when they face the failing health of parents and need to make long-term decisions about their care. It's extremely difficult for a family to have to acknowledge the demise of its elders, evoking buried fears of death and abandonment. Often, the grown children don't feel ready for the changing of the guard. "I look in the mirror and see an older, white-haired man, but inside I still feel 25 and way too young to become the older generation," says one therapist, whose elderly father recently came to live with him. "I look at his shrunken body and I can't help feeling repulsed. He used to be a strapping, handsome guy. Now the chronic pain from arthritis doesn't let him sleep. I have to feed him by hand as if he were a baby. It's very sad, and very surreal." Is this what will happen to us, siblings wonder?

Not only does the individual's relationship with the parent change dramatically as the older generation loses its authority, but the need to collaborate closely with a sibling, sometimes after 40 years of mutual alienation, can revive feelings of insecurity, competitiveness, and resentment. In the face of huge existential issues like death, some adult siblings find it is easier to fall back on picking on one another, feeding the illusion that they will be children forever instead of accepting terminal adulthood.

Boston family therapist David Treadway worked with three siblings in their 60s—an eminent jurist, a history professor, and a successful businesswoman. They were not interested in talking about the past, but needed a facilitator

Our word *cad* originally meant a younger brother.
—Bergen Evans

A brother is born for adversity.
—Proverbs 17:17

Some uninformed newspapers printed: "Mrs. C.L. Lane, Sister of the Famous Comedian Will Rogers." They were greatly misinformed. It's the other way around. I am the brother of Mrs. C.L. Lane, the friend of humanity. . . . It was the proudest moment of my life that I was her brother.
—Will Rogers, after the funeral of his sister Maud

In siblinghood we may experience more intense emotions than in any other relationship that follows.

to help them come to an agreement about their aging mother.

"They didn't acknowledge that their struggle had anything to do with their childhood roles, but the roots of the conflict surfaced within the first 10 minutes," says Treadway. They found that they could not come to any agreement without first understanding the curse of each one's sibling position. After this exercise, they could begin the hard work of real negotiation and compromise.

In some families, a parent's death removes the force that holds siblings in their habitual orbits. The question then becomes, Will the brothers and sisters drift apart, finally dissolving the tenuous threads of connection? Most of the time siblings find the pull among them is strong enough to draw them into a new configuration. In a family of two brothers and two sisters, after the parents died no one came forward at first to organize family gatherings during the holidays. After spending the first Thanksgiving of their lives apart, they set up a rotation so they would each plan one holiday a year.

When adult siblings maintain their connection in later life, the relationship takes on a special importance because, as veterans of multiple losses—deaths, divorce, children moving away—they realize that no one else alive can remember the way it was when they were children. The parents' deaths may even open up a space for siblings to know each other for the first time without competitive friction. "I never really thought, 'Would I like this person if he were not my brother?'" says a 56-year-old therapist. "After our parents were gone, I found myself calling him up, and he'd call me. We enjoy each other's company now. It's comfortable in a way I don't feel with anyone else because we've known each other forever." It can be a sweet and unexpected discovery to realize that the people with whom one feels the most affinity and closeness after a lifetime of struggle or emotional distance are our own siblings.

Many of us take our siblings for granted. They simply are, as unavoidable as gravity. Even as adults, we may not have devoted much thought to figuring out how they fit into our lives and how they shaped us. There's something in us that resists giving our sibling relationships the credence and attention they deserve. Cherishing our adult autonomy and freedom, we strive to bury our childish vulnerabilities and reinvent ourselves, but our sibs get in the way.

The boy who was teased by the neighborhood kids and grows up to be a confident, successful businessman doesn't want to remember those days of hot tears and humiliation. He may feel uneasy in the presence of the older sister who remembers all too clearly a time he'd rather forget. In a sense, our siblings don't let us put the past behind us. "Every time I see you, I try to be open to the idea that you are a different person than the one I used to know," one brother told his sister. "But it's hard, because I know you so well."

In this knowledge is, perhaps, the paradox of the sibling relationship. Siblings are the living remnant of our past, a buffer against the loss of our own history, the deepest, oldest memories of us. But in these memories lies a terrible power: Our siblings hold up a mirror before us, forcing us to look at an image of ourselves that may be either comforting or devastating, perhaps evoking self-acceptance and pride, perhaps shame and humiliation.

There is a fateful perpetuity about sibling relationships: Our brothers and sisters will always be our contemporaries; we can't ever quite leave them. However convenient it would be, we can't consign them to irrelevancy. No wonder that when sibling relationships are bad, they leave deep, irreparable scars of bitterness, betrayal, and rage. No wonder that when they are good, they are a source of profound satisfaction, one of the best and most fulfilling of human ties. Whether our siblings are thorns in our side or balm for our wounds, they are fellow travelers who have witnessed our journey, living bridges between who we once were and who we have become.

I worry about people who get born nowadays because they get born into such tiny families— sometimes into no family at all. When you're the only pea in the pod, your parents are likely to get you confused with the Hope Diamond.
—Russell Baker

Relations are simply a tedious pack of people, who haven't got the remotest knowledge of how to live, nor the smallest instinct about when to die.
—Oscar Wilde

Crises—Challenges and Opportunities

Family Violence and Chaos (Articles 29–32)
Sexual Issues and Infidelity (Articles 33 and 34)
Work/Family Stress (Articles 35 and 36)
Divorce and Remarriage (Articles 37 and 38)
Caring and Caregiving (Articles 39–41)

Stress is life and life is stress." Sometimes stress in families gives new meaning to this statement. When a crisis occurs in families, many processes occur simultaneously as families and their members cope with the stressor and its effects. The experience of a crisis often leads to conflict and reduces the family members' ability to act as resources for each other. Indeed, a stressor can overwhelm the family system, and family members may be among the least effective people in coping with each other's responses to a crisis.

Family crisis comes in many forms; it can be drawn out or the crisis event can be clearly defined. The source of stress can be outside or inside the family, or it can be a combination of both. It can directly involve all family members or as few as one, but the effects will ripple through the family, affecting all of its members to one degree or another.

In this unit, we consider a wide variety of crises. Family violence and chaos are the initial focus. "Behind Closed Doors" is a powerful description of the descent of a family into chaos and filth and overwhelmed by the alcoholism of the parents. The remainder of this section specifically focuses on children. John Leo, in "Things That Go Bump in the Home," questions whether abuse should be seen in terms of gender and proposes that partner battering can no longer be seen from a "male against female" viewpoint. "Helping Children Cope with Violence" shows how children growing up in violent surroundings can come away scarred for life, while "Resilience in Development" documents characteristics of children who show amazing ability to recover and adjust, even in highly dysfunctional families.

The next section deals with problems in sexuality and sexual relationships, with infidelity as the focus. In "Beyond Betrayal: Life after Infidelity," Frank Pittman recounts the emotional and practical wreckage that results from extramarital sex. In the next essay, Tamar Lewin reports on research suggesting that infidelity and other sexual stressors are less common in American marriages than has been assumed.

The section that follows looks at the work/family connection, with interesting results. "The Myth of the Miserable Working Woman" confronts many of the myths regarding women's balancing work and home. Many of the assumptions we have about the overwhelming nature of this balancing act are found to be untrue. Means by which couples can maintain egalitarian relationships while they balance work and family are presented in "Remaking Marriage & Family."

Divorce and remarriage are the subjects of the next section. Programs that have been developed to reduce the negative impacts of divorce or to reduce the likelihood of divorce are reviewed in "Should This Marriage Be Saved?" In "Lessons from Stepfamilies," Virginia Rutter takes an optimistic look at stepfamilies. In both essays, the reader has an opportunity to examine the way our culture has set stepfamilies in an impossible position. Rutter shows that stepfamilies, although more complex than traditional families, are not doomed to failure and unresolved conflict.

The nature of stress resulting from caring for others in the family is the subject of the final section. Two articles, "Caregiving: Continuities and Discontinuities in Family Members Relationships with Alzheimer's Patients" and "Hard Lessons," address issues of providing care for a family member with a debilitating, ultimately fatal condition, first from a scholarly perspective and second from a personal perspective. When these are read together, they present a picture of challenging, sometimes frustrating, work that also contains some reward. As a result of the 1997 death of Diana, Princess of Wales, we have seen increased awareness of the unique character of children's grief. "How Kids Mourn" presents a picture of the special needs of children when they have experienced loss.

Looking Ahead: Challenge Questions

How does an abusive relationship develop? What can be done to prevent it? How can we help someone involved in such a relationship? If you found that someone you knew was obsessively in love with another person, what would you do? What would you do if someone you knew was a victim of abuse in a relationship?

How would you react if you learned that your spouse or partner had been unfaithful? Under what circumstances would you consider extrarelational sex?

What is the best way to work out the competing demands of work and family? Assuming there is an option, discuss whether or not both partners should work outside the home if there are small children in the home.

Discuss how divorce affects the people involved. Should the rate of divorce be reduced? If so, how? If not,

why not? How has divorce affected someone you know? If the person has children, how have the children been affected?

Is your family, or that of a friend, a remarried or blended family? If so, how have you, or your friend, been affected?

What is your responsibility to the members of your family? What is their responsibility to you? What would you give up to care for your parents? What would you expect your children to give up for you? How about your spouse or partner?

What makes the grief of children unique? What can be done to help them deal with loss?

BEHIND CLOSED DOORS

A Schaumburg family rebuilds after a shattering descent into chaos

Bonita Brodt

Bonita Brodt is a Tribune *staff writer.*

At 4:30 that morning, Kelly Mahnke sat alone in her living room, cross-legged and all hunched over. Her face was puffy after hours of hysterical tears. She was calmer, now. Talking on the phone.

Listening, mostly.

Then her head snapped up. She couldn't believe it. Someone was at the door.

"Who could that be?" she whispered into the receiver.

"Oh, Kelly. It's probably the police. I was so worried I called 911."

Still a little drunk, Kelly regarded the door dumbly.

"My God," she mumbled when it finally hit her. "You did *what?*"

Slowly Kelly put the phone down. At that moment, words seemed of little use. It would have been impossible to explain the inevitability of what was about to happen, for even her best friend did not know how they were living.

No one did.

The doorbell kept ringing. Heart racing, Kelly got to her feet. She wasn't wearing much, just a cream-colored underthing, but that wasn't on her mind just then. She stepped carefully and when she got to the door, she opened it just enough to slide her slender body through. Kelly had often wondered if the nightmare had an ending. She was scared.

Yes, she told the officer, she had argued with her husband and, yes, she had swallowed pills. But she said she was feeling better and her friend had overreacted and her husband and three children were upstairs sleeping.

"*Hey! Wait a minute. No! You can't go in there. No. No! It's a mess!*"

"She started grabbing at me," recalled Gerard Thommes, a patrolman for the Village of Schaumburg. "She was telling me I couldn't go in there and I said I had to. I had to make sure everyone was all right."

Kelly lunged and tried to block him. But by that time, paramedics were coming up the sidewalk, and faces appeared in neighbors' windows, watching curiously as she was moved out of the way. With all his might, Thommes pushed, but it felt as if the door was hitting something. His first thought was that the husband might be lying behind it, dead.

Eventually he was able to force the opening wide enough. But for the longest time, he just stood there, eyes following the beam of his flashlight as it danced over a mighty sea of garbage and debris.

He distinctly heard flies.

He was wondering about rats when he heard a voice. It was his and he was muttering: "What the hell?"

Until that moment, there was no "before" or "after" for the Mahnke family. Their lives were divided into two incongruous worlds.

In one, visible from the outside, the couple owned a modest townhome in a comfortable white-bread suburb. The father went to work; the mother stayed home. They did things like take their three kids fishing. Went to church sometimes. But kept to themselves, mostly.

In the other world, known only on the inside, life had totally broken down.

Fragments of toys jutted up from a thick carpeting of trash that buried the floor two-feet-under. Whole pieces of furniture had been camouflaged with debris. There were mountains of soiled clothing. Decaying leftovers still on plates. Piles of beer cans and liquor bottles in every room.

From *Chicago Tribune Magazine,* September 15, 1996, pp. 13, 16, 18-22. © 1996 by the Chicago Tribune Company. All rights reserved. Reprinted by permission.

Though they didn't know it then, Roger and Kelly Mahnke were alcoholics. They drank to have fun, to avoid, to escape, to medicate.

Then drinking took from them without asking. Or maybe they just let go.

It hadn't always been like this. Custom portraits of the children—Meghan, 10, Matt, 8, and Brendan, 3—were displayed proudly on walls covered with grass cloth. A carved wooden heart that said, "Mom's kitchen" hung from a nail. But as life disintegrated, pages of family photo albums got ripped out, stepped on and matted with last night's fast food. It was a bewildering paradox even to the people who lived here. One day Kelly remembers looking around the living room and asking Roger: "What would we do if Ed McMahon came to our house with the check for a million dollars? We couldn't open the door."

Life does not afford any of us the luxury of knowing what waits around the corner. Nor do we know how we will deal with circumstance when it arrives. We may not see it coming, and we may not understand as it is happening.

We don't really know what we are capable of until we are there.

On May 5, 1995, the Mahnkes lost everything that mattered. Their self-respect. Their privacy. Their kids.

But they have surprised a lot of people in the 16 months since. A needlepoint plaque that says, "Nobody's perfect" is displayed in their living room window, facing out. They have thought a lot about what might have happened if not for the defining episode that blew up their lives.

Roger: "I would have been the same, probably."
Kelly: "I would have been dead."

Roger and Kelly married young, but they did not have a wedding. They drove to Wisconsin one day in 1982 and made it official in front of a judge. Both grew up in the same working-class neighborhood on the Northwest Side of Chicago. They dated for three months and became inseparable, feeling stronger together than they did apart.

Kelly was 18, a high school senior and working a waitress job that she hated so she could afford the $25 a week rent to live in a friend's basement. Roger was seven years older, a neighborhood longhair who played bass guitar in a garage band. He had gone from community college to steady work as a skilled laborer in heating and cooling repairs. On her key ring, Kelly still keeps the plastic-handled key from their first night in a motel.

Their first grocery receipt as a married couple is tucked inside a worn red wallet in which Kelly keeps sentimental things. She also saved a folded-up piece of lined notebook paper On one side is a heart that says, "Kelly L's Roger." On the other side, she wrote, "Mr & Mrs. Mahnke," then twice practiced a note she imagined someday writing to a teacher. It asked that her daughter be excused from having missed school on Tuesday because she had a sore throat.

Those were elements of normal life Kelly hoped for but that she and Roger never quite managed. Their picture had problems with its composition, cluttered with props that didn't belong or detracted or just plain overwhelmed.

By the time she met Roger, Kelly already had taken the initiative to distance herself from a troubled relationship with her father. Her childhood memories include punishments for not cleaning the house well enough. Though her father acknowledges Kelly could be difficult and was disciplined, he denies any of the physical abuse she says she remembers, such as being pulled down a flight of stairs by her hair. Her parents were divorced and both remarried, her mother to a man she met while both were patients in a psychiatric hospital. Kelly was close to her mother, who died at 31 from head injuries that were never fully explained. That was the year Kelly got drunk for the first time. She was 9.

Roger's upbringing was nothing out of the ordinary. His father drove buses and taxis and sometimes worked two and three jobs, while his mother was mostly at home. When he was 13, Roger took his first drink—to be different from his friends. He remembers sneaking the bottle out of a cabinet and deliberately drinking himself incoherent. Soon, he was part of the hangout at the forest preserve.

They had a lot of fun together. Roger was laid-back, Kelly feisty. Drinking was the most reliable ritual of their married lives.

This is what Roger says, his simple mantra: "We messed up."

By the time their first child was born in 1985, the Mahnkes had moved to the suburbs. A repair job had taken Roger to Schaumburg, and he found himself driving around, liking how it felt. Children bicycled freely. Playgrounds were close.

"Financially it was a real jump for us," Roger said of the two-bedroom townhouse they bought in a modest subdivision. It also meant a change in lifestyle, the move isolating them some what. Kelly does not drive; life in the car-dependent suburb isolated her, too.

Roger liked being the one to earn the money, and Kelly, though not exactly the domestic type, enjoyed the freedom of staying home. The first two children were born 17 months apart; the third in 1992.

Eventually though, they found themselves living in a world that felt as if it had been tailored to somebody else's measurements. It didn't always fit.

Life changed insidiously. Roger fell into a habit of staying out to have a couple of drinks because he felt he deserved that after a day's work. Kelly began waking up to wine coolers, unhappy at home.

"At some point, we started to drift apart," said Kelly. "I'd be at home all day angry because Roger wouldn't come home until late, and feeling like I should have gotten my high school diploma. Then I'd feel worse, because I knew I couldn't get a job anyhow because I drank all the time."

"We really didn't talk," Roger said.

The house was a barometer of what was happening.

When things were on an even keel between them, clothes made it to hangers and objects had a place of importance. There were periods when it was cleaned up enough to have a birthday party or to welcome family and friends.

But there were also darker swatches of time when the blinds were always closed, the inside carefully hidden. Whole parts of 1994 were like that.

Debbie Pyers dialed 911 the morning the house was discovered. She is a mother of two, and had met Kelly almost 10 years earlier in a Lamaze class. They were instantly drawn to each other, their eyes meeting with mutual amusement as others obediently panted through imaginary pain.

"I was brought up so differently from Kelly," said Pyers, who lives in a more affluent part of the village. The two talk on the phone every day, sometimes two and three times.

"There would be times when she would tell me something and I'd try to understand it. Their family structure was different," said Pyers. "My kids went to bed at 8:30, and it would be late, after 10:30, and we'd be on the phone talking and I'd say, 'Aren't you going to put them to bed?'"

Pyers knew Roger and Kelly drank. The friendship was clearly defined by things they couldn't do, like go out as couples to the movies because theaters didn't serve beer. But Pyers had never seen either out of control. She also noticed their children seemed cared for and happy. She was not a judgmental friend.

What she also knew was that Kelly wasn't just drinking. She was also using alcohol to dull the terror of panic attacks she battled as an adult.

"It got to the point where I was afraid to go to sleep, because I was afraid to wake up, because I would get an attack," said Kelly "I'd drink to deal with it. I know now that alcohol probably made [the attacks] worse."

Going back about six years, Pyers can recall Kelly's talking about how the house was a mess and Roger's complaining because she wouldn't clean. But Kelly was skillful keeping her at arm's length when necessary, confining their friendship to the phone for sometimes months at a time.

"One day" Pyers remembered, "I was driving and I had to go to the bathroom real bad. I was not far from Kelly's house, so I called her from the car. But she would not let me come by. She said it was just really, really a mess, and I said, 'Well, Kelly, how bad can it be?'"

It was like this:

There were flies. Dead ones. Live ones. A Polaroid tacked to the wall was so thickly covered with fly-specks the image was marred.

The inside of the refrigerator was splotched with mold, the shelves stocked with rotting food.

It had been a long time since anyone cooked a meal.

The kitchen sink was useless, without knobs or a faucet. The oven door was broken, the stove a greasy shelf where unwashed pots and bowls had come to rest. A man's suit jacket dangled from a hanger at one end of the counter. When the eggs were gone, the empty carton didn't make it to the garbage. Nothing did.

Just about every dish the family owned was dirty and lying out, not always in the kitchen. Utensils were washed on an as-needed basis, except at some point, that stopped, too. Food, then, was eaten with plastic and served on paper plates that became encrusted reminders of where meals took place. One plate was on the stairway. Another rested on the bare mattress where the whole family slept.

The family lost track of seven telephones under something. They bought clothing or appliances to replace what disappeared.

In the upstairs bathroom, plastic boxes crammed the toilet and beer cans swam in the sink.

Walking required careful detours around and over things like overturned chairs and broken fans. Underfoot, the terrain was sometimes soggy and the accompanying sound was a crunching of things being compacted or the clanging together of bottles of Zima, wine coolers and cans of Miller Lite.

The floor was not always visible, buried by piles of things that normally would have been dropped into a hamper or folded up in a drawer.

Or dumped in a bag and set outside for the garbage truck. The house smelled from a mélange of cigarette smoke, soiled clothing, decaying leftovers still in the foam carton from the drive-through window, spilled beer and human waste. The only working toilet was the one in the room behind the kitchen. But it was not stocked with toilet paper. Feces had been wiped across two walls and no one bothered to scrub it off.

This is what authorities found.

Family life went on a crash dive about 18 weeks before that, just after Christmas. But the mess had been accumulating for months. Roger and Kelly had been sliding for a year, and now they were scared—mostly about what they had become.

Roger found himself not calling home and staying out later to avoid what was waiting. It bothered him to do this, but he did it anyway. Sometimes he ignored his beeper even when he knew it was Kelly. Each time that happened, she got mad all over about the time she beeped to let him know their youngest had said "Da-da" for the first time. Roger, out drinking, did not bother to call.

When Roger finally got home at night, Kelly would sometimes stay just long enough for a good argument before taking her turn at the bars. As often as not, Roger would drink more at home, watching TV and smoking, eventually passing out in his chair.

Kelly was sick. A doctor diagnosed a problem with her liver and politely suggested she was allergic to alcohol. But even as she watched her face puff up, her skin turn pasty and her body grow lethargic, she drank.

"At first, I thought it was just a depression, but then it became physical," said Kelly. "I lost a lot of weight. At one point, I couldn't get out of bed and threw up if I did. I had Brendan on a schedule so he'd sleep until afternoon, and I remember lying there watching reruns, holding his hand as it stuck through the slats of the crib beside the bed. I couldn't remember things, not even someone's name from the TV. My hands got numb."

As the holidays approached, Roger gave the family an ultimatum: He said he would not buy a Christmas tree unless everyone helped clean.

"I wanted the kids to help me," said Roger. "I'd say 'Come on, guys. If we just get going here, we'll get it cleaned.' But they weren't used to picking up."

Nobody helped, so Roger relented. He didn't want to rob the children of a holiday and thought a good one might do everyone some good. So he cleaned alone, as best he could, and family snapshots tell the story of a happy, bountiful Christmas. But it was one that sent the family on a quick spiral down.

"We managed to get the tree and the wrapping paper out of the house, but that's about where it stopped," Kelly said. "We were getting madder and madder at each other. Some of our arguments were just like this: 'You clean it up.' 'No, you clean up.' 'No! You clean it up.'"

After Christmas, neither did.

Life, then, adjusted to the shrinking contours defined by warring parents in a house filling up with garbage. Ultimately there were no clear spots even for children to play. It was a confusing time in par-

ticular for Meghan, and Matt. Every morning, they left for a tidy suburban school with orderly classrooms, but came home to a world where they walked on trash and had to reach down into piles for pieces of clothing or shoes. Most evenings, when the yelling started, they were ordered upstairs and along with their younger brother, they'd huddle on top of the bare mattress to watch TV.

"I was kind of sad," Meghan remembered. "I could not have friends over. They were always kind of suspicious because I didn't have sleepovers, and they were always like, 'Well, why can't we come to your house?' I would say, 'Because my mom and dad don't like me to have friends over,' but I was thinking, 'I hope they don't find out.'"

Family life was a free-for-all. No bedtimes. No chores. No rules except for the one about opening the front door to visitors. If the family chose to answer, it would be "just a minute," then someone would sneak out the patio door and walk around.

"We really didn't deal with things like homework," said Kelly. "I do remember them asking for help and it depended on my mood whether I would help them or not."

For their 13th wedding anniversary in February 1995, the Mahnkes renewed their vows with the church wedding they had never had, and hosted a small reception in a private hall. Kelly addressed formal invitations sitting near a pedestal ashtray spilling over with days' worth of Roger's cigarette butts. Their theme was "Dreams Do Come True."

"It did renew us to some degree," said Roger. After the festivities, they drove to Jollet and spent the weekend on a gambling boat, where they sat in a whirlpool and drank in the room.

"It was like coming out of a dream," said Kelly of coming home. "Everything just went back to the way it was."

Worse, actually. The whole affair cost them close to $3,000, and they hadn't yet paid for Christmas.

There was a comical aspect to some of their drunken bouts. Roger would come home late and stomp heavily in his big work shoes, kicking things in all directions. He'd smoke in silence, calculating where he figured Kelly would walk next and that's where he'd toss his beer cans.

Kelly, who had been flinging hers all day, simply changed targets. Once she got so angry she hurled a can at Roger, spraying beer everywhere. She missed, however, and broke the blinds. Roger did nothing, which he knew would infuriate her. He just said "great!"

Savagely, in their lowest moments, they betrayed and turned on each other. They fought, sometimes leaving red marks and bruises. Roger remembers twisting Kelly's arm hard, trying to keep her from going out without him. Kelly remembers attacking Roger in full view of the neighbors when he got home late.

The night everything fell apart, they decided, as they did sometimes, to go out together and leave Meghan at home and in charge of her two brothers with Roger's beeper number programmed into the phone.

They spent a couple of hours at a neighborhood bar but the night ended quickly when Roger accused her of flirting. They yelled all the way home.

"I remember telling Kelly something like 'That's it. I'm out of here,' like I was going to leave her," said Roger. He stumbled upstairs, but Kelly grabbed a bottle of pills prescribed for a female problem and dumped six into her palm.

"I just tried to kill myself," she told Pyers, hysterical on the phone.

This had happened once before, a year earlier, but Pyers did not call police that time, then second-guessed herself through a sleepless night.

"She does this when she gets real upset," Pyers said of Kelly's pill-swallowing. "I don't know if it's a cry for help or if she's trying to punish the one who upset her or punish herself."

Whatever it was, Meghan was at her mother's side through much of it.

"I didn't want her to die," Meghan said.

The last thing Roger remembered was passing out on the mattress.

"Next thing I knew, there were six people standing around the bed, all in uniform. It was just like a scene out of 'Cops.'"

As he sat in an interview room at the police station, his mind cobwebbed and his face unshaven, he could hear police officers talking about him. "I'd like to kill that son-of-a-bitch," one said.

Police had taken protective custody of the children. Kelly was admitted to a hospital psychiatric ward and both she and Roger were named on misdemeanor charges of child endangerment and neglect.

He needed $100 to make bail.

"Roger looked like someone who just had the life kicked out of him," said Pyers, who drove to the police station with the money, then drove Roger home.

In the few hours he was gone, the village had found the home unfit for humans and police roped the front entry off with yellow tape that said "Crime Scene Do Not Enter" Roger ripped down the tape, then wrestled with the front door, which had been taken off the hinges and heaved by the walkway. Then he just sat down.

"I must have sat in the same spot for hours," Roger remembered. "I was stunned. Humiliated. I had lost everything. I had the phone down there with me, I had to call my mom, my work.

"Then I turned on the television and all of a sudden, it was showing exactly the spot where I was sitting. Our living room was all over the 4:30 news. I remember thinking, 'Oh, my God! The whole world can see me!' And to have the whole world see you at your most devastating moment, well, that's when I looked around that room, really for the first time, and asked myself, 'How did you let it get like this?'"

What Mary Passaglia remembered first was that she couldn't just walk in: She had to take a big step up. Passaglia, the village's environmental health supervisor, had been called out to inspect houses filled with trash, but never anything like the Mahnke house.

"It was just so unbelievable that a family could have lived in that environment. Walking through that house, I was trying to figure out where life would take place. I was able to touch the master bedroom ceiling because the piles reached the top of the mattress, and I am 5-foot-5."

She wrote this in a report:

"The odors were strong. Their sources included human feces and a variety of decaying food waste. I also found gross amounts of both live and dead flies, in addition to large amounts of fly fecal matter on the walls, ceiling, counter tops."

Passaglia also found that she liked Roger. The more she talked with him, the more she felt he was a genuinely nice man who loved his family. She was struck by a feeling that under the same set of circumstances, another man's instinct might be to bolt.

"I figured something just tragic had happened in this family," said Passaglia. "I wanted them to get their lives together and live a normal life."

Roger did not ask anyone for help.

But help arrived anyway. A nephew. Debbie Pyers. His half-brother. The wife of a guy at work. Kelly's father. As soon as Roger had cleared paths, he allowed his mother inside.

"When he opened the door, I noticed my hand had gone over my heart and I was saying, 'My God. My God. My God,'" recalled Ruth Mahnke. "I remember I turned to him and I said, 'I would have helped you.' And he said, 'Mom, it just started to get so bad and I was ashamed.'"

Roger's boss gave him vacation time for the cleanup, a job that required two 20-foot industrialized dumpsters and scores of black garbage bags.

"I had to tell myself, 'Just keep going. Just keep going,'" said Roger.

He threw just about everything out.

"The cleaning was kind of creepy" said Pyers. "It was like a hush-hush organization was doing it. We kept the blinds shut and stayed inside. I was really mad about the way those children had been living. But I loved Kelly. I loved Roger. I did not walk away."

The phone rang with crank calls and hang-ups. Passing cars slowed; the people gawked. One night, an eager gossip befriended Roger and his mother as they walked, unaware of who they were.

"Didja hear about that family that lives around here?" the young boy asked anxiously. "They all pooped in a bucket and wiped it on the walls!" Roger's mother was speechless. "You know," Roger said evenly, "I'll just bet it wasn't that bad."

The school called, and Roger stopped by to pick up envelopes for Meghan and Matt. Classmates at Collins Elementary sent notes:

Dear Matt: You are very nice to everyone. Your desk has been very clean and you have been getting good grades. I feel sorry for you and your family. You didn't do anything wrong.

Dear Meghan: We hope you come back to school. We understand that you think we will tease you, but we won't.

New kitchen tile was donated by a father at the grade school. A resident called the village to arrange to give the family a sofa. A relative bought sacks of building materials but refused Roger's money. Fresh new coatings of donated paint slathered the walls.

After hurling yet another bag into the dumpster one day, Roger walked to the townhomes' common mailbox and found himself standing next to a neighbor he did not know. She smiled, studying his face and extended a friendly hand.

"Are you sure you want to touch 'the squalor guy'?" Roger asked in all seriousness.

She hugged him. And Roger cried.

The first lawyer Roger and Kelly talked to suggested they refinance their house to pay for his services.

The second one looked at them squarely and said: "I don't know if I want *you*." Mike Ruzicka was unnerving. He was big and when he talked, which he did a lot, his voice sounded as though it could move furniture. Mostly though, he seemed to understand where they had been and where they wanted to go.

They hired him. They wanted their kids.

Ruzicka, who specializes in juvenile matters, was once a part of the state's child welfare agency, the Department of Children and Family Services. Originally he was an investigator on the front lines, recommending if children should be removed from a home.

"You run into a lot of dirty houses," said Ruzicka, who remembers one in particular that was so far gone he walked in, ran out, and vomited at the doorstep. Typically he would find substance abuse, alcohol, low intelligence or mental illness—underlying problems that tended to explain, not excuse.

By the time Ruzicka got involved, Roger and Kelly had chosen to accept full responsibility. They pleaded guilty to misdemeanor charges of child neglect and endangerment in a separate Circuit Court proceeding. Their punishment: a suspended six-month jail term and probation for 18 months. The day after, their doorbell rang and a deliveryman handed them a large bouquet of flowers, sent by a stranger. "I decided to be one of the people to encourage you," the card read.

Already, they had come a long way.

After Kelly spent six days in psychiatric care she came home on antidepressants. After a month of intensive out-patient therapy, she was handed her marble, a symbolic gift to remind her that if she took a drink, she could lose hers all over again.

Roger and Kelly worked with a certain resolve about doing what was necessary to mend their lives. Roger was able to adjust his work schedule so he could drive them to individual and group therapy sessions as well as parenting classes and family counseling. They also attended frequent meetings to follow a 12-step program to live without alcohol.

The night before his first Juvenile Court appearance on their behalf, Ruzicka visited the house to get to know Roger and Kelly better. They asked him to help remove an overhead light so they could wipe out the bugs.

"I guess I was kind of surprised the way the house looked—new floor, new carpet, the kitchen pretty much spotless," said Ruzicka. "The kids' rooms were looking good. It hit me that these people had taken a look at the problem and recognized what the problem was: them."

Ruzicka's goal was to reunite the family as quickly as possible.

The system, however, moved with deliberate caution. The children were not returned for 4½ months.

The Mahnkes were among 77,082 reports of neglect or abuse investigated by DCFS in fiscal 1995. Theirs was among the 40 percent found to be credible complaints. And their situation, no matter what its particulars, would be ultimately evaluated alongside some stark examples of how the state had failed to protect kids.

Having the state take custody of the Mahnke children ran counter to the judgment of Richard Zemon, a veteran DCFS investigator of 10½ years. To this day Zemon believes the state overreacted in assuming custody and did so for the wrong reasons, putting fear of bad publicity ahead of other concerns.

Zemon began assembling facts. There was no history of contact with the police, but the family had come to DCFS attention four years earlier when a neighbor complained the children had been left home alone. Zemon noted that DCFS did not intervene.

Interviewing first Roger, then the children and Kelly, he came away with a picture of a caring, though colossally dysfunctional, family. From Roger, for example, he learned that even at their worst, he and Kelly did a load of wash most nights so the children would have clean clothes.

Of particular significance was his conversation with Joel Karr, a school social worker, who told him that generally Meghan and Matt came to school clean and did not stand out except there had been a recent concern that Matt was disheveled. Karr said he talked with the Mahnkes and Kelly reacted badly when he suggested that Matt might be "neglected." But the boy's appearance immediately improved.

"All this told me something," said Zemon, "that these were not bad people, but that they let a situation get out of control. To me, unless there is an urgent risk, try to work out something without taking the kids. In removing kids, you traumatize someone. Custody is necessary when there's a real risk and when you don't have a responsible relative to help out."

Zemon drew up a plan that a copy of his official log shows was agreed to by his supervisor. He would not take formal custody, but would instead go to court for a protective order that would ensure Roger's and Kelly's cooperation while the children lived with Kelly's cousin, a Chicago police officer, who volunteered to keep them while Roger and Kelly put their lives back on track. At any point, DCFS could go to court for custody if the Mahnkes did not comply.

However, Zemon's log notes that three hours later he got a call from a higher-up saying the media wanted details. He said he was told to scrap his plan and put the children back under protective custody He was overruled.

"I had never *had* a phone call like that," said Zemon. "I was furious. I was flat-out told that because the press was asking questions, the depart-

ment's position would have to be to take custody of these kids.

"I think we hung this family out to dry," said Zemon, who retired three months later from DCFS.

But DCFS noted there isn't always agreement about what is the right thing to do when protecting the best interests of children, and pointed to a history replete with examples of why caution was the most appropriate route. DCFS was already under a blistering attack from many directions for being too overburdened to effectively safeguard children. The Mahnke case triggered the memory of the house on Keystone Avenue in Chicago where police went on a drug raid in February of 1994 and discovered 19 children living amid rat droppings and garbage, most of their mothers on welfare, some on drugs.

There also was the haunting memory of 3-year-old Joseph Wallace. Though DCFS intervened, his mother, a woman with a history of mental problems, won her custody dispute, then in 1993, she hanged her son. This was a red flag in view of Kelly's emotional history. In the midst of the case, a psychologist suggested she be evaluated as manic-depressive. Kelly already noticed she was doing peculiar things, such as waking up at 3 a.m. to scrub the toilet bowl. It was determined, however, that her medication created these symptoms, which disappeared when her prescription changed.

M eghan, Matt and Brendan spent five of their first days in state custody as patients in a hospital, where they were evaluated by therapists and social workers. Then they were placed in the Chicago home of Kelly's father, James Scriven, and his wife, Carol, who themselves were parenting two young children. Scriven said it was difficult to care for three more, but felt it was his responsibility as the grandfather.

About two months into the placement, Ruzicka filed court papers alleging that the antagonistic relationship between Kelly and her father was having a negative effect on the children. Ruzicka said he had seen the children show up dirty at the DCFS office for a visit. He also alleged the Scrivens allowed the children to be baby-sat by Carol's son, who she acknowledged was an ex-convict who served time on a weapons charge. Carol Scriven said he was sometimes in the house, but denied that the Mahnke children were ever left in his care.

During the placement, the Scrivens' household, too, would come under the scrutiny of DCFS. Carol Scriven blamed Kelly for this and said it included an incident that happened while the Mahnke children were there, when Carol disciplined one of her boys for using foul language by rubbing hot pepper on his lips.

At various points, professionals who evaluated the Mahnke children found them to be wrestling with the kind of emotional problems one might expect from living in a house filled with garbage and with parents who made sure they had food and clean clothes yet left them to fend largely for themselves. All the children, Meghan in particular, were also described as having problems stemming from the separation from their parents.

"This case did not belong in Juvenile Court," said Ruzicka, who took his own kids to the Mahnke house one day and cooked steak fajitas for everyone. "Everyone panicked. Court holds a bat over your head, but these people reacted when they were slapped. Yes, they were drunks. Yes, the house was a pigsty. Yes, the kids lived like animals. But look at what they've done."

Roger and Kelly used their time without the children to learn how to walk without "crutches." They got to know each other, this time sober. They weren't exactly sure if they'd like each other but they were pleasantly surprised. They went out to dinner. Went to movies. Joined a sober bowling league. To their relief, they discovered they shared the same wicked wit as when they drank.

When the new oven arrived, the deliveryman kept peering over for a good look at the living room. He recognized the outside of the house from television, and they all talked about how bad the garbage must have been.

"You'd never know this was the same place," he said, thinking they were new owners who rehabbed. "You guys really did a great job. Those people, man, what was their name?"

Kelly and Roger looked at one another sidelong, answering together:

"Us!"

It has been a year now since Meghan, Matt and Brendan were allowed to return to their parents. The Mahnkes live as a family, two adults and now four children. Connor, the youngest, was born in July. They share the house with a parakeet, a mouse, a rabbit, a large tortoise and three hamsters.

There are rules.

No shoes on the carpet. No food anywhere except the kitchen. No playing outside until rooms are clean, and that means everything picked up off the floor.

No alcohol. Neither Roger nor Kelly has taken a drink since the moment they lost everything. They are sober, now, for a year and four months. And no excuses. Though Roger and Kelly debate end-

lessly about whether alcoholism is something the will can conquer or if it is a disease that can fell even the strongest of people, this is their explanation:

"We were wrong. It's that simple," said Roger.

"We blame ourselves," Kelly said.

Today, the Mahnkes raise their children in a house that is almost obsessive in its cleanliness.

"We both get kind of edgy when anything is out of place," said Kelly. "I'm starting to sound like my grandmother, and that scares me. The kids were eating popcorn in the kitchen the other day and I was telling them not to make a mess on 'my floor.'"

The home has been painstakingly reassembled with things of particular meaning, such as a crucifix in the living room and a kitchen plaque that says, "Home Sweet Home." Family snapshots are displayed on a sideboard and Kelly, like a museum curator, divides them into three distinct periods of Mahnke history: "Before it got bad"; "When the kids were gone"; "After we got the kids back."

Upstairs, the two bedrooms were reinvented, much to the delight of the children. Meghan has one. Matt shares the other with Brendan. Kelly and Roger sleep on the fold-out couch in the living room with Connor in a portable crib alongside. Kelly looks at him, thankful that she had the presence of mind to drink less when she was pregnant with the other three.

The house is close quarters. When Kelly was overdue with the baby, she sent the children to their rooms to play more often than usual, admitting she needed space. One day she grabbed the phone and dialed Pyers to conspire about how she might convince the doctor to help the baby along.

"It's got to come out," Kelly said. "I'm going to tell him I'm depressed."

"But he expects you to be depressed," Pyers said. "You're pregnant."

"OK," said Kelly, thinking a moment. "Then how about if I tell him I don't feel like cleaning my house?"

This kind of humor has endured through misery. It's survival instinct, Roger thinks. When he spotted his van in the parking lot after a family shopping trip recently, his favorite sentence from a newspaper story chronicling the cleanup popped into his head.

"And the maroon van sagged with the weight of garbage bags," Roger announced, voice booming. It is a family joke and Meghan and Matt giggle even though they've heard it many times.

They still get embarrassed when they go to the grocery store or order a pizza and wonder if someone recognizes them or their address. Some neighbors still look at them funny. One in particular has a habit of peering around her grill to check on their activities. When the telephone rings, no one answers before first checking the number displayed on Caller ID.

Theirs was a costly mess.

"We're completely wiped," Roger says. He estimates close to $20,000 was spent on two lawyers, counseling, building materials and all of the possessions to start over. Roger's mother gave them money and the Mahnkes cashed about $12,000 in savings bonds, some of which had not yet matured. An insurance policy had to be cashed in, too.

One night recently Roger and Kelly were sitting with Brendan at the kitchen table when he looked up and asked: "When you went away, why didn't you take me with you?"

"He thought we abandoned him," Kelly said. They explained as best they could in language a 4-year-old could understand, just as they have talked openly with both Matt, now 10, and Meghan, almost 12, about how, if alcoholism can truly be inherited, they too, could be at risk.

The family tends to cling to one another. They pile on top of each other on the sofa. Hold hands when they walk. Roger now 38, and Kelly 32, like to say they live one day at a time, never claiming to be "cured" of anything but stronger because of what they have learned. The children go with them to family counseling. They find themselves watching Matt and Meghan, wondering how they have digested things they do not always talk about.

"At dinner the other night, I set out a bottle of sparkling grape juice," said Roger. "Matt's eyes went straight to the label and he started reading it. I told him there was no alcohol, but it got me to wondering if he trusts us. I hope he does."

For Sweetest Day, Roger went out shopping and came home with a symbolic gift that made Kelly laugh out loud when he offered it: a ceramic figurine of two happy, hugging pigs. Meghan studied it thoughtfully and then disappeared upstairs to her room.

When she came back down, she was holding a miniature bottle from her Barbie doll collection and placed it carefully between the two pigs.

"I didn't really know drinking was bad at the time," said Meghan, a slight girl who used to lie awake sometimes until after 2 in the morning, her stomach churning to the sound of angry voices. "My parents are different now. They are always working hard to make things right.

"I just think we're really lucky," said Meghan. "We're so happy now. It's like that was somebody else's house."

Things that go bump in the home

JOHN LEO

A Page 1 headline in the *Los Angeles Times* announces "A New Side to Domestic Violence." This "new side," apparently quite puzzling to the reporter, is that under mandatory arrest laws, a large number of women are now being arrested after domestic battles. In Los Angeles, arrests of women in such cases have almost quadrupled in eight years. In Wisconsin, the number of abusive men referred by the courts for counseling has doubled since 1989, while the number of abusive women referred for counseling increased 12-fold.

You could sense that the reporter was grappling with a baffling question: How is it that laws intended to protect women are producing so many arrests of women themselves? Luckily, he was able to come up with three explanations: a backlash against women, spiteful action by police officers who resent mandatory arrest laws, and outright male trickery.

Under the heading of trickery came tales of a man who smashed a brick on his head and blamed his wife, a man who bloodied himself by scratching his ear and a man, born with on odd bump on his head, who repeatedly showed the bump to police and got his wife arrested three times.

There is another explanation, one that has nothing to do with lucky head bumps or rogue cops. The explanation is this: If mandatory arrest laws are fairly applied, we will eventually see roughly equal numbers of men and women arrested, because the amount of domestic violence initiated and conducted by men and women is roughly equal. In fact, women may well be ahead.

Newsroom taboo. No, you haven't read this in your local newspaper, and certainly not in elite papers like the *Los Angeles Times.* The obvious reason is that publishing this news would create a severe political problem in the newsroom. To their credit, feminists made domestic violence a political issue. But they shaped this issue around a theory: This violence is an expression of patriarchy as a social force and marriage as a patriarchal institution. It is something men do to women because of the way society is organized.

An enormous amount of evidence now shows this paradigm is wrongheaded. But feminists are unwilling to adapt it to reality, and since the modern newsroom is supportive of feminism, news stories on domestic violence are carefully crafted, consistently unreliable and often just wrong.

Follow the work of the National Family Violence Survey. The original 1975 survey showed rather high rates of female-on-male domestic violence, but these were fitted to the paradigm and explained as understandable reactions to male violence. But the second survey in 1985 clearly showed equality in turning to violence: In both low-level assaults and severe assaults, only the wife was violent in a quarter of the cases, only the husband in another quarter, both in half of the cases. These findings came from self-reports.

This signaled a split in research: Feminist researchers keep churning out work that fits feminist theory, while independent researchers keep finding equality in the use of violence. Men are more dangerous—they kill partners twice as often—and more likely to inflict serious damage. But women are just as inclined to be violent with their partners as men are. (The rather high rates of violence in lesbian homes echoes this finding.) The equality findings undercut the feminist theory of partner violence as patriarchy in action, with its dark view of men and marriage. Instead, they support the common-sense view that violence between partners has more to do with problems of individuals in a difficult culture rather than with any vast ideological scheme.

The feminist insistence on using theory to mug facts has unfortunate results. One is that a generalized view of men as uniquely violent and dangerous to women ("men batter because they can," "the most dangerous place for a woman to be is in the home") has leached deep into popular culture. In a recent TV ad for girls' athletics, a young girl says if she plays sports, she will be more likely to leave an abusive relationship. A recent national list of what children want actually included the wish that daddies would stop hitting mommies.

In fact, children are now more likely to see mommy hit daddy. The rate of severe assaults by men on women in the home fell by almost 50 percent between the first National Family Violence Survey (1975) and the most recent update of data in 1992. It dropped from 39 percent per 1,000 couples per year to 20. Give the feminists credit for this. They did it mostly by themselves. But the rate of dangerous female assaults on males in the home stayed essentially static over that period—45 per 1,000 couples—and is now twice as high as the male rate. Give feminists responsibility for this, too. By defining partner violence as a male problem they missed the chance to bring about the same decline in violence among women.

Feminist studies of partner violence rarely ask about assaults by women, and when they do, they ask only about self-defense. Journalists, in turn, stick quite close to the feminist-approved studies for fear of being considered "soft" on male violence. The result is badly skewed reporting of domestic violence as purely a gender issue. It isn't.

Helping Children Cope With Violence

Lorraine B. Wallach

Lorraine B. Wallach, M.A., is one of the founders of the Erikson Institute in Chicago and is presently a faculty member there. Her recent work includes staff training around issues of children and violence.

Children who grow up in violent communities are at risk for pathological development because growing up in a constant state of apprehension makes it difficult to establish trust, autonomy, and social competence.

Violence is epidemic in the United States today. The murder rate in this country is the fifth highest in the world. It is 10 times higher than England's and 25 times that of Spain. For many inner-city children, violence has become a way of life. In a study of more than 1,000 children in Chicago, 74% of them had witnessed a murder, shooting, stabbing, or robbery (Kotulak, 1990; Bell, 1991). Almost half (47%) of these incidents involved friends, family members, classmates, or neighbors. Forty-six percent of the children interviewed reported that they had personally experienced at least one violent crime. These figures are similar to those found in other U.S. urban areas, such as Baltimore (Zinsmeister, 1990), Los Angeles County (Pynoos & Eth, 1985), and New Orleans (Osofsky, Wewers, Hann, Fick, & Richters, 1991).

Children are exposed to several kinds of violence, including child abuse and domestic violence. And there are communities where violence is endemic, where gang bangers, drug dealers, petty crimi-

nals, and not-so-petty criminals rule the streets. For children living in these conditions, feelings of being safe and secure do not exist.

Children who are not designated victims of assault can be unintended victims. Shoot-outs between gangs and drive-by shootings result in the wounding, and often killing, of innocent bystanders. In addition, the psychological toll of living under these conditions is immeasurable. The children in these neighborhoods see violence and hear it discussed. They are surrounded by danger and brutality.

Child abuse, other domestic violence, and neighborhood violence can harm development

The effects of this kind of violence on children are widespread and can permeate all areas of development, beginning in infancy and continuing through childhood. The first task a baby faces is the development of trust—trust

in the caregiving environment and eventually in himself. Achieving a sense of trust is compromised by growing up in a violent community. Many families find it difficult to provide infants with support, love, and affection in a consistent and predictable manner when they live in a constant state of apprehension—not knowing when they are going to be victims of violence. Toddlers have difficulty developing a sense of autonomy when their families cannot help them explore their environments because their surroundings are filled with danger. Preschoolers, too, are inhibited from going out into the world. Just at the age when they should be expanding their social contacts and finding out about people beyond the family, they are restricted by the dangers lurking outside. Many children living in high-rise housing projects and other dangerous neighborhoods are cooped up inside all day because it is unsafe to go out-of-doors. The situation is even more tragic when children experience violence within the family. Where can a child find protection when she is victimized within her own home? Although domestic violence occurs in *every* kind of neighborhood, the effects may be even more damaging when compounded by the harmful effects of growing up in *violent* neighborhoods.

Children who grow up under conditions that do not allow them to develop trust in people and in themselves or learn to handle day-to-day problems in socially acceptable ways are at risk for pathological development; they are at risk for resorting to violent behaviors themselves. The anger that is instilled in children when they are mistreated or when they see their mothers or siblings mistreated is likely to be incorporated into their personality structures. Children learn by identifying with the people they love. They also identify with the people who have power and control. When children see and experience abuse and violence as a way of life, when the people who are responsible for them behave without restraint, the children often learn to behave in the same manner.

Another serious problem for children living in chaotic communities is that the protectors and the dangerous people may be one and the same. The police, who are supposed to be protectors, are often seen as dangerous by community members. In his book *There Are No Children Here,* Alex Kotlowitz (1991) describes how a young man who is idolized by his housing project community be-

---

The young child's protectors and the dangerous people in her life may be one and the same.

It is particularly important for children who come from chaotic environments to have firm but appropriate limits, even though children who feel powerless may try to provoke adults into a battle of wills in an effort to make themselves feel important.

cause he is successful, has graduated from high school, is not caught up in gangs, and is still his own person is mistakenly killed by the police. What do children think when their idol is gunned down by the people who are supposed to protect them?

Children are confused when they cannot tell the good guys from the bad guys. Their teachers and the media tell them that drug dealers are bad and are the cause of the problems in the community, but the children may know that cousins or friends or even older brothers are dealing. Some people have likened the inner city, especially housing projects, to war zones; but in a war the enemy is more often than not on the outside, and usually everyone knows who he is.

Children growing up with violence face risks other than becoming violent themselves. Children who live with danger develop defenses against their fears, and these defenses can interfere with their development. When children have to defend themselves constantly from outside or inside dangers, their energies are not available for other, less immediately urgent tasks, such as learning to read and write and do arithmetic and learning about geography and history and science. In addition to not having enough energy to devote to schoolwork, there is evidence that specific cognitive functions such as memory and a sense of time can be affected by experiencing trauma (Terr, 1981).

Boys and girls who are victims of abuse and who see abusive behavior in their families can grow up feeling as if they are responsible for what is happening. Young children cannot always differentiate between what is real and what is part of their inner lives. The literature on divorce has made clear that many children believe that they have caused the breakup of the family, even though it had nothing to do with them (Wallerstein & Kelly, 1980; Hetherton, Cox, & Cox, 1982). Children who feel guilty about the violence in their families often perceive themselves as being bad and worthless. Feelings of worthlessness can lead children to the idea that they

When children have to defend themselves constantly from inside and outside dangers, there is little energy for schoolwork. There is also evidence that specific cognitive functions such as memory and a sense of time can be affected.

are not capable of learning, which leads, in turn, to a lack of motivation to achieve in school.

Children who experience trauma may have difficulty seeing themselves in future roles that are meaningful. Lenore Terr (1983), in her study of the schoolchildren of Chowchilla who were kidnapped in their school bus, found that the views of their future lives were limited and often filled with anticipation of disaster. Children who cannot see a decent future for themselves cannot give their all to the present task of learning and becoming socialized.

Living in unpredictably frightening situations makes children feel as if they have no control over their lives. We know that young children need to feel as if they can direct some parts of their lives,

but children who are victims of violence learn that they have no say in what happens to them. This sense of helplessness interferes with the development of autonomy.

It is difficult for children to keep on growing and maturing when they have been traumatized because an almost universal reaction of children to traumatic occurrences is regression. Children slip back to stages at which they felt more secure. This is particularly true when they have only a tenuous hold on their current status.

What makes some children more resilient than others, and what can we do?

As depressing as all this sounds, however, it does not mean that all children who experience violence are doomed. It is known that some children are more resilient and withstand trauma and stress better than others. If a child has an easy temperament and makes a good fit with his primary caregiver, he or she is more likely to be off to a good start. Some lucky children are born to strong parents who can withstand the ravages of poverty and community violence and still provide some security and hope for their children. Children are shaped not only by their parents' behavior but also by their parents' hopes, expectations, motivations, and view of the future—including their children's future.

It is important to remember that children are malleable, that what happens in the early years is im-

A kindergarten teacher in a Chicago public school was discussing her dilemma concerning two boys in her classroom. All of the children were at their tables, engaged in drawing, when the teacher noticed these boys crawling under the tables, pretending to have guns. When one of the boys saw the teacher watching them, he reassured her, "Don't worry, we're just playing breaking into an apartment." The teacher questioned whether she should let the play continue or offer a more socially acceptable view of behavior. How should she react? A Head Start teacher in the group said that the boy who was taking the lead in this game had been in her class the year before, and that his family's apartment had been burglarized. The boy had been very frightened and, after that experience, had changed from a confident, outgoing youngster to a quiet and withdrawn child. Here it was a year later, and he was just beginning to play out his experience. He was becoming the aggressor in the play instead of the helpless victim. And he was regaining some of his old confidence.

portant, but that many children can overcome the hurts and fears of earlier times. Many can make use of positive experiences that occur both inside and outside their families. Child care centers, recreation programs, and schools can be resources for children and offer them alternative perceptions of themselves, as well as teaching them skills. One of the things that help determine the resiliency of children is the ability to make relationships and to make use of the people in their environments, people who provide to children what they do not get in their families or who supplement what their families cannot offer.

Child care professionals can help offset the negative effects of violence in the lives of young children by providing that supplement. Although teachers, social workers, and human service personnel cannot cure all of the hurts experienced by children today, they can make a difference.

1. **The first thing they need to do is to make sure that their programs provide opportunities for children to develop meaningful relationships with caring and knowledgeable adults.** Teachers and other staff members can offer each child a chance to form an important relationship with one of them, a relationship within which the child can learn that there are people in the world who can be of help. The best thing to offer children at risk is caring people, people who are available both physically and emotionally.

Some years ago the famous Chicago analyst Franz Alexander (1948) coined the term *corrective emotional experience* to explain the curative power of therapy, and that term best describes what child care professionals can do for children at risk. A corrective emotional experience means having a relationship with another person that touches one's deepest core—not a relationship that

is superficial or intellectual, but one that engages the emotions. It means having a relationship within which a person can redo old patterns and ties. It means feeling safe enough within a relationship to risk making basic changes in one's psychic structure. Children cannot be forced into these kinds of relationships; they can only be offered the opportunities with the hope that they take advantage of them.

Some children attach easily, and it does not take much effort on the part of the adults for these children to form attachments; these are usually the children who have had a good relationship in their past. Other children have not been lucky enough to have had the kind of relationship that makes them want to seek out others and repeat this satisfying experience; these children need more help in forming ties and trusting alliances.

What can adults do to stimulate relationships with children who do not come easily to this task? They can look into themselves and see if they are ready

for this kind of relationship—a relationship that makes demands on their emotions, their energies, and their time. Relationships with children who have inordinate needs and who do not have past experiences in give-and-take partnerships are not 50–50 propositions; adults must meet these children more than halfway.

2. **Child care professionals can organize their schedules and their time with the children so that they provide as much consistency as possible.** Attachment can be encouraged by reducing the number of people a child encounters during the day and by maximizing the amount of meaningful time and activity the child has with one adult. In this way each child is allowed to form an attachment to one person. There are several models—including therapeutic centers, child-life programs, and primary-care nursing—that use relationship as the principal tool in their interventions. Establishing significant relationships with the children who

A nine-year-old boy in a shelter for battered women told a story about his recurring dream. This is what he said: "I dreamed of someone taking me away. He was dressed like a lady, but he had a moustache. I went inside the house. It was dark. The lights were out, and there were people inside having a party. It was ugly. They were eating worms and they asked me to try one. I took one and threw it away. Then I opened the door, and the light came on in there, and I saw there were no more ghosts, and I saw I was sleeping. When I dream like that, I become afraid."

It was obvious that the boy was expressing his fears, but the exact meaning of the details was not evident—not until one of the child care workers who knew the mother reported that the abusive father was bisexual and brought his male sexual partners to the family's apartment. It then became clear that in addition to struggling with feelings about an abusive father, the boy was also frightened and confused about the meaning of his father's behavior and probably about his own sexual identification. In this case the child was able to tell about a disturbing dream through the telling of a story, and the adults were able to understand it with additional information about his family.

have suffered from trauma is the most important thing that can be done, and it is the basis for all of the work that follows. What is this other work?

3. **Child care professionals must provide structure and very clear expectations and limits.** All children, especially young children, need to know where they stand, but it is particularly important for children who come from chaotic environments to have firm but appropriate limits. It should be noted that they do not take to this kind of structure easily. It is not something they have experienced before, and the newness of it may cause anxiety and tension, just as any new situation does.

Some children see the structure of a new setting as an opportunity to assert themselves and force the adults into power struggles. Children who feel powerless may try to provoke adults into a battle of wills in an effort to make themselves feel important. But even though some of the neediest children may rebel against structure, no matter how benign, it is important to provide it so that the boundaries are clear.

4. **Early childhood professionals should offer children many opportunities to express themselves** within the confines of a comfortable and consistent schedule, with clear expectations about behavior. Children need to air their emotions; they need to tell their stories. They can do this in several activities that can be a part of any good program for children.

Except for life-sustaining activities, play is, of course, the most universal activity of children

Through play, children learn about the physical and social world. As they play, children develop a map of the world, a map that helps them make sense of the

Josephine, the child of an abused mother, told a story about a girl with red eyes who bit and scratched her mother because she was angry at her and the devil got into her body. The child care worker listened and accepted her story, thereby accepting the child's feelings. In subsequent sessions, after establishing a more trusting relationship with the child, the worker told her a story about the same little girl who told the devil not to bother her and who talked to her mother about how she was going to try harder to be nicer. By using the same characters and theme, she offered the little girl another way of relating to her mother. At the same time, the mother's worker helped her understand her own anger and supported her in trying to alter her behavior toward her daughter.

complexities that define the world today. Play, in the context of a corrective experience, offers children who live with chaos and violence a chance to redraw their world map.

Play provides an avenue for children to express their feelings. Children who are angry or hurt can take their anger out on toys, dolls, and stuffed animals. Children who feel isolated or lonely can find solace in pretending to live in a world with lots of friends. Children who are frightened can seek safety within a game by pretending to be big and strong. In other words, children can play out their own scenarios, changing their real life situations to their own design. They can invent happy endings. They can reverse roles and become the big—instead of the small—people. They can become the aggressors rather than the victims.

Play also allows children to repeat some of the bad things in their lives. Some people think that children want to forget the frightening or horrible things that they have experienced and try to put these events out of their minds. Some people think that children's play reflects only happy experiences; and many times it does. But some children gain strength from repeating situations that were overwhelming to them, as a way of trying to come to terms with the experiences.

Traumatic events have a way of staying with us. Sometimes they are repeated in dreams. Adults may review these events by talking about them with their friends and even with strangers. Adults, through discussion—and children, through play—gain control over trauma by repeating it again and again. Repetition allows the trauma victim to absorb the experience little by little, come to grips with what happened, and learn to accept it or live with it.

Expressive art is very therapeutic

In addition to being given many opportunities for dramatic play, children can benefit from a chance to paint and draw. Just as some children make sad or frightening events into happy occasions in their play, others may draw pictures of happy times, even when they are living in far-from-happy circumstances. They draw pictures of nice houses with flowers and trees and sunshine. Others draw pictures that are, or that represent, disturbing things in their lives. They draw angry or violent pictures and find solace in expressing their feelings through art and conquering their fears by putting them on paper.

Storytelling can bridge to valuable conversation

Storytelling is another way in which children can handle difficult situations and express their inner thoughts. Sharing the telling of stories can be an excellent way to open up communication between adults and children. It can establish rapport between the two and lay the basis for further discussions of a child's difficulties. It is easier for the adult to understand stories than to interpret drawings or play, and the adult is able to engage a child in a conversation about her or his story.

This does not mean that the stories children tell can be accepted verbatim. Just as play and drawing allow children to express themselves symbolically, so do stories offer them a chance to communicate an idea or feeling without acknowledging its closeness to reality. Adults often cannot understand a child's story without having some outside information about the child's life.

If we understand what children are telling us through their stories, we can help them by participating with them in storytelling. Gardner (1971) used this method in his therapy with children. After the child told a story, Gardner told the same story but with a different, healthier ending. Although teachers are not therapists, they can engage children in joint storytelling sessions and offer alternative endings to the stories told by the children.

Collaboration with families is critically important

Direct work with children is invaluable, but if it can be combined with help for parents, its effectiveness can be increased. Young children are best understood in the context of their families and communities. Professionals need to know the facts about a child's life situation, and that information can be gained from the adults who know the child well.

In addition to obtaining information from parents, the most effective help for a child is in collaboration with help for the family. Because the child is entwined with his family for many years, it is important to make changes in his familial relationships, if possible; even small changes can be important.

It is not possible for teachers and other child specialists to also be social workers and parent therapists. The person who makes contact with a child, however, is often in a good position to establish a working alliance with the child's parents. This alliance can then be used to refer parents to community agencies, clinics, churches, or self-help groups for the support, guidance, or therapy that they need. Making a good referral takes skill and patience. It cannot be done quickly, which means that teachers and child care workers must have the time to talk to parents and to make home visits if necessary. They must have time to establish contact with families as an essential part of their work with children who suffer the consequences of violence.

The problems spelled out here are formidable. They will not be easy to solve, but professionals who see children on a daily basis can be an important part of the solution. They cannot cure all of the ills and solve all of the problems that confront children today, but they can offer these children a chance to face and accept their feelings and to see alternative ways of relating to others. If child care professionals can help some—not all, but some—children find alternatives to destructive behavior, be it toward themselves or others, they have helped break the cycle of violence.

References

Alexander, F. (1948). *Fundamentals of psychoanalysis.* New York: W.W. Norton.

Bell, C. (1991). Traumatic stress and children in danger. *Journal of Health Care for the Poor and Underserved, 2*(1), 175–188.

Gardner, R. (1971). *Therapeutic communication with children: The mutual storytelling technique.* New York: Science House.

Hetherton, E.M., Cox, M., & Cox, R. (1982). Effects of divorce on parents and children. In M. Lamb (Ed.), *Non-traditional families.* Hillsdale, NJ: Lawrence Erlbaum.

Kotlowitz, A. (1991). *There are no children here.* New York: Doubleday.

Kotulak, R. (1990, September 28). Study finds inner-city kids live with violence. *Chicago Tribune,* pp. 1, 16.

Osofsky, J., Wewers, S., Hann, D., Fick, A., & Richters, J. (1991). *Chronic community violence: What is happening to our children?* Manuscript submitted for publication.

Pynoos, R., & Eth, S. (1985). Children traumatized by witnessing personal violence: Homicide, rape or suicide behavior. In S. Eth & R. Pynoos (Eds.), *Posttraumatic stress disorder in children* (pp. 19–43). Washington, DC: American Psychiatric Press.

Terr, L. (1981). Forbidden games: Posttraumatic child's play. *Journal of American Academy of Child Psychiatry, 20,* 741–760.

Terr, L. (1983). Chowchilla revisited: The effects of psychic trauma four years after a schoolbus kidnapping. *American Journal of Psychiatry, 140,* 1543–1550.

Wallerstein, J.S., & Kelley, J.B. (1980). *Surviving the breakup: How children and parents cope with divorce.* New York: Basic Books.

Zinsmeister, K. (1990, June). Growing up scared. *The Atlantic Monthly,* pp. 49–66.

Resilience in Development

Emmy E. Werner

Emmy E. Werner is Professor of Human Development at the University of California, Davis. Address correspondence to Emmy E. Werner, Department of Applied Behavioral Sciences, University of California, Davis, 2321 Hart Hall, Davis, CA 95616.

During the past decade, a number of investigators from different disciplines—child development, psychology, psychiatry, and sociology—have focused on the study of children and youths who overcame great odds. These researchers have used the term resilience to describe three kinds of phenomena: good developmental outcomes despite high-risk status, sustained competence under stress, and recovery from trauma. Under each of these conditions, behavioral scientists have focused their attention on protective factors, or mechanisms that moderate (ameliorate) a person's reaction to a stressful situation or chronic adversity so that his or her adaptation is more successful than would be the case if the protective factors were not present.[1]

So far, only a relatively small number of studies have focused on children who were exposed to biological insults. More numerous in the current research literature are studies of resilient children who grew up in chronic poverty, were exposed to parental psychopathology, or experienced the breakup of their family or serious caregiving deficits. There has also been a growing body of literature on resilience in children who have endured the horrors of contemporary wars.

Despite the heterogeneity of all these studies, one can begin to discern a common core of individual dispositions and sources of support that contribute to resilience in development. These protective buffers appear to transcend ethnic, social-class, and geographic boundaries. They also appear to make a more profound impact on the life course of individuals who grow up in adversity than do specific risk factors or stressful life events.

Most studies of individual resilience and protective factors in children have been short-term, focusing on middle childhood and adolescence. An exception is the Kauai Longitudinal Study, with which I have been associated during the past three decades.[2] This study has involved a team of pediatricians, psychologists, and public-health and social workers who have monitored the impact of a variety of biological and psychosocial risk factors, stressful life events, and protective factors on the development of a multiethnic cohort of 698 children born in 1955 on the "Garden Island" in the Hawaiian chain. These individuals were followed, with relatively little attrition, from the prenatal period through birth to ages 1, 2, 10, 18, and 32.

Some 30% of the survivors in this study population were considered high-risk children because they were born in chronic poverty, had experienced perinatal stress, and lived in family environments troubled by chronic discord, divorce, or parental psychopathology. Two thirds of the children who had experienced four or more such risk factors by age 2 developed serious learning or behavior problems by age 10 or had delinquency records, mental health problems, or pregnancies by age 18. But one third of the children who had experienced four or more such risk factors developed instead into competent, confident, and caring adults.

PROTECTIVE FACTORS WITHIN THE INDIVIDUAL

Infancy and Early Childhood

Our findings with these resilient children are consistent with the results of several other longitudinal studies which have reported that young children with good coping abilities under adverse conditions have temperamental characteristics that elicit positive responses from a wide range of caregivers. The resilient boys and girls in the Kauai study were consistently characterized by their mothers as active, affectionate, cuddly, good-natured, and easy to deal with. Egeland and his associates observed similar dispositions among securely attached infants of abusing mothers in the Minnesota Mother-Child Interaction Project,[3] and Moriarty found the same qualities among infants with congenital defects at the Menninger Foundation.[4] Such infants were alert, easy to soothe, and able to elicit support from a nurturant family member. An "easy" temperament and the ability to actively recruit competent adult caregivers were also observed by Elder and his associates[5] in the resourceful children of the Great Depression.

By the time they reach preschool

age, resilient children appear to have developed a coping pattern that combines autonomy with an ability to ask for help when needed. These characteristics are also predictive of resilience in later years.

Middle Childhood and Adolescence

When the resilient children in the Kauai Longitudinal Study were in elementary school, their teachers were favorably impressed by their communication and problem-solving skills. Although these children were not particularly gifted, they used whatever talents they had effectively. Usually they had a special interest or a hobby they could share with a friend, and that gave them a sense of pride. These interests and activities were not narrowly sex typed. Both the boys and the girls grew into adolescents who were outgoing and autonomous, but also nurturant and emotionally sensitive.

Similar findings have been reported by Anthony, who studied the resilient offspring of mentally ill parents in St. Louis;[6] by Felsman and Vaillant, who followed successful boys from a high-crime neighborhood in Boston into adulthood;[7] and by Rutter and Quinton, who studied the lives of British girls who had been institutionalized in childhood, but managed to become well-functioning adults and caring mothers.[8]

Most studies of resilient children and youths report that intelligence and scholastic competence are positively associated with the ability to overcome great odds. It stands to reason that youngsters who are better able to appraise stressful life events correctly are also better able to figure out strategies for coping with adversity, either through their own efforts or by actively reaching out to other people for help. This finding has been replicated in studies of Asian-American, Cauca-

sian, and African-American children.[2,9,10]

Other salient protective factors that operated in the lives of the resilient youths on Kauai were a belief in their own effectiveness (an internal locus of control) and a positive self-concept. Such characteristics were also found by Farrington among successful and law-abiding British youngsters who grew up in high-crime neighborhoods in London,[11] and by Wallerstein and her associates among American children who coped effectively with the breakup of their parents' marriages.[12]

PROTECTIVE FACTORS WITHIN THE FAMILY

Despite the burden of chronic poverty, family discord, or parental psychopathology, a child identified as resilient usually has had the opportunity to establish a close bond with at least one competent and emotionally stable person who is attuned to his or her needs. The stress-resistant children in the Kauai Longitudinal Study, the well-functioning offspring of child abusers in the Minnesota Mother-Child Interaction Project, the resilient children of psychotic parents studied by Anthony in St. Louis, and the youngsters who coped effectively with the breakup of their parents' marriages in Wallerstein's studies of divorce all had received enough good nurturing to establish a basic sense of trust.[2,3,6,12]

Much of this nurturing came from substitute caregivers within the extended family, such as grandparents and older siblings. Resilient children seem to be especially adept at recruiting such surrogate parents. In turn, they themselves are often called upon to take care of younger siblings and to practice acts of "required helpfulness" for members of their family who are ill or incapacitated.[2]

Both the Kauai Longitudinal

Study and Block and Gjerde's studies of ego-resilient children[9] found characteristic child-rearing orientations that appear to promote resiliency differentially in boys and girls. Resilient boys tend to come from households with structure and rules, where a male serves as a model of identification (father, grandfather, or older brother), and where there is some encouragement of emotional expressiveness. Resilient girls, in contrast, tend to come from households that combine an emphasis on risk taking and independence with reliable support from a female caregiver, whether mother, grandmother, or older sister. The example of a mother who is gainfully and steadily employed appears to be an especially powerful model of identification for resilient girls.[2] A number of studies of resilient children from a wide variety of socioeconomic and ethnic backgrounds have also noted that the families of these children held religious beliefs that provided stability and meaning in times of hardship and adversity.[2,6,10]

PROTECTIVE FACTORS IN THE COMMUNITY

The Kauai Longitudinal Study and a number of other prospective studies in the United States have shown that resilient youngsters tend to rely on peers and elders in the community as sources of emotional support and seek them out for counsel and comfort in times of crisis.[2,6]

Favorite teachers are often positive role models. All of the resilient high-risk children in the Kauai study could point to at least one teacher who was an important source of support. These teachers listened to the children, challenged them, and rooted for them—whether in grade school, high school, or community college. Similar findings have been reported by Wallerstein and her associates from their long-term observations of youngsters who coped effectively with their parents' divorces[12] and by Rutter and his associates from their studies of inner-city schools in London.[13]

Finally, in the Kauai study, we found that the opening of opportunities at major life transitions enabled the majority of the high-risk children who had a troubled adolescence to rebound in their 20s and early 30s. Among the most potent second chances for such youths were adult education programs in community colleges, voluntary military service, active participation in a church community, and a supportive friend or marital partner. These protective buffers were also observed by Elder in the adult lives of the children of the Great Depression,[14] by Furstenberg and his associates in the later lives of black teenage mothers,[15] and by Farrington[11] and Felsman and Vaillant[7] in the adult lives of young men who had grown up in high-crime neighborhoods in London and Boston.

PROTECTIVE FACTORS: A SUMMARY

Several clusters of protective factors have emerged as recurrent themes in the lives of children who overcome great odds. Some protective factors are characteristics of the individual: Resilient children are engaging to other people, adults and peers alike; they have good communication and problem-solving skills, including the ability to recruit substitute caregivers; they have a talent or hobby that is valued by their elders or peers; and they have faith that their own actions can make a positive difference in their lives.

Another factor that enhances resilience in development is having affectional ties that encourage trust, autonomy, and initiative. These ties are often provided by members of the extended family. There are also support systems in the community

that reinforce and reward the competencies of resilient children and provide them with positive role models: caring neighbors, teachers, elder mentors, youth workers, and peers.

LINKS BETWEEN PROTECTIVE FACTORS AND SUCCESSFUL ADAPTATION IN HIGH-RISK CHILDREN AND YOUTHS

In the Kauai study, when we examined the links between protective factors within the individual and outside sources of support, we noted a certain continuity in the life course of the high-risk individuals who successfully overcame a variety of childhood adversities. Their individual dispositions led them to select or construct environments that, in turn, reinforced and sustained their active approach to life and rewarded their special competencies.

Although the sources of support available to the individuals in their childhood homes were modestly linked to the quality of the individuals' adaptation as adults, their competencies, temperament, and self-esteem had a greater impact. Many resilient high-risk youths on Kauai left the adverse conditions of their childhood homes after high school and sought environments they found more compatible. In short, they picked their own niches.

Our findings lend some empirical support to Scarr and McCartney's theory[16] about how people make their own environment. Scarr and McCartney proposed three types of effects of people's genes on their environment: passive, evocative, and active. Because parents provide both children's genes and their rearing environments, children's genes are necessarily correlated with their own environments. This is the passive type of genotype-environment effect. The evocative type refers to the fact that a person's partially heritable characteristics, such as intelligence, personality, and physical

attractiveness, evoke certain responses from other people. Finally, a person's interests, talents, and personality (genetically variable traits) may lead him or her to select or create particular environments; this is called an active genotype-environment effect. In line with this theory, there was a shift from passive to active effects as the youths and young adults in the Kauai study left stressful home environments and sought extrafamilial environments (at school, at work, in the military) that they found more compatible and stimulating. Genotype-environment effects of the evocative sort tended to persist throughout the different life stages we studied, as individuals' physical characteristics, temperament, and intelligence elicited differential responses from other people (parents, teachers, peers).

IMPLICATIONS

So far, most studies of resilience have focused on children and youths who have "pulled themselves up by their bootstraps," with informal support by kith and kin, not on recipients of intervention services. Yet there are some lessons such children can teach society about effective intervention: If we want to help vulnerable youngsters become more resilient, we need to decrease their exposure to potent risk factors and increase their competencies and self-esteem, as well as the sources of support they can draw upon.

In *Within Our Reach*, Schorr has isolated a set of common characteristics of social programs that have successfully prevented poor outcomes for children who grew up in high-risk families.[17] Such programs typically offer a broad spectrum of health, education, and family support services, cross professional boundaries, and view the child in the context of the family, and the family in the context of the community. They provide children with sustained access to competent and caring adults, both professionals and volunteers, who teach them problem-solving skills, enhance their communication skills and self-esteem, and provide positive role models for them.

There is an urgent need for more systematic evaluations of such programs to illuminate the process by which we can forge a chain of protective factors that enables vulnerable children to become competent, confident, and caring individuals, despite the odds of chronic poverty or a medical or social disability. Future research on risk and resiliency needs to acquire a cross-cultural perspective as well. We need to know more about individual dispositions and sources of support that transcend cultural boundaries and operate effectively in a variety of high-risk contexts.

Notes

1. A.S. Masten, K.M. Best, and N. Garmezy, Resilience and development: Contributions from the study of children who overcame adversity, *Development and Psychopathology, 2*, 425–444 (1991).

2. All results from this study that are discussed in this review were reported in E.E. Werner, Risk resilience, and recovery: Perspectives from the Kauai Longitudinal Study, *Development and Psychopathology, 5*, 503–515 (1993).

3. B. Egeland, D. Jacobvitz, and L.A. Sroufe, Breaking the cycle of child abuse, *Child Development, 59*, 1080–1088 (1988).

4. A. Moriarty, John, a boy who acquired resilience, in *The Invulnerable Child*, E.J. Anthony and B.J. Cohler, Eds. (Guilford Press, New York, 1987).

5. G.H. Elder, K. Liker, and C.E. Cross, Parent-child behavior in the Great Depression, in *Life Span Development and Behavior*, Vol. 6, T.B. Baltes and O.G. Brim, Jr., Eds. (Academic Press, New York, 1984).

6. E.J. Anthony, Children at risk for psychosis growing up successfully, in *The Invulnerable Child*, E.J. Anthony and B.J. Cohler, Eds. (Guilford Press, New York, 1987).

7. J.K. Felsman and G.E. Vaillant, Resilient children as adults: A 40 year study, in *The Invulnerable Child*, E.J. Anthony and B.J. Cohler, Eds. (Guilford Press, New York, 1987).

8. M. Rutter and D. Quinton, Long term follow-up of women institutionalized in childhood: Factors promoting good functioning in adult life, *British Journal of Developmental Psychology, 18*, 225–234 (1984).

9. J. Block and P.F. Gjerde, Early antecedents of ego resiliency in late adolescence, paper presented at the annual meeting of the American Psychological Association, Washington, DC (August 1986).

10. R.M. Clark, *Family Life and School Achievement: Why Poor Black Children Succeed or Fail* (University of Chicago Press, Chicago, 1983).

11. D.P. Farrington, *Protective Factors in the Development of Juvenile Delinquency and Adult Crime* (Institute of Criminology, Cambridge University, Cambridge, England, 1993).

12. J.S. Wallerstein and S. Blakeslee, *Second Chances: Men, Women and Children a Decade After Divorce* (Ticknor and Fields, New York, 1989).

13. M. Rutter, B. Maughan, P. Mortimore, and J. Ousten, *Fifteen Thousand Hours: Secondary Schools and Their Effects on Children* (Harvard University Press, Cambridge, MA, 1979).

14. G.H. Elder, Military times and turning points in men's lives, *Developmental Psychology, 22*, 233–245 (1986).

15. F.F. Furstenberg, J. Brooks-Gunn, and S.P. Morgan, *Adolescent Mothers in Later Life* (Cambridge University Press, New York, 1987).

16. S. Scarr and K. McCartney, How people make their own environments: A theory of genotype → environment effects, *Child Development, 54*, 424–435 (1983).

17. L. Schorr, *Within Our Reach: Breaking the Cycle of Disadvantage* (Anchor Press, New York, 1988).

Recommended Reading

Haggerty, R., Garmezy, N., Rutter, M., and Sherrod. L., Eds. (1994). *Stress, Risk, and Resilience in Childhood and Adolescence* (Cambridge University Press, New York).

Luthar, S., and Zigler, E. (1991). Vulnerability and competence: A review of research on resilience in childhood. *American Journal of Orthopsychiatry, 61*, 6–22.

Werner, E.E., and Smith, R.S. (1992). *Overcoming the Odds: High Risk Children From Birth to Adulthood* (Cornell University Press, Ithaca, NY).

Beyond Betrayal: Life After

INFIDELITY

Frank Pittman III, M.D.

Hour after hour, day after day in my office I see men and women who have been screwing around. They lead secret lives, as they hide themselves from their marriages. They go through wrenching divorces, inflicting pain on their children and their children's children. Or they make desperate, tearful, sweaty efforts at holding on to the shreds of a life they've betrayed. They tell me they have gone through all of this for a quick thrill or a furtive moment of romance. Sometimes they tell me they don't remember making the decision that tore apart their life: "It just happened." Sometimes they don't even know they are being unfaithful. (I tell them: "If you don't know whether what you are doing is an infidelity or not, ask your spouse.") From the outside looking in, it is insane. How could anyone risk everything in life on the turn of a screw? Infidelity was not something people did much in my family, so I always found it strange and noteworthy when people did it in my practice. After almost 30 years of cleaning up the mess after other people's affairs, I wrote a book describing everything about infidelity I'd seen in my practice. The book was *Private Lies: Infidelity and the Betrayal of Intimacy* (Norton). I thought it might help. Even if the tragedy of AIDS and the humiliation of prominent politicians hadn't stopped it, surely people could not continue screwing around after reading about the absurd destructiveness of it. As you know, people have *not* stopped having affairs. But many of them feel the need

to write or call or drop by and talk to me about it. When I wrote *Private Lies,* I thought I knew everything there was to know about infidelity. But I know now that there is even more.

ACCIDENTAL INFIDELITY

All affairs are not alike. The thousands of affairs I've seen seem to fall into four broad categories. Most first affairs are cases of *accidental infidelity,* unintended and uncharacteristic acts of carelessness that really did "just happen." Someone will get drunk, will get caught up in the moment, will just be having a bad day. It can happen to anyone, though some people are more accident prone than others, and some situations are accident zones.

Many a young man has started his career as a philanderer quite accidentally when he is traveling out of town on a new job with a philandering boss who chooses one of a pair of women and expects the young fellow to entertain the other. The most startling dynamic behind accidental infidelity is misplaced politeness, the feeling that it would be rude to turn down a needy friend's sexual advances. In the debonair gallantry of the moment, the brazen discourtesy to the marriage partner is overlooked altogether.

Both men and women can slip up and have accidental affairs, though the most accident-prone are those who drink, those who travel, those who don't get asked much, those who don't feel very tightly married, those whose running buddies

screw around, and those who are afraid to run from a challenge. Most are men.

After an accidental infidelity, there is clearly the sense that one's life and marriage have changed. The choices are:

1. To decide that infidelity was a stupid thing to do, to confess it or not to do so, but to resolve to take better precautions in the future;

2. To decide you wouldn't have done such a thing unless your husband or wife had let you down, put the blame on your mate, and go home and pick your marriage to death;

3. To notice that lightning did not strike you dead, decide this would be a safe and inexpensive hobby to take up, and do it some more;

4. To decide that you would not have done such a thing if you were married to the right person, determine that this was "meant to be," and declare yourself in love with the stranger in the bed.

ROMANTIC INFIDELITY

Surely the craziest and most destructive form of infidelity is the temporary insanity of *falling in love.* You do this, not when you meet somebody wonderful (wonderful people don't screw around with married people) but when you are going through a crisis in your own life, can't continuing living your life, and aren't quite ready for suicide yet. An affair with someone grossly inappropriate—someone decades younger or older, someone dependent or dominating, someone with problems even bigger than your own—is so crazily stimulating that it's like a drug that can lift you out of your depression and enable you to feel things again. Of course, between moments of ecstasy, you are more depressed, increasingly alone and alienated in your life, and increasingly hooked on the affair partner. Ideal romance partners are damsels or "dumsels" in distress, people without a life but with a lot of problems, people with bad reality testing and little concern with understanding reality better.

Romantic affairs lead to a great many divorces, suicides, homicides, heart attacks, and strokes, but not to very many successful remarriages. No matter how many sacrifices you make to keep the love alive, no matter how many sacrifices your family and children make for this crazy relationship, it will gradually burn itself out when there is nothing more to sacrifice to it. Then you must face not only the wreckage of several lives, but the original depression from which the affair was an insane flight into escape.

People are most likely to get into these romantic affairs at the turning points of life: when their parents die or their children grow up; when they suffer health crises or are under pressure to give up an addiction; when they achieve an unexpected level of job success or job failure; or when their first child is born—any situation in which they must face a lot of reality and grow up. The better the marriage, the saner and more sensible the spouse, the more alienated the romantic is likely to feel. Romantic affairs happen in good marriages even more often than in bad ones.

MYTHS OF INFIDELITY

The people who are running from bed to bed creating disasters for themselves and everyone else don't seem to know what they are doing. They just don't get it. But why should they? There is a mythology about infidelity that shows up in the popular press and even in the mental health literature that is guaranteed to mislead people and make dangerous situations even worse. Some of these myths are:

1. Everybody is unfaithful; it is normal, expectable behavior. Mozart, in his comic opera *Cosi Fan Tutti,* insisted that women all do it, but a far more common belief is that men all do it: "Higgamous, hoggamous, woman's monogamy; hoggamous, higgamous, man is polygamous." In Nora Ephron's movie, *Heartburn,* Meryl Streep's husband has left her for another woman. She turns to her father for solace, but he dismisses her complaint as the way of all male flesh: "If you want monogamy, marry a swan."

We don't know how many people are unfaithful; if people will lie to their own husband or wife, they surely aren't going to be honest with poll takers. We can guess that one-half of married men and one-third of married women have dropped their drawers away from home at least once. That's a lot of infidelity.

Still, most people are faithful most of the time. Without the expectation of fidelity, intimacy becomes awkward and marriage adversarial. People who expect their partner to betray them are likely to beat them to the draw, and to make both of them miserable in the meantime.

Most species of birds and animals in which the male serves some useful function other than sperm donation are inherently monogamous. Humans, like other nest builders, are monogamous by nature, but imperfectly so. We can be trained out of it, though even in polygamous and promiscuous cultures people show their true colors when they fall blindly and crazily in love. And we have an escape clause: nature mercifully permits us to survive our mates and mate again. But if we slip up and take a new mate while the old mate is still alive, it is likely to destroy the pair bonding with our previous mate and create great instinctual disorientation—which is part of the tragedy of infidelity.

2. Affairs are good for you; an affair may even revive a dull marriage. Back at the height of the sexual revolution, the *Playboy* philosophy and its *Cosmopolitan* counterpart urged infidelity as a way to keep men manly, women womanly, and marriage vital. Lately, in such books as Annette Lawson's *Adultery* and Dalma Heyn's *The Erotic Silence of the American Wife,* women have been encouraged to act out their sexual fantasies as a blow for equal rights.

It is true that if an affair is blatant enough and if all hell breaks loose, the crisis of infidelity can shake up the most petrified marriage. Of course, any crisis can serve the same detonation function, and burning the house down might be a safer, cheaper, and more readily forgivable attention-getter.

However utopian the theories, the reality is that infidelity, whether it is furtive or blatant, will blow hell out of a marriage. In 30 odd years of practice, I have encountered only a handful of established first marriages that ended in divorce without someone being unfaithful, often with the infidelity kept secret throughout the divorce process and even for years afterwards. Infidelity is the *sine qua non* of divorce.

3. People have affairs because they aren't in love with their marriage partner. People tell me this, and they even remember it this way. But on closer examination it routinely turns out that the marriage was fine before the affair happened, and the decision that they were not in love with their marriage partner was an effort to explain and justify the affair.

Being in love does not protect people from lust. Screwing around on your loved one is not a very loving thing to do, and it may be downright hostile. Every marriage is a thick stew of emotions ranging from lust to disgust, desperate love to homicidal rage. It would be idiotic to reduce such a wonderfully rich emotional diet to a question ("love me?" or "love me not?") so simplistic that it is best asked of the petals of daisies. Nonetheless, people do ask themselves such questions, and they answer them.

Falling out of love is no reason to betray your mate. If people are experiencing a deficiency in their ability to love their partner, it is not clear how something so hateful as betraying him or her would restore it.

4. People have affairs because they are oversexed. Affairs are about secrets. The infidelity is not necessarily in the sex, but in the dishonesty.

Swingers have sex openly, without dishonesty and therefore without betrayal (though with a lot of scary bugs.) More cautious infidels might have chaste but furtive lunches and secret telephone calls with ex-spouses or former affair partners—nothing to sate the sexual tension, but just enough to prevent a marital reconciliation or intimacy in the marriage.

Affairs generally involve sex, at least enough to create a secret that seals the conspiratorial alliance of the affair, and makes the relationship tense, dangerous, and thus exciting. Most affairs consist of a little bad sex and hours on the telephone. I once saw a case in which the couple had attempted sex once 30 years before and had limited the intimacy in their respective marriages while they maintained their sad, secret love with quiet lunches, pondering the crucial question of whether or not he had gotten it all the way in on that immortal autumn evening in 1958.

Both genders seem equally capable of falling into the temporary insanity of romantic affairs, though women are more likely to reframe anything they do as having been done for love. Women in love are far more aware of what they are doing and what the dangers might be. Men in love can be extraordinarily incautious and willing to give up everything. Men in love lose their heads—at least for a while.

MARITAL ARRANGEMENTS

All marriages are imperfect, and probably a disappointment in one way or another, which is a piece of reality, not a license to mess around with the neighbors. There are some marriages that fail to provide a modicum of warmth, sex, sanity, companionship, money. There are awful marriages people can't get all the way into and can't get all the way out of, divorces people won't call off and can't go through, marriages that won't die and won't recover. Often people in such marriages make a *marital arrangement* by calling in marital aides to keep them company while they avoid living their life. Such practical affairs help them keep the marriage steady but distant. They thus encapsulate the marital deficiency, so the infidel can neither establish a life without the problems nor solve them. Affairs can wreck a good marriage, but can help stabilize a bad one.

People who get into marital arrangements are not necessarily the innocent victims of defective relationships. Some set out to keep their marriages defective and distant. I have seen men who have kept the same mistress through several marriages, arranging their marriages to serve some practical purpose while keeping their ro-

In general, monogamous couples have a lot more sex than the people who are screwing around.

5. Affairs are ultimately the fault of the cuckold. Patriarchal custom assumes that when a man screws around it must be because of his wife's aesthetic, sexual, or emotional deficiencies. She failed him in some way. And feminist theory has assured us that if a wife screws around it must be because men are such assholes. Many people believe that screwing around is a normal response to an imperfect marriage and is, by definition, the marriage partner's fault. Friends and relatives, bartenders, therapists, and hairdressers, often reveal their own gender prejudices and distrust of marriage, monogamy, intimacy, and honesty, when they encourage the infidel to put the blame on the cuckold rather than on him- or herself.

One trick for avoiding personal blame and responsibility is to blame the marriage itself (too early, too late, too soon after some event) or some unchangeable characteristic of the partner (too old, too tall, too ethnic, too smart, too experienced, too inexperienced.) This is both a cop-out and a dead end.

One marriage partner can make the other miserable, but can't make the other unfaithful. (The cuckold is usually not even there when the affair is taking place). Civilization and marriage require that people behave appropriately however they feel, and that they take full responsibility for their actions. "My wife drove me to it with her nagging"; "I can't help what I do because of what my father did to me"; "She came on to me and her skirt was very short"; "I must be a sex addict"; et cetera. Baloney! If people really can't control their sexual behavior, they should not be permitted to run around loose.

There is no point in holding the cuckold responsible for the infidel's sexual behavior unless the cuckold has total control over the sexual equipment that has run off the road. Only the driver is responsible.

6. It is best to pretend not to know. There are people who avoid unpleasantness and would rather watch the house burn down than bother anyone by yelling "Fire!" Silence fuels the affair, which can thrive only in secrecy. Adulterous marriages begin their repair only when the secret is out in the open, and the infidel does not need to hide any longer. Of course, it also helps to end the affair.

A corollary is the belief that infidels must deny their affairs interminably and do all that is possible to drive cuckolds to such disorientation that they will doubt their own sanity rather than doubt their partner's fidelity. In actuality, the continued lying and denial is usually the most unforgivable aspect of the infidelity.

One man was in the habit of jogging each evening, but his wife noticed that his running clothes had stopped stinking. Suspicious, she followed him—to his secretary's apartment. She burst in and confronted her husband who was standing naked in the secretary's closet. She demanded: "What are you doing here?" He responded: "You do not see me here. You have gone crazy and are imagining this." She almost believed him, and remains to this day angrier about *that* than about the affair itself. Once an affair is known or even suspected, there is no safety in denial, but there is hope in admission.

I recently treated a woman whose physician husband divorced her 20 years ago after a few years of marriage, telling her that she had an odor that was making him sick, and he had developed an allergy to her. She felt so bad about herself she never remarried.

I suspected there was more to the story, and sent her back to ask him whether he had been unfaithful to her. He confessed that he had been, but had tried to shield her from hurt by convincing her that he had been faithful and true but that she was repulsive. She feels much worse about him now, but much better about herself. She now feels free to date.

7. After an affair, divorce is inevitable. Essentially all first-time divorces occur in the wake of an affair. With therapy though, most adulterous marriages can be saved, and may even be stronger and more intimate than they were before the crisis. I have rarely seen a cuckold go all the way through with a divorce after a first affair that is now over. Of course, each subsequent affair lowers the odds drastically.

It doesn't happen the way it does in the movies. The indignant cuckold does scream and yell and carry on and threaten all manner of awful things—which should not be surprising since his or her life has just been torn asunder. But he or she quickly calms down and begins the effort to salvage the marriage, to pull the errant infidel from the arms of the dreaded affairee.

When a divorce occurs, it is because the infidel can not escape the affair in time or cannot face going back into a marriage in which he or she is now known and understood and can no longer pose as the chaste virgin or white knight spotless and beyond criticism. A recent *New Yorker* cartoon showed a forlorn man at a bar complaining: "My wife understands me."

Appropriate guilt is always helpful, though it must come from inside rather than from a raging, nasty spouse; anger is a lousy seduction technique for anyone except terminal weirdos. Guilt is good for you. Shame, however, makes people run away and hide.

The prognosis after an affair is not grim, and those who have strayed have not lost all their value. The sadder but wiser infidel may be both more careful and more grateful in the future.

mance safely encapsulated elsewhere. The men considered it a victory over marriage; the exploited wives were outraged.

I encountered one woman who had long been involved with a married man. She got tired of waiting for him to get a divorce and married someone else. She didn't tell her husband about her affair, and she didn't tell her affairee about her marriage. She somehow thought they would never find out about one another. After a few exhausting and confusing weeks, the men met and confronted her. She cheerfully told them she loved them both and the arrangement seemed the sensible way to have her cake and eat it too. She couldn't understand why both the men felt cheated and deprived by her efforts to sacrifice their lives to satisfy her skittishness about total commitment.

Some of these arrangements can get quite complicated. One woman supported her house-husband and their kids by living as the mistress of an older married man, who spent his afternoons and weekend days with her and his evenings at home with his own children and his sexually boring wife. People averse to conflict might prefer such arrangements to therapy, or any other effort to actually solve the problems of the marriage.

Unhappily married people of either gender can establish marital arrangements to help them through the night. But men are more likely to focus on the practicality of the arrangement and diminish awareness of any threat to the stability of the marriage, while women are more likely to romanticize the arrangement and convince themselves it is leading toward an eventual union with the romantic partner. Networks of couples may spend their lives halfway through someone's divorce, usually with a guilt-ridden man reluctant to completely leave a marriage he has betrayed and even deserted, and a woman, no matter how hard she protests to the contrary, eternally hopeful for a wedding in the future.

Philandering

Philandering is a predominantly male activity. Philanderers take up infidelity as a hobby. Philanderers are likely to have a rigid and concrete concept of gender; they worship masculinity, and while they may be greatly attracted to women, they are mostly interested in having the woman affirm their masculinity. They don't really like women, and they certainly don't want an equal, intimate relationship with a

Every marriage is a thick stew of emotions ranging from lust to disgust.

member of the gender they insist is inferior, but far too powerful. They see women as dangerous, since women have the ability to assess a man's worth, to measure him and find him wanting, to determine whether he is man enough.

These men may or may not like sex, but they use it compulsively to affirm their masculinity and overcome both their homophobia and their fear of women. They can be cruel, abusive, and even violent to women who try to get control of them and stop the philandering they consider crucial to their masculinity. Their life is centered around displays of masculinity, however they define it, trying to impress women with their physical strength, competitive victories, seductive skills, mastery of all situations, power, wealth, and, if necessary, violence. Some of them are quite charming and have no trouble finding women eager to be abused by them.

Gay men can philander too, and the dynamics are the same for gay philanderers as for straight ones: the obvious avoidance of female sexual control, but also the preoccupation with masculinity and the use of rampant sexuality for both reassurance and the measurement of manhood. When men have paid such an enormous social and interpersonal price for their preferred sexuality, they are likely to wrap an enormous amount of their identity around their sexuality and express that sexuality extensively.

Philanderers may be the sons of philanderers, or they may have learned their ideas about marriage and gender from their ethnic group or inadvertently from their religion. Somewhere they have gotten the idea that their masculinity is their most valuable attribute and it requires them to protect themselves from coming under female control. These guys may consider themselves quite principled and honorable, and they may follow the rules to the letter in their dealings with other men. But in their world women have no rights.

To men they may seem normal, but

women experience them as narcissistic or even sociopathic. They think they are normal, that they are doing what every other real man would do if he weren't such a wimp. The notions of marital fidelity, of gender equality, of honesty and intimacy between husbands and wives seem quite foreign from what they learned growing up. The gender equality of monogamy may not feel compatible to men steeped in patriarchal beliefs in men being gods and women being ribs. Monogamous sexuality is difficult for men who worship Madonnas for their sexlessness and berate Eves for their seductiveness.

Philanderers' sexuality is fueled by anger and fear, and while they may be considered "sex addicts" they are really "gender compulsives," desperately doing whatever they think will make them look and feel most masculine. They put notches on their belts in hopes it will make their penises grow bigger. If they can get a woman to die for them, like opera composer Giacomo Puccini did in real life and in most of his operas, they feel like a real man.

Female Philanderers

There are female philanderers too, and they too are usually the daughters or ex-wives of philanderers. They are angry at men, because they believe all men screw around as their father or ex-husband did. A female philanderer is not likely to stay married for very long, since that would require her to make peace with a man, and as a woman to carry more than her share of the burden of marriage. Marriage grounds people in reality rather than transporting them into fantasy, so marriage is too loving, too demanding, too realistic, and not romantic enough for them.

I hear stories of female philanderers, such as Maria Riva's description of her mother, Marlene Dietrich. They appear to have insatiable sexual appetites but, on closer examination, they don't like sex much, they do like power over men, and underneath the philandering anger, they are plaintively seeking love.

Straying wives are rarely philanderers, but single women who mess around with married men are quite likely to be. Female philanderers prefer to raid other people's marriages, breaking up relationships, doing as much damage as possible, and then dancing off reaffirmed. Like male philanderers, female philanderers put their victims through all of this just to give themselves a sense of gender power.

Spider Woman

There are women who, by nature romantics, don't quite want to escape their own life and die for love. Instead they'd rather have some guy wreck his life for them. These women have been so recently betrayed by unfaithful men that the wound is still raw and they are out for revenge. A woman who angrily pursues married men is a "spider woman"—she requires human sacrifice to restore her sense of power.

When she is sucking the blood from other people's marriages, she feels some relief from the pain of having her own marriage betrayed. She simply requires that a man love her enough to sacrifice his life for her. She may be particularly attracted to happy marriages, clearly envious of the woman whose husband is faithful and loving to her. Sometimes it isn't clear whether she wants to replace the happy wife or just make her miserable.

The women who are least squeamish and most likely to wreak havoc on other people's marriages are victims of some sort of abuse, so angry that they don't feel bound by the usual rules or obligations, so desperate that they cling to any source of security, and so miserable that they don't bother to think a bit of the end of it.

Josephine Hart's novel *Damage,* and the recent Louis Malle film version of it, describe such a woman. She seduces her fiancee's depressed father, and after the fiancee discovers the affair and kills himself, she waltzes off from the wreckage of all the lives. She explains that her father disappeared long ago, her mother had been married four or five times, and her brother committed suicide when she left his bed and began to date other boys. She described herself as damaged, and says, "Damaged people are dangerous. They know they can survive."

Bette was a spider woman. She came to see me only once, with her married affair partner Alvin, a man I had been seeing with his wife Agnes. But I kept up with her through the many people whose lives she touched. Bette's father had run off and left her and her mother when she was just a child, and her stepfather had exposed himself to her. Most recently Bette's man-

All marriages are imperfect, a disappointment in one way or another.

———

ic husband Burt had run off with a stripper, Claudia, and had briefly married her before he crashed and went into a psychiatric hospital.

While Burt was with Claudia, the enraged Bette promptly latched on to Alvin, a laid-back philanderer who had been married to Agnes for decades and had been screwing around casually most of that time. Bette was determined that Alvin was going to divorce Agnes and marry her, desert his children, and raise her now-fatherless kids. The normally cheerful Alvin, who had done a good job for a lifetime of pleasing every woman he met and avoiding getting trapped by any of them, couldn't seem to escape Bette, but he certainly had no desire to leave Agnes. He grew increasingly depressed and suicidal. He felt better after he told the long-suffering Agnes, but he still couldn't move in any direction. Over the next couple of years, Bette and Alvin took turns threatening suicide, while Agnes tended her garden, raised her children, ran her business, and waited for the increasingly disoriented and pathetic Alvin to come to his senses.

Agnes finally became sufficiently alarmed about her husband's deterioration that she decided the only way she could save his life was to divorce him. She did, and Alvin promptly dumped Bette. He could not forgive her for what she had made him do to dear, sweet Agnes. He lost no time in taking up with Darlene, with whom he had been flirting for some time, but who wouldn't go out with a married man. Agnes felt relief, and the comfort of a good settlement, but Bette was once again abandoned and desperate.

She called Alvin hourly, alternately threatening suicide, reciting erotic poetry, and offering to fix him dinner. She phoned bomb threats to Darlene's office. Bette called me to tell me what a sociopathic jerk

Alvin was to betray her with another woman after all she had done in helping him through his divorce. She wrote sisterly notes to Agnes, offering the comfort of friendship to help one another through the awful experience of being betrayed by this terrible man. At no point did Bette consider that she had done anything wrong. She was now, as she had been all her life, a victim of men, who not only use and abuse women, but won't lay down their lives to rescue them on cue.

Emotionally Retarded Men in Love

About the only people more dangerous than philandering men going through life with an open fly and romantic damsels going through life in perennial distress, are emotionally retarded men in love. When such men go through a difficult transition in life, they hunker down and ignore all emotions. Their brain chemistry gets depressed, but they don't know how to feel it as depression. Their loved ones try to keep from bothering them, try to keep things calm and serene—and isolate them further.

An emotionally retarded man may go for a time without feeling pleasure, pain, or anything else, until a strange woman jerks him back into awareness of something intense enough for him to feel it—perhaps sexual fireworks, or the boyish heroics of rescuing her, or perhaps just fascination with her constantly changing moods and never-ending emotional crises.

With her, he can pull out of his depression briefly, but he sinks back even deeper into it when he is not with her. He is getting addicted to her, but he doesn't know that. He only feels the absence of joy and love and life with his serenely cautious wife

Once an affair is known or even suspected, there's no safety in denial but there is hope in admission.

———

and kids, and the awareness of life with this new woman. It doesn't work for him to leave home to be with her, as she too would grow stale and irritating if she were around full time.

What he needs is not a crazier woman to sacrifice his life for, but treatment for his depression. However, since the best home remedies for depression are sex, exercise, joy, and triumph, the dangerous damsel may be providing one or more of them in a big enough dose to make him feel a lot better. He may feel pretty good until he gets the bill, and sees how much of his life and the lives of his loved ones this treatment is costing. Marriages that start this way, stepping over the bodies of loved ones as the giddy couple walks down the aisle, are not likely to last long.

Howard had been faithful to Harriett for 16 years. He had been happy with her. She made him feel loved, which no one else had ever tried to do. Howard devoted himself to doing the right thing. He always did what he was supposed to do and he never complained. In fact he said very little at all.

Howard worked at Harriett's father's store, a stylish and expensive men's clothiers. He had worked there in high school and returned after college. He'd never had another job. He had felt like a son to his father-in-law. But when the old man retired, he bypassed the stalwart, loyal Howard and made his own wastrel son manager.

Howard also took care of his own elderly parents who lived next door. His father died, and left a nice little estate to his mother, who then gave much of it to his younger brother, who had gotten into trouble with gambling and extravagance.

Howard felt betrayed, and sank into a depression. He talked of quitting his job and moving away. Harriett pointed out the impracticality of that for the kids. She reminded him of all the good qualities of his mother and her father.

Howard didn't bring it up again. Instead, he began to talk to Maxine, one of the tailors at the store, a tired middle-aged woman who shared Howard's disillusionment with the world. One day, Maxine called frightened because she smelled gas in her trailer and her third ex-husband had threatened to hurt her. She needed for Howard to come out and see if he could smell anything dangerous. He did, and somehow ended up in bed with Maxine. He felt in love. He knew it was crazy but he couldn't get along without her. He bailed her out of the frequent disasters in her life. They began to plot their getaway, which consumed his attention for months.

Harriett noticed the change in Howard, but thought he was just mourning his father's death. They continued to get along well, sex was as good as ever, and they enjoyed the same things they had always enjoyed. It was a shock to her when he told her he was moving out, that he didn't love her anymore, and that it had nothing whatever to do with Maxine, who would be leaving with him.

Harriett went into a rage and hit him. The children went berserk. The younger daughter cried inconsolably, the older one

Most affairs consist of a little bad sex and a lot of telephoning.

became bulimic, the son quit school and refused to leave his room. I saw the family a few times, but Howard would not turn back. He left with Maxine, and would not return my phone calls. The kids were carrying on so on the telephone, Howard stopped calling them for a few months, not wanting to upset them. Meanwhile he and Maxine, who had left her kids behind as well, borrowed some money from his mother and moved to the coast where they bought into a marina—the only thing they had in common was the pleasure of fishing.

A year later, Harriett and the kids were still in therapy but they were getting along pretty well without him. Harriett was running the clothing store. Howard decided he missed his children and invited them to go fishing with him and Maxine. It surprised him when they still refused to speak to him. He called me and complained to me that his depression was a great deal worse. The marina was doing badly. He and Maxine weren't getting along very well. He missed his children and cried a lot, and she told him his preoccupation with his children was a betrayal of her. He blamed Harriett for fussing at him when she found out about Maxine. He believed she turned the children against him. He couldn't understand why anyone would be mad with him; he couldn't help who he loves and who he doesn't love.

MEN AND WOMEN WHO CHEAT

Howard's failure to understand the complex emotional consequences of his affair is typically male, just as Bette's insistence that her affair partner live up to her romantic fantasies is typically female. Any gender-based generalization is both irritating and inaccurate, but some behaviors are typical. Men tend to attach too little significance to affairs, ignoring their horrifying power to disorient and disrupt lives, while women tend to attach too much significance, assuming that the emotions are so powerful they must be "real" and therefore concrete, permanent, and stable enough to risk a life for.

A man, especially a philandering man, may feel comfortable having sex with a woman if it is clear that he is not in love with her. Even when a man understands that a rule has been broken and he expects consequences of some sort, he routinely underestimates the extent and range and duration of the reactions to his betrayal. Men may agree that the sex is wrong, but may believe that the lying is a noble effort to protect the family. A man may reason that outside sex is wrong because there is a rule against it, without understanding that his lying establishes an adversarial relationship with his mate and is the greater offense. Men are often surprised at the intensity of their betrayed mate's anger, and then even more surprised when she is willing to take him back. Men rarely appreciate the devastating long-range impact of their infidelities, or even their divorces, on their children.

Routinely, a man will tell me that he assured himself that he loved his wife before he hopped into a strange bed, that the women there with him means nothing, that it is just a meaningless roll in the hay. A woman is more likely to tell me that at the sound of the zipper she quickly ascertained that she was not as much in love with her husband as she should have been, and the man there in bed with her was the true love of her life.

A woman seems likely to be less concerned with the letter of the law than with the emotional coherence of her life. It may be okay to screw a man if she "loves" him, whatever the status of his or her marriage, and it is certainly appropriate to lie to a man who believes he has a claim on you, but whom you don't love.

Women may be more concerned with the impact of their affairs on their children than they are with the effect on their mate, whom they have already devalued and discounted in anticipation of the affair. Of course, a woman is likely to feel the children would be in support of her affair, and thus may involve them in relaying her messages, keeping her secrets, and telling her lies. This can be mind-blowingly seductive and confusing to the kids. Sharing the secret of one parent's affair, and hiding it from the other parent, has essentially the same emotional impact as incest.

Some conventional wisdom about gender differences in infidelity is true.

More men than women do have affairs, but it seemed to me that before the AIDS epidemic, the rate for men was dropping (philandering has not been considered cute since the Kennedy's went out of power) and the rate for women was rising (women who assumed that all men were screwing around saw their own screwing around as a blow for equal rights.) In recent years, promiscuity seems suicidal so only the suicidal—that is, the romantics— are on the streets after dark.

Men are able to approach sex more casually than women, a factor not only of the patriarchal double standard but also of the difference between having genitals on the outside and having them on the inside. Getting laid for all the wrong reasons is a lot less dangerous than falling in love with all the wrong people.

Men who get caught screwing around are more likely to be honest about the sex than women. Men will confess the full sexual details, even if they are vague about the emotions. Women on the other hand will confess to total consuming love and suicidal desire to die with some man, while insisting no sex ever took place. I would believe that if I'd ever

seen a man describe the affair as so consumingly intense from the waist up and so chaste from the waist down. I assume these women are lying to me about what they know they did or did not do, while I assume that the men really are honest about the genital ups and downs—and honestly confused about the emotional ones.

Women are more likely to discuss their love affairs with their women friends. Philandering men may turn their sex lives into a spectator sport but romantic men tend to keep their love life private from their men friends, and often just withdraw from their friends during the romance.

On the other hand, women are not more romantic than men. Men in love are every bit as foolish and a lot more naive than women in love. They go crazier and risk more. They are far more likely to sacrifice or abandon their children to prove their love to some recent affairee. They are more likely to isolate themselves from everyone except their affair partner, and turn their thinking and feeling over to her, applying her romantic ways of thinking (or not thinking) to the dilemmas of his increasingly chaotic life.

Men are just as forgiving as women of their mates' affairs. They might claim ahead of time that they would never tolerate it, but when push comes to shove, cuckolded men are every bit as likely as cuckolded women to fight like tigers to hold on to a marriage that has been betrayed. Cuckolded men may react violently at first, though cuckolded women do so as well, and I've seen more cases of women who shot and wounded or killed errant

husbands. (The shootings occur not when the affair is stopped and confessed, but when it is continued and denied.)

Betrayed men, like betrayed women, hunker down and do whatever they have to do to hold their marriage together. A few men and women go into a rage and refuse to turn back, and then spend a lifetime nursing the narcissistic injury, but that unusual occurrence is no more common for men than for women. Marriage can survive either a husband's infidelity or a wife's, if it is stopped, brought into the open, and dealt with.

I have cleaned up from more affairs than a squad of motel chambermaids. Infidelity is a very messy hobby. It is not an effective way to find a new mate or a new life.

It is not a safe treatment for depression, boredom, imperfect marriage, or inadequate gender splendor. And it certainly does not impress the rest of us. It does not work for women any better than it does for men. It does excite the senses and the imaginations of those who merely hear the tales of lives and deaths for love, who melt at the sound of liebestods or country songs of love gone wrong.

I think I've gotten more from infidelity as an observer than all the participants I've seen. Infidelity is a spectator sport like shark feeding or bull fighting—that is, great for those innocent bystanders who are careful not to get their feet, or whatever, wet. For the greatest enjoyment of infidelity, I recommend you observe from a safe physical and emotional distance and avoid any suicidal impulse to become a participant.

Sex in America: Faithfulness in Marriage Is Overwhelming

Tamar Lewin

While several previous studies of sex in America have created a popular image of extramarital affairs, casual sex and rampant experimentation, an authoritative new study of American sexual practices—widely described as the most definitive ever—paints a much more subdued picture of marital fidelity, few partners and less exotic sexual practices.

In the new study, based on surveys of 3,432 men and women 18 to 59 years of age, 85 percent of married women and more than 75 percent of married men said they are faithful to their spouses. And married people have more sex than their single counterparts: 41 percent of all married couples have sex twice a week or more, compared with 23 percent of the singles.

But cohabiting singles have the most sex of all, with 56 percent reporting that they had sex twice a week or more.

"We have had the myth that everybody was out there having lots of sex of all kinds," said John H. Gagnon, a co-author of the study. "That's had two consequences. It has enraged the conservatives. And it has created anxiety and unhappiness among those who weren't having it, who thought, 'If I'm not getting any, I must be a defective person.'

"Good sense should have told us that most people don't have the time and energy to manage an affair, a job, a family and the Long Island Rail Road," said Mr. Gagnon, a sociology professor at the State University of New York at Stony Brook.

The study is considered important because it is one of the first to rely on a randomly selected nationally representative sample. Most previous sex studies—from the Kinsey reports in the 1940's and the Masters and Johnson study in the 1960's to more recent popularized studies—by, for example, Playboy magazine, the researcher Shere Hite and Redbook magazine—relied on information from volunteers, a method that may seriously skew the results, experts say, because those who are interested in sex and are most sexually active tend to participate.

"A lot of the people we approached initially said, 'Oh, you don't want to talk to me, I haven't had a partner in three years,' and those people wouldn't have taken part in previous studies, where self-selection decided who would fill out the questionnaires," said Edward O. Laumann, a sociology professor at the University of Chicago who is one of the coauthors of the study.

For an American man, the median number of sexual partners over a lifetime is six; for a woman, the median is two. But the range in the number of lifetime sexual partners varied enormously, with 26 percent reporting only one lifetime partner, while one man in the study reported 1,016 partners and one woman reported 1,009.

To one of the most politicized questions in human sexuality—how common is homosexuality—the study offers a fuzzy answer: It depends.

A subdued picture of few partners and less exotic sexual practices.

For many years, the conventional wisdom was that 1 in 10 Americans was homosexual, a number that came from a 1948 Kinsey report that 10 percent of the men surveyed had had exclusively homosexual relations for at least three years between the ages of 16 and 55. Many recent studies have debunked that figure, including a study last year finding that only 1 percent of the male population was homosexual.

In the new study, 2.8 percent of the men and 1.4 percent of the women identified themselves as homosexual or bisexual. But when the question is asked differently the numbers change.

About 9 percent of the men and 5 percent of the women reported having had at least one homosexual experience since puberty. Forty percent of the men who had a homosexual experience sometime in their life did so before they were 18, and not since. Most women, though, were 18 or older when they had their first homosexual experience.

And when asked whether having sex with someone of the same sex seemed appealing, 5.5 percent of the women said the idea was somewhat or very appealing. About 6 percent of the men said they were attracted to other men.

The survey also found that homosexuals cluster in large cities. More than 9 percent of the men in the 12 largest cities identified themselves as homosexual, compared with less than 4 percent of the men in the suburbs of those cities and only about 1 percent of the men in rural areas. Lesbians also tend to cluster in cities, but not to the same extent as gay men.

The study asked about many different sexual practices, but found that only three were appealing to more than a small fraction of heterosexual Americans.

The vast majority of heterosexual Americans said they included vaginal intercourse in almost every sexual encounter. Many people said that oral sex and watching a partner undress were also appealing, but men were substantially more likely to enjoy both practices than women.

Most men and women said they did not find such practices as anal intercourse, group sex or sex with strangers very appealing, but again, the men were more interested than the women.

Among the other findings were these:

• More than half the men said they thought about sex every day, or several times a day, compared with only 19 percent of the women.

• More than four in five Americans had only one sexual partner, or no partner, in the past year. Generally, blacks reported the most sexual partners, Asians the least.

• Three-quarters of the married women said they usually or always had an orgasm during sexual intercourse, compared with 62 percent of the single women. Among men, 95 percent said they usually or always had an orgasm, married or single.

• Less than 8 percent of the participants reported having sex more than four times a week. About two-thirds said they have sex "a few times a month" or less, and about 3 in 10 have sex a few times a year or less.

• Both men and women who, as children, had been sexually touched by an adult were more likely, as adults, to have more than 10 sex partners, to engage in group sex, to report a homosexual or bisexual identification and to be unhappy.

• About one man in four and one woman in 10 masturbates at least once a week, and masturbation is less common among those 18 to 24 years of age than among those who are 24 to 34.

• Among marriage partners, 93 percent are of the same race, 82 percent are of similar educational level, 78 percent are within five years of each other's age and 72 percent are the same religion.

To gather data for the study, conducted by the National Opinion Research Center at the University of Chicago, 220 researchers spent several months in 1992 conducting face-to-face interviews. Those who agreed to participate—almost four out of five of those contacted—were also given written forms to place in a sealed envelope, so that the oral answers to some of the most intrusive, potentially embarrassing questions could be checked against what they wrote privately.

"There were some differences, but it never amounted to much, percentage-wise," Professor Laumann said. "Of course, you can't be sure that everyone told the truth all the time, but most of the time our interviewers had the sense that people were being extremely candid."

The sex survey grew out of a 1987 attempt by the Federal Government to develop data on sexual practices that would help in the fight against AIDS. The authors got money from the Government to develop a methodology for such a survey, but Senator Jesse Helms, a North Carolina Republican, persuaded the Senate in 1991 to block the financing to carry out the survey. The authors then got money to continue their work from several private foundations.

Among the survey's important implications was the finding that more than a third of the younger women said that peer pressure had made them have sex for the first time, compared with only 13 percent of those from previous generations. The authors suggest, therefore, that one important part of preventing teen-age pregnancy is helping young women learn to resist peer pressure.

The survey results are being published in two forms, one a paperback book, "The Social Organization of Sexuality" (University of Chicago Press), written by Mr. Gagnon, Mr. Laumann, Robert T. Michael, dean of the graduate school of public policy studies at the University of Chicago, and Stuart Michaels, a researcher at the University of Chicago.

The other version is a general-interest hard cover book, "Sex in America: A Definitive Survey" (Little, Brown and Company), by Mr. Gagnon, Mr. Laumann, Mr. Michael and Gina Kolata, a science reporter for The New York Times.

The Myth of the Miserable Working Woman

She's Tired, She's Stressed Out, She's Unhealthy, She Can't Go Full Speed at Work or Home. Right? Wrong.

Rosalind C. Barnett and Caryl Rivers

Rosalind C. Barnett is a psychologist and a senior research associate at the Wellesley College Center for Research on Women. Caryl Rivers is a professor of journalism at Boston University and the author of More Joy Than Rage: Crossing Generations With the New Feminism.

"You Can't Do Everything," announced a 1989 USA Today *headline on a story suggesting that a slower career track for women might be a good idea. "Mommy Career Track Sets Off a Furor," declaimed the* New York Times *on March 8, 1989, reporting that women cost companies more than men. "Pressed for Success, Women Careerists Are Cheating Themselves," sighed a 1989 headline in the* Washington Post, *going on to cite a book about the "unhappy personal lives" of women graduates of the Harvard Business School. "Women Discovering They're at Risk for Heart Attacks," Gannett News Service reported with alarm in 1991. "Can Your Career Hurt Your Kids? Yes, Say Many Experts," blared a* Fortune *cover just last May, adding in a chirpy yet soothing fashion, "But smart parents—and flexible companies—won't let it happen."*

If you believe what you read, working women are in big trouble—stressed out, depressed, sick, risking an early death from heart attacks, and so overcome with problems at home that they make inefficient employees at work.

In fact, just the opposite is true. As a research psychologist whose career has focused on women and a journalist-critic who has studied the behavior of the media, we have extensively surveyed the latest data and research and concluded that the public is being engulfed by a tidal wave of disinformation that has serious consequences for the life and health of every American woman. Since large numbers of women began moving into the work force in the 1970s, scores of studies on their emotional and physical health have painted a very clear picture: Paid employment provides substantial health *benefits* for women. These benefits cut across income and class lines; even women who are working because they have to—not because they want to—share in them.

There is a curious gap, however, between what these studies say and what is generally reported on television, radio, and in newspapers and magazines. The more the research shows work is good for women, the bleaker the media reports seem to become. Whether this bizarre state of affairs is the result of a backlash against women, as *Wall Street Journal* reporter Susan Faludi contends in her new book, *Backlash: The Undeclared War Against American Women,* or of well-meaning ignorance, the effect is the same: Both the shape of national policy and the lives of women are at risk.

Too often, legislation is written and policies are drafted not on the basis of the facts but on the basis of what those in power believe to be the facts. Even the much discussed *Workforce 2000* report, issued by the Department of Labor under the Reagan administration—hardly a hotbed of feminism—admitted that "most current policies were designed for a society in which men worked and women stayed home." If policies are skewed toward solutions that are aimed at reducing women's commitment to work, they will do more than harm women—they will damage companies, managers and the productivity of the American economy.

THE CORONARY THAT WASN'T

One reason the "bad news" about working women jumps to page one is that we're all too willing to believe it. Many adults today grew up at a time when soldiers were returning home from World War II and a way had to be found to get the women who replaced them in industry back into the kitchen. The result was a barrage of propaganda that turned at-home moms into saints and backyard barbecues and station wagons into cultural icons. Many of us still have that outdated postwar map inside our heads, and it leaves us more willing to believe the horror stories than the good news that paid employment is an emotional and medical plus.

In the 19th century it was accepted medical dogma that women should not be educated because the brain and the ovaries could not develop at the same time. Today it's PMS, the wrong math genes or rampaging hormones. Hardly anyone points out the dire predictions that didn't come true.

You may remember the prediction that career women would start having more heart attacks, just like men. But the Framingham Heart Study—a federally funded cardiac project that has been studying 10,000 men and women since 1948—reveals that working women are not having more heart attacks. They're not dying any earlier, either. Not only are women not losing their health advantages; the lifespan gap is actually widening. Only one group of working women suffers more heart attacks than other women: those in low-paying clerical jobs with many demands on them and little control over their work pace, who also have several children and little or no support at home.

As for the recent publicity about women having more problems with heart disease, much of it skims over the important underlying reasons for the increase: namely, that by the time they have a heart attack, women tend to be a good deal older (an average of 67, six years older than the average age for men), and thus frailer, than males who have one. Also, statistics from the National Institutes of Health show that coronary symptoms are treated less aggressively in women—fewer coronary bypasses, for example. In addition, most heart research is done on men, so doctors do not know as much about the causes—and treatment—of heart disease in women. None of these factors have anything to do with work.

But doesn't working put women at greater risk for stress-related illnesses? No. Paid work is actually associated with *reduced* anxiety and depression. In the early 1980s we reported in our book, *Lifeprints* (based on a National Science Foundation–funded study of 300 women), that working women were significantly higher in psychological well-being than those not employed. Working gave them a sense of mastery and control that homemaking didn't provide. More recent studies echo our findings. For example:

• A 1989 report by psychologist Ingrid Waldron and sociologist Jerry Jacobs of Temple University on nationwide surveys of 2,392 white and 892 black women,

conducted from 1977 to 1982, found that women who held both work and family roles reported better physical and mental health than homemakers.

• According to sociologists Elaine Wethington of Cornell University and Ronald Kessler of the University of Michigan, data from three years (1985 to 1988) of a continuing federally funded study of 745 married women in Detroit "clearly suggests that employment benefits women emotionally." Women who increase their participation in the labor force report lower levels of psychological distress; those who lessen their commitment to work suffer from higher distress.

• A University of California at Berkeley study published in 1990 followed 140 women for 22 years. At age 43, those who were homemakers had more chronic conditions than the working women and seemed more disillusioned and frustrated. The working mothers were in good health and seemed to be juggling their roles with success.

In sum, paid work offers women heightened self-esteem and enhanced mental and physical health. It's unemployment that's a major risk factor for depression in women.

DOING IT ALL—AND DOING FINE

This isn't true only for affluent women in good jobs; working-class women share the benefits of work, according to psychologists Sandra Scarr and Deborah Phillips of the University of Virginia and Kathleen McCartney of the University of New Hampshire. In reviewing 80 studies on this subject, they reported that working-class women with children say they would not leave work even if they didn't need the money. Work offers not only income but adult companionship, social contact and a connection with the wider world that they cannot get at home.

Doing it all may be tough, but it doesn't wipe out the health benefits of working.

Looking at survey data from around the world, Scarr and Phillips wrote that the lives of mothers who work are not more stressful than the lives of those who are at home. So what about the second shift we've heard so much about? It certainly exists: In industrialized countries, researchers found, fathers work an average of 50 hours a week on the job and doing household chores; mothers work an average of 80 hours. Wethington and Kessler found that in daily "stress diaries" kept by husbands and wives, the women report more stress than the men do. But they also handle it better. In short, doing it all may be tough, but it doesn't wipe out the health benefits of working.

THE ADVANTAGES FOR FAMILIES

What about the kids? Many working parents feel they want more time with their kids, and they say so. But does maternal employment harm children? In 1989 University of Michigan psychologist Lois Hoffman reviewed 50 years of research and found that the expected negative effects never materialized. Most often, children of employed and unemployed mothers didn't differ on measures of child development. But children of both sexes with working mothers have a less sex-stereotyped view of the world because fathers in two-income families tend to do more child care.

However, when mothers work, the quality of non-parental child care is a legitimate worry. Scarr, Phillips and McCartney say there is "near consensus among developmental psychologists and early-childhood experts that child care per se does not constitute a risk factor in children's lives." What causes problems, they report, is poor-quality care and a troubled family life. The need for good child care in this country has been obvious for some time.

What's more, children in two-job families generally don't lose out on one-to-one time with their parents. New studies, such as S. L. Nock and P. W. Kingston's *Time with Children: The Impact of Couples' Work-Time Commitments,* show that when both parents of pre-schoolers are working, they spend as much time in direct interaction with their children as families in which only the fathers work. The difference is that working parents spend more time with their kids on weekends. When only the husband works, parents spend more leisure time with each other. There is a cost to two-income families—the couples lose personal time—but the kids don't seem to pay it.

One question we never used to ask is whether having a working mother could be *good* for children. Hoffman, reflecting on the finding that employed women—both blue-collar and professional—register higher life-satisfaction scores than housewives, thinks it can be. She cites studies involving infants and older children, showing that a mother's satisfaction with her employment status relates positively both to "the quality of the mother-child interaction and to various indexes of the child's adjustment and abilities." For example, psychologists J. Guidubaldi and B. K. Nastasi of Kent State University reported in a 1987 paper that a mother's satisfaction with her job was a good predictor of her child's positive adjustment in school.

Again, this isn't true only for women in high-status jobs. In a 1982 study of sources of stress for children in low-income families, psychologists Cynthia Longfellow and Deborah Belle of the Harvard University School of Education found that employed women were generally less depressed than unemployed women. What's more, their children had fewer behavioral problems.

But the real point about working women and children is that work *isn't* the point at all. There are good mothers and not-so-good mothers, and some work and some don't. When a National Academy of Sciences panel reviewed the previous 50 years of research and dozens of studies in 1982, it found no consistent effects on children from a mother's working. Work is only one of many variables, the panel concluded in *Families That Work,* and not the definitive one.

What is the effect of women's working on their marriages? Having a working wife can increase psychological stress for men, especially older men, who grew up in a world where it was not normal for a wife to work. But men's expectations that they will—and must—be the only provider may be changing. Wethington and Kessler found that a wife's employment could be a significant buffer *against* depression for men born after 1945. Still, the picture of men's psychological well-being is very mixed, and class and expectations clearly play a role. Faludi cites polls showing that young blue-collar men are especially angry at women for invading what they see as their turf as breadwinners, even though a woman with such a job could help protect her husband from economic hardship. But in highly educated, dual-career couples, both partners say the wife's career has enhanced the marriage.

THE FIRST SHIFT: WOMEN AT WORK

While women's own health and the well-being of their families aren't harmed by their working, what effect does this dual role have on their job performance? It's assumed that men can compartmentalize work and home lives but women will bring their home worries with them to work, making them distracted and inefficient employees.

Perhaps the most dangerous myth is that the solution is for women to drop back—or drop out.

The only spillover went in the other direction: The women brought their good feelings about their work home with them and left a bad day at home behind when they came to work. In fact, Wethington and Kessler found that it was the *men* who brought the family stresses with them to work. "Women are able to avoid bringing the contagion of home stress into the workplace," the researchers write, "whereas the inability of men to prevent this kind of contagion is pervasive." The researchers speculate that perhaps women get the message early on that they can handle the home front, while men are taking on chores they aren't trained for and didn't expect.

THE PERILS OF PART-TIME

Perhaps the most dangerous myth is that the solution to most problems women suffer is for them to drop back—or drop out. What studies actually show is a significant connection between a reduced commitment to work and increased psychological stress. In their Detroit study, Wethington and Kessler noted that women who went from being full-time employees to full-time housewives reported increased symptoms of distress, such as depression and anxiety attacks; the longer a woman worked and the more committed she was to the job, the greater her risk for psychological distress when she stopped.

What about part-time work, that oft-touted solution for weary women? Women who work fewer than 20 hours per week, it turns out, do not get the mental-health work benefit, probably because they "operate under the fiction that they can retain full responsibility for child care and home maintenance," wrote Wethington and Kessler. The result: Some part-timers wind up more stressed-out than women working full-time. Part-time employment also provides less money, fewer or no benefits and, often, less interesting work and a more arduous road to promotion.

That doesn't mean that a woman shouldn't cut down on her work hours or arrange a more flexible schedule. But it does mean she should be careful about jumping on a poorly designed mommy track that may make her a second-class citizen at work.

Many women think that when they have a baby, the best thing for their mental health would be to stay home. Wrong once more. According to Wethington and

Kessler, having a baby does not increase psychological distress for working women—*unless* the birth results in their dropping out of the labor force. This doesn't mean that any woman who stays home to care for a child is going to be a wreck. But leaving the work force means opting out of the benefits of being in it, and women should be aware of that.

As soon as a woman has any kind of difficulty—emotional, family, medical—the knee-jerk reaction is to get her off the job. No such solution is offered to men, despite the very real correlation for men between job stress and heart attacks.

What the myth of the miserable working woman obscures is the need to focus on how the *quality* of a woman's job affects her health. Media stories warn of the alleged dangers of fast-track jobs. But our *Lifeprints* study found that married women in high-prestige jobs were highest in mental well-being; another study of life stress in women reported that married career women with children suffered the least from stress. Meanwhile, few media tears are shed for the women most at risk: those in the word-processing room who have no control at work, low pay and little support at home.

Women don't need help getting out of the work force; they need help staying in it. As long as much of the media continues to capitalize on national ignorance, that help will have to come from somewhere else. (Not that an occasional letter to the editor isn't useful.) Men need to recognize that they are not just occasional helpers but vital to the success of the family unit. The corporate culture has to be reshaped so that it doesn't run totally according to patterns set by the white male workaholic. This will be good for men *and* women. The government can guarantee parental leave and affordable, available child care. (It did so in the '40s, when women were needed in the factories.) Given that Congress couldn't even get a bill guaranteeing *unpaid* family leave passed last year, this may take some doing. But hey, this is an election year.

REMAKING MARRIAGE&FAMILY

BY BETTY CARTER AND JOAN K. PETERS

Betty Carter has been a family therapist for more than two decades. During that time, she has pioneered a way of working with couples that looks at the social structure in which they exist. Family histories, economic pressures, and gender expectations are all part of Carter's notion of a "family tree." In this excerpt from her new book, *Love, Honor & Negotiate*, written with Joan K. Peters, Carter argues that modern couples are gripped in an unforgiving vise, caught between traditional role models and a changing world—particularly once they have children. The problem, she says, is that "our society forces couples to backslide into traditional marriages when they have children, which reduces the woman's power in a previously equal marriage." Key to this is what she calls the Golden Rule: "Whoever has the gold, makes the rules." In *Love, Honor & Negotiate*, Carter offers solutions to this Golden Rule that are both personal and political. The advice is down-to-earth, practical—and strongly feminist. Although the book refers to married couples—they are Carter's main clients—the analysis of where we need to go from here is relevant not only for wives and husbands, but for any couple struggling to forge a path through the work/family dilemma.   —The Editors

When I started my work with couples in the seventies, I assumed that since women now worked and considered themselves the equals of men, we'd solved the gender problems I had struggled with in the early years of my own marriage. In therapy, I treated every marriage as if it were as unique as a snowflake. But as I began to notice the repetition of complaints, I couldn't help but realize that I was caught in a blizzard of sex-role issues that had not gone away.

The more I explored couples' "communication" problems, the more I found that one of the main things they can't communicate about is the power to make decisions. The more I questioned younger couples, the more I heard about their constant arguments. The more I questioned them about the content of their arguments, the more I heard about who spends what money, who does what housework and child care, and—if both partners work—whose work comes first. Or else I heard about the backlash from these conflicts in their sex lives—if they still had any. Older couples complained about the emptiness between them or argued bitterly about every detail of their lives. But the more I questioned them, the more I heard from the women about how much they resented their husbands' high-handedness or indifference to family life. The men, on the other hand, were defensively dismissive of these complaints.

Finally, I began to see the reason for this pattern—*most American couples backslide into traditional sex roles as soon as their children are born.* Women cut back at work, quit, or play superwoman because they are *automatically* the ones in charge of children. Meanwhile, men toil even more to "be good providers," ending up the bewildered breadwinner. Many are just furious because of what they see as their spouse's incessant complaints. And the divorce rates skyrocket.

I saw all this, but I was stymied. There was no way to use tra-

From *Ms.*, November/December 1996, pp. 57-65. Adapted from *Love, Honor & Negotiate: Making Your Marriage Work* by Betty Carter and Joan K. Peters. © 1996 by Betty Carter and Joan K. Peters. Reprinted by permission of Pocket Books, a division of Simon & Schuster.

We have to give up the myths that women can't have it all except by doing it all and that men don't have to do it all but can have it all.

ditional family therapy theory to respond to the problems of gender. So, with a few like-minded colleagues—Marianne Walters, Peggy Papp, and Olga Silverstein—in 1977 I cofounded the Women's Project in Family Therapy, where we developed our own techniques. But it meant thinking in an entirely new way for a family systems therapist. To explain the new thinking, though, I should first describe what family systems therapy is.

Family systems therapy was developed in the fifties as an improvement on individual therapy. The classic Freudian approach treats the individual in a vacuum, as if a person has an emotional problem within himself or herself. Family systems theorists say that the individual doesn't exist alone emotionally but in dynamic relationship with other family members. This means that emotional problems exist not inside the person who happens to exhibit or experience the problem but among all the family members.

Except in rare circumstances, the family is the most powerful emotional system we ever belong to. It shapes and continues to determine the course and outcome of our lives. A three- or four-generation family operates as a finely tuned system with roles and rules for functioning as a unit. For example, if one member behaves "irresponsibly," an "overresponsible" member will step in and pick up the slack; if one person is silent and withdrawn, another is usually the one to talk and engage, and vice versa—the sequences are circular.

Everyone in the family maintains problem behavior, such as that of an alcoholic father or depressed mother or runaway son. They don't do this because they want or need to but because their "common sense" responses to the problem are also part of the problem. The wife who empties her husband's bottles of scotch, the husband who suggests his wife go on antidepressants, and the parents who send their runaway son to therapy to "get fixed" are all trying to be helpful. But they're only making the problem worse, partly because these "solutions" imply that the person's symptom is the problem. Instead of looking for the factors in the family system that are producing the person's anxiety or depression, they try to get rid of the symptoms.

Most people don't realize the extent to which the marriage and family we create is a product of the family we were raised in, whether we are trying to re-create that original family or do the opposite. Our family relationships—the gears that run the clock, so to speak—are highly patterned and reciprocal. Rules are spoken and unspoken. They are based on our family history, which produces themes, stories, taboos, myths, secrets, he-

roes, and rebels. This history is passed on, consciously and unconsciously, to the next generation and to all new marriages.

That's what we mean when we say that family relationships aren't optional. They're also not equal or fair. You might say that our original family is like a hand of cards dealt by fate. And that our life's task, emotionally, is dealing with this hand.

For all these reasons, the family therapist will help patients actively work out problems with their parents on the assumption that, as I always put it, if you can work them out with your parents, you can work them out with anyone. And you'd better, I tell them, because your parents will always play a significant, if silent, part in all your relationships, particularly in your marriage. The more unresolved the problems of the past, the more they influence the present.

Even when people flee their "families of origin," as we call them, the impact of the family doesn't end. In fact, it actually increases. Not speaking to family members who caused us difficulty may temporarily relieve the pain of trying to deal with them. But the poison of the cutoff spreads throughout the family as members expend enormous emotional energy taking sides, justifying some people's actions and vilifying others. Every subsequent family event takes place in the shadow of the cutoff, and when the conflict that supposedly caused it is almost forgotten, what remains are families whose members are disconnected from one another and who live with broken hearts or hearts covered with calluses. Worst of all, the legacy suggests to future generations that family members we disagree with should be discarded. This is not a healthy resolution of conflict.

The other side of the coin—what we call enmeshment or fusion—comes up when family members become overinvolved and entangled in their relationships, taking inappropriate responsibility for one another, wanting peace at any price, insisting on ignoring differences through denial and compromise. There is no "live and let live" in this smothering system.

Family therapists normally believe that for a person to have a mature relationship with family members, he or she must be authentically true to self—even in ways that may break the family rules—while still having a meaningful personal connection. Of course, as anyone who has ever tried to achieve this with parents, spouses, and siblings knows, it is very difficult to do. Most of us will spend a lifetime trying to do it. Family therapy just helps us move in that direction.

But the family context wasn't enough to explain the gender complaints I was constantly hearing. So I had to discover on my own that family systems therapy—like Freudian therapy—wasn't drawing a large enough picture. Marriages, I realized, were not only two people enmeshed in family structures, they were also families enmeshed in cultural structures—structures that often exert unbearable pressures on these families, making spouses blame each other for what are really social problems.

Each family tries to teach its members the "right way" to live in our time and the "right values" to have about things like money, marriage, work, parenting, and sex. A family does this without realizing the degree to which these "truths" are dictated by the family's place in our very stratified culture—for example, their race, gender, ethnicity, social class, or sexual orientation—and how those values play out not only against the family, but also within it.

Without an understanding of the impact of family and cultural beliefs, couples are left with the crazy idea that they are inventing themselves and their lives, or that they could, if only their spouses would change. It is this false notion of independence that leads to marital power struggles and, often, divorce.

Improved communication is supposed to solve a couple's problems, but in the majority of cases, it cannot. For example, if a woman who works outside the home still does the lion's share of housework and child care, communication can only name the problem or identify the source of the wife's unhappiness. Unless the talk leads to a change in how the couple divide up housework and child care, it won't help at all. Too often, "communication" can become an argument without end and lead to mutual blame and psychological name-calling. With a cultural perspective on their problems, as well as a psychological one, couples can start to evaluate their problems in the context of their families and our culture.

American culture intrudes upon the inner sanctum of marriage. On one hand, it has given us new expectations of marriage; on the other, it has failed to allow the new marriage to fulfill these expectations. The American economy requires that most husbands and wives work outside the home but offers little workplace or social support for the two-earner family. And couples have changed—but not enough.

That's why I've come to believe in resolutions that combine the personal, social, and political. First, we have to give up the myths that women can't have it all except by doing it all and that men don't have to do it all but can have it all. We seriously have to question the idea that men's careers must never be disturbed and that mothering is different from—and more involving than—fathering.

The problem with contemporary marriage is that the lives of men and, especially, women have changed dramatically, radically, in this century, but the rules about marriage have not. Partly because of economics and partly because of the women's movement, women's behavior has changed drastically since the sixties. The vast majority of women are now in the workforce and half of them are providing as much—or more—of the family's income as their husbands. But men's behavior has changed far less. For personal, social, and economic reasons, they have not accommodated themselves to women's working by participating equally in the home. Although they now "accept" that a woman will work, they also "expect" her to be a homemaker. It is this lag in men's role change (combined with women's ambivalence about insisting on greater change) that results in contradictory wishes that weaken so many marriages.

In addition to blaming their husbands, women in this predicament often blame the women's movement for "taking away their 'right' to stay home." Instead of joining with other women to find support and solutions, they join the backlash that paints feminism as the enemy of men and family. Some may end up losing themselves in the excesses of the self-help movement, focusing on their "codependency" or their "inner child," as if these were the real problems in their marriages.

Men in these harried marriages also blame women. Instead of helping men to become more involved in the daily emotional and practical lives of their families, the men's movement blames contemporary women for "making them marginal." Spokesmen encourage men to take back their rightful place at the "head" of the family. As my colleague and friend Marianne Walters points out, the men's movement is about "male bonding" against women's "domination," not about developing men's capacities for emotional connection with wives and children and adjusting to equal partnership.

The changes women have made by coming into the world of work and politics have been a step up for them, a gain of power. For men, however, family involvement seems like a step down, a loss of power. This standstill reflects our continued valuing of power over connectedness and the continued association of power and money. Yet men have everything to gain by being more emotionally engaged in their lives.

While the traditional definition of masculinity is surely being challenged, it still holds sway in most men's lives. And the rules for "man the provider" are still very slippery. Is his wife fully committed to being a coprovider for life, or will she suddenly decide she has to stay home with the children? If his children are a priority for him, will he be penalized at work for taking paternity or family emergency leaves?

Men are also often afraid of the intimacy of family life. They are afraid that they don't know how to be intimate, and they're afraid of their own feelings, which they've been taught to suppress. Intimacy and connection have traditionally been the feminine sphere. Recognizing that "feminine" part of himself threatens a man's identity.

Unfortunately, avoiding intimacy also means that men cut themselves off from their deepest feelings, from their spouses, and from their children. Men who don't "feel" are as haunted and unhappy as women who aren't autonomous. They might grin and bear it, drink, gamble, have affairs, or become TV zombies, but escape is never satisfying. The demons are there when the high or the numbness wears off.

What does finally motivate men to change? Recognizing their own pain. Most men I work with begin to realize how much they suffered because their own fathers were distant and overworked. In their own longing and pain, they find the will to be a different kind of husband and father.

Men's reluctance to change has certainly been an obstacle to family life today. But to a large extent, society hasn't allowed them to change. It certainly hasn't helped them. If there is a villain in the contemporary marriage problem, it is our society. Women at work and men in the family are this century's revo-

Here we are, working such long hours for security, only to find ourselves feeling lost in an obsessive concern with marketplace values.

lution and problem. Society pays lip service to equality and to marriage, but there has been so little support of the two-paycheck marriage that I've come to think of the American workplace as the iron vise squeezing the life out of otherwise resilient, viable couples.

It's taken me a lifetime to realize that how we live and work as a nation is our own choice. And mostly I feel as if we don't even try to make our lives better, though it wouldn't be so very difficult to do so; we did it in the early part of the twentieth century by legislating an eight-hour workday and workplace safety standards. But now, women—who suffer most—don't dare challenge the status quo for fear we might sound "unrealistic" or "unable to make the grade in a man's world."

The Family and Medical Leave Act of 1993 sounded good, but it didn't actually change our lives. In the first place, the legislation only applies to companies with more than 50 employees, while most Americans work for smaller ones. Second, employers can exempt "key employees," so women and men who want to take parental leave can kiss the best jobs good-bye. Third, the provision is for three months of unpaid leave with the birth of a child or a medical emergency. If parents need the income, they can't take off. But still, we don't join together to challenge the workplace rules that leave no time for family. And one thing we need, desperately, is more time with our families.

The real reason most parents don't take sufficient time off when a child is born or a family member is ill is because they are afraid of losing their jobs. Justifiably. As much talk as there has been in the business community about the "work-family" problem, there's been precious little action. Why?

• Because many companies believe that work-family programs are too costly, even though it has been proven that companies don't actually lose money.

• Because most bosses are male, and they just don't see what the problem is. Or if there is some problem for working mothers, their bosses believe it's up to the mothers to solve it.

• Because women don't yet have enough power in the business community to change the work-family conflict.

Add to these problems several more: over half of all working women still earn less than $25,000 a year; child care is expensive and often of very poor quality; there are few after-school programs, no elder care for infirm parents, and no coverage on school holidays. And giving in to economic pressure, or careerism, or greed, parents work so much overtime that they often can't be home to put their children to sleep, let alone eat dinner with them.

In the past, the Puritan work ethic caused no conflict because the wife was the homemaker. Now that nearly everyone works, home life is often as hectic as work. Work has become the cen-

ter of our universe, our raison d'être, even though most salaries today no longer buy either the free time or the upward mobility enjoyed by many of our parents. Today both partners usually have to work just to stay in place. But—and here's the shock—most don't really have to work as hard as they do.

And so here we are, striving so fiercely and working such long hours for security, only to find ourselves feeling lost in an obsessive concern with marketplace values and an out-of-control whirlwind of activity that we don't know how to stop long enough to take care of our relationships.

Whenever asked, people here in the United States say that family life and betterment of society are more important than having a nice home, car, and clothes. Clearly, our beat-the-clock lives are not in sync with our deep belief in family and community. The result is that not only do we suffer from overwork, but we also betray ourselves daily. Overworked Americans cannot raise their children well, cannot contribute to their communities, and cannot sustain the companionship they once found in their marriages. They also can't live according to their expressed values; they just don't have the time.

Society also drives us. We don't want to be workaholics, but we just can't stop. In a Los Angeles *Times* survey, nearly 40 percent of men say they would change jobs to have more family and personal time; and in another survey, cited by *Time* magazine, half of the men interviewed said they would refuse a promotion that involved sacrificing family time. The problem is they can't work fewer hours or refuse the promotion and hold on to their jobs. Even more women than men would give up money and status if they could have more family time. But they can't.

The lucky few can work shorter hours if they let themselves, but the average couple have to work outside the home at inflexible jobs, confronting a terrible choice between work and family. Clearly, sweeping changes are necessary.

What would improve the workplace for people who also want fulfilling personal and family lives? In the last several years, social critics and workers have come up with a list of suggestions. These are the most frequently cited:

• On-Site Day Care. Or: subsidies or discounts at child care centers near the workplace.

• Flextime. This allows employees to choose their hours and days. Compressed workweeks help, too, especially when there's a long commute.

• No Mandatory Overtime.

• Family Leave. What would a really supportive plan look

To thrive, couples have to repair their deep emotional connections to their original families and put out new shoots into the community.

like? Swedes are guaranteed 15 months of paid parental leave after the birth or adoption of a child, four months paid leave for sick children under 12, and the right to work part-time without losing their job or benefits until their children are 12.

• Telecommuting. Many companies are now experimenting with employees working at home two or more days a week. Some companies go a step further to the "ultimate flexibility" of the virtual office. With laptops, e-mail, cellular phones, and beepers, people can work wherever they work best.

Given how much better family support programs could make the lives of today's men, women, and children, wouldn't it be wonderful if the men's movement turned its energies to advocating such programs? Men could bond by sharing fathering problems and the challenges of their new roles. Men's groups could explore the work-family problem to see how business today might support them as fathers and equal partners in their marriages. Finally, men could use the very real power they have to campaign for changes in the workplace.

The clients who come to my office to try to repair their family relationships want to believe that their lives have some meaning beyond their own narrow self-interest. Caught up, like the rest of us, in the scramble and the individualism of the competitive marketplace, they nevertheless readily acknowledge that "there must be more to life than this."

The positive side of any crisis that brings a couple to therapy is the opportunity to reflect in just this way: Is my life meaningful? Do my relationships work? Are we teaching our children what they need to know? Do I like my work? Is money as important as I thought it was? Do I have caring connections? Do I belong? Among my clients and friends, some search for this kind of meaning or spirituality through religion, but many seek it through a connection with others in a positive, mutually helpful way. That is, by being part of a caring community.

To thrive, couples have to repair their deep emotional connections to their original families and also put out new shoots into the community, whose support may make a life-or-death difference to their relationships. So few people seem to understand how interconnected the personal and public levels of experience are. So few couples make the time to invest themselves beyond their family and friends, beyond their own ambition and pleasure. And most couples suffer because they don't. Ending the isolation of marriage is as important as changing the emotions and behavior within it. We have overloaded the marital circuits by expecting one relationship to meet all of our needs.

It may seem odd that a family therapist should issue a call for social and political involvement, but it is precisely the misaligned connection between marriage and society that has put marriage in such jeopardy and will continue to do so if the so-

cial contract isn't repaired. We must recognize the degree to which we are all interdependent. Just as we benefit from understanding how a family functions as a system, we can benefit from understanding how society functions as a system and how, as individuals and couples, we are all a part of it.

I teach my therapist trainees that it is their job to connect the clients' complaints not only to what is going on in the family system, but also to what is happening in the social system they live in. A truly systematic therapy encourages clients to question their role in every system they belong to. Alienation, cynicism, and despair poison relationships, whether their source is the family system or the larger systems of society, or typically, both.

As a culture, we have begun to understand the importance of connectedness and what we have lost by devaluing it. This is one of the reasons why the issue of "family values" strikes home for so many people. But family values need not be defined according to a notion of rigid family forms and traditional sex roles. Real family values are more appropriately defined as those created by parents who are as involved in their marriage and their children as they are in their own achievement. Real family values are reflected by a family's involvement in society and by a society that supports the needs of its families whatever those families might look like: two-paycheck marriages, single-parent households, remarried couples with their children, gay and lesbian couples with children, as well as traditional wage earner-homemaker partners.

The so-called family values debate now raging has become a code phrase to signify support for the traditional family structure of yesterday. But wage-earner father/stay-at-home mother is a family structure few of today's families want or can afford. Nor do women want the contemporary variation on that structure that "allows" wives to work if the family needs the income but preserves the traditional role of husband-money manager and wife-homemaker. We cannot turn the clock back to a marriage contract meant for a different social system. But we can certainly uphold family values. Who could possibly be against "family values" if it means what it always has: adults caring about each other and teaching their children to be loving, responsible, productive people? Bad values, an equal opportunity problem, can be learned from family or peers in the slums, in the heartland, in school, in the corporation or the country club.

The traditional nuclear family structure led to an extremely high divorce rate, and certainly produced at least as much alcoholism, drug addiction, incest, and physical abuse as any other family structure. It could exist only through the sacrifice of women's autonomy. We need to strengthen the family values in the actual present-day structures of the American family. And this view was upheld recently by the men and women interviewed in a national survey. The vast majority of them did not define family values as having a traditional family. Nine out of ten of the women interviewed said, "Society should value all types of families." And the families that make up these new structures must in turn make their voices heard in their local communities and in the American polity.

That may sound very grandiose, but as Madeleine Kunin, three-time governor of Vermont and current U.S. Ambassador to Switzerland, has said, "The difference between community activities and political action is merely one of scale." As Kunin organized to better her children's lives, she took the next obvious step and got involved in local politics. But she never deviated from her family focus. The result of her efforts and the efforts of so many idealistic young families that settled in Vermont during the sixties and seventies was that Vermont was ranked the number one state for environmental policy, children's services, and mental health during much of Kunin's tenure as governor. And Kunin was rated one of the nation's top ten education governors. I am reminded of my favorite quo-tation, something credited to Margaret Mead: "Never doubt that a small group of thoughtful, committed citizens can change the world. Indeed, it's the only thing that ever has."

The more that men are involved with the daily workings of family life, the easier it will be to get legislation that supports family needs. And the more that women learn to translate their personal needs into political action, the more that public policy will reflect real American values. There has seldom been a time when we have so urgently needed to return an ethos of caring about others to the American dialogue. We need a new vision of communal life that we can relate to—one that calls forth our caring, not our fears; one that describes more than the "information superhighway" that lies ahead. And this new vision should include an extension of family values into the larger society, such values as taking responsibility for ourselves and being responsible toward others, particularly those in need. As someone once said, we are not here to see through each other, but to see each other through.

Betty Carter is the director of the Family Institute of Westchester in White Plains, New York, and cofounder of the Women's Project in Family Therapy. Joan K. Peters is a journalist and the author of the novel "Manny and Rose" (St. Martin's Press).

Should This Marriage Be Saved?

Many Americans are trying to make marriages more permanent—and divorce more difficult

ELIZABETH GLEICK

ON A CHILLY MONDAY NIGHT, Laura Richards and Mark Geyman are sitting in a living room in Jeffersonville, Indiana, their hands clasped tightly together in Laura's lap. This attractive, clean-cut couple met last May through a mutual friend and got engaged in November, and they are happy to tell John and Patti Thompson, their mentors in the St. Augustine Catholic Church's marriage-preparation program, all about their wedding plans. It will be a big June affair, Laura says, with eight bridesmaids and eight groomsmen, two flower girls, a ring bearer and two priests. Patti Thompson cuts through the chatter. "How much time have you put into your marriage?" she asks, adding pointedly, "Your wedding is just one day. Your marriage is the rest of your life."

The conversation grinds to a brief, awkward halt, then takes a turn into the wilderness—into the thicket of this young couple's most intimate concerns and darkest fears. Patti tells Laura, a 29-year-old department store salesclerk, that in her opinion it is O.K. to take birth-control pills on the advice of her doctor to help with PMS. Then John, coordinator of family ministry at St. Augustine, says, "Is either one of you jealous?"

"Yeah," admits Mark, who works in international customer service for United Parcel Service. He laughs and adds, "She gets jealous of some of the girls in the office," then explains how Laura once visited him at his previous job and became uncomfortable after she overheard him repeatedly compliment a female co-worker on her job performance. Laura smiles nervously, fidgets with a pen and says nothing.

Patti urges Laura and Mark to continue discussing Laura's jealousy when they are alone together. Soon the Thompsons hit upon other prickly topics: Mark's compulsive neatness and Laura's worry that her future mother-in-law has reservations about the pending nuptials.

After Mark and Laura leave, the first of four 90-minute sessions completed, the Thompsons—who have been married 31 years and have raised four children—offer an assessment of this couple's chances at marital harmony. It is based not just on gut impressions but also on a computer printout of the pair's "premarital inventory"— more than 100 questions about everything from the number of children they want to whether they are comfortable being naked in front of each other. Mark and Laura, who scored 72 out of 100 on this compatibility test, should do just fine, says Patti, but "there are just some things that smack you in the face that say they've got some work to do."

Working on a relationship, of course, is an activity that everyone—save for perhaps the most wildly romantic and misguided among us—has come to regard as a sometimes thrilling, sometimes infuriating, but always necessary exercise. But Mark and Laura, well meaning, full of love and hope, with their lives ahead of them and their family values just taking shape, are actually on the cutting edge—even if it is an old blade. Although the Catholic Church has always required engaged couples to undergo pre-Cana counseling—usually just one day of talks from a priest and a married couple about finances, communication and family planning—a more intensive form of preparation is coming into practice not only among Catholics but also among churchgoers of all denominations across America. Last November clergy in the Louisville, Kentucky, area became the 26th religious coalition in the U.S. to adopt standard premarital procedures that, in the words of the Kentuckiana

Marriage Task Force, express "the seriousness with which we view marriage and the preparation we are convinced is vital." Says Michael McManus, author of the 1993 *Marriage Savers* and a national leader of this particular bandwagon: "We're preventing bad marriages. If it is the job of a church to bond couples for life, it has to provide more help before and after."

If this new marital *gravitas* were simply a church-based phenomenon, it would not be a phenomenon at all; the clergy has traditionally attempted to shore up the moral foundations of people's private lives. But a growing recognition that marriages are not to be entered into—or dissolved—lightly because of the enormous social and economic costs is dawning in some unlikely places and crossing political lines. Conservatives who espouse "family values" have long lamented the trend toward throwaway marriage and quickie divorce. But in President Clinton's recent State of the Union speech he too took time out to introduce the Revs. John and Diana Cherry, whose ministry convinces couples "to come back together to save their marriages and to raise their kids." Meanwhile, there is a new sensitivity among divorce lawyers that breakups can have a devastating effect on everyone involved—and so comes a nudge toward reconciliation or mediation, lost revenues be damned! An increasing number of marital therapists believe it is their job to save the relationship rather than simply help each party pursue his or her chosen path.

Several people have gone so far as to suggest imposing a waiting period for marriage licenses, modeled after gun laws. "Both kinds of licenses," explains historian Glenda Riley, author of *Divorce: An American Tradition*, "create a volatile situation." And just last week, a group of mostly

From *Time*, February 27, 1995, pp. 48–53, 56. © 1995 by Time Inc. Magazine Company. Reprinted by permission.

female state lawmakers in Washington introduced a bill that would require marriage licenses to come with warnings about spousal abuse. "I would say, simply, 'Beware. Stop, look, listen and be cautious,' " said state senator Margarita Prentice, a cosponsor of the bill, which is expected to pass the Democratic Senate but run into trouble in the Republican House. "Marriage is serious business."

In 1993, 2.3 million couples—in living rooms and city halls, in churches and synagogues and backyards, on mountaintops and while scuba diving—performed that most optimistic of human rituals and got married. That same year, 1.2 million couples agreed, officially, that their marriages could not be saved. Again in 1993, the Bureau of the Census projected that four out of 10 first marriages would end in divorce. Indeed, the number of divorces began soaring in the mid-60s and has declined only slightly since peaking at a little over 1.2 million in 1981. Thus, despite sporadic cheers about falling divorce rates, couples have not gotten much better at staying together—not yet anyway. Divorce, Glenda Riley claims, reflects the true American spirit; after the country achieved independence, she says, people wrote divorce petitions that read something like: "My husband is tyrannical. If the U.S. can get rid of King George, I can get rid of him."

T HE INSTITUTION OF MARRIAGE underwent a particularly rebellious and dramatic shift when women entered the work force. "People don't have to stay married because of economic forces now," explains Frank Furstenberg Jr., co-author of the 1991 Divided Families and a sociology professor at the University of Pennsylvania who has been studying divorce for 20 years. "We're in the midst of trying to renegotiate what the marriage contract is—what men and women are supposed to do as partners." But the chips in these negotiations are often young children, emotionally fragile, economically vulnerable—for despite their work outside the home, most women still suffer a severe income drop after divorce. The by-product of what remains the world's highest divorce rate is millions of children thrown into poverty, millions more scarred by bifurcated lives and loyalties.

Almost no one disputes there are many valid reasons for divorce—among them, domestic violence, child abuse and substance abuse. Mere incompatibility seems reason enough, when no children are involved. But the breakup of families is increasingly seen not only as a personal tragedy but also as a social crisis. Which may be why, suddenly, there seems to be so much attention being paid to preventing divorce. "We're seeing a trend in the past couple of years toward cou-

ples doing more work to preserve and strengthen relationships," says Froma Walsh, co-director of the Center for Family Health at the University of Chicago.

Certainly marital therapy has become big business in the past decade or so, though few hard figures are available. Some 4.6 million couples a year visit 50,000 licensed family therapists, up from 1.2 million in 1980. Thousands of couples swear by such programs as PAIRS (Practical Application of Intimate Relationship Skills), the semester-long relationship class offered by the PAIRS Foundation in 50 U.S. cities (as well as 16 other countries), or Retrouvaille, a church-sponsored program in which couples who have weathered their own marital difficulties run weekend seminars for other couples in trouble.

"People are poorly trained for marriage today," says Joyce Clark, a coordinator for Retrouvaille in Youngstown, Ohio. From her 34-year marriage she recognizes all the stages of matrimony: romance, casual irritation, (he doesn't put the toilet seat down; she stays on the phone too long), then total disillusionment. "This is when many couples decide to bail out. They don't realize that they can still work back to romance," says Clark, who suffered through five years of misery after discovering her husband Pat had had an affair. Then she and Pat attended a Retrouvaille weekend and learned how to forgive, how to get over it—and how to fight. "Everyone I knew who had the same problem was divorced," says Joyce of the crisis in her marriage. "I wanted to find one person who survived and was in good shape. Now we work in the movement because somebody out there is waiting to see us."

Perhaps the newest, and most unlikely, recruits in the battle against divorce are lawyers. Last fall Lynne Gold-Bikin, a divorce attorney in Norristown, Pennsylvania, who chairs the family law division of the American Bar Association, founded the Preserving Marriages Project. "Divorce lawyers as individuals have no vested interest in saving marriages," Gold-Bikin says. "It's not our business. But we know the problems more than anyone else. Every day we see kids being yanked back and forth. Enough. I'm sick of people not recognizing what they're doing."

Last October, Gold-Bikin took her project—to which some 3200 lawyers have contributed time and money—to more than 50 high-school classrooms nationwide. During five sessions, juniors and seniors do role-playing exercises and homework designed to give an overview of family law and show how difficult it can be to maintain a serious relationship. "We're trying to teach these things to kids because many are not learning them at home," Gold-Bikin says. In March, Gold-Bikin will conduct a weekend seminar for couples who have been married one year; after that, she hopes to create a marriage-

Taking Stock

PREPARE (Premarital Personal and Relationship Evaluation), a set of 125 questions developed by University of Minnesota family social science professor David Olson to assess a couple's compatibility, has been administered to some 500,000 couples worldwide. The results are computer scored, and, claims Olson, can determine with 80% to 85% accuracy which couples will divorce. "Ten percent [of those who take the inventory] are so shocked by their poor scores, they break their engagement," contends Michael McManus, author of Marriage Savers. "That can be painful, but much less painful than a divorce with two kids." Individuals are asked if they ·"Agree Strongly," "Agree," are "Undecided," "Disagree," or "Disagree Strongly" with statements such as the following:

▶ I believe most disagreements we currently have will decrease after marriage.

▶ I expect that some romantic love will fade after marriage.

▶ I am concerned about my partner's drinking/smoking.

▶ I wish my partner was more careful in spending money.

▶ I am satisfied with the amount of affection I receive from my partner.

▶ My partner and I sometimes disagree regarding our interest in sex.

▶ I have some concerns about how my partner will be as a parent.

▶ We disagree on whether the husband's occupation should be a top priority in deciding where we live.

▶ I can easily share my positive and negative feelings with my partner.

▶ My partner is less interested in talking about our relationship than I am.

▶ We have some important disagreements that never seem to get resolved.

▶ I enjoy spending some time alone without my partner.

▶ At times I feel pressure to participate in activities my partner enjoys.

▶ My partner and I agree on how much we will share the household chores.

▶ We sometimes disagree on how to practice our religious beliefs.

preservation program for corporations, which she claims suffer tremendous productivity losses because of divorce.

All such efforts are applauded by Judith Wallerstein, the California clinical psychologist who first raised public consciousness about the lasting damage of divorce. After studying 131 children of divorce over a span of 15 years, she found them to be at higher risk for depression, poor grades, substance abuse and intimacy problems. "We started to report this," she says, "and people got angry. They said, 'Impossible! If it's good for the parents, it's good for the children.' They wanted to believe that divorce and women's lib would take care of everything."

Though Wallerstein's results are debatable, they have definitely seeped into the zeitgeist and affected not only efforts to stay married but also how people approach divorce. More and more often, couples are seeking to avoid ugly fights over custody, property and money. A St. Louis, Missouri, couple who do not want their names used are dissolving their marriage after 17 years, two daughters, couples therapy and individual counseling. They have chosen to use a mediator and work out the details at the kitchen table. "It's a much healthier environment for [the children]," says the wife, a Presbyterian minister. "They see that we still treat each other with respect." The six- to eight-month process will cost $2,500 and produce a divorce decree, a property agreement and a parenting plan to be submitted for court approval.

On the state level too, there is a growing belief that if divorcing couples cannot reconcile, they should at least be taught how to split in a reasonable fashion. Bucking the trend to make divorce ever easier and quicker, Utah and Connecticut have mandatory education programs for all parents of minor children entering the family court. Six states are considering such regulations in a current session of their legislature. "This is the latest trend in family courts," says Michael Pitts, who until recently was executive director of the Children's Rights Council in Washington, "and it is a lasting one. "

In many other states, including Maryland, Virginia, New Jersey and Florida, divorce-education classes are required in some counties, or at the discretion of some family court judges. Some family judges have even taken it upon themselves to involve the children directly. As of last November, divorcing parents in Dade County, Florida, attend one mandatory course, while children attend another, called Kids in Divorce Succeeding (KIDS). Sherri Thrower, a 30-year-old mother of five, says the parenting classes have really helped her. "There were a lot of cobwebs in my mind," she says. "A lot of confusion." She and her husband tried several times to reconcile for the sake of the children, but the attempts ultimately failed. Now her main concern is for her kids. "I don't want to teach them anything bad about their father," she says. "My son has been missing him more and more. He doesn't know how to deal with it." Thrower's children have attended the KIDS program, which uses a curriculum called Sandcastles.

IN SANDCASTLES THE CHILDREN ARE divided into small groups by age, and each group is run by a therapist and a teacher. Older children may write poems, do role-playing or create their own talk shows, while the younger kids draw pictures of their families and talk about them, or write letters to their parents and read them aloud. "When you come home from court, I want you to have a happy face, not a sad one," reads Edward, 10, during the Saturday morning session. "Mom, I love you. Dad, I miss you," says Dave. Another child reads, "If you were divorced, you wouldn't fight. I wish you were divorced." Explains psychotherapist Gary Neuman, who developed Sandcastles: "When kids see there are all these other kids experiencing the same type of things, it immediately alleviates the intense feelings of isolation children of divorce experience."

Though the Federal Government has no jurisdiction over marriage and divorce, indirectly the impact of federal programs is enormous. Current welfare policy, for example, pays AFDC benefits only when there is no man in the house, thus fueling divorce and abandonment. And in a broader sense says University of California, Berkeley, sociology professor Arlie Hochschild, author of the landmark study about two-career marriages, *The Second Shift*, "we do not have a family-friendly society." Better day care, plentiful jobs at decent wages, flex- time and job sharing would all help to reduce the stresses on American households, which are overtaxed, overburdened and overwhelmed. And while entering into marriage with the utmost care and deepest consideration can only be to the good, it may be marriage itself—along with the most basic institutions like the workplace—that continues to need refining. "I would say we're in a stalled revolution," says Hochschild, "Women have gone into the labor force, but not much else has changed to adapt to that new situation. We have not rewired the notion of manhood so that it makes sense to men to participate at home. Marriage then becomes the shock absorber of those strains."

Mark Geyman and Laura Richards are convinced that they are increasingly prepared to handle those strains. Since they began meeting with Patti and John Thompson, says Mark, "we have done a lot of talking, more than we were." They have had conversations about whose family they will see during holidays and how they will handle their finances. And they have tried to grapple with the problem of Laura's jealousy. "It's been helpful," says Mark. "I think she's beginning to open up a little more. She's being more trusting." The fact that one of Laura's sisters is going through a divorce makes the idea of building a secure marriage from the outset feel all the more urgent to this young couple. And in spite of the problems that have begun to crop up during a time when they wish only to focus on the excitement of planning a wedding, Laura insists she is looking into her future with, well, a somewhat tempered confidence. As she puts it, "I'm still sure we want to get married, and everything."

—*Reported by* *Ann Blackman/Washington, Gideon Gil/Jeffersonville, Jenifer Mattos/New York, Elizabeth B. Mullen/San Francisco, Sophfronia Scott Gregory/Miami, and Leslie Whitaker/Chicago*

lessons from stepfamilies

Yes, they are more complicated. But they're also richer. Stepfamilies turn out to be living laboratories for what it takes to create successful relationships. They have surprising things to tell us all about marriage, gender relations, parenting, and the intricacies of family life.

Virginia Rutter

Virginia Rutter is a freelance writer living in Seattle who reports on family, marital, and sex research, among other things. She has worked as public affairs director at the Johns Hopkins School of Public Health and the American Association for Marriage and Family Therapy. She is currently coordinating a project on collaborative, psychosocial health care.

Here we are, three decades into the divorce revolution, and we still don't quite know what to make of stepfamilies. We loved the Brady Bunch, but that was before we discovered how unreal they were. Now that stepfamilies embrace one of three children and, one way or another, impact the vast majority of Americans, we can't seem to get past seeing them as the spawn of failure, the shadow side of our over-idealized traditional family. When we think of them at all, we see only what they are not—hence their designation as "nontraditional" families, heaped with unwed moms, gay parents, and other permutations that make up the majority of families today. By the year 2000, stepfamilies will outnumber all other family types.

Despite their ambiguous standing, stepfamilies are getting first-class attention from social scientists. Much of what they are discovering is eye-opening. Although, for example, it is widely known that second marriages are less stable than first ones—with a break-up rate of 60 percent, versus 50 percent for first marriages—that statistic paints stepfamilies with too broad a brush; it conceals their very real success. A far more useful, more important fact is that stepfamilies do indeed face instability, but that shakiness occurs early in the re-marriage—and may ultimately be traced to lack of support from the culture. In denying them the status of "real family," we may be doing much to undermine their chances of success. Nevertheless, once re-marriage families make it over the early hurdle, they are even stronger than traditional families.

Let this turnabout truth serve as a metaphor for what is now coming to light about stepfamilies. They are certainly more complex than first-marriage families—but they are also richer. New information about what really goes on, and what goes wrong, in stepfamilies will definitely change the way you think about them. It also promises to change the way you think about *all* families. Among the new findings:

• Contrary to myth, stepfamilies have a high rate of success in raising healthy children. Eighty percent of the kids come out fine.

• These stepkids are resilient, and a movement to study their resilience—not just their problems—promises to help more kids succeed in any kind of family, traditional or otherwise.

• What trips stepkids up has little to do with stepfamilies per se. The biggest source of problems for kids in stepfamilies is parental conflict leftover from the first marriage.

•A detailed understanding of the specific problems stepfamilies encounter now exists, courtesy of longitudinal research—not studies that tap just the first six months of stepfamily adjustment.

•Stepfamilies turn out to be a gender trap—expectations about women's roles and responsibilities are at the root of many problems that develop in stepfamilies.

•After five years, stepfamilies are more stable than first-marriage families, because second marriages are happier than first marriages. Stepfamilies experience most of their troubles in the first two years.

•Stepfamilies are not just make-do households limping along after loss. All members experience real gains, notably the opportunity to thrive under a happier relationship.

•The needs of people in stepfamilies are the needs of people in all families—to be accepted, loved, and cared about; to maintain attachments; to belong to a group and not be a stranger; and to feel some control by maintaining order in their lives. It's just that these needs are made acutely visible—and unavoidable—in stepfamilies.

THE MYTHS AND THE RESEARCH

Despite the prevalence of stepfamilies, myths about them abound. You probably know some of them: There's an Evil Stepmother, mean, manipulative, and jealous. The stepfather is a molester, a sexual suspect—Woody Allen. The ex-wife is victimized, vindictive, interfering—a She-Devil. The ex-husband is withdrawn, inept, the contemporary Absentee Father. And the kids are nuisances intent on ruining their parents' lives; like Maisie in Henry James' story of 19th century post-divorce life, they play the parents and stepparents like billiard balls.

The familiarity of these myths can't be blamed solely on Dan Quayle, nor on nostalgia for the 1950s. Stepfamilies are a challenge. There are attachments that must be maintained through a web of conflicting emotions. There are ambiguities of identi-

Reprinted with permission from *Psychology Today,* May/June 1994, pp. 30-33, 60, 62, 64, 66, 68-69. © 1994 by Sussex Publishers, Inc.

ty, especially in the first years. Adults entering stepfamilies rightly feel anxious about their performance in multiple roles (spouse, instant parent) and about their acceptance by the kids and by the ex-spouse, who must remain a caring parent to the children. When an ex-spouse's children become someone else's stepchildren and spend time in a "stranger's" home, he or she worries about the children's comfort, their role models—and their loyalty.

Out of this worry are born the mythic stereotypes—and the fear of reliving a bad fairy tale. A stepmother, for example, forced to take on the role of disciplinarian because the children's biological father may lack a clear understanding of his own responsibilities—is set up to be cast as evil.

'Stepfamilies turn out to be a gender trap—expectations about women's roles are at the root of many problems that develop in stepfamilies.'

Still, there is a growing recognition among researchers that for every real pitfall a myth is built on, stepfamilies offer a positive opportunity in return. Researchers and stepfamilies are asking questions about resilience and health, not just pathology. In "The Family In Transition," a special issue of the *Journal of Family Psychology* in June 1993, editors and stepfamily researchers Mavis Hetherington, Ph.D., and James Bray, Ph.D., explained it this way: "Although divorce and remarriage may confront families with stresses and adaptive challenges, they also offer opportunities for personal growth and more harmonious, fulfilling family and personal relationships. Contemporary research is focusing on the diversity of responses to divorce, life in a single-parent household, and remarriage."

It is now clear from detailed research that the adaptation to stepfamily relation-ships depends on the timing of the transition in the children's lives, the individuals involved, and the unique changes and stresses presented to the group.

THE 80 PERCENT WHO SUCCEED
Take Hetherington's research, considered the definitive, longitudinal study of post-divorce families, conducted at the University of Virginia. She found that children in post-divorce and remarriage families may experience depression, conduct disorders, lower academic performance, and delinquency. Such problems are the result of reductions in parental attention that may immediately follow divorce or remarriage. There are the distractions of starting a new marriage. Such lapses may also be the outgrowth of parental conflict. They may reflect a noncustodial parent's withdrawal from the scene altogether. There's the stress of reductions in resources—typically, the lowered income of divorced mothers—and the disruption of routines, so highly valued by children, when two residences are established.

Hetherington, however, is quick to point to her finding that 80 percent of children of divorce and remarriage do *not* have behavior problems, despite the expectations and challenges, compared to 90 percent of children of first marriage families. Kids whose parents divorce and remarry are not doomed.

This high success rate, Hetherington and others recognize, is a testament to the resilience of children. Further study, she believes, can teach us more about the strengths summoned up in stepfamilies—and how to support them. But that would also contradict the gloom-and-doom scenarios that, though they do not actually describe most stepfamilies, often get trotted out on state occasions.

Needless to say, scientifically researching strength and resilience in stepfamilies, complete with a control group, poses great challenges. Building a scientific model of stepfamilies isn't simply trying to pin down a moving target, it's like trying to pin down many moving targets—up to four sets of kids from previous marriages in as many residences at different times—with none of them on the same radar screen at once.

From the standpoint of the kids, yes, they feel loss going into a stepfamily—it certifies that their original family exists no more. And it takes time to adjust to a new set of people in family roles. But the new arrangement is not just a problem appearing in their lives by default. Elizabeth Carter, M.S.W., director of the Westches-ter Family Institute, points to specific opportunities a stepfamily affords. Children acquire multiple role models, they get a chance to see their parents happier with other people than they were with each other. They learn how to be flexible.

Because they come into the world with no relationship ties but must forge their own, stepfamilies provide a living laboratory for studying what makes all families successful, insists psychologist Emily Visher, Ph.D., who cofounded the Stepfamily Association of America in 1979 with her husband, psychiatrist John Visher, M.D., after finding herself in a stepfamily and no rules to go by. For their pioneering efforts, the Vishers jointly received a Lifetime Contribution Award from the American Association for Marriage and Family Therapy at its annual meeting last fall.

Addressing an audience packed to the rafters in a mammoth sports arena, Visher

'Stepfamilies provide lessons for all families, because their emotions and problems are common—but they are exposed by an open structure.'

emphasized that "stepfamilies provide lessons for all families, because their emotions and problems are common to all people—but they are exposed by the open structure of stepfamilies." The process of bonding and belonging is made entirely, sometimes painfully, visible.

THE COPARENTING FACTOR
It turns out that it's the parents, not the stepfamily, that make the most difference in the success of stepfamilies.

"Remember, divorce isn't ending the family. It is restructuring it," explains Carter. "Parents and children don't get divorced. Parents and children aren't an optional relationship. One of the biggest issues for stepfamilies is: How can we stay in touch?" The steady, regular involvement of both biological parents in their children's lives come what may is known in the family biz as coparenting.

Today's most familiar stepfamily setup is a mother and her biological children living with a man who is not their birth father, and a noncustodial father in another residence—although the dilemmas of maintaining parenting responsibilities are much more complicated than who lives with whom. The U.S. Bureau of the Census reports that 14 percent of children in stepfamilies live with their biological father, 86 percent live with their biological mother and their stepfather. Whatever the situation, the parents' job is to find a way to stay in touch with each other so that both can remain completely in touch with their children.

Study after study shows that divorce and remarriage do not harm children—parental conflict does. That was the conclusion of research psychologists Robert Emery, Ph.D., of the University of Virginia, and Rex Forehand, Ph.D., of the University of Georgia, in a 1993 review of the divorce research. Sociologist Andrew Cherlin, Ph.D., author of the classic *Divided Families*, reported in *Science* magazine that children with difficulty after divorce started having problems long before divorce took place, as a result of parental conflict.

While divorce forces temporary disruption and a period of adjustment to loss and to new routines, marital conflict produces long-term disturbances. Depression and anger, often acted out in behavior problems, substance abuse, and delinquency, are all especially common among children in families where conflict rages. Following divorce, adversarial coparenting or the withdrawal of one of the parents from his or her (but usually his) role undermines children's healthy development.

The solution, of course, is cooperation of the parents in coparenting following divorce and remarriage. Desirable as it is, cooperative parenting between divorced spouses is rare, attained only in a minority of cases, Hetherington and Bray note.

WHY IS COPARENTING SO DIFFICULT?
Most marriages don't end mutually with friendship—so jealousy and animosity are easily aroused—and ex-spouses aren't two folks practiced at getting along anyway. Yet the ability of exes to get along is a key to the success of a new stepfamily.

Remarriage of one or both ex-spouses only enlarges the challenge of getting along —while possibly increasing tension between the ex-spouses responsible for coparenting. A stepparent who becomes a part of the kids' lives usually has no relationship to the child's other biological parent; if anything there is hostility.

The ideal, says John Visher, is creation of a "parenting coalition" among the parents and stepparents in both households. "From the beginning, the new couple needs to work together in making family decisions." One of the most important is how, and by whom, the children will be disciplined, and on that score the evidence is clear: only a birth parent has the authority to discipline his or her children.

Betty Carter is quick to warn, however, that stepparents cannot interfere with their spouse in parenting. Involved but not interfering? A parenting coalition requires the parents include their new spouses in family decisions. The new spouses, for their part, must support the parenting duties and the coparenting bond between the ex-spouses.

IT TAKES RESPECT
The glue that makes it all happen is respect, the Vishers report. Both parents must require kids and stepparents to treat one another with respect. Only then can bonds between them develop. Despite feelings of jealousy and animosity, first and second spouses must also accord one another respect to accomplish the coparenting tasks the children need to do well.

For their part, the kids also need each of the coparents to refer to the other parent with respect. Children are quick to pick up hints of hostility on either side. For them, hostility becomes an invitation to play the grown-ups off each other, and to imitate unkind behavior.

> 'Children are quick to pick up hints of hostility on either side. For them, it becomes an open invitation to play the grown-ups off each other.'

When the parents are adversarial, their hostility inhibits children from freely spending time with both parents, and the kids suffer. They lack the one-on-one attention that breeds a sense of self-value. And they are torn in half. All in all, it's a recipe for disappointment and anger.

ANY HELP?
"If you can help parents and stepparents early on to deal with issues of child-rearing appropriately, they have a lot of potential for giving stability to children and exposing them to appropriately happy relationships," says Australian research psychologist Jan Lawton. Lawton is spokesperson for The Stepfamily Project at the University of Queensland, a major government study of behavioral interventions for stepfamilies with troubled children.

What kind of help do stepfamilies need? Information and support. Stepfamily support groups exist across the United States, many of them organized by the Stepfamily Association. The organization responds to about 400 information requests each week from stepfamilies—while 7,000 new stepfamilies are forming weekly.

Stepfamily functioning improves dramatically when participants know which problems are normal, which are temporary, and that it takes time for people to integrate themselves and feel comfortable in a stepfamily. Lawton's study has demonstrated the benefits of practical guidance, and she has found that even a little help goes a long way. "The positive part of this study is that we can help stepfamilies with a very minimal amount of therapy and self-help, aimed at the right areas." The components of the Queensland program are a map of stepfamily problem areas.

•Child-Management Training, for parents and stepparents, to help them focus their attention on the children at a time when there's a tendency to slip a little on monitoring and disciplining the kids. The adults often get overly absorbed in their new romance.

•Partner-Support Training for newly remarried couples, since they don't automatically work together as a team during the first two years, when they are also at high risk for divorce. Such support helps them while their relationship is undergoing trial by fire in the new stepfamily.

•Communication and Problem-Solving Training for the entire new stepfamily helps everyone learn to talk together, understand each other, and learn how to solve problems and reach consensus.

Lawton reports as much as a 60 percent reduction in behavior problems and about 50 percent improvement in child adjustment, self-esteem, and parent/stepparent conflict. While therapy had a slight margin over self-help, persons in both groups outperformed by far the control group that received no help during the study. Those with the most troubled children do best with formal therapy; the rest do fine with self-help. Indeed, programs families could apply at home are especially useful, since stepfamilies involve people already weighed down by multiple demands, and coordinating a formal appointment can be formidable.

The key, Lawton says, is to reach stepfamilies at the beginning when they need basic information about what to expect. Lawton's next project is a prevention study, seeking the most effective ways to help all stepfamilies—not just ones where the children have behavior problems.

MORE HELP: A HAPPY MARRIAGE

If coparenting can be accomplished, children benefit in at least two ways. They feel loved by both biological parents; no child can thrive without affectionate connections. And they gain from being exposed to remarried adults in a successful intimate relationship. Especially when remarriage occurs before the children are teenagers, there is great potential for easy adaptation and smooth development.

A remarriage at adolescence, however, poses added challenges to adjustment and success of the stepfamily, Bray and Hetherington report. It's a critical time of identity formation. Daughters are particularly apt to get into fights with stepmothers. Sexual tension may develop between stepfather and a budding adolescent stepdaughter, manifest in aloofness and what every parent knows as snottiness. Even if the divorce occurred many years before, a parent's remarriage during a child's teen years can revive adjustment difficulties that may have cropped up during the divorce.

Generally, though, a successful second marriage helps to reduce—if not eliminate—kids' problems. Divorced people are generally more compatible with their second partner than their first—even though there is a higher divorce rate among second marriages.

Clinical psychology lore has it that the high divorce rate is because the spouses are making the same mistake again. Divorcing spouses have problems with intimate relationships, not with a particular partner, the

thinking goes, and they are more apt to bail out a second time.

But this view is totally contradicted by those who have closely scrutinized many stepfamilies. The Vishers are among them. So is University of Southern California sociologist Constance Ahrons, Ph.D. They point out that a lot of second divorces are the result not of conventional marital deterioration but of problems in integrating into a household children and adults who are not related to each other.

"The divorce rate among remarried families is high in the first two years—then it slows down," says Lawton. "By about the five-year period, second relationships are more stable than first relationships. I see these couples at very high risk during the first few years, but thereafter offering great benefits to the children."

LOOKING AT THE PROBLEMS

While stepfamilies are doing a lot better than they're generally given credit for, a not insubstantial 20 percent of them—or twice the number of first-marriage families—do have problems with the kids. The research illuminating the specific problems in stepfamilies points to the basic requirements of stepfamilies as the major stumbling blocks. Cooperative coparenting. Equal involvement of both parents after the divorce. Noninterference by stepparents.

> 'Sexual tension may develop between stepfather and adolescent stepdaughter, and manifest in aloofness and snottiness.'

Support for the coparenting relationship.

Bray's longitudinal study of stepfamilies has tracked mothers, stepfathers, and children, who were around six years old at the time of remarriage, over the next seven years. During the early months of remarriage, behavior problems rise steeply among the children. This is a time when stepfamilies are not yet cohesive—they are not likely to think of themselves as a unit.

Gradually, behavior problems subside over the next two years. By then stepfamilies are just as likely as first-marriage families to have developed useful ways of communicating, rules of behavior, and discipline. They may not consider themselves as cohesive, but objective evaluation finds few practical differences.

In Bray's study, trouble with the children developed when there was a reduction in time and attention from one or both parents, and reduced resources. These parental lapses, Bray notes, arise most often from problems of coparenting, and difficulties of stepparents in supporting the coparenting role.

But even the reduced parental attention does not doom the children. Hetherington observes that the reduced parental attention can also be seen as an opportunity for the children to take on responsibility. The end result is that some children—almost always daughters—wind up more capable and competent.

Others, however, particularly at adolescence, respond to the lapse of parental attention by going off and experimenting with sex or drugs. Younger children may display more conduct problems and depression. Both younger and older kids are at risk for lower academic achievement.

While few distinctions turn up between the ways daughters and sons react to being in a stepfamily, Bray did find increased conflict between stepfathers and stepdaughters at puberty. Hetherington also found difficulties with teenage daughters, and warns that remarriage when a daughter is entering adolescence promises to produce tremendous tension and resentment on the part of the daughter.

Daughters, who have grown close to their mothers and increasingly identify with them at the onset of puberty, will have difficulty with the addition of either a mother's new spouse, who is competition for her, or a father's new spouse—who is competition for her mother. What the girls are feeling is divided loyalty.

DIVIDED LOYALTIES

Stepfamilies are littered with possibilities for loyalty conflicts, say the Vishers. A particularly common one revolves around entry of new stepparent. A mom feels hostile toward her ex-husband's new partner; kids understand that their mom wants them to feel the same way. The same kids are also being asked by their dad to love the new wife, whom he loves. The kids feel torn because their parents are pulling them in opposite ways.

It is an axiom of psychology that when kids feel torn, they erupt in symptoms—like bad behavior or depression. It may be a desperate attempt to draw attention away from the unresolvable conflict between the parents. Whatever the source of divided loyalties, once kids feel them, they develop problems—if not behavior problems or depression, then the symptoms of anxiety. The solution? Back to coparenting. It is up to the adults to rise above jealousy or romanticism and work together for the good of the kids.

The respect they use to make the system operate must include appreciation for the inevitability of ambivalent feelings in the kids. And that, says Emily Visher, is one of the most important lessons from stepfamilies for all families. "The ability of adults to share with children ambivalence over loss and change determines how well they will do in the future. It paves the way for sharing other thoughts. It leads to a sense of mastery of whatever life presents."

'Lesson #1: The ability of adults to share with kids ambivalence over loss and change determines how well they will do in the future.'

One of the sizable traps in remarriage is the temptation a new spouse may feel to interfere with the coparenting process, observes William Doherty, Ph.D., family social scientist at the University of Minnesota. The new spouse may feel insecure or jealous of the coparent's continuing attachment to the former spouse. Still, that only succeeds in dividing the loyalty of the biological parent. A weekly conversation with an ex-spouse about the kids might trouble an anxious new spouse—but the communication is essential and the stepparent has the obligation to adjust, just as the parents do, for the good of the kids.

On the other hand, no stepparent should be expected to love, or even like, a partner's kids, nor must demands be placed on kids to love the stepparent. Loyalty just can't be forced. A strong couple relationship is necessary to the success of the stepfamily, but it cannot hinge on whether the stepparent likes the kids, marital therapists agree. After all, a stepfamily essentially brings together strangers.

THE BASIC NEED: ACCEPTANCE

Stepfamilies can't push members into close relationships; still, they may feel the pain of absence of intimacy. Stepfamily life throws into bold relief very fundamental human needs—above all, says John Visher, the need to be a part of something. Entry into a stepfamily puts members in a position of assessing whether they are an insider or an outsider. A new wife belongs to her new husband, and he to her, but she is not a natural part of the husband's children's life. Feeling like an outsider to their relationship may be upsetting to her.

There's no fast solution for the inside/outside dilemma; stepfamilies come with a big catch in their very structure. The relationship between the parents and children predates the new marital relationship. It may even seem to outweigh it. A parent's love for a child must always be unconditional; couple love is not.

Joan Giacomini, a remarried parent and university administrator in Seattle, warns that it is hard for stepmothers to adjust to the fact that they are not number one to their new spouse. "There may be a handful of number ones, but you aren't the only number one," she says.

That gives rise to an all-too-common scenario: a remarried stepparent—often the stepmother—asks, "who is it going to be, me or your kids?" It's a false question—it leads to what Carter calls a "fake fight"—because it erroneously equates parent–child relationships and marital relationships, apples and oranges. Children are dependents; parental obligations to them are always unconditional.

Because the loyalty challenge rests on a mistaken assumption, Carter says, the proper solution is acceptance that relationships between parent and child are qualitatively different from those between spouses. Still, such conflicts can recur from time to time, as life continually presents new situations that assault the loyalties, resources, and time of kids and spouses.

THE ULTIMATE TRAP

Name a stepfamily dilemma and women—biomothers, stepmothers, even stepdaughters—are at the center of the problem. Psychologists know that women are always more likely to express distress wherever troubles exist. But stepfamilies are the ultimate gender trap. Ever-sensitive to interpersonal problems, women sense problems all over the place in stepfamilies.

Traditional male and female roles are troublesome enough, for the marriage and the children, in first-marriage families. But they wreak havoc on stepfamilies, Carter explains; they don't work at all. Indeed, researchers report that there's more equality in the marriage and in the distribution of domestic tasks in stepfamilies. But they still have a lot to learn—or unlearn—about gender roles and domestic life.

"No matter what we say or how feminist you are, everybody knows that women take care of children and men bring in most of the money. This sucks the stepmother into a quagmire of traditional domestic roles; it's not only that somebody makes her do it, she also does it to herself," explains Carter, coauthor of *The Invisible Web: Gender Patterns in Family Relationships.*

"We are raised to believe that we are responsible for everybody. A stepmother sees the children as unhappy and the husband as ineffectual, and she moves in to be helpful. Mavis Hetherington's research shows the consequence of this: a lot of fighting between teenage stepdaughters and stepmothers." Nevertheless, women move toward a problem to work on it—whether it's theirs to work on or not.

Trouble is, explains Carter, "in stepfamilies, everybody has to be in charge of their own children. A biological father has to understand that it is his responsibility to take charge. The stepmother has to back off, let the father do the monitoring and caretaking of the kids—even let him do it wrong. This is very hard to do; it flies in the face of all our gender training."

What's more, a large body of research on depression and marriage demonstrates that women's self-esteem becomes contingent upon relationships going smoothly; it holds in stepfamilies, as well. Women get depressed when stepfamily life goes badly, and they blame themselves.

For all its difficulty, the way parents in stepfamilies devise to take care of their own children contains another lesson for all families. "Stepfamilies demonstrate the importance of one-on-one relationships," says Emily Visher. "Parent–child alone time maintains the security of relationships. It requires conscious planning in all families. The health of all families resides in the quality of the relationships between members."

THE MYTH OF THE HAPPY FAMILY

If stepfamilies make it out of the gender trap, there's one more to avoid—the myth of the nuclear family. Successful stepfamilies let go of their fantasy of a traditional family life, reports James Bray. They become more realistic, less romantic, and more flexible about family. They can cope with what life deals.

But remarriage often sets up conditions pulling the other way. "There's often a sense of defensiveness," explains Betty Carter. "There's a feeling of 'let's not rock the boat this time. Let's be a happy family immediately so we can prove that this complicated thing—the divorce, the new marriage—was the right move.' People try to achieve an instant family, they don't allow for disgruntlement, fear, anxiety. Now we know it takes about five years for a stepfamily to become fully integrated."

Carter advises stepfamilies to "kiss the nuclear family good-bye. Stepfamilies simply cannot draw a tight circle around the household in the same way that nuclear families do. That always excludes somebody." The stepfamily's task is to keep permeable boundaries around the household, to facilitate coparenting, and to allow children access to the noncustodial parent.

It's a lot like tightrope-walking. "At the very time a stepfamily is trying to achieve its own integration, it has to keep the doors wide open and stay in touch with another household. You are not the lord of all you survey, as in the traditional family myth. You are on the phone regularly with someone about whom you feel, at best, ambivalent."

WHAT TO CALL IT?

Perhaps the most concrete evidence that old-fashioned family ideas don't work for stepfamilies is in the labels stepfamilies prefer for themselves.

Some people reject the label "stepfamily" altogether. Joan Giacomini is one. She is divorced from her grown children's father; he is remarried and has a toddler boy. Joan's husband has grown children from his first marriage, too, but she doesn't want to be referred to as a stepmother, nor does she like the idea of someone being referred to as the "stepmother" of her children.

"In our cases, we don't do any mothering. No one else is mother to my children, and my husband's children have their own mother," she explains. "One of my main goals is to respect their first family, so that they can have their relationships without worry about me." Despite dropping the "step" terminology, Giacomini's various families comprise a successful stepfamily that has respect, shared responsibility, even shared holidays.

Many stepfamilies who start off using step terminology eventually drop it all, reports James Bray. It may be the surest sign of integration. The terms "stepmother" and "stepfather" help clarify roles and remind everybody who belongs to whom, and under what terms, in the transition. Later, though, they don't bother with such names. "Labels connote a struggle for identity that doesn't exist anymore for these groups," says Bray.

For other stepfamilies, such as Ned and Joanna Fox—my mother and her husband—in Charlotte, North Carolina, there is little thought of stepfamily integration.

Nobody considers it a stepfamily, nor is anyone a stepsibling or stepparent. The kids were grown when the divorces and remarriages occurred, and none of the kids seem particularly interested in getting involved with the others. While Joanna's children treat Ned like an uncle, and value his love for Joanna, Ned's children don't warm up to the situation.

The moral of the story: Every stepfamily is different.

Some reject not merely the "stepfamily" label but stepfamily roles as well. In fact, the best way for a new spouse to move into stepparent life, suggests Barry Dym, Ph.D., a family psychologist (and remarried father) in Cambridge, Massachusetts, may be to find a different role than that of stepparent. The term itself may force the relationships into an unrealistic, and even intrusive, parental mold.

Dym suggests that stepmothers might do better modeling themselves after a favorite aunt—involved, but not the mother. My favorite aunt provides acceptance, guidance, honesty, but the obligation on either side is voluntary. If I become a stepmother, I think I'll be an aunt.

The naming issue underscores what stepfamilies have that original families don't always get: there is no monolithic view of what a stepfamily is supposed to be, or even be called. To catalog stepfamily experiences would be to catalog all relationships—there is endless variety, and unlimited routes to success or failure. Unlike traditional families, stepfamilies allow much more room for diversity. And equality. Count that as the ultimate lesson from stepfamilies.

CONTINUITIES AND DISCONTINUITIES IN FAMILY MEMBERS' RELATIONSHIPS WITH ALZHEIMER'S PATIENTS*

Thirty families who cared for a family member with Alzheimer's Disease were asked to provide narratives of daily care over one and one-half years. A key finding of the hermeneutic analysis of their narratives was that different family members experience their relationship with the AD patient to be continuous, continuous but transformed, or radically discontinuous with their relationship prior to the disease. Responsiveness to these qualities of family relations by professionals may ease family members' caregiving efforts.

Catherine Chesla, Ida Martinson,
and Marilou Muwaswes

Catherine Chesla is an Assistant Professor and Ida Martinson is a Professor in the Department of Family Health Care Nursing, University of California, San Francisco, California, 94143. Marilou Muwaswes is an Associate Clinical Professor, Physiological Nursing, University of California, San Francisco.

The central concern in research on families and Alzheimer's Disease (AD) in the past ten years has been to identify factors that place family members at risk for negative outcomes because of their involvement in AD care (Bowers, 1987; Colerick & George, 1986; Liptzin, Grob, & Eisen, 1988; Ory et al., 1985; Quayhagen & Quayhagen, 1988). This research has identified AD family caregivers to be at risk for poor physical health, mental health, and quality of life, when compared with family members who are not caregivers (Kuhlman, Wilson, Hutchinson, & Wallhagen, 1991). Family burden, resources (including social support), and AD patient characteristics and symptoms im-

*This research was conducted as part of a larger study "Impact of Alzheimer's Disease on the Family and Caregiver," by Ida Martinson, P.I., Catherine Gilliss, Glen Doyle and Marilou Muwaswes, Co-Investigators. The project was funded by Biomedical Research Support Grant, School of Nursing, University of California, San Francisco; Academic Senate Grant, UCSF; NRSA Post-Doctoral Fellowship Grant #1F31 NR06020, National Center for Nursing Research, NIH; Alzheimer's Disease and Related Disorders Association Paine-Knickerbocker Graduate Research Award.

Key Words: Alzheimer's disease, dementia, family caregiving, family relationships, intergenerational relationships.

(*Family Relations*, 1994, 43, 3-9.)

pact negative family outcomes, although factors that place family members most at risk remain to be specified (Baumgarten, 1989). In all of this research, however, AD patients are assumed to be a demand or a drain on family members.

Persons with AD are frequently described as experiencing a loss of self as the disease unfolds (Cohen & Eisdorfer, 1986). Progressive loss of memory, along with personality and behavior changes common to the disease, are thought to overwhelm those with the disease. AD patients are characterized as suffering from a biomedical disorder that severs them from their history and severely restricts their potential in life. The biomedicalization of dementia (Lyman, 1989) has restricted the scope of research to disease progression and biologic processes that give rise to the disease. Research about those who care for demented elders has similarly been restricted by the pervasiveness of the biomedical perspective to the questions about how the disease, in its various stages of progression, impacts family members. Largely unasked, and therefore unanswered, are questions about the lived experience of AD for the person with the disease, the family member's experience of living with and caring for the person with AD, and how qualities of the caregiving environment might influence disease progression (Lyman, 1989).

Research on caregivers of AD patients often progresses from the implicit assumption of particular relations between the ill family member and others in the family. One member in the relationship is assumed to be the passive recipient of care, holding less interpersonal power yet imposing demands and burdens. In a parallel way, the caregiving member is assumed to be an active provider, possessing relatively greater interpersonal power, but at risk of negative outcomes because of the burdens and risks experienced. Recent caregiver research suggests that the quality of relations between ill and other family members is complex, and that factors such as centrality of the relationship, personal qualities of both members, and the degree of reciprocity in the relationship may impact outcomes for both the ill and non-ill family members (Walker, Pratt, & Oppy, 1992; Wright, Clipp, & George, 1993).

One aim of this investigation was to question the assumption of a fixed relation between the family and the person with AD and additionally to specify the range of relations that were apparent in the day-to-day lives of family members living with a person with AD. As part of a larger study aimed at understanding the *experiences* of family members who cared for a person with AD over time, we critically examined family members' self-initiated discussion of relations with the person with AD, as well as the content and nature of those relations. Working directly from family members' narratives, we attempted to understand these relations in ways that formal theories, such as exchange or friendship theory, may have missed. We were interested in the whole of the family's experience; what was salient and meaningful for the family members themselves, the difficulties or demands they encountered (Martinson, Chesla, & Muwaswes, 1993) and the skills and practices they developed in living with a person with AD. Through family members' narratives over an 18-month time span, it was evident that relationship issues were paramount to family members in their everyday lives and that qualitatively distinct forms of relations between ill members and other family members were evident.

Relationships Between Caregivers and Family Members with AD

Although little attention has been paid to the positive or sustaining aspects of caring for a family member with AD, detailed studies of the relationship between the AD patient and the family show that: (a) relationships change over time and intimacy declines with time for some but not for all family members (Blieszner & Shifflett, 1990); (b) care of a family member with AD brings both suffering and rewards; and (c) reciprocity in the relationship with a family member with dementia seems to be a key aspect reported by families, but can take many forms (Farran, Keane-Hagarty, Salloway, Kupferer, & Wilken, 1991; Hirschfeld, 1983; Orona, 1990).

Blieszner and Shifflett (1990) produced a sensitive analysis of caregivers' responses to the first 18 months of care after AD had been diagnosed. They found that intimacy between AD patients and family caregivers diminished over the first 18 months of care and that a host of emotional responses was elicited for family caregivers at each point in time. At diagnosis, there was relief at having an understanding of what was happening, but also anger, sadness, and grief. Six months into the disorder, family members focused on the loss of the previously established relationship with the AD patient. One year and six months after diagnosis, caregivers were found to be coping with a dramatically changed but continuing relationship. Coping strategies that predominated were redefining the relationship, working on closure in the relationship, and working on expanding caregiver role responsibilities. These investigators found that, although caregivers on average felt less intimate with the person with AD, some caregivers reported increased intimacy as the disease progressed (Blieszner & Shifflett, 1989).

Hirschfeld (1983) developed in her grounded theory study a concept of "mutuality" in caregiver, care receiver relations. Mutuality was defined as the caregiver's capacity to find: (a) gratification in the relationship with the impaired person; (b) positive meaning from the caregiving situation; and (c) a sense of reciprocity, even in situations where the elder had severe dementia. The sample of 30 caregivers included both spouses and children of elders with senile brain disease. Most striking was Hirschfeld's finding that the higher the mutuality in the relationship, the less likely the caregiver was to consider institutionalization of the elder.

In a small grounded theory study of family members who cared for a member with AD, Orona (1990) focused on identity loss of the AD patient and its impact on the dyadic relationship over time. Using a social constructionist framework, Orona noted temporality as an important subjective aspect of the caregiving experience. Facets of temporal experience were: (a) the use of memories to maintain the identity of the AD person, (b) the re-enactment of meaningful social interactions with the AD person, and (c) the use of memories as a basis for constructing new images for the future. Caregivers were found to engage in "identity maintenance" via everyday activities with the AD family member, and when reciprocity was lost, these relatives "worked both sides of the relationship," or took on both the caregiver's and the AD patient's social roles, in order to continue some part of the past relating.

In summary, detailed studies that have examined a family member's experience with a relative with dementia over time undermine any standard depiction of the process. Rather, they demonstrate complex variability in issues of intimacy, reciprocity, and management of life tasks given the unbalanced capabilities of well and ill members. Questions remain about the basic nature of these relations and how they evolve over time.

METHOD

This study was designed within a tradition known as hermeneutic phenomenology (Benner & Wrubel, 1989; Packer & Addison, 1989; Van Manen, 1990). The aim of the method is to explain particular and distinct patterns of meaning and action in the lives of those studied, taking into account the context in which they live, their history, and their particular concerns. Rather than trying to characterize a modal or group response, research within this method provides detailed explanations of varied patterns of human understanding and action. The method is: (a) systematic in its use of practiced modes of questioning the informant about experiences; (b) explicit in its attempt to articulate, through careful interpretation of a text, the meanings embedded in human experience; (c) self-critical and self-corrective in its continual examination of interpretations made on a text; and (d) a shared interpretation that is consensually agreed upon by multiple readers (Van Manen, 1990).

This phenomenological study was part of a multifaceted, longitudinal study of the impact of Alzheimer's Disease on the family and caregiver (Martinson, Gilliss, Doyle, & Muwaswes, 1983). Only the phenomenologic interview data are reported here. Fifteen spouses and fifteen adult-child family members were recruited from support groups and clinics serving AD patients. Semistructured, intensive interviews were conducted at intake and every six months for 18 months. In each interview, family members were asked to reflect on their experiences in the previous 6 months and on changes in the AD patient, family members' feelings, and care arrangements. They were asked to provide narratives of salient, difficult, or memorable episodes of care that had arisen in the past 6 months. Full narratives of the episodes, preceding events, caregivers' emotions, thoughts, and actions throughout the episodes and outcomes were elicited. The interviews, which lasted approximately one hour, were audiotaped and transcribed verbatim.

Hermeneutic interpretation (Packer & Addison, 1989; Van Manen, 1990) of texts from the interviews comprise this paper. The first author, educated in Heideggerian philosophy and hermeneutics, directed the interpretive process and interpreted all texts with the third author. The second author was familiar with all interview texts and provided consensus on summary interpretations.

Interpretation was comprised of two interwoven processes: thematic interpretation and interpretation of exemplars. Three levels of thematic interpretation were used to uncover and isolate themes in a text: (a) the holistic approach, (b) the selective approach, and (c) the detailed or line-by-line approach. In the holistic approach, the whole text was read through and described as a piece in an attempt to capture the fundamental meaning of the text as a whole. In the selective approach, aspects of the text that stood out as essential or revealing of the phenomenon under study were the focus. A line-by-line detailed reading was then completed in which the text was examined for what it revealed about the experience. After completing all three steps, the text was examined in its entirety, in its particular salience, and for fine-grained nuances.

Interpretation of exemplars occurred simultaneously with the search for general themes. Exemplars are narratives of whole incidents of family care elicited from participants in the interviews. All relevant aspects of each exemplar were coded together, including the family member's recollection of what preceded the episode, how the episode unfolded, emotions at the start and throughout the episode, actions considered and taken, direct and indirect clues to what was at stake for the family, and the family member's retrospective reworking of the situation. These episodes, in their complete form, served as examples of particular patterns of action that included a rich description of the situation and responses that evidenced family member's understandings, concerns, and practical involvements with the AD patient.

FINDINGS

Description of Informants

Eighteen of the family members interviewed were female (7 wives and 11 daughters), and twelve were male (8 husbands and 4 sons). The mean age of family members was 57 years. Family members were predominantly Caucasian and from middle socioeconomic strata.

Eight male and 22 female persons with AD entered the study. Their mean age was 74 years (range 59-86) and the mean duration of the illness was 4 years (range 1-11 years). Twenty persons with AD at the start of the study resided in the home of a family member, seven were institutionalized in a nursing or board and care home, and three lived alone. Residence status changed with each data collection period, and at six months 17 AD patients lived in their caregiver's home, 11 lived in institutions, 1 lived alone, and 1 person with AD died. By 18 months, 8 were living in the caregiver's home, 8 were institutionalized, 1 was still living alone, 8 persons with AD had died, and 5 family members had withdrawn from the study.

Severity of the AD patients' illness, as measured by the Mini-Mental Status Exam (Folstein, Folstein, & McHugh, 1975) indicated moderate to severe cognitive dysfunction. Mean scores for AD patients were 9.4 (SD = 6.7) at induction and 6.4 (SD = 8.06) six months later on a 30-point scale, where a score below 24 indicates some cognitive impairment. On a second measure of illness severity, the Older Adults Multifunctional Assessment Questionnaire (Fillenbaum & Smyer, 1981), the AD patients scored significantly lower (p < .001) on measures of physical health and activities of daily living than a comparison group of institutionalized elderly.

Interpretive Findings

Continuity and discontinuity in the relationship between the family member and the person with AD were salient issues in two paradigm cases in an early reading of the narratives. A paradigm case is an outstanding instance of a pattern of narratives that seem to go together, the coherence of which is visible only through the whole reading of a particular case. Continuity and discontinuity in these two cases seemed to set up the kind of care that the family member had with the AD patient. The finding challenged our assumption of what AD relations might be, which most closely resembled a third pattern we eventually observed and labeled *continuous but transformed*. After recognition and identification of three predominant forms of relating through paradigm cases, the texts from the remaining informants were identified as being strongly similar to the aspects of relating evident in these three predominant forms.

One aspect of the experience of living with and caring for a family member with AD is presented in this article: the existential relation that family members had with their spouse or parent with AD as evidenced by their narratives of providing day-to-day care. Three forms of relationship will be presented: (a) a relationship that is maintained as continuous with the relationship between caregiver and AD patient prior to the disease, (b) a relationship that is continuous but is transformed by the disease, and (c) a relationship in which there is radical discontinuity between the present and prior relationship.

Relationship as Continuous

Some family members found possibilities in their relationships to continue to be a wife, daughter, husband or son to the person with AD. Despite the changes in the person with AD, family members continued to define themselves "in relation to" the patient in ways that paralleled their relations prior to the disease. These family members interpreted small gestures or statements made by the AD patient as continuous with past behavior and found remnants of the AD patient's intentions, wishes, likes and dislikes in present behavior. Dramatic losses and changes in the relationship were not denied and there was particular sensitivity in this group to patients' functional and memory losses. Despite realistic assessment and grieving, these family members felt a sense of connection to and continuity with the patient. They watched for, held precious, and felt comforted by, familiar responses and behaviors by the patient.

One woman exemplifies continuous relating with an AD spouse. She is a 75-year-old woman who had been married to her husband for more than 54 years. The husband had shown signs of AD for the past 10 years and during the course of the study declined from almost complete dementia to death.

This woman's narratives provide evidence that her relationship to her husband is almost unaltered from the life they shared prior to the illness. Despite the AD, she finds access to his person, his intelligence, and his capacity to comfort her. She is distressed that her husband, who never used profanity, now curses her in anger and tries to hit her if he is confused. However, the man with whom she built a life and a family, the person that comprised her world prior to the illness, continues to define her world and focus her daily concerns. She finds comfort that they can share a bed together and feels his presence very strongly in her life. In the first two interviews, when they lived together in their retirement apartment, she noted repeated instances where her husband seemed present and interacted with her in familiar ways:

> Wife: The other morning, for instance, he woke up early and I was just barely awake, and he reached over and held my hand. So you know that is a lot really. He's here. He always has been a very gentle, caring sort of person.

She noted incidents where he commented on her clothes, "I always liked you in that," or tried to comfort her when she became tearful. From an outsider's perspective, his behavior could have been interpreted as random or meaningless, but the woman interprets it as meaningful, coherent, and indicative of his past and present personhood.

This woman's respect for her husband's continuity of person appears in the way she approaches his physical care. She values his lifelong habits and practices and continues them for him now that he cannot carry them out.

> Wife: My son said 'Well you don't have to shave Dad everyday.' I said, 'I know he doesn't have much of a beard but he likes being shaved.' He sometimes sings when I'm shaving him. I remember he always used to clean his finger nails every morning when he was getting ready to go. So why not do that?

In a similar way, this woman relied on past relationship patterns with her husband to comfort *her*. She told of two stressful incidents in which her husband wandered away from her. In both incidents, her husband was found within minutes, but she experienced extreme anxiety and distress, fearing he might be harmed or permanently lost. Both times, she calmed her husband and comforted herself by sitting and talking with him.

Wife: Well, I talk to him. I just say, 'you know, you really scared me, and you worry me when you wander away like that. I can't keep track of you all the time.' I just talk like you would in general.

Interviewer: And that helps you?

Wife: Yea.

Interviewer: Do you think that sinks in?

Wife: No. It's helpful for me to talk to him. We always talked a lot.

Conversing with her husband re-enacted a 54-year-old ritual in which they sat together and had a glass of wine each night when her husband returned from work. This ritual was time-honored and practiced no matter what was happening with their household of seven children.

One year into the study, the husband had a stroke and had to be placed in a nursing home. While this dramatically changed the nature of her care responsibilities, her relationship with her husband continued largely unchanged. She went to the nursing home for many hours each day to monitor his care and bring him foods he liked. In the final interview, after her husband died, she recounted her sense of continuity with her husband.

Interviewer: So the Alzheimer's disease didn't take that away from you, that happy feeling of being married to Ron and that relationship you felt with him?

Wife: No, it never did. Never. I would have been happy to bring him home again. . . . I mean, I would have gone on indefinitely. One of the books I read said they usually have Alzheimer's for about 15 years. So I figured that I had about another 7 years to go. He'd come home from the hospital before, so I thought he'd be coming home again, I really did.

Interviewer: So you really felt you had an ongoing relationship with him?

Wife: Yes.

This case demonstrates several aspects of a continuous relationship with an AD family member: (a) the interpretation that the AD patient is still present despite the disease, (b) the interpretation that the person with AD reciprocates in positive ways, and (c) the AD patient continues to define the spouse's or child's world in stable and relatively unchanging ways.

In a similar way, adult children maintained the parent in a place of respect and esteem despite the advance of the disease. Although the parent could not provide advice or support, he or she was still respected and honored by the child as his or her parent. Adult children in this group expressed concern that they "try to maintain her dignity" and "not strip everything away from her."

One daughter's capacity to see her mother in small aspects of the mother's behavior remained present, as in the prior case, throughout the 18-month study. During that time, the mother's physical and mental health declined, she suffered numerous strokes, and the AD progressed to the extent that the mother required placement in a board and care home and eventually a nursing home. Still, the daughter felt an attachment to what she saw in her mother's behavior and appearance that still represented "mother." The daughter continued practices that her mother had maintained throughout her lifetime: coloring her hair red and manicuring her nails. Until the end of the study, the daughter claimed that her relationship with her mother was alive and vibrant.

Interviewer: So you still very much have that bond with her?

Daughter: Oh yes. I will sit there with her in the evenings. I'll sit on the bed and she's in the wheelchair, and I'll put my arm around her and cuddle with her.

Interviewer: She still likes affection from you?

Daughter: Oh yes. She responds to that. Awhile back when I told her I loved her, I was very richly rewarded because she told me, 'I love you.' That just leveled me. I try to hang on to what's still left of her. She still knows me; she still knows chocolate; she still remembers hymns; she's not gone yet. There's still Mama there.

Relationship is Continuous but Transformed

Another group of family members described the AD patient as fairly lost to them because of AD. These spouses and children saw minimal, residual, and fleeting signs of the AD person's personality and either had doubts about their accessibility or saw them as totally inaccessible. What remained, however, was a strong commitment to the relationship, to maintaining contact with the person that the patient had *become* in the disease. Because of the changes in the AD patient, past relations were mourned, and current relations were on a new footing.

Interviewer: Is she still the same person to you?

Daughter: No. Oh no! She's a totally different person. She's not Helen anymore. She's not my mom. No. She's just there in body.

These family members found ways to relate to the patient as the symptoms progressed, and continued to adapt their ways of relating as the AD person's capacities became more constricted. For example, one man reported in the first three interviews that his greatest fear was that his wife would no longer recognize him. In the abstract, he feared that her lack of recognition would break the thin continuity that he felt with her. Additionally, he said he was most sustained by his wife's contentment and recognition. Then in the last interview, his wife increasingly did not recognize him. He then found a new way to stay connected to her in her current capacities. He no longer worried that she recognize him but found it essential that she appreciate him and accept his care. Her willingness to eat what he prepared and her cooperation with the caregivers he hired were taken as signs of her acceptance of his care.

Family members who experienced their relationships as transformed lived more in synchrony with the actual decline in the AD patient's functioning than did those family members who experienced continuity in relations with the AD member. Their relationship with the patient evolved and changed with the changes in the disease. They saw their possibilities for relating to the person with AD as being more firmly bounded by the actual symptomatic changes in the person than did those family members who experienced a continuous relationship with the family member with AD.

In the continuous but transformed relationship, reciprocity between the patient and family members was seen as minimally possible and always in doubt. The patient's fleeting smiles or signs of pleasure were noted by family members and brought them satisfaction. What distinguished these family members from those in the continuous relationship category is the fact that small gestures by the AD patient were not interpreted as indications that the patient was still "there" in the same way that those who had continuous relationships interpreted these signs.

Daughter: I just feel like I've already lost her. She's here but she isn't here. It's probably the most difficult thing.

Spouses found living in this ambiguous relationship difficult because they could no longer relate to their partner as an intimate friend or sexual partner and at the same time they remained married and deeply committed to the spouse. Children also experienced the ambiguity in relations as a dilemma, although the day-to-day impact on their lives was less than for spouses. The children never talked of finding a replacement relationship for that which they had lost, but many of the spouses wished this were possible.

In families where the relationship was transformed, the primary relationship concerns were to provide sensitive care that maintained the dignity of the person and to sustain the AD patient's functional abilities. One spouse, who exemplifies these concerns, demonstrated that to be a good husband to his wife meant providing good care. To this end, he gave up his job in international business and turned his energies entirely to the care of his wife. In his interviews he was exclusively focused on his wife's care requirements and how to sensitively meet them in a way that maintained her current functioning and dignity. He was deeply committed to taking good care of his wife, deeply grieved when there was any evidence that he was not doing a good job, and satisfied when he was successful.

Relationship is Radically Discontinuous

In the third form of relating to a family member with AD, the relationship with the spouse or parent was radically discontinuous with the relationship that existed prior to the illness. These family members found no continuity in the AD patient's personhood and instead found that the AD rendered the patient unrecognizable. They found the behaviors and symptoms of AD to be an affront to the person he or she had been prior to the disease. The relationship these family members experienced was less emotional, less personal and more clinical than that of the first two groups. In their interpretation, the spouse or parent was lost in the disease, and therefore the family member could not continue a truly personal relationship. The concern of these family members for the patient was more objective, abstract, and less tailored to the particular needs of their AD family member.

The coping narratives of these family members focused on caregiving arrangements and problems. When the AD patient gave signs of recognition or pleasure, these family members, like others, were pleased and touched. They did not, however, attempt to elicit such signs and did not interpret such signs as evidence of purposeful, personalized behavior. They diminished the importance of instances of recognition. Instead, there was more of a clinical distancing

and evaluation of the person's disease process.

Emotional distancing was evident in a daughter whose mother had contracted the disease eight years earlier. The daughter described a recent incident where her mother said something that actually seemed to make sense. The daughter was about to take her mother off the commode and the mother said "no" because she needed to stay longer. This moment of possible lucidity in a woman who had not been lucid for 2 years surprised the daughter. But when the interviewer probed about how the incident affected her, she replied:

> Daughter: I don't think it made a difference. I found it interesting that she said 'no' definitely. I thought to myself, how does the correlation go there?

The mother's statement raised for the daughter a clinical question, rather than a relational response. The daughter wondered about how the disease worked, rather than how her mother experienced the disease. Witnessing her mother make sense, and thus have some possibility of making meaningful contact with current reality, made the daughter feel neither closer to nor more distant from her mother. In this daughter's understanding of the situation, the possibility of connecting with her mother simply was not present.

One husband provides some insight about how this emotional break in his relationship with his wife occurred. He recounted that prior to the AD they were "best friends," "did everything together" and in many ways she defined his life. When facing up to her illness, he recognized the only way that he could stay in a relationship with his wife was if he were to "die" himself.

> Husband: I think somehow I'm hardened. If I can say it like that. I've become hardened to a lot of it. It may be by design. Because I had to decide, when I talked about that turning point, whether I was going to live, or whether I was going to sit here and curl up and die because she's got that disease. I don't know if the word's martyr or. . . . Anyway I'm not going to sit around here and let it kill me. I think that's what it was doing.

The dissolution of the relationship with his wife is also evident in this man's hopes and fears for the future. The best possible life he hoped for was: "I would feel good if she died, the sooner the better." He also felt that the worst life for him would be if his wife were to continue to live, and hold him in this "limbo" of being "married, but not married."

Family members who realized radical discontinuities in their relationships

with the AD patient may have had a wide variety of predisposing factors. Perhaps they as a group had more conflicted relations with the person with AD prior to the disease, and thus the disease introduced unsurmountable distance. Perhaps they had difficulty coping with the pervasive losses that one must face as a loved one progresses through AD and distancing was one way of warding off the pain of these losses. We lack the data to thoroughly understand *how* family members came to a discontinuous relationship with the AD patient. What was evident was that these family members found few, if any, possibilities for relating to the person with AD that paralleled their relationship prior to the disease.

Despite the emotional distance that typified the discontinuous relationship, providing good care was a central and focusing concern for family members who experienced this relationship. Proper diet, supervision, safety, and comfort of the AD patient were all raised as issues in the family members' narratives. Providing or arranging care demanded extensive daily effort and time and some of these family members were the primary or sole providers of care. What distinguished the care concerns of this group of families was their relative lack of concern that the care be tailored to the present or past personal needs of the AD patient.

DISCUSSION

In this intensive study of the relationships between family members and AD patients over time, we discovered qualitatively distinct ways that family members interpreted the AD patient's accessibility, capacity to reciprocate affection and concern, and capacity to *relate* as parent or spouse to the family member. For some family members of persons with AD, the loss of self and transformation of the person with AD by the disease were not complete. For these family members, the life and capacities of the person with AD were still a part of their ongoing relationship either fully or in a diminished and transformed way. For other family members, however, the disease covered over the person, overrode their relational possibilities, and care became much more strategic or objectified.

All three forms of relating (continuous, transformed, or discontinuous) presented here were evident in both the children's and spouses' relations with the person with AD. With the exception of continuous relating, both male and female caregivers experienced each form of relating. In our group of informants, there were no male caregivers who demonstrated the continuous form of relating, and wives of persons with AD were the most predominant in this group of caregivers. We acknowledge that the forms of relating that we present may not represent all of the possibilities for how relations between family and the person with AD might evolve. For example, we interviewed only persons who maintained some kind of relationship with the person with AD, whether that relationship was personal or merely organizational. Thus, we have no information on the ways in which family members may sever their relationship with the person with AD.

The severity of illness in the person with AD did not seem to determine the form of relationship that was described by the family member. Moderate to severe Alzheimer's disease was evident in all three forms of relationships when data from both family member ratings and interviewer ratings were considered. The disease itself, and the progression of the disease, was not a clear determinant of what the relationship might be.

Our findings support and further articulate detailed qualitative studies of AD family relationships reported to date. Like Blieszner and Shifflett (1990), we found that closeness between the person with AD and the family members diminished for some but remained strong for others over time, despite sometimes dramatic progression of the dementia and, thus, a decrease in the AD person's "objective" capacities to relate. Orona (1990) reported interactions similar to those we observed in the first two groups of our sample: the reenactment of familiar rituals and the searching for and success at finding familiar behaviors and expressions in the AD patient. She similarly reported the phenomena we observed in the continuous relationships of "working both sides" of the relationship, filling in additional meanings for vague or difficult to interpret behaviors by the person with AD.

Hirschfeld (1983) combined three dimensions of mutuality in a single concept. Considering Hirschfeld's concept of mutuality in light of our own findings, we believe that her three aspects of mutuality might offer greater explanatory power in terms of caregivers' involvements if they are examined independently. In this study, we found that: (a) the caregiver's capacity to find gratification in the *relationship* with the impaired person, (b) *positive* meaning of caregiving, and (c) a sense of *reciprocity* with the care recipient, all aspects of mutuality, did not combine in meaningful ways in our groups of family members who provided care. For example, family members in the continuous group seemed to experience all three dimensions of mutuality in a consistent, coherent fashion. Family members in the con-

tinuous but transformed group also experienced positive meanings from the care situation, questionable reciprocity, and some gratification from the relationship, but here it was a relation acknowledged to be changed by the disease. Finally, family members in the discontinuous group experienced substantial positive meanings from giving care, but found no sense of reciprocity in the caregiving relationship and made almost no mention of relationship gratifications with the AD patient. We believe that Hirschfeld identified important explanatory dimensions in the relationship of family and persons with AD and argue for further refinement of the "mutuality" concept so that each dimension be examined as qualitatively distinct.

Our findings are not in conflict with, but are distinct from, the prevailing themes in the literature on family factors and AD care. This literature has largely ignored the quality of the relationship between the person with AD and the family member who provides care, assuming instead that the former is a passive, uninvolved recipient of care and the latter is burdened by the responsibility for this passive object/person. We wish to argue that the qualitative aspects of the relationship between the AD person and the family members described in this research deserve a more prominent place in research on family processes in relation to AD care. Alongside continuing efforts to identify factors that place the family at risk for negative outcomes, conceptualizations and investigations of family care processes must begin to include an awareness of relationships that may be sustaining and meaningful. As Hirschfeld's research demonstrated a decade ago, the relational qualities may have powerful explanatory power in how families function over time.

CLINICAL IMPLICATIONS

Recognizing that family members who care for a person with AD have distinct relations with that person is vital to their sensitive care and support. Relying on standardized responses to the family situation, or relying on the pervasive literature that emphasizes the losses, burdens, and difficulties in AD care, may lead professionals to overlook the family members' possibilities for hope, satisfaction, and continuity in their relations with and care of the AD patient.

Care for family members who experience their relationship as continuous might explicitly legitimatize their experience of the person as present and encourage their efforts to continue the AD patient's habits and practices. The biomedicalization of dementia (Lyman,

1989) may be so complete that family members feel criticized or isolated because they continue to relate to the person with AD. In recognizing the two-way nature of the family relations, health professionals should give credence to the AD patient as a person with a history and recognize further the AD patient's capacity to carry on in a meaningful way in relationships despite the debilitations of the dementia. Rather than emphasizing the negative changes wrought by the disease, health professionals might learn from family members how the disease makes possible continued exercise of lifelong marital or parental relations. Family members additionally might inform practitioners about authentic commitments to the care of beloved family members that are neither self-sacrificing nor "loving too much." For some, care of the person with AD is the genuine working out and fulfillment of a lifelong relationship; therefore, it is not experienced as burdensome but sustaining and meaningful.

The group of family members who experience a continuous relationship with the person with AD might have the most difficulty, however, with recognizing the true limitations that occur over time in the AD person's abilities. Although all caregivers we observed provided safe and protective environments, some had their choices for care restricted because they believed that the person with AD was capable of doing things that seemed unlikely. Respectful solicitation of what family members perceive as the capabilities of the AD person, and feedback by the professional regarding these perceptions are warranted.

Family members who experienced their relationship with the AD patient as continuous but transformed might similarly benefit from interventions that respect their efforts at continued close relations with the person with AD. These family members, who are more in synchrony with the changes of the disease, are particularly apt to observe firsthand a decline in the AD patient's abilities. Care of these family members may involve helping them find ways to maintain their commitment to closeness, while at the same time being respectful of the AD patient's new restrictions. Providing examples of how other family members have coped with this dilemma, like the spouse who no longer needed his wife's recognition, but merely needed her acceptance of his care, might make these transitions easier.

Work with family members who experience their relationship with the person with AD as discontinuous could focus on helping them find some continuities in the person despite the AD, assisting them with appropriate care arrangements, and showing appreciation for their existential experience of distance from their prior relations with the person with AD. These family members may need help in recognizing that AD dementia does not immediately and totally transform a person, and that she or he may actively contribute to and participate in the life of the family. These family members may also benefit from a frank discussion about how we live in a culture where caring for others is seldom valued, and how the person providing care may be misunderstood as "addicted" to or dependent upon his or her need to care for others (Dreyfus & Rubin, in press). Offering a positive connotation for care of a family member who has AD may make closer relations possible for these families. Both of these interventions, however, must be tempered by attention to the family member's current possibilities in relation to the AD patient. Some family members, because of their background with the AD patient or because of their current social context, cannot tolerate closer emotional proximity to the AD patient, and thus their distance must be honored.

REFERENCES

Baumgarten, M. (1989). The health of persons giving care to the demented elderly: A critical review of the literature. *Journal of Clinical Epidemiology*, 42, 1137-1148.

Benner, P., & Wrubel, J. (1989). *The primacy of caring, stress and coping in health and illness*. Menlo Park, CA: Sage.

Blieszner, R., & Shifflett, P. A. (1989). Affection, communication and commitment in adult-child caregiving for parents with Alzheimer's disease. In J. A. Mancini (Ed.), *Aging parents and adult children* (pp. 231-242). Lexington, MA: Lexington Books.

Blieszner, R., & Shifflett, P. A. (1990). The effects of Alzheimer's disease on close relationships between patients and caregivers. *Family Relations*, 39, 57-62.

Bowers, B. J. (1987). Intergenerational caregiving: Adult caregivers and their aging parents. *Advances in Nursing Science*, 9(2), 20-31.

Cohen, D., & Eisdorfer, C. (1986). *The loss of self*. New York: Norton.

Colerick, E. J., & George, L. K. (1986). Predictors of institutionalization among caregivers of patients with Alzheimer's Disease. *Journal of the American Geriatrics Society*, 34, 493-498.

Dreyfus, H., & Rubin, J. (in press). Kierkegaard on the nihilism of the present age: The case of commitment as addiction. *Synthese*.

Farran, C. J., Keane-Hagerty, E., Salloway, S., Kupferer, S., & Wilken, C.S. (1991). Finding meaning: An alternative paradigm for Alzheimer's Disease family caregivers. *The Gerontologist*, 31, 483-489.

Fillenbaum, G. G., & Smyer, M. A. (1981). The development, validity and reliability of the OARS Multidimensional Functional Assessment Questionnaire. *Journal of Gerontology*, 36, 428-434.

Folstein, M., Folstein, S., & McHugh, P. (1975). Mini-mental state: A practical method for grading the cognitive state of patients for the clinician. *Journal of Psychiatric Research*, 12, 189-198.

Hirschfeld, M. (1983). Homecare versus institutionalization: Family caregiving and senile brain disease. *International Journal of Nursing Studies*, 20, 23-32.

Kuhlman, G. J., Wilson, H. S., Hutchinson, S. A., & Wallhagen, M. (1991). Alzheimer's disease and family caregiving: Critical synthesis of the literature and research agenda. *Nursing Research*, 40, 331-337.

Liptzin, R., Grob, M., & Eisen, S. (1988). Family burden of demented and depressed elderly psychiatric inpatients. *The Gerontologist*, 28, 397-401.

Lyman, K. A. (1989). Bring the social back in: A critique of the biomedicalization of dementia. *The Gerontologist*, 29, 597-605.

Martinson, I. M., Chesla, C., & Muwaswes, M. (1993). Caregiving demands of patients with Alzheimer's Disease. *Journal of Community Health Nursing*, 10, 225-232.

Martinson, I., Gilliss, C. L., Doyle, G., & Muwaswes, M. (1983). *The impact of Alzheimer's Disease on the family and caregiver*. San Francisco: University of California.

Orona, C. J. (1990). Temporality and identity loss due to Alzheimer's Disease. *Social Science in Medicine*, 30, 1247-1256.

Ory, M. G., Williams, T. F., Emr, M., Lebowitz, B., Rabins, P., Salloway, J., Sluss-Radbaugh, T., Wolff, E., & Zarit, S. (1985). Families, informal supports and Alzheimer's Disease. *Research on Aging*, 7, 623-644.

Packer, M. J., & Addison, R. B. (1989). *Entering the circle: Hermeneutic investigation in psychology*. Albany: SUNY Press.

Quayhagen, M. P., & Quayhagen, M. (1988). Alzheimer's stress: Coping with the caregiving role. *The Gerontologist*, 28, 391-396.

Van Manen, M. (1990). *Researching lived experience*. London, Ontario: Althouse.

Walker, A. J., Pratt, C. C., & Oppy, N. C. (1992). Perceived reciprocity in family caregiving. *Family Relations*, 41, 82-85.

Wright, L. K., Clipp, E. C., & George, L. K. (1993). State of the art review: Health consequences of caregiver stress. *Medicine, Exercise, Nutrition & Health*, 2, 181-195.

Embracing Our Mortality
♦ ♦ ♦ ♦ ♦ ♦

Hard Lessons

Learning to let go of the uncontrollable

ELLEN PULLEYBLANK

Ellen Pulleyblank, Ph.D., is a psychologist in private practice. Address: 230 California Avenue, Suite 200, Palo Alto, CA 94301.

HANGING ON THE WALL OF OUR LIVing room in Palo Alto was a photograph of my 3-year-old daughter, Sarah, hands on her hips, her name emblazoned on her sweatshirt. She was formidable even at that age, taking on her six-foot father, never flinching as he towered above her, challenging her typical response of "No." She would build a fort in her room and decide who could enter and who would be barred. No easy child to live with, but how I admired her will. When she was a teenager, Sarah looked at that photograph on the wall, and then at her father, inert in his wheelchair, hooked up to a ventilator. The now 14-year-old Sarah asked me where I thought that feisty little girl had gone. I imagined that, like me, she had been slammed so hard by circumstance that she had simply disappeared.

In the summer of 1985, during a sabbatical year in Europe, my husband, Ron, began having trouble tying knots. Then came difficulty with riding a bicycle and undoing buttons. In October, at a hospital in the Netherlands, he was diagnosed with Amyotrophic Lateral Sclerosis, or Lou Gehrig's Disease. By the end of the year, he could not dress himself and fell frequently. Just before Christmas, a year later, he could no longer breathe on his own and was put on a ventilator. He came home from the hospital–via ambulance–to round-the-clock nursing care. He could not feed himself, and it became progressively harder for him to swallow and speak. His body, below the neck, became utterly still. And that is how we lived–Ron and I and our daughters Caitlin and Sarah–for seven years.

During those years, part of me vanished. I am embarrassed when I remember how strong and certain I used to be. Until Ron was diagnosed, I believed unquestioningly in personal responsibility and free will. I had faith in human beings' capacity for change, and I took that faith forward into my life, into my work as a therapist, and into my relationships.

Such beliefs had shaped my life since the time in my early twenties when I was hospitalized with what was then called a nervous breakdown. Ron and I were newly married, and he was in graduate school, studying electrical engineering. I had no idea what I was going to do with my life and I couldn't stop crying. One day a young woman, also a patient at the hospital, jumped off the roof. At that moment, I realized that I was the only one who could keep myself safe and alive.

I went to graduate school, began to work as a family therapist, got my Ph.D., and took care of my growing family. In the 1970s and early 1980s, when we lived in Stockton, California, I was part of a group of women who raised $1 million dollars to start a multi-service womens' center. I was often admired for my guts, my energy and my willingness to help—qualities that I took for granted, without even noticing the personal and societal supports that held me up and made it possible for me to be so confident.

That is the part of me that vanished after Ron got sick. At first, I tried to take charge, make do, run the show, but I couldn't keep it up. I began to see the world as a place containing tragic forces beyond our understanding, beyond our ability to adapt. I was humbled by how little I knew about myself, others and the universe.

Now, after Ron's illness and death, my psychology practice is less about relieving suffering or changing experience or circumstances and more about learning how to bear suffering and stay alive. Before, I believed that right thinking, feeling and acting led to relief, and that I could help show the way. But tragedy showed me that sometimes there can be no relief, at least not at first. There was nothing I could do that even touched the depth of my family's pain and difficulties.

Watching Ron become more and more disabled and ultimately choose to die changed what I now pay attention to and how I respond. My work with my clients now is built on what I learned:

To bear pain by paying attention to it;

I remember sitting on the deck one afternoon with Ron. He was cold. I massaged his arms and hands, got him more warm clothing, and moved his chair into the sun. He was still cold and he was crying. I realized that all I could do was sit next to him and bear the pain with him. It was so little, but it was all I could do and I couldn't do it for long.

To witness the suffering of others by staying present and doing only what is possible;

To stop expecting rational explanations for the unexplainable;

To ask the community for help;

To let go of control of the uncontrollable; and

To focus less on our responsibility to ourselves, and more on what we have to offer each other.

FOR MONTHS AFTER RON CAME home from the hospital and was on the ventilator, I would sometimes sit bolt upright in the middle of the night, thinking that something horrible was about to happen, and then realize that it already had. I would try to figure out what to do, try to distract myself, and then give up and lie awake. One night, in desperation, I went toward my fear instead of moving away from it—I gave it all my attention, feeling the physical sensation in the pit of my stomach, and watching: I didn't fight my sensations; I let go of control. I stopped trying to protect myself from the stark terror of the unknown. I was swept up and knocked out by my fear.

By then, Ron was sleeping alone in a hospital bed, his ventilator beeping regularly through the night. For months I could not decide where to sleep. Sometimes I spent the night on the living room couch or in a spare upstairs bedroom. Wherever I lay, I began to follow the nightly ritual of going toward my pain. When I couldn't stand it, I would count backwards for relief, follow my breath, and then go toward my fear

again. One night, I had the unmistakable feeling that I was being held in loving arms. This feeling came back from time to time, giving me comfort and a sense of well-being. After a while, I learned how to summon it at will, by breathing, staying with my pain and remembering and thinking of loving arms.

SIMON, A SHORT, PUDGY, BEARDED man, wearing a yarmulke, his clothes in disarray, asked for a session alone. Usually I see him with his wife or with other family members. He tells me that he has brought a list of reasons why he's having such a hard time looking for a job.

"I am too old. I am too fat," he reads. "The market is very bad right now. If I move to where the children are, they might move away and then where would I be? I am depressed and have little enthusiasm."

I fidget, wondering if I remembered to turn off the oven. I ask questions designed to show him how he is giving up his power and refusing to take responsibility for himself. He goes along with me for a while and then says, with surprising clarity, "You just don't get what is happening to me."

Three years earlier, his father, aged 86, had died suddenly. Simon had called on Sunday, as he usually did, and his mother had told him his father was out for a walk. Later that night, Simon's father had a heart attack, but his mother didn't let Simon know, because she didn't want to upset him. The following Thursday, his father was dead.

Simon dissolves into tears. "I miss my father," he wails.

"I am sorry," I say, "and I am sorry I didn't understand what a hard time you are having and how hard it must have been to write that list. Please read it to me again."

"I am too old. I am too fat. The market is very bad right now. If I move to where the children are, they might move away and then where would I be? I am depressed."

I listen intently, my own tears flowing as he focuses on his losses, finally offering him the attention he needs to stay with the pain.

◆　◆　◆　◆

I remember sitting on the deck one afternoon with Ron, trying to help him. He was having a bad day. He was cold. I massaged his arms and hands, got him more warm clothing, and moved his chair into the sun. He was still cold and he was crying. I realized that all I could

do was sit next to him and bear the pain with him. It was so little, but it was all I could do and I couldn't do it for long. My pain welled up, threatening to overwhelm me. I got up and went inside, leaving Ron on the deck, retreating from his suffering into my own.

Sometimes, now, I can bear incredible pain, and sometimes I can help my clients bear it too. Sometimes all we can do for one another is witness suffering by staying present.

SUSAN, WHOSE FATHER HAS COMmitted suicide, complains of confusion, exhaustion and feelings of anxiety when she is with her mother. She tells me all she is doing to try and help, while her mother stays mired in grief.

I suggest we sit together and just watch our breathing. It is a miracle: we don't have to do anything, the breath just comes. I ask her to imagine her mind as a sky and let thoughts, feelings and images fly by, in and out, not minding what flies through. Then I ask her to direct her attention to her body and suggest she locate where the strongest sensations are. I tell her to focus her attention on these sensations, to go toward them rather than move away from them.

Susan says it is unbearable knowing how sad her mother feels. She desperately wants to help. Obviously, we could work on boundary issues (and no doubt we will in other family sessions) but now I find myself working with Susan's desire to help. I ask her if she is willing to learn to witness her mother's pain and not try to change it. She struggles with this idea for a while and then I ask her to close her eyes again and practice watching her mother in pain. Silently she weeps as she watches her mother grieve, but her own breathing slows and deepens. She leaves the session later with a sense of relief.

◆　◆　◆　◆

Before Ron was diagnosed, I thought that I could make sense of almost anything. I had lived in other cultures and worked with families from different ethnic backgrounds. I knew how to step aside and hear and appreciate different versions of reality and other experiences of suffering. Ron and I had always tried to understand each other and to communicate, and by and large we'd succeeded. Nothing, I felt, was insurmountable. But that began to change on the day in the Netherlands that I went to Ron's hospital room and met the doctor in the corridor. He was grave. Without looking me in the eye, he told me that

Ron would die within the year. He said it would be better if I did not tell him.

I immediately went into Ron's room and told him what the doctor had said. I was determined that whatever happened, we would face it together and talk about it. He looked at me without saying very much, and then we cried. We cried, along with our two daughters, for about two weeks.

Afterward, Ron decided he would go on with his life, as much as he could, as though nothing had changed. He continued his sabbatical, and when the year was over, he went back to work as an electrical engineer at Hewlett Packard in Palo Alto. I helped him dress in the mornings, and his colleagues gave him rides to work and carried his lunch tray for him. In December, after he woke up unable to breathe, the doctor in the emergency room told me that if we didn't put him on a ventilator, he would die. We didn't understand then that if you choose to turn a ventilator on, you will someday have to choose to turn it off.

Ron came home and worked half-time, using a special computer. He focused on staying alive, on keeping things the same. He continued to enjoy life and to value every day. Although his determination to go on was inspiring, he found it hard to understand why the children and I were grieving and why we felt so overwhelmed. His unspoken demand to us was that everything be as normal as possible, and that we not be too sad. As he struggled to stay alive, his world narrowed and he became oblivious to us. He stopped thinking about money and didn't notice when things were broken in the house. His most significant relationships were often with the nurses who cared for him 24-hours-a-day and who saw his illness from his perspective.

We lived parallel lives. I needed Ron to understand my fear and grief. He needed me to be unemotional and accept him as he was. He was angry with me for grieving, for trying to separate, although we never gave up the effort to understand each other. I was appalled at my inability to accept our circumstances. Nothing made sense.

Only in the last months of his life could Ron acknowledge the effects his illness had on him and on us. Just before Ron died, when even I could barely understand his labored speech, we talked about what had happened to us. It was beyond understanding. Only at the end could we look at each other with kindness and forgiveness, realizing

that we both had tried our best, but for the most part, we had failed. Things sometimes just don't make sense, and no amount of understanding and empathy or talk will explain them.

GABRIELLE, AGED 12, CAME IN with her father, George, and her new stepmother, Joan. Her parents divorced three years ago, after her mother fell in love with a neighbor and asked her father to leave. Her father has since remarried, and Joan has two children of her own. For months, Gabrielle has been raging and throwing tantrums, both at her own mother's house and with Joan.

She has decided not to speak to Joan either in my office or at home. Her rage has turned into a silent protest. Her father cares for her deeply and is worried about her. Joan is angry and disappointed because no matter what she does, Gabrielle does not like her and will not cooperate.

Gabrielle's father patiently describes his daughter's feelings to me. He tries to coax her to talk. She won't. I become interested in her silence and wonder out loud if, with her silence, Gabrielle has found a way to express her anger without hurting herself or others. I ask George and Joan to talk about what it will take to allow her silence, to respect it and to admire her honesty. Gabrielle looks out from behind the pillows she is hiding under. I ask them if we might sit together in silence and acknowledge with Gabrielle how difficult things have been, and how, from her point of view, none of it makes any sense. At the end of the session, Gabrielle cautiously begins to speak.

About two years after Ron went on the ventilator, we started to run out of money. I couldn't think straight and I wasn't sleeping. One day I had lunch with my friends from the Stockton women's center. I had always been seen as the strong one, and they still saw me that way. They marveled at how I could do it.

Finally, I looked at them and said, "Help me. I can't do it. I can't." I felt such shame. How often I had offered to help others, feeling so magnanimous, blithely unaware of how hard it is to turn to others, to say you cannot manage your life on your own.

Of course they helped me. A community formed around us. People raised money—about $300,000 over the next

few years. Others visited or gave me respite time or helped us take Ron on extravagant outings to the symphony and even on vacations to a cabin near the sea. Near the end of Ron's life, a group of friends began meditating at our house weekly.

I had never thought of myself as the kind of person who would need help. Without the help that I asked for and received, we would have become destitute in every way.

NAOMI CAME TO SEE ME WITH HER parents, deeply confused about the source of her sadness. She is 14, very depressed, and refuses to go to school. She says she feels like an outsider and is treated like one. She tells me she lives in a community where everyone looks and tries to act the same. Her father, whose parents were Holocaust survivors, remembers going through much the same thing when he was younger. Her mother thinks Naomi has always been very sensitive, and mentions her own family's history of depression.

But when I meet with Naomi alone, she tells me more about the tangled communal and familial roots of her sorrow. Once, she tells me, her father came to her school and talked about what had happened to his parents in Auschwitz, and the kids snickered. None of their families had known similar experience. Since then, she has told other kids very little about her background. How is she to feel part of her community when her experience is so different, and she has shared so little of it? As she talks, I am reminded of how I felt walking around the streets of Palo Alto when Ron was disabled, looking at all the perfect houses and wondering what I was doing there with my disheveled life.

In family sessions, Naomi's father talks more about his own feelings of isolation when he was growing up. He tells Naomi how identifying with his history and with other Holocaust survivors had helped him. He realizes he hadn't told her this before because he hoped that she could be unaffected by the tragedy, but now he helps her become part of a community stretching through space and time.

The more Naomi acknowledges, to herself and to others, how the Holocaust has influenced her, the easier her life becomes. She makes a new friend at Wednesday-night school at Temple. At school, she begins to build community not by trying to fit in, but by identifying with her history and asking her friends to listen to her experiences. She is surprised to find out that most of the time, they are interested and friendly.

IN THE SPRING OF 1993, RON wrote a letter to our families, telling them that he had begun to think about dying. It had become almost impossible for him to use the computer. He was losing all speech. When I asked him whether we should sell the house, he finally realized that we were $150,000 in debt. I was exhausted; both of our daughters had stayed close to home, their lives on hold. For eight years, he had been determined to stay alive and keep things the same, and now he began to let go. Month by month, conversation by conversation, Ron got clearer and clearer. One day he decided to die, just as he decided so many other things in his life. He would think and think, and suddenly he would know.

Once he made the decision, he began to say goodbye in one halting conversation after another. By then, very few of us could understand him. I could do so only by focusing all my attention on each word. If I got a word wrong, even if it was close in meaning, Ron would ignore my attempt and repeat his word again and again, until I got it right. He said all of his goodbyes in his own way.

Then it was time. We sat in the living room—Ron, our daughters, Caitlin and Sarah, me, the doctor and a woman friend. The doctor gave Ron a small dose of morphine so he could relax.

Therapy is more than helping clients to take appropriate and responsible action to achieve their goals. I meet regularly with a group of therapists and physicians to explore what might be called "the work of the soul"–learning how to face the broad questions of human existence and to tolerate the realization that much of life is beyond our control.

Ron wanted to die naturally, without tubes or drugs. The doctor first removed the gastrostomy tube and then the ventilator. As soon as the tubes were gone, Ron's face changed. The strained, frozen look on his face melted, and my handsome husband returned. I found myself breathing more deeply, letting go deeper and deeper, as if my life depended on it. It was as if I was birthing Ron's death. My daughters, our friend and I held onto each other. Ron's body did not move as he died, and yet we all felt him leap out of that chair. Sarah later said she had literally held us down, because the energy was so strong that she was afraid

it would lift us all away. She had held onto me especially, because she thought I might want to leave with him, and she was right.

It is only recently that I feel glad that I am still here and not with Ron. Death seems so close. Life paled in the face of death. Only time, tears and loving arms made it possible for me to return to what I think of as "normal."

What I learned in all this is that birth and death are somehow the same, but each has its time and place. Ron's choice to go on the ventilator extended his life until the time when he was ready, after exploring all the possibilities he could see, to die.

In my work with clients, I find that quite often they, too, are talking about either their fear of death or their fear of life. I find myself asking them more about their views of life and death, and more about their spiritual beliefs and the practice of prayer. Over the past year, I have contemplated suicide, not knowing how to reattach myself to the earth. I wanted to die, partly out of curiosity, partly to follow Ron. Mostly I was caught in a flood of pain that did not let me see anything beyond my own suffering. But I chose to live: my suicide would have disrupted my possibilities here on earth. I once heard Carl Whitaker speak about all the forms of suicide he had considered, and how he ultimately chose life as the best form, since it, too, leads to death. I see the choices that Ron and I made in that same light: Though they may both sound like acts of will—choosing life, choosing death—I see them both as a letting go of control, as reentering a stream that is hurtling us to who knows where.

Dealing with death: Let children grieve, the experts say. Don't shield them from loss, but help them express their fear and anger. BY JERRY ADLER

How Kids Mourn

THE PAIN NEVER GOES AWAY," SAYS Geoff Lake, who is 15 now, and was 11 when his mother, Linda, died of a rare form of cancer. He is only starting to realize it, but at each crucial passage of life—graduation, marriage, the birth of children—there will be a face missing from the picture, a kiss never received, a message of joy bottled up inside, where it turns into sorrow. His sleep will be shadowed by ghosts, and the bittersweet shock of awakening back into a world from which his mother is gone forever. If he lives to be 100, with a score of descendants, some part of him will still be the boy whose mother left for the hospital one day and never came home.

A child who has lost a parent feels helpless, even if he's a future King of England; abandoned, even in a palace with a million citizens wailing at the gates. But children have ways of coping with loss, if they are allowed to mourn in their own ways. Grief can be mastered, even if it is never quite overcome, and out of the appalling dysfunction of the Windsor family, one of the few positive signs psychologists could point to was the sight of William and Harry trudging manfully behind their mother's bier, both brushing away tears during the service. "There is something very healing," says Catherine Hillman, coordinator of the Westminster Bereavement Service, "about openly sharing pain."

The death of a parent can have devastating psychological consequences, including anxiety, depression, sleep disturbances, underachievement and aggression. But so can a lot of other things, and losing a parent is actually less devastating than divorce. "We know that children tend to do better after a parental death than a divorce," says sociolo-

gist Andrew Cherlin of Johns Hopkins, "and that's a stunning statistic, because you'd think death would be harder." Historically, people have always had mechanisms for coping with the early death of a parent, a fairly common event until recently.

As late as 1900, a quarter of all American children had lost at least one parent by the age of 15. The figure today is about 6 percent. A century ago most people lived on farms and died at home, so children had a fairly intimate, routine acquaintance with death. In the genteel, antiseptic suburban culture of midcentury, death became an abstraction for most American children, something that happened on television (and, in the case of cartoon characters, was infinitely reversible). Growing up as what psychologist Therese Rando calls "the first death-free generation," Americans forgot the rituals of grief so ancient that they predate civilization itself. So the mental-health profession has had to fill the gap. In the last few decades more then 160 "bereavement centers" have opened around the country, directed at allowing children to express and channel their grief over the death of a parent or sibling. The one thing they can't do is make the grief disappear, because it never does.

If they could enroll, William and Harry would be prime candidates for bereavement counseling. Experts consider them almost a case study in risk factors for future emotional problems, with the notable exception that, unlike many other children who have lost a parent, their social and financial status is not in any jeopardy. But children who experience "multiple family transitions"—such as a death on top of Charles and Diana's acrimonious and humiliatingly public divorce—"don't do as well as children who experience just one," Cherlin warns. David

Zinn, medical director of Beacon Th[...] tic Center in Chicago, thinks this [...] especially true if there is some cau[...] nection, however remote, between [...] vorce and the death. It is not such [...] leap of logic, for a child, to blame h[...] for the circumstances that put his m[...] the back seat of a speeding car with [...] at the wheel.

Moreover, the princes are each a[...] that has been identified—by diffe[...] perts—as being at particular risk [...] parent dies. An adolescent, such a[...] year-old William, is already un[...] difficult life changes, says Rabbi E[...] man, author of 25 books on coping [...] "You're not only dealing with the [...] a parent, you're dealing with the [...] your own childhood," he says. "Yo[...] you were beginning to know yourself, but now the road ahead is uncertain." "I think it's hardest when you're 9 to 12," says Maxine Harris, author of "The Loss That Is Forever." (Harry was just short of his 13th birthday when Diana died.) "You're not a little kid, so you feel more shy about crying or sitting on someone's lap, but you're also not an adolescent, with all the independence that comes with that."

Worse yet, in the opinions of most armchair specialists, is the famously reticent and undemonstrative temperament of the Windsor family. "The way to handle grief is to allow the expression of feelings and the sharing of sadness," declares Dr. Dennis Friedman, a psychiatrist who has written a book on the psyche of the British royal family. "This particular family doesn't allow the expression of grief. . . . There has been a pattern of deprivation of love beginning with Victoria, then gathering momentum, and ending up with Charles. [The princes] are

"Can't we just fly up to heaven and get her and bring her back when God isn't looking?"

Some mourning children draw or paint, others pound a toy in frustration

This is, as it happens, almost the exact opposite of what was accepted wisdom a generation ago, when children were encouraged to get on with their lives and parents advised not to depress them with reminders of the departed. Lori Lehmann was 6 when her mother died of leukemia, 30 years ago. Lori was dropped off at a neighbor's house for the funeral, and afterward her father packed up all her mother's belongings and took down all her photographs, and no one ever talked about her. "He was so sad that you didn't feel like you could ask him about it," she remembers. Her father died himself nine years later, and now she is trying to reconstruct her parents, her mother especially, from her relatives' memories. "It's the little things they tell me that I really love," she says. "Like what she cooked for desert. I don't think my aunts realize how I cling to these things." Of course, by not talking to her, her father was sparing his own feelings as well; men of that generation didn't like to be seen crying.

And it's easy for parents to overlook the grief of young children. A child of 6, says New York psychiatrist Elliot Kranzler, is just on the cusp of mastering the four essential attributes of death: that is has a specific cause, involves the cessation of bodily function, is irreversible and is universal. Before that, children may nod solemnly when told of their father's death, and still expect him to be home for dinner. Young children process their loss a bit at a time; they may be sad for 10 minutes, then ask to go outdoors to play. And they are captives of childhood's inescapable solipsism. "It hits them over the head that they have needs to be met, and one key provider is gone," says Kranzler. "They pretty quickly tell their surviving parents to remarry." That isn't callous, merely practical on the child's part; and, of course, when the parent finally does remarry, it is one of the invariable rules of human psychology that the children will hate the new spouse. "There has not been a person I've interviewed who liked their stepparents when they were children," says Harris.

Children mourn piecemeal; they must return to it at each stage of maturity and conquer grief anew. Over the years, the sharp pang of loss turns to a dull ache, a melancholy that sets in at a certain time of year, a certain hour of the night. But every child who has lost a parent remains, in some secret part of his or her soul, a child forever frozen at a moment in time, crying out to the heedless heavens, as Geoff Lake did, when his mother died just days before his 12th birthday: "Mom, why did you die? *I had plans.*"

With PAT WINGERT *in Washington,* KAREN SPRINGEN *in Chicago,* BRAD STONE *in New York,* PATRICIA KING *in San Francisco,* CLAUDIA KALB *in Boston and* DONNA FOOTE *in London*

bereaved not only by the loss of a mother who was very close to them, but also for a father who is quite often unavailable to them because of his duties and temperament."

It will be hardest at night, when the routines of the day wind down and the memories crowd in. Nighttime is when 11-year-old Dennis Heaphy leaves his bedroom and pads down the hall of his home in New York's Long Island to take his place on the floor of the master bedroom. His 7-year-old sister, Catherine, is already sleeping in bed alongside their mother, Mary Beth, who lies awake with her own thoughts of Brian, the husband who died of a brain tumor last January. He was 37, a big, strong man until he got sick. Dennis remembers his father's teaching him to play basketball and the hockey games they would play in the street until 9 o'clock at night. The memories make him miss his father even more, but they are precious all the same. "My sister doesn't remember my dad so well," Dennis says. "She remembers him from when he was sick, when he would get mad at the littlest things and not act like himself. We have to help her out."

Children cling to their memories, try to fortify them against the passage of the years. "They're always afraid they're going to forget how their mother looked, what her voice sounded like, how she smelled," says Debby Shimmel, a volunteer at the St. Francis Center in Washington. They paint their memories

onto the quilts that are ubiquitous at bereavement centers, little shards of a shattered family, sharp enough to pierce the heart: "Mommy read Matty bedtime stories." "Leo and Mommy played Candyland." Or they draw their parents as angels in heaven. Envisioning what heaven is like for their dads, says Stefanie Norris of the Good Mourning program in Park Ridge, Ill., children sometimes draw a giant football stadium. At the end of each eight-week group session, children hold a memorial for their dead parents; they wear something their parent wore, or perhaps make one of their favorite dishes. This is a more concrete form of memorial than a church eulogy, and a lot more meaningful to a 7-year-old.

The other thing children can't do in church is get angry, but bereavement centers provide for that as well. The Dougy Center in Portland, Ore., the model for scores of bereavement houses around the country, includes a "splatter room," where kids throw violent sploches of paint, an innovation suggested by a child who came to the center after his father had been accidentally shot to death in his home by police. And most centers have some variation of the "volcano room," thickly padded with foam and supplied with large stuffed animals that are periodically pummeled into piles of lint. Barney is said to be the favorite of many teenagers.

Families, Now and into the Future

What is the future of the family? Does the family even have a future? These questions and others like them are being asked. Many people fear for the future of the family. As previous units of this volume have shown, the family is a continually evolving institution that will continue to change throughout time. Still, certain elements of family appear to be constant. The family is and will remain a powerful influence in the lives of its members. This is because we all begin life in some type of family, and this early exposure carries a great deal of weight in forming our social selves, who we are and how we relate to others. From our families, we take our basic genetic makeup, while we also learn and are reinforced in health behaviors. In families, we are given our first exposure to values, and it is through families that we most actively influence others. Our sense of commitment and obligation begins within the family as well as our sense of what we can expect of others.

Much writing about families has been less than hopeful and has focused on ways of avoiding or correcting errors. The four articles in this unit take a positive view of family and its influences on its members. The emphasis is on health rather than dysfunction.

Increasing evidence of genetic factors in physical as well as mental health serves to promote the need for awareness of our family's health history. "To See Your Future Look into Your Past" considers how charting your relatives' medical history can save your life. Steven Finch provides a useful technique for mapping out your family health history so that you can anticipate, plan, and possibly change your health behaviors. The next article, "What's Ahead for Families: Five Major Forces of Change," identifies five societal trends that Joseph Coates believes will impact the future direction of families. Geoffrey Cowley and Karen Springen's "Rewriting Life Stories" describes narrative therapy, a new and promising approach in family therapy that sees life as a series of stories that can be rewritten to find one's own strengths rather than weaknesses. Concluding this volume, "Rituals for Our Times," by family therapists Evan Imber-Black and Janine Roberts, describes the ways in which rites and ceremonies are used to strengthen families. Through examples, readers see how they might use ritual in their own families.

Looking Ahead: Challenge Questions

After having charted your family's health history, what type of future do you see for yourself? What changes do you see yourself making in your life?

What decision have you made about long-term commitments—marriage or some other relationship? How about children? Do you see divorce as a viable option, even before marriage? Do you expect to live "happily ever after"?

How would rewriting your life story, or aspects of it, benefit you?

What is the state of rituals in your family? What rituals might you build in your family? Why?

TO SEE YOUR
FUTURE
look into your past

Tracing your family health history may be the most important step you ever take toward long life

BY STEVEN FINCH

AS A CHILD Kathi Marangos always found her birthday cake a bit hard to swallow. Each sugary bite reminded her of a mother who gave her up for adoption and of a family she didn't know. But she recalls her 18th birthday as especially bittersweet.

"That's when my mother found me," she says. "She hired a private detective so she could give me information about my family."

Marangos felt at once transformed—into the proud daughter of a ski lodge manager and a Harvard graduate. But at the same instant she felt the chill from her family's dark side: its frightening predisposition for depression, heart disease, and colon cancer.

Today, at 35, Marangos, with her doctor's help, keeps an eye out for any sign of cancer while she makes sure her family sticks to a low-fat diet. "I'm so glad to know my medical history," she says, "to know I can use it to protect myself and my kids from our genetic shortcomings."

If only more Americans would see the light, says Michael Crouch, director of the Baylor Family Practice Residency Program in Houston and a leading expert on inherited risks. Trac-

ing your roots to learn your family's health history may be the single most important thing you ever do to bolster your well-being.

> "People who see illness patterns in their families tend to note the red flags in their own lives, then they seek help."

Why? Because any disease that runs in your family puts *you* at risk. And regardless of whether the risks stem from your genetic code or from habits nurtured in your childhood, many family-linked ills can be kept at bay if you know the right steps to take.

If a woman and her husband both have insulin-dependent diabetes, for example, any child of theirs runs a one-

in-ten chance of getting the disease herself. But she greatly lowers her risk if she eats well, exercises regularly, and maintains a healthy weight. For problems such as alcoholism, the genetic connection is less certain. Children of alcoholics are between two and four times more likely to become alcoholics than other people.

"People who recognize patterns of alcoholism in their families tend to note the red flags in their own lives and are more likely to seek help or avoid a problem in the first place," says Crouch. What's more, doctors alerted by family histories can aggressively look for and treat specific health problems.

"Take breast cancer," says Steven Esrick, a family physician who helps direct Kaiser-Permanente's preventive care programs in the northeastern United States. "It's reasonable for most women to start having mammograms at age 50, but I'd want a woman with a family history to start at 40." And many physicians who'd normally recommend counseling for depressed patients, says Esrick, are quicker to consider antidepressant drugs if the family history includes suicide attempts.

"I know one woman who lost her mother and one sister to ovarian cancer at

Preventable Perils: Are You at Risk?

ONCE YOU FIND OUT which health problems various family members have had, your doctor can help you figure out how that affects your risk—or refer you to a genetic counselor if necessary. Many inherited conditions, alcoholism or obesity for example, are passed on by a mix of inborn tendencies and family habits, such as cocktail hour every night or a love of fried foods. But here's one rule of thumb: The more close relatives who suffered one of the conditions listed below—and the younger they were at the time—the likelier you are to have inherited a predisposition to the illness. Here's how to size up your risk—and improve your odds.

HEART DISEASE If your father or grandfather had a heart attack or bypass surgery before age 55 or your mother or grandmother before 65, your risk rises significantly, especially if you're African American. *If it runs in your family:* Swear off smoking, and have your cholesterol tested. If it's over 240, you need to have your blood analyzed for LDL, or "bad" cholesterol. An LDL level over 160 will likely prompt your doctor to prescribe cholesterol-lowering drugs and to advise you to exercise and cut back on fatty foods.

HIGH BLOOD PRESSURE A family history of high blood pressure increases your risk of developing the condition, which in turn boosts your odds of having a stroke sixfold. *If it runs in your family:* Have your pressure checked regularly, watch your weight, exercise, and eat a diet low in fat and high in calcium, potassium, and magnesium. Your doctor may advise you to cut down on salt or to take calcium supplements or blood pressure drugs.

DIABETES If you have one parent with type I (insulin-dependent) diabetes, you typically have a 4 to 6 percent chance of getting it yourself. If one parent has type II (non-insulin-dependent), your risk is 7 to 14 percent. African Americans, Mexican-Americans, and Pima Indians are at highest risk. *If it runs in your family:* Exercise regularly, lose weight if you're obese, and eat a low-fat, high-fiber diet.

BREAST CANCER Many women assume they have a genetic predisposition to breast cancer if a family member developed the disease. But only 5 to 10 percent of all breast cancers are inherited. Scientists have pinpointed a mutated gene, BRCA1, linked to both breast and ovarian cancer, and 1 percent of Jewish women carry it. *If it runs in your family:* You may want to start yearly mammograms at 40 instead of 50. If many members of your family developed the disease at a young age, you might ask your doctor about being tested for the mutated form of BRCA1.

COLON CANCER Ten to 15 percent of all colon cancers are inherited; family genes lead to about 20,000 new cases each year. *If it runs in your family:* Ask your doctor whether you should get a sigmoidoscopy. Regular, low doses of aspirin may offer protection, as does a low-fat, high-fiber diet.

ALCOHOLISM Thirteen to 25 percent of children of alcoholics are likely to become alcoholics. *If it runs in your family:* You need to be especially vigilant about your drinking habits; dependence develops over time. If you've ever found it hard to keep your drinking under control, or anyone close to you thinks your drinking is a problem, you may want to seek treatment.

DEPRESSION Some types of depression run in families and occur generation after generation. Not everyone with a vulnerable genetic makeup will develop depression, but stress is believed to trigger its onset. *If it runs in your family:* Your doctor is more likely to suggest early intervention with antidepressants if you become depressed and your family history includes suicide attempts or major depressions requiring hospitalization. —*S.F.*

a young age," says Esrick. Because this cancer tends to be fatal and is difficult to detect early, even with frequent screening, the patient chose to have her ovaries removed. Not the decision for everyone, to be sure. "But because this woman knew her risks," says Esrick, "she was better able to weigh the options and to make the right decision *for her.*"

People in this country are hardly strangers to unearthing family history. Nearly half say they've at least dabbled in genealogy, and tens of millions have compiled some kind of family tree.

Still, Crouch and Esrick are amazed by how few people know even the barest details of their relatives' medical histories. Only now, thanks to health maintenance organizations and other managed care groups, is this trend starting to change. Under Esrick, for example, Kaiser recent-

> "It's not just that family trees prompt more people to come in for tests. The right people are getting the right tests."

ly began an ambitious effort to gather family health information from all 114,000 of its patients in New York, Connecticut, and Massachusetts.

"What you're really looking for is patterns," says Crouch. Most crucial, he explains, are cases of cancer, high blood pressure, heart disease, diabetes, depression, and alcoholism—all common, life-threatening hereditary diseases that you can do something about.

"Another important pattern," Crouch says, "is the age at which your relatives developed a disease." For example, women whose mothers had breast cancer prior to menopause run a much higher risk themselves. "It's hardly worrisome if several relatives died in their eighties due to heart disease," says Crouch. "But it's a different kettle of fish if they died at 35 or even 55."

Crouch constructs a health history for every patient but tells people not to worry just because a couple of relatives

Family Facts: Where to Find Them

FEW AMERICANS KNOW even the highlights of their family's health history, but no group knows less than the 5 million people who were adopted. Confidentiality has been the watchword for adoption agencies since the 1930s. Today only Hawaii and Kansas allow open records. That means someone adopted in any other state has no right to his or her health history—although judges have sometimes ordered records to be opened in emergencies. Of course, you don't have to be adopted to be blind to some bogeyman in your bloodline. The following agencies can help you track down your relatives, research your heritage, and, after you've compiled a health history, gauge your risks or those facing your children.

IF YOU'RE BUILDING A FAMILY TREE

NATIONAL GENEALOGICAL SOCIETY Offers two publications ($6 each) that explain ways to track down family health records. 4527 17th St. N., Arlington, VA 22207.

FAMILY HISTORY LIBRARY OF THE CHURCH OF JESUS CHRIST OF LATTER-DAY SAINTS Houses the world's largest collection of genealogical records (church members are only a fraction of the database), with 2 million rolls of microfilm and 300,000 bound volumes containing 2 billion names. The staff can answer brief questions and refer you to sources. You can also check the databases at more than 1,800 Family Search Centers in the United States and Canada; call for the nearest location. 35 Northwest Temple, Salt Lake City, UT 84150; 801/240-2331.

NATIONAL SOCIETY OF GENETIC COUNSELORS Gives referrals to professionals who flag hereditary illnesses and determine your risks as well as the chances of passing an illness on to a child. Once you've compiled your family health history, send the society a written request. 233 Canterbury Dr., Wallingford, PA 19086.

IF YOU'RE SEEKING YOUR PARENTS

NATIONAL ADOPTION INFORMATION CLEARINGHOUSE Sends important facts on state adoption laws and on searching for birth relatives, including a list of mutual consent registries as well as other organizations and support groups. 5640 Nicholson Ln., Suite 300, Rockville, MD 20852; 301/231-6512.

INTERNATIONAL SOUNDEX REUNION REGISTRY Matches data on adopted children with data on biological parents who have given up a child for adoption (a free service). Call for a registration form. The registry will contact you if the computer turns up a match. P.O. Box 2312, Carson City, NV 89702; 702/882-7755.

AMERICAN ADOPTION CONGRESS Has local support groups across the country for adoptees, birth parents, and adoptive parents. Each group offers psychological as well as search guidance. 1000 Connecticut Ave. NW, Suite 9, Washington, DC 20036; 202/483-3399.

CONCERNED UNITED BIRTHPARENTS Provides support and some search help through a monthly newsletter and 14 local branches around the country. First-year membership is $50. 2000 Walker St., Des Moines, IA 50317; 800/822-2777.

ADOPTEE LIBERTY MOVEMENT ASSOCIATION Holds search workshops at 62 chapters worldwide. Also provides a registry for people adopted from foreign countries who are seeking their biological relatives. P.O. Box 727, Radio City Station, New York, NY 10101; 212/581-1568. —S.F.

have suffered from heart disease or struggled with addiction. "My guess is that there's a genetic component to almost every disease," he says. "But few of them are caused entirely by genetics." In other words, having a diabetic grandfather raises your risk—it doesn't necessarily doom you to the disease.

Neither does a clean record mean you can quit taking good care of yourself, says Bruce Bagley, public health chairman of the American Academy of Family Physicians. "Just because you don't have a history of hypertension or heart disease doesn't mean a doctor won't still urge you to have your blood pressure checked, to eat healthily, and to exercise." But when doctors can tie in family history, he says, blanket health warnings are made personal.

"Sure, no one should smoke," Bagley says. "But if somebody looks at their family history and sees low cholesterol coupled with a two-pack-a-day cigarette habit, they may come to realize it was really Dad's smoking that caused his heart attack. That's a pretty strong impetus for a person to quit."

This type of nudge can be crucial for people with silent conditions like high blood pressure and elevated cholesterol, says Esrick. Why change your habits if the disorder doesn't make you feel bad? "What feels bad," he points out, "is what happened to your parents."

No wonder Esrick often finds that his patients aren't ready to discuss their family's medical past until they're about the same age as a mother or brother was when she or he became ill or died.

"I had one patient who finally came in because he's 47 and his father had a heart attack at 50," says Esrick. "Now he's taken up walking two days a week, he's reduced his weight, and because he lost someone he cared about, he's agreed to take cholesterol-lowering medication."

Esrick's gospel is steadily sinking in. "A lot more people here are being counseled and screened," he says. "And it's not just that more people are getting mammograms and Pap smears and cholesterol tests. It's that the *right* people are being given the *right* tests."

Getting yourself to that stage doesn't have to be difficult, Esrick says, but it does take a little time. An ideal health tree includes details on all your close relatives, both living and dead. Focus first on older family members, since they're more likely to have suffered whatever ailments run in your bloodline. After tracking down information on your parents, grandparents, aunts, uncles, and siblings, you can compile the data for your spouse and children. If you're ambitious, you can even fill in facts on cousins, nieces, and nephews.

Placing a few phone calls is all it takes for some people. Others send out questionnaires or plan a big reunion so family members can swap medical details. Of course, close-knit families have a distinct edge over those separated by geography or personal disputes. But even deep gaps can be bridged. One method is to send any estranged relatives a note describing how a comprehensive health tree will benefit the whole family.

Locating relatives is the easy part, says Crouch. Often tougher, he says, is convincing them to open up about their mal-

> "Some may be afraid of finding an illness in their bloodline. But knowledge is a good thing, even when the news is bad."

adies—and provide details. Health topics are highly sensitive; some are taboo to older people. Remember that not long ago it was the norm in this country to keep mum on miscarriages, mental illnesses, and even cancer.

Ethnicity, too, remains a delicate topic, albeit an important one. "For example, we worry about hypertension in blacks because they suffer more damage from the disease earlier in life. But in the South especially," Crouch says, "if a mother was Creole it's often not talked about because some people don't want to know what the racial background really is."

If one relative is tight lipped, see if your chatty aunt might be more forthcoming. But in the end, says Crouch, don't sweat a few unknown details about an unreachable uncle or long-lost grandparent. Your goal is simply to gather as much information as you can. For all your close relatives, try to find out:

◆ full name and dates of birth, marriage, divorce, and remarriage.

◆ ethnic background.

◆ height and weight.

◆ average amount that he or she drank or smoked.

◆ any health problems, from recurring headaches and frequent colds to allergies and even limps. Pay special attention to heart attacks, strokes, cancers, diabetes, high blood pressure, high cholesterol, miscarriages, and major surgeries. List the age at which an event occurred or a condition was diagnosed.

◆ any depression or substance abuse and all suicide attempts.

◆ date and cause of death. Tease out as much information as you can. If a grandmother died of stroke, was it caused by a blood clot or by bleeding in the brain? Did she also have high blood pressure? If she died of cancer, what kind?

Organize your tree so that you and your physician can easily compare the health histories of two or more family members. The more close relatives you see who developed a hereditary illness and the younger they were at the time they got sick, the more significant your own risk. Some illness patterns—all your aunts had osteoporosis—will be obvious. But your doctor might notice threats that you miss and possibly refer you for tests or even suggest that you see a genetic counselor, who can help gauge your risk of, say, kidney disease or multiple sclerosis.

"Some people will always be worried about finding an incurable disease in their bloodline—though I'm of the school of thinking that knowledge is a good thing even if the news is bad," says Crouch.

Not everyone agrees. Both patients and doctors worry that insurance companies might use this information to deny coverage to high-risk individuals, such as women who carry the gene mutation that raises the odds of breast cancer. Still, 11 states already have laws on the books banning this type of discrimination.

And though there's no advantage to finding out that a relative had an incurable illness such as Alzheimer's or Lou Gehrig's disease, the day will come when doctors can actually repair defective genes. Until then, Crouch says, there's a lot we can do about the big things people die from—heart disease, hypertension, cancer—especially if a family tree leads to an early diagnosis.

"In the balance of things," Crouch says, "learning more about your family history is about as close as you can get to controlling your destiny."

Steven Finch is a writer and research editor for Hippocrates *magazine.*

BY JOSEPH F. COATES

What's Ahead for Families: Five Major Forces of Change

A research firm identifies key societal trends that are dramatically altering the future prospects for families in America and elsewhere.

No adequate theory in the social sciences explains how values change, so it is very difficult to anticipate changing social values. On the other hand, the social sciences are outstanding in reporting and exploring historic patterns of social change and in reporting contemporary social values through surveys, opinion polls, and observational research.

Identifying long-term shifts in values is complicated by the great deal of attention given to fads—that is, transient enthusiasms. A good example is "family values," a topic of great interest in recent political seasons. Both the family and values are undergoing shifts, and the challenge for futurists and other observers of social change is to identify the long-term trends and implications in both of these important areas. Social values are slowly evolving trends.

To help you understand the myriad of evolving patterns in families, this article describes several major trends and forecasts in families and values and suggests what they may imply for the future.

TREND 1

Stresses on Family Functions

The family in the United States is in transition. While the forces at play are clear and numerous, the outcomes over the next decades remain uncertain.

Anthropologists agree that the family is a central, positive institution in every society. It performs two functions: the nurturing and **socialization** of children and the regulation of the expression of **sexuality**. In European and North American society, the family serves another basic function: **companionship**. Also important are the **economic** functions of families, such as providing care for the elderly and sick and social support for unemployed members.

All of these family functions are being stressed by structural changes in society. Among the patterns that have long-term implications are:

• Increased life-spans mean that adults live well past the period in which nurturing and socialization of children is central to their lives. In many cases, longevity leads to the death of one spouse substantially before the other, creating a companionship crisis.

• Sexual behavior is increasingly being separated from its procreative function, thanks to reproductive technologies such as artificial insemination and *in vitro* fertilization, as well as contraceptives.

• New patterns of work and leisure mean that people are developing interests and activities that are different from other members of their family. In many cases, this leads to conflicting interests and ex-pectations rather than convergence and mutual support. As a result, the companionship function of families comes under increasing stress.

• Television and magazines create images of lifestyles, which may influence people's expectations of each other and the roles of families.

• The anonymity of metropolitan life eliminates many of the social and community pressures on families. There are no watchful and all-knowing eyes in the big city that compare with those in smaller and more cohesive communities, where "What will the neighbors think?" is a critical socializing factor.

These forces will not wipe out the family or the commitment to family, but they will continue to reshape it.

Implications of Stress on Family Functions:

• **Substitutes for family functions will develop.** As family members seek other sources of companionship, and nurturing children becomes less important in matured families, institutions will have a challenge and opportunity to meet human needs. Already, people are finding companionship and even forming committed relationships on the Internet. Schools, businesses, and governments are all under more demand for meeting human services once provided in families, such as health and medical care, child care,

From *The Futurist*, September/October 1996, pp. 27-35. © 1996 by The World Future Society, Bethesda, MD. http://www.wfs.org/wfs. Reprinted by permission.

About the Report

This article expands on research prepared for "Social and Value Trends," the third in a series of reports by Coates & Jarratt, Inc., on critical trends shaping American business in the next 30 years.

The reports were collected under the general project title, American Business in the New Millennium: Trends Shaping American Business, 1993–2010, which was prepared for and sponsored by 15 U.S. organizations: Air Products and Chemicals, Battelle Pacific Northwest Laboratory, CH2M Hill, Discover Card Services, Dow Chemical Company, E.I. DuPont de Nemours & Company, Eastman Chemical Company, Motorola, Niagara Mohawk Power Corporation, NYNEX Corporation, Ohio Edison, Sony Corporation of America, Southwestern Bell Corporation, Goodyear Tire & Rubber, and U.S. West.

Other reports in the series covered trends in U.S. and world demography, politics, the global economy, science and technology, environment and resources, information technology, health and safety, transportation and habitats, and more.

For more information on the reports, contact: Coates & Jarratt, Inc., 3738 Kanawha Street, N.W., Washington, D.C. 20015. Telephone 202/966-9307; fax 202/966-8349.

retirement care, unemployment compensation, etc.

• **Interest groups will proliferate.** Support groups have burgeoned in recent years to help people with special health or emotional problems. Similarly, special-interest groups such as book-discussion salons, travel and adventure societies, or gourmet dinner circles could see a renaissance as individuals seek others with similar interests outside their own families.

• **"Recreational sex" may become more acceptable** as the connection between sexual activity and child-bearing diminishes. Greater access to information on health and "safe sex" will allow people—including the very young and the very old—to engage in sexual activity more safely, both physically and emotionally.

TREND 2

Economics Drives Family Changes

The greatest changes in families have to do less with the family structure and more with economics. The change richest in implications is the rise of the two-income household. The United States has a way to go. Sweden and Denmark are the standards for mothers participating in the labor force. Sixty-five percent of U.S. mothers with children under age 18 are in the work force, compared with 86% in Denmark and 89% in Sweden. For children under 3, the figures are 53% in the United States, 84% in Denmark, and 86% in Sweden. Among the significant patterns emerging are:

• By 2000, women will make up just under half of the work force.

• Women are older when they marry and have their first child, deferring family formation until after they finish their education and get their first job. In 1988, the median age of mothers of firstborn children was 26, the oldest at any time in U.S. history.

• Although the average income of the family household has stayed relatively flat over the last 15 years, the growth of the two-income household is allowing couples to make a higher average income.

Implications of Changes in Family And Economics

• **Two incomes, two decision makers.** Both breadwinning members of two-income households will have broader opportunities to start a new career or business initiative. Any change of job or relocation offer will thus affect two incomes rather than just one, making life/career planning doubly complicated.

• **Women disappear from the community.** Women's greater commitment to work means a long-term change in their commitment to home and the community. Like male breadwinners of the past, women may be rarely seen in stores, in their neighborhood, at home, and so on. In the shopping mall of the future, for instance, the only daytime customers may be the very old, the very young with their mothers or minders, and after-school teenagers.

• **A masculinization of the home** will spread to the community. Telecommuting allows one or both

Enduring Family Values

(Percentage of adults saying these values are important)

Respecting your parents	70%
Providing emotional support for your family	69%
Respecting people for who they are	68%
Being responsible for your actions	68%
Communicating your feelings to your family	65%
Respecting your children	65%
Having a happy marriage	64%
Having faith in God	59%
Respecting authority	57%
Living up to your potential	54%
Being married to the same person for life	54%
Leaving the world in a better shape	51%

Source: *American Demographics* (June 1992), from the Massachusetts Mutual American Family Values Study, 1989.

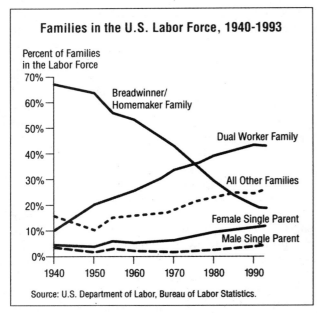

Families in the U.S. Labor Force, 1940-1993

Percent of Families in the Labor Force

Breadwinner/Homemaker Family

Dual Worker Family

All Other Families

Female Single Parent

Male Single Parent

Source: U.S. Department of Labor, Bureau of Labor Statistics.

breadwinners of the dual-income household to work at home. Many men are choosing this option in order to be more available for domestic responsibilities such as cooking, cleaning, and chauffeuring children to various activities. Men may also increasingly become involved in volunteer activities, especially those that directly benefit their own families, such as neighborhood crime-watch groups and the PTA.

• **An economy of convenience will emerge.** A working lifestyle for most families will also continue to shape their preferences in eating, at home, for entertainment, and in shopping. Many families will be willing to pay a premium for convenience in all goods and services they purchase.

TREND 3

Divorce Continues

Divorce may be viewed as a way to correct social mistakes and incompatibility. In the 1940s, for example, there was a surge of marriage in the early 1940s as young Americans went off to war, and at the end of the war there was a surge of divorces in 1945–1947, apparently correcting impetuous mistakes. There was an even greater surge in postwar marriages.

Divorce is seen by many as the death knell of family values. On the other hand, a high divorce rate could be seen as a positive social indicator. It represents an unequivocal rejection of a bad marriage. For the first time anywhere in a mass society, the United States has had the income, the wealth and prosperity, and the broad knowledge base to allow people previously trapped in lifelong misery to reject that state and search for a better marriage. The evidence is clear, since the majority of divorced people either remarry or would remarry were the opportunity available.

Among the patterns emerging in divorce are:

• Divorce rates fell below 10 per 1,000 married women between 1953 and 1964, then surged to a high of almost 23 per 1,000 married women in 1978. Divorces have continued at about 20 to 21 per 1,000 for the last decade.

• Commitment to marriage continues, as demonstrated in the fact that the majority of divorced people remarry. One-third of all marriages in 1988 were remarriages for one or both partners. The average time until remarriage is about two and a half years.

• The shorter lifespans of many families has led to serial marriages. Almost surely there will continue to be people who have three, four, or five spouses, without any intervening widowhood. In the long term, it is much more likely that society will settle down into a

pattern of later marriage, earlier sexual engagement, and much more careful and effective selection of life mates.

• **Marriages and families will be businesses.** Families may increasingly be treated as business units, which form legal partnerships and plan and evolve their own lifecycles as an integrated activity. Families may even incorporate to obtain tax and other benefits. Divorces will be handled as simple business or partnership dissolution. [Ed. note: The rise of "families as businesses" was predicted by Lifestyles Editor David Pearce Snyder in his article, "The Corporate Family: A Look at a Proposed Social Invention," THE FUTURIST, December 1976.]

• **Teenage sex—but not pregnancy—will increase.** Teenagers will observe and emulate their parents' distinct separation of sexuality and commitment.

• **Companies will share and care.** Businesses will offer their employees training in household economics and management, as well as family and divorce counseling. These courses could also be marketed as a service to the community.

• **Opportunities for marketing to new families will emerge.** Many of

U.S. Divorce Rate, 1940-1992

Rate per 1,000 married women, aged 15 and over

Source: National Center for Health Statistics.

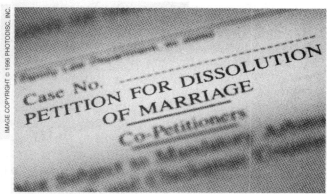

Divorce petition. Author Coates anticipates a movement to improve matchmaking in order to strengthen marriages and families.

the families in the top income segments will include remarriages and second and third families, in which the parents will have a strong incentive to tie together the new relationships. Aiming at this concern could offer opportunities. For example, a new blended family may want financial planning and related services to reallocate its resources. Club memberships for the new family, new homes, etc., all could be important among this group.

• **A "pro-family" movement will take new directions.** One of the most important underlying causes of divorce is that no institution in the United States—school, church, Boy Scouts, or other—teaches and trains people about what it is like to be married, to live in a two-income household, or to share and be involved in a new division of domestic labor. The search for a good marriage is not supported by the right tools to aid that search. Over the next decade, society will focus more on creating more-effective families. A new "pro-family" movement will encourage better and more effective matchmaking, as well as better teaching and training on marriage lifestyles and on economic and household management.

TREND 4

Nontraditional Families Proliferate

A variety of nontraditional family forms are evolving in the United States, shaped by economic and so-

cial changes. For example, higher expectations for education mean young people spend more years in the educational system and marry later. The greater tolerance of divorce and remarriage affects how often people dissolve and re-form families. Many people enter long-term cohabiting relationships before marriage. And many single-parent families are being formed among low- and middle-income communities, as a result of divorce, widowhood, or out-of-wedlock childbearing.

The emerging patterns include:

• More couples are cohabiting. In 1988, one-third of all women aged 15–44 had been living in a cohabiting relationship at some point.

• The number of "boomerang" families is increasing. Young people—post-high school or post-college children who would otherwise be on their own—are returning home to live with Mom and Dad. To a large extent, this is a money-saving move more commonly practiced by men than by women.

• Blended families are becoming the norm. Blended families result from divorced parents who remarry, either linking stepfamilies together

or linking the children of one partner to the subsequent children of both. It is estimated that, for nearly 16% of children living with two parents in 1990, one of those parents is a stepparent.

• Technology is creating new families. These may involve adopted children matched for similar genetic inheritance, children from surrogate parents, and eventually children from cloned embryos.

• Gay families are surfacing as a result of the new openness in society. Aside from the social approval so valuable to many in the gay community, acknowledgment offers substantial economic benefits in corporate or business health and recreation benefits packages. Time will make family resources available to members of nontraditional families.

• Group living, with or without sexual intimacy, is likely to remain a transitional life stage for an increasing number of people, often as an alternative to living alone.

• Single-parent families are increasingly common across all socioeconomic groups. The unmarried woman who bears a child is one of these family styles. It is unclear what the consequences are for middle- and professional-class mothers and children in these voluntary single-parent households. Evidence is strong that teenage childbearing, particularly by unmarried mothers, is so-

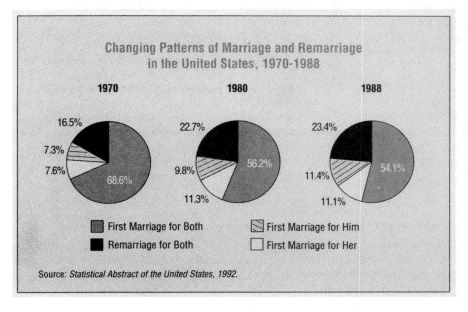

Changing Patterns of Marriage and Remarriage in the United States, 1970-1988

1970
- 16.5%
- 7.3%
- 7.6%
- 68.6%

1980
- 22.7%
- 9.8%
- 11.3%
- 56.2%

1988
- 23.4%
- 11.4%
- 11.1%
- 54.1%

☐ First Marriage for Both   ☑ First Marriage for Him
■ Remarriage for Both   ☐ First Marriage for Her

Source: *Statistical Abstract of the United States, 1992.*

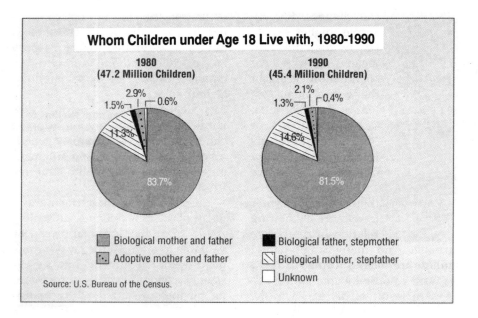

Whom Children under Age 18 Live with, 1980-1990

1980
(47.2 Million Children)

2.9%   0.6%
1.5%
11.3%
83.7%

1990
(45.4 Million Children)

2.1%   0.4%
1.3%
14.6%
81.5%

■ Biological mother and father
⬛ Biological father, stepmother
▨ Adoptive mother and father
▧ Biological mother, stepfather
☐ Unknown

Source: U.S. Bureau of the Census.

cially destructive of the future well-being of both the mother and the child. Some single-parent families are single by divorce or separation.

Implications of the Proliferation of Nontraditional Families

• **Rearranged families will rearrange the workplace.** The work force will continue to be profoundly affected by new family structures. The proliferation of family arrangements will create new pressures on employers to be flexible and responsive in relation to working hours.

• **Businesses will make attitude adjustments.** Employers will be hard-pressed to justify accepting one type of family arrangement among their employees and not another. One company decided to offer benefits to gay couples because they could *not* get married and deny them to male-female couples living together because they *could.* Workers did not accept this justification.

• **"Nonfamily" families will gain in status.** Many groups of people consider themselves families, even though they do not fit traditional definitions (e.g., gay couples, unmarried couples with or without children, foster parents, long-term housemates, etc.). This has implications for business and nonbusiness issues, for example in marketing,

housing codes and covenants, loans, billing, leasing, and so on.

• **Family-oriented organizations will reinvent themselves.** For example, Parent-Teacher Associations may broaden into Family-Teacher or Community-Teacher Associations. Schools may provide more counseling for students in nontraditional families.

• **Flexible architecture will be mandatory.** Housing will become more flexible, with walls that can be easily taken down and rearranged to form new rooms depending on the needs of new family members.

TREND 5

An Aging Society Will Redefine Families

The traditional family in past decades was the nuclear family: a working father, a homemaker mother, and children. As the children aged and left home, the traditional family was two adults with no children living at home; then one or the other died, leaving an elderly single person alone.

Aging creates a crisis in traditional families' lifecyles. The patterns to watch now include:

• Death rates of men are relatively high compared with women. Men also tend to marry women younger than themselves. As a result, at age

75 and older, 66% of men but only 24% of women are living with a spouse. At age 65, for every 100 men there are 150 women. At age 85, for every 100 men there are 260 women.

• The savings rate among working adults is now just 4.1% of personal income, compared with 7.9% in 1980; this low rate bodes ill for Americans' economic status in retirement.

• Voting rates among seniors are traditionally higher than for younger people (60.7% of those 65 years and older voted in 1994, compared with 16.5% for 18- to 20-year olds and 22.3% for 25- to 34-year olds). It is likely that the baby boomers' influence on public policy will gain strength as they approach retirement years.

Implications of Age and Family

• **The end of retirement?** A combination of several factors may lead to the end of retirement: the emotional need of seniors to feel useful when their families no longer demand their daily attention, the financial needs of seniors who didn't save enough during their working years, the improved mental and physical health of older people, and the need in businesses for skilled, experienced workers.

• **Economic priorities shift away from children.** There is already concern among the elderly about balancing their economic assets against commitments to their children. Personal savings during their working years for their kids' college education may have left them ill-prepared for retirement.

• **Parents will "boomerang" back to their kids.** Just as adult children of the 1980s and 1990s moved back into their parents' home for economic security, elderly parents in the twenty-first century may increasingly move into the homes of their grown children. "Granny flats" and mother-in-law apartments will be common additions to houses.

• **No retirement from sex.** The sexual experimentation characteristic of baby boomers' youth may be brought to their old age. New drugs and therapies, such as penile implants, will help.

• **Elders will have roommates** or form other shared-living arrangements. A substantial increase in cohabitation offers the benefits of companionship without compromising the individual's financial survival or reducing the children's inheritance. We may see some college campuses convert into retirement communities, with dorm-style living.

The Effects of Population Changes on Values

Changes in values in the United States will depend to some extent on demographic change. Social institutions will continue to be stressed when population groups such as the aging baby boomers pass through society.

The baby boomers' children, the echo generation, now number more than 80 million people; they will be an even larger generation and a bigger social force than the baby boom was. They may be expected to stress and reshape education, justice, and work in turn, beginning now and accelerating through 2005, when they reach 20 and are ready to go to work.

Through the 1990s, the young echo boomers will increase school enrollment, then college enrollment. As they reach their late teens and move into their violence-prone years, the United States could experience an increase in violent crimes after the turn of the century. At around the same time there may be some risk of social unrest either in universities or in cities, as the echo boom goes through its years of youthful idealism and discontent.

The aging of the baby boom in the 1990s and 2000s may push the dominant values of U.S. society to be more conservative, more security conscious, and more mature and less driven by youthful expectations. In 2010, the first of the baby boomers

turn 65. If the conservatism of their elders becomes repressive, the echo boomers could have more to rebel against.

As the U.S. population grows, if the economy affords only shrinking opportunities, this may promote more conservative views. At the same time, there may be an emerging social activism around worker rights, employment stability, and related issues.

Effects of Shifting Family Patterns

As a flexible institution, the family will continue to accommodate itself to the economy and the values of the Information Age. In many societies, this means an ongoing shift to dual-income partnerships.

It has also meant a shift in what work is available for the family to earn its income—away from agriculture and manufacturing and to information and services. This shift has brought millions of women into the work force because the work now requires education rather than raw physical might—mind, not muscle.

In many societies, men are finding it more difficult to find work unless they, too, can shift to information-based work. It is possible that women will become the higher wage earners in millions of families. It is also possible that as a result child care and family responsibilities will be more equally distributed between men and women.

People will continue to want to be part of families, but for some the economic necessity to do so will be less. For example, young people will need to spend more time in acquiring their education, and they will form their families later. Women with substantial careers will have less economic need to remarry after divorce.

Education, prosperity, and a decline in regard for authority will continue to secularize U.S. society, but concern for the family and com-

munity will tend to promote ties with religion. The church will continue to be a source of support for those who feel in some way disadvantaged by current values and attitudes. The other attractions of religion are its rituals, its shared experiences, its mysteries, and its social events. These will continue to bring in and keep people in religious groups, unless urban society develops some alternatives.

Conclusion: Belief in the Family Remains High

Anticipations of family life have not diminished to a significant degree in the last decades. In general, Americans are committed to the family as the core of a successful life. It is particularly gratifying to see this view widely maintained by young people. The percentage of college freshmen saying that raising a family is "essential" or "very important" has been fairly constant in the past quarter century: 67.5% in 1970 and 69.5% in 1990.

Adults' commitment to the family has become somewhat tempered by the higher likelihood of divorce. But most people still agree that being happily married and having a happy family is an important goal.

About the Author
Joseph F. Coates is president of Coates & Jarratt, Inc., 3738 Kanawha Street, N. W., Washington, D.C. 20015. Telephone 202/966-9307; fax 202/966-8349.

This article is based on the "Social and Value Trends" section of a major report by Coates & Jarratt for its clients, *American Business in the New Millennium: Trends Shaping American Business, 1993–2010*. The author acknowledges the assistance of Christine Keen of the Domani Group and the team support of Jennifer Jarratt, John Mahaffie, Andy Hines, Andrew Braunberg, Sean Ryan, and Nina Papadopoulos of Coates & Jarratt, Inc.

Rewriting Life Stories

Mind: Instead of looking for flaws in people's psyches, 'narrative therapy' works at nurturing their forgotten strengths

Geoffrey Cowley and Karen Springen

Last August, Lorraine Grieves fell into a familiar pattern: "The rule in my head was, I couldn't have any food, and if I did, I had to purge." Fearing for her life, the 21-year-old Vancouver woman's doctor sent her to a psychiatric ward where, for three weeks, she sat surrounded by fellow sufferers with feeding tubes dangling from her nose. Under the house rules, anyone who left a meal unfinished was fed liquid calories or plugged into a feeding machine. And if a patient resisted that drill, she was eligible for a straitjacket. Hospital staffers monitored the ward closely, but the women found ways to evade them. Though Grieves weighed just 103 pounds, she did sit-ups in bed and ran in the shower. When hooked up to a feeding machine, she would wait until no one was looking and then disconnect the tubes. "we'd all sit there sometimes with our tube dripping into the garbage," she recalls. "After all, they were giving you the thing you're most afraid of."

Narrative therapy recognizes that one's psyche is not a fixed, objective entity but a fluid social construct that can be "re-authored" to correct mental problems.

Today, Grieves carries a healthy 125 pounds on her 5-foot, 5-inch frame, and she's no longer dominated by the craving to be thinner. What finally kept her from starving herself was not the prison-style discipline of the hospital, she says, but the perspective she gained through her conversations with a local psychotherapist named Stephen Madigan. Unlike the professionals she'd consulted in the past, Madigan didn't reinforce her sense that there was something wrong with her. Instead, he worked at driving a wedge between her and her problem. He got her to think about the rare moments when anorexia and bulimia *didn't* control her life. He coaxed her to focus on what that experience felt like. And as she began to think of anorexia as a hostile oppressor, not the whole of her own being, he inspired her to fight back. If a person told you to deprive yourself of food and water, he asked, wouldn't you revolt? Yes, she realized, she would revolt. And with the support of other sufferers, she did.

Like Madigan, a small but growing number of psychotherapists are shedding ideas that have dominated their field for a century. Loosely united by what they call a "narrative" approach, they're forging a new conception of mental suffering and devising new strategies for easing it. The psyche, from their perspective, is not a fixed, objective entity but a fluid social construct—a story that is subject to revision. And the therapist's job is to help people "re-author" stories that aren't doing them justice. The new approach is still far from orthodox, but its adherents—mainly family therapists in Australia, New Zealand and North America—are applying it to everything from marital conflict to psychosis. And as Lorraine Grieves's experience suggests, their efforts are changing people lives. Narrative therapy is "more than a new set of techniques," Omaha therapist Bill O'Hanlon wrote recently in The Family Therapy Networker. "It represents a fundamentally new direction in the therapeutic world."

At the heart of the new approach is the postmodernist idea that we don't so much perceive the world as interpret it. The buzz of sensory experience would overwhelm us without some frame of reference, says Michael White, an Australian therapist who helped launch the narrative movement in the late 1980s. So we collapse our experience into narrative structures, or stories, to make it intelligible. As we forge identities, we inevitably give some patterns of experience more weight than others, and cultural pressures help determine which patterns define us. If our "dominant stories" happen to center on problems, they can become spiritual prisons, As the Berkeley, Calif.-based therapists Jennifer Freeman and Dean Lobovits have written, a "problem-saturated" dominant story tends to "filter problem-free experiences from a person's memories and perceptions," so that "threads of hope, resourcefulness and capability are excluded from a person's description of self."

That's where therapy comes in. Conventional Freudian psychotherapy tends to assume that people's problems stem from internal pathologies that need to be identified, scrutinized and corrected. Narrative therapy, as conceived by White and his colleague David Epston of Auckland, New Zealand, takes a different tack. Instead of looking for flaws in people's psyches, the therapist helps people spot omissions in their stories. "No problem or diagnosis ever captures the whole of a person's experience," says Epston. "The person has other ways of acting and thinking, but they get neglected because they lie in the shadows of the dominant story." Practitioners have different tricks for helping people recover forgotten strengths, but the process follows a predictable arc.

Small discoveries can have big effects. One small discovery can be when a person seeking help feels, even for an instant, that they are not dominated by their problem.

Danny's story: The first step is to initiate what's known in the trade as an externalizing conversation. "People come in thinking, 'I'm depressed. This diagnosis defines me. I'm a failure'," says Freeman, the Berkeley therapist. "There's usually very little distance between the person and the problem. That feeling of being defective can immobilize people." To counter that feeling, the therapist typically invites the client to personify the problem—to give it a name and talk about how it's affecting his life. As you see from a videotaped conversation between White and a 5-year-old named Danny, the effect can be transformative. Danny has already seen many counselors when his mom brings him to White's office at the Dulwich Centre in Adelaide, Australia. No one has been able to toilet-train the bubbly, sweet-natured kindergartner; he won't bother with a trip to the bathroom, no matter how awful the consequences. But White engages Danny in a conversation about two characters named Sneaky Poo and Sneaky Wee, and within minutes the child is talking about how they take advantage of him.

How does Sneaky Poo make you feel?
I start to have tears. It just sneaks out.
So it makes you feel sad. How else does it make you feel?
It makes me feel angry.
Anything else?
Yes, it stinks and it sticks to me. It hurts and its hard to get off.
Does Sneaky Poo cause trouble in your friendships with other kids?
Sometimes they just want to go away.
I can see that Sneaky Poo is causing a lot of trouble in your life. What would you like instead?
I'd be happy if it didn't come out any time except in the toilet!

Danny is soon scheming to put Sneaky Poo in his place, and doing timed laps around the office to show that he's a faster runner than his newfound adversary. Throughout the exchange, White proposes nothing directly. He simply asks questions that create an opening for the boy to act on the problem without acting against himself. "[The other] therapists had succeeded in making him think of himself as the problem," White says. "No one had invited him to recount the problem's effects on his own life." Danny returned for several visits, but within six weeks Messrs. Poo and Wee had been vanquished.

Sparkling moments: To "externalize" a problem is not necessarily to solve it. The next step in the therapeutic process is to identify "unique outcomes"—those sparkling moments when the person seeking help has *not* been dominated by the problem. Those small discoveries can have big effects. Consider what happened last year when Epston had an hourlong conversation with Jermaine, a black 17-year-old from Ann Arbor, Mich. Jermaine has always suffered from life-threatening asthma, and as a teenager he'd grown so indifferent about treating and monitoring it that he was rarely out of the hospital for more than three days at a stretch. Despairing over his irresponsibility (he had also started committing petty juvenile offenses), his mother had recently placed him in a state institution.

In chatting with Epston, Jermaine quickly establishes that asthma has been messing up his life, and that he'd like to assert some control over it. Then Epston asks a pivotal question: "Tell me, has there ever been a time when asthma tried to pull the wool over your eyes and somehow you didn't keel over?" It turns out that he had staved off a trip to the hospital just that morning, by testing himself and taking his medication. Epston bears down enthusiastically on the meaning of the event, and Jermaine is soon proclaiming himself "asthma smart" and predicting a winning streak. A year later, the streak is all but unbroken.

New identities: There's more to changing a life than noticing a "unique outcome." The value of those moments is that they illuminate the resources a person can use to succeed on a larger scale. "we're not just telling people, 'You can do it!'" says therapist Jill Freedman of the Evanston Family Therapy Center, outside Chicago. "we're asking questions, in the hope that they'll help people see things about themselves that they weren't seeing before."

Liz Gray, a 52-year-old, self-employed accountant, used to think of herself as a servant. That was the assigned role of girls in her Irish Catholic household. and she continued to play the role as an adult. She laughs when she remembers teaching a course for tax preparers at an H&R Block office—and voluntarily cleaning the bathroom while she was there. When she started suffering panic attacks a few years ago, the therapists she consulted declared her "codependent" and told her she'd been psychologically damaged as a toddler. But the conversation changed when she started seeing Gene Combs at the Evanston Family Therapy Center.

Combs wanted to know how Gray, 20 years divorced, had managed to run a household, raise two children, look after her aging mother and run her own business. What did it say about her that she was able to do all that? Was she a victim, or was she a survivor? What resources had she drawn on? "As the patient identifies the exceptions to the dominant story of pathology," says New York psychiatrist Christian Beels, "the plot becomes thick and many-stranded." After two years of monthly sessions with Combs, Gray still suffers occasional panic attacks, which she treats with a tranquilizer. But she says she doesn't feel "broken" anymore. "I'm rewriting a story that someone told me a long time ago about what happens to women in this world," she says. "The idea of a queen keeping track of a house is a very different story from a victim saying, 'Oh my god, I'm overwhelmed'."

Going public: Unlike most other approaches, narrative therapy isn't a secretive transaction between the therapist and the client. Since the stories that define us are "negoti-ated and distributed within communities," White observes it's only reasonable to "engage communities in the renegotiation of identity." In Vancouver, Lorraine Grieves and others have organized an "anti-anorexia/anti-bulimia league" to fight the social pressures that encourage women to starve themselves. In Berkeley, Jennifer Freeman encourages the children she sees to chronicle their struggles for anthologies like "The Temper Tamer's Handbook" and "The Fear Facer's Handbook." And narrative therapists everywhere are incorporating audiences into the therapeutic process.

It's not an entirely new idea.

With the client's consent, a family therapist will often have other therapists observe a session from behind a screen. Normally, the observers share their impressions only with the therapist who recruited them. But narrative practitioners often invite their clients to watch the "reflecting team" deliberate. The Moore family had that experience last fall, when they spent an hourlong session with Michael White at the Evanston Family Therapy Center. Jane Moore and her second husband, Clint, an Episcopal priest, had been married for several years when Jane's 16-year-old daughter, Jennifer, left her father to live with them. They felt they needed help in becoming a family, but as they listened to the reflecting team, they realized they had already started to function as one. "It was a wonderful surprise to find out that other people perceived you as having the qualities you thought you were looking for," says Jane.

Narrative therapy doesn't have all the answers people need, but it incites them to ask different questions that may well lead to positive life choices.

There are of course limits to what any of these exercises can accomplish. No form of talk therapy is likely to eliminate a biologically based depression or psychosis. And traumatic experiences, such as childhood abuse, don't just go away when people focus on their strengths. "There is such a thing as true mental illness," says San Diego psychiatrist Harold Bloomfield, "Some people just need drugs." Many proponents of narrative therapy would agree, but they would add that there's more than one way of living with an illness. "The question is how you want to face the experiences you're stuck with," says

Beels. ""What kind of relationship are you going to have with depression? What have you found effective? It's not an either-or situation, where you're cured or defeated. It's a lifetime battle."

Some experts worry that narrative enthusiasts, in their reluctance to "pathologize" people, will give their problems short shrift. They fear that by focusing solely on the problem at hand—anorexia, pants-soiling or panic attacks—a therapist may ignore larger issues that need to be confronted. But to narrative purists, such questions simply reflect a particular view of the world. "In traditional therapy, the audience is the therapist," say Beels. "What does the therapist expect? He expects that we have not gotten to the bottom of this problem yet. He expects that things are not better than we thought, but worse." In fact, he says, the sources of people's suffering—traumatic memories, low self-esteem, whatever—are not that mysterious. Any line of inquiry will draw them out, and they need to be acknowledged. But they don't need monuments built to them. As Epston puts it, "Every time we ask a question, we're generating a possible version of a life." Narrative therapy doesn't have all the answers people need. Its beauty is that it incites them to ask different questions.

FOR OUR TIMES

Evan Imber-Black and Janine Roberts

Evan Imber-Black is the director of the Family and Group Studies program of the Department of Psychiatry at Albert Einstein College of Medicine. Janine Roberts is the director of the Family Therapy program of the School of Education at the University of Massachusetts.

EVERY FOURTH OF JULY, PAUL and Linda Hoffman pack their three children and their dog into the station wagon and drive 250 miles to Paul's sister's home, where all of the Hoffmans gather. The event is fairly unpleasant. The women spend the day cooking, which Linda resents, while the men watch sports, an activity Paul doesn't care for. The young cousins spend most of the day fighting with one another. In the evening, Grandpa Hoffman sets off fireworks, but no one really pays attention. On the fifth of July, Paul and Linda drive home, wearily vowing that this is the last year they will spend their holiday this way.

The following June, however, when Paul and Linda dare mention that they are thinking about doing something different for Independence Day, Paul's sister calls and tells them how upset their parents will be if the couple and their children don't come this year. Alternate plans fall by the wayside, and on the Fourth of July into the car they go.

Does this story sound at all familiar to you? Because of experiences like the Hoffmans', in which celebrations are static and meaningless, many of us have minimized the practice of rituals in our lives. One

• • • • • • • • • •

How today's families are developing innovative rites and ceremonies to ease difficult transitions, heal relationships, and celebrate life.

• • • • • • • • • •

woman we know who grew up in a family whose rituals were particularly confining put it this way: "I don't want any rituals in my life. Rituals are like being in prison!"

Yet in these times of rapid and dramatic change in the family—with more children being raised by single parents, more mothers working outside the home, fewer extended families living in close proximity —rituals can provide us with a crucial sense of personal identity as well as family connection. Despite the changing status

of the family, membership within a family group is still the primary way that most people identify themselves. Rituals that both borrow from the past and are reshaped by relationship needs of the present highlight for us continuity as well as change. A family in which ritual is minimized may have little sense of itself through time. Everything simply blends into everything else.

As family therapists who have been working with and teaching the use of rituals since the late '70s, we have encountered an increasing number of people who are longing to revitalize the rituals in their lives. They just don't know how. Rituals surround us and offer opportunities to make meaning from the familiar and the mysterious at the same time. Built around common symbols and symbolic actions such as birthday cakes and blowing out candles, or exchanging rings and wedding vows, many parts of rituals are well known to us.

A ritual can be as simple as the one that sixty-two-year-old Eveline Miller practices when she needs to sort things through. She goes to her grandmother's rocking chair, sits, and rocks. When she was a child and needed comfort, this was where she used to go to lay her head upon her grandmother's lap. Her grandmother would stroke her hair and say, "This too will pass." Now, as Eveline rocks and thinks, she repeats those words to help calm herself and provide perspective.

Rituals also can be more elaborate and creative, such as one that Jed and his wife, Isabel, a couple in their early twenties, designed for Jed's brother. Several months after Jed married Isabel, his mother died suddenly, leaving Jed's nineteen-year-old brother, Brian, orphaned. Brian came to live with Jed and Isabel. The young couple thus found themselves not only newly-weds but also new "parents." One day Brian told them, "You know, I feel like I don't have a security blanket. My friends at school, other people in my classes—most of them have at least one parent still alive. Their parents can help them if they're having trouble in school, or if they need a place to stay, or can't find a job. And I don't have that security blanket because both of my parents are dead."

What Brian had said seemed so important to him that Jed and Isabel talked about it between themselves and eventually came up with an idea: They would make Brian a quilt—a security blanket. Jed's sister had an old nurse's uniform of their mother's that they could use for material. An older brother had a Marine camouflage shirt of their father's. They found some other old fabric among their mother's things. Then, as they began to cut the material into squares, they realized that they would need help sewing them together into a quilt. Jed thought of his maternal grand-mother, who had sewn a number of quilts for other family members.

The siblings and the grandmother began gathering in secret to sew the quilt and share memories of Brian's parents and their earlier life. And when the family gathered to celebrate the grandmother's eightieth birthday, Brian was given the quilt—a blanket that symbolized both the ability of Jed and Isabel to "parent" in cre-ative ways and the new network of contact that had been built between the siblings and their grandmother. Together, these family members had proved to be Brian's "security blanket."

The symbols and symbolic actions of rituals embrace meaning that cannot always be easily expressed in words. Eve-line Miller's rocking chair, for example, was much more than a place to sit; it evoked safety, reassurance, and the memo-ry of her grandmother. Brian's quilt was not just a cover; it represented the inter-connected people in his life—from the past and the present—whom he could carry with him into the future. The tex-tures, smells, and sounds of ritual sym-bols—an heirloom rocking chair, a family-made quilt—can be powerful activators of sensory memory. Family members may recall scenes and stories of previous times when similar rituals were enacted or some of the same people were together. Rituals connect us with our past, define our pre-sent life, and show us a path to our future.

FAMILY RITUALS TAKE A VARIETY OF FORMS. There are daily practices, such as the read-ing of a child's bedtime story or the shar-ing of a mealtime. There are holiday tradi-tions, some celebrated with the communi-ty at large (seasonal events such as the sol-stice, religious events such as Passover, national events such as the Fourth of July) and others exclusive to a particular family (birthdays, anniversaries, reunions). Then there are life-cycle rituals, which mark the major transitions of life.

All human beings throughout the world and throughout time are born, and all die. All of us experience emerging sexuality. And most create sustained adult relation-ships to form new family units and new generations. Such changes are enormously complicated, involving both beginnings and endings; holding and expressing both pain and joy. They may shape and give voice to profoundly conflicting beliefs about our personal existence and our rela-tionships. It's little wonder that every cul-ture in the world has created rituals to cel-ebrate and guide our way through these life-cycle passages.

The truly magical quality of rituals is embedded in their capacity not only to announce a change but to actually create the change. Given that volumes have been written advising people how to change, and that people spend countless hours in therapy, often agonizing over their inabili-ty to make needed changes, it is easy to see why rituals exist in all cultures, to ease our passage from one stage of life to another. Using familiar symbols, actions, and words, rituals make change manage-able and safe. Simply knowing which ritu-als lie ahead during a day, a year, or a life-time stills our anxiety. Change is *enacted* through rituals and not simply talked about—couples don't change from being single to being married by talking about marriage, but rather by participating in a wedding ceremony. Teens don't graduate from high school when a teacher says "you're finished now"; they attend proms, picnics, and the graduation ceremony itself.

As families have changed, life-cycle events have changed too, and there are many crucial transitions for which there are no familiar and accepted rituals in our culture. Changes that often go unmarked include divorce, the end of a nonmarried relationship, adoption, forming a commit-ted homosexual relationship, leaving home, pregnancy loss, and menopause. Since life-cycle rituals enable us to begin to rework our sense of self and our rela-

tionships as required by life's changes, the lack of such rituals can make change more difficult.

Rituals tend to put us in touch with the profound circle of life and death, so it is not surprising that healing moments emerge spontaneously during these cele-

• • • • • • • • •

A family in which ritual is minimized may have little sense of itself through time.

• • • • • • • • •

brations. If you keep that in mind when changes are occurring in your life or in the lives of those close to you, you can plan a ritual to specifically generate healing.

Healing a Broken Relationship
The crisis of shattered trust and broken promises can lead to genuine atonement, forgiveness, reconciliation, and relation-ship renewal or, alternatively, to chronic resentment, bitterness, parting, and isola-tion. Since rituals are able to hold and express powerful contradictory feelings, such as love and hate, anger and connect-edness, they enhance the possibility of relationship healing.

For Sondra and Alex Cutter, ritual pro-vided a way to bury that past. The Cutters had spent seven of their twelve years of marriage in bitter arguments about a brief affair Alex had had just before their fifth anniversary. Sondra didn't want to leave her marriage, but she felt unable to let go of the past. Alex, in turn, had become extremely defensive about his behavior and was unable to genuinely show Sondra that he was sorry. In couple's therapy, Son-dra and Alex were asked to bring two sets of symbols of the affair. The first set of symbols was to represent what the affair meant to each of them at the time it occurred. The second set was to symbolize what the affair had come to mean in their current life together. As a symbol of her feelings at the time of the affair, Sondra brought a torn wedding photograph to show that the affair meant a break in their vows. Sondra was surprised by Alex's symbol: an old picture of his father, who had had many affairs. "I thought this was just what husbands did," said Alex. "I thought this was what made you a man, but I found out quickly that this didn't work for me and for what I wanted my marriage to be. Then we couldn't get past it." Sondra had never heard Alex speak about the affair in this way. Her belief that the affair meant he didn't love her and that he loved another woman began to shift for the first time in seven years.

As a symbol of what the affair meant currently, Alex brought the wheel of a hamster cage, remarking, "We just go round and round and round and get nowhere." Sondra brought a bottle of bitters, and said, "This is what I've turned into!" After a long conversation engendered by their symbols, Sondra said quietly, "This is the first time in seven years that we've talked about this without yelling and screaming." When the therapist asked if they were ready to let go of the past, both agreed that they were. They decided to revisit a favorite spot from early in their relationship and to bury these symbols there. During the ceremony, Alex cried and for the first time asked Sondra to forgive him, which she readily did. They followed this with a celebration of their anniversary, which they had stopped celebrating seven years earlier.

This healing ritual was created as part of couple's therapy, but you don't need the help of a therapist to create rituals to effect healing. Common to all healing rituals is a dimension of time—time for holding on and time for letting go. Selecting symbols to express painful issues generally allows for a new kind of conversa-

tion to emerge. Taking some joint action together, such as symbolically burying the past, can impart a new possibility of collaboration. Creating a ritual together can help you to rediscover the playful parts of your relationship, such as the couple who "put an affair on ice," placing symbols in their deep freezer and agreeing that they could only fight about the affair after they had thawed these symbols out!

A Ceremony for Grieving

There is no life that is lived without loss. We all experience the death of people we love and care for deeply. When healing rituals have not occurred, or have been insufficient to complete the grief process, a person can remain stuck in the past or unable to move forward in meaningful ways. Even the unhealed losses of previous generations may emerge as debilitating symptoms in the present. When this happens, new rituals can be created to address the need for healing.

Joanie and Jeralynn Thompson were identical twins who had a close and loving

Rituals shape our relationships and give us a basis for a healthy society. Simply having a family meal together helps establish a stronger sense of self.
(UN photo/John Isaac)

relationship. They went away to the same college and planned to graduate together. During their junior year, however, Jeralynn developed leukemia. She died within the year. Before her death, Jeralynn talked with Joanie about how important it was that Joanie continue college and graduate. Joanie did go back to school after her sister's funeral, but she found it impossible to study. At the urging of friends, she took a year off in order to be with her family and begin to deal with the terrible loss of her sister. But a year turned into two years, two years into three. Finally, her family insisted that she go back to college. Joanie returned to school and finished all of her courses, but remained unable to do her senior thesis. She didn't graduate that June. "I don't know how I can graduate without Jeralynn," she told her mother. "It'll mean that she's really gone." Once her mother began to understand what was stopping Joanie from finishing, she talked with her daughter about how they might honor Jeralynn's life while still celebrating Joanie's entering adulthood with her college graduation. After developing a plan with her mother, Joanie finished her thesis in time to graduate the following December.

Joanie and her mother planned a special ceremony to be held two nights before graduation. They invited extended family and close friends, asking them to bring symbols of Jeralynn and to speak about her openly. During a very moving ceremony, many people spoke about what they thought Jeralynn would have wished for Joanie. One aunt made a video that showed places the two sisters had both loved, and after showing it told Joanie, "These places still belong to you." Joanie's father brought photographs of several pets the twins had raised, carefully pointing out the individual contributions each twin had made to these animals. Then, in a five-minute talk, he highlighted the strengths and gifts of each young woman and gave Joanie permission to be her own person. People grieved the loss of Jeralynn openly and then embraced Joanie for finishing school and going on in life.

Several months later, settled in a new job as a teacher, Joanie talked about this ceremony and her graduation: "They all helped me to graduate. If we hadn't had our memorial first, I know all I would have been wondering about on graduation day was what my family was feeling about Jeralynn's death. Instead, all of it was out in the open. We could be sad together and then we could be happy together on my graduation day. They call graduation a

Rituals connect us with our past, define our present life, and show us a path to our future.

commencement, an ending that's really a beginning, and that's what mine was. I miss my sister terribly—I'll always miss her—but my family and friends helped me take the next step in my life, and Jeralynn's spirit was right there with me."

Celebrating Recovery from Illness

Sometimes very important changes take place but remain unacknowledged. This may be because the changes are difficult to talk about, because they bring up the pain of how things used to be, or because no one had thought about how to mark the change. In our experience, recovery from medical or psychiatric illness is an aspect of change that is seldom marked by a ritual. Families, relationships, and the individual's own identity remain stuck with the illness label, and behavior among family members and friends remains as it was when the person was ill.

Adolescents who have recovered from cancer or adults who are now healthy after heart surgery often maintain an "illness identity," and others treat them accordingly. A ritual can declare in action that a person has moved from illness to health. Such a ritual might include a ceremony of throwing away no-longer-needed medicines or medical equipment, burning or burying symbols of a long hospital stay, or writing a document declaring new life and health.

After recovering from breast cancer,

Gerry Sims had a T-shirt made that read HEALTHY WOMAN! She wore this T-shirt to a family dinner and announced to everyone that they were to stop treating her as a patient, and that, in particular, she wanted people to argue with her as they had before she became ill. Then she handed out T-shirts to her husband and children that read HUSBAND OF A HEALTHY WOMAN, CHILD OF A HEALTHY WOMAN, and TEENAGER OF A HEALTHY WOMAN. Everyone put on his or her T-shirt and for the first time spontaneously began to talk about what they had been through together during Gerry's year-long illness. They cried out loud to each other. Following this, Gerry's teen-age daughter picked a fight with her, just as Gerry had hoped!

A Rite of Passage

Like many life-cycle passages, a child leaving home is an event that carries deeply mixed feelings, including a sense of joy and accomplishment, fear regarding what lies ahead, sadness over the loss of relationships in their present form, and curious anticipation about what life will look like next. This life-cycle passage of leaving home may be even more difficult when the leaving is unanticipated or when the child has grown up with a handicap. Creating a leaving-home ritual whose symbols and symbolic actions speak to the many contradictory issues can ease this passage for everyone in the family.

Jennifer Cooper-Smith was born with some severe disabilities that affected her capacity to read, write, and speak. During her childhood she took the handicap in stride despite the cruel teasing of other children and despite coming from a family where high academic achievement was the norm. Through it all she taught her family a lot about perseverance in the face of enormous struggles and about building on strengths rather than focusing on weaknesses.

When Jennifer reached nineteen, since her disabilities would preclude her going to college, it was clear that high school graduation was to be her rite of passage. The family wanted to create a ritual that would both honor all that she had accomplished and send her forth into the adult world with confidence.

Jennifer wanted a party at a Chinese restaurant with her favorite festive food. Her mother and stepfather invited people who were important to Jennifer—extended family who lived far away, friends who had supported her, special teachers and co-workers from her part-time job. The invitation included a secret request for special items—poems, letters, photos, stories, drawings, and so on—to help make a "becoming an adult woman" album for Jenni. During the weeks before the party, her mom worked secretly to construct the album, which began at the time Jennifer joined the family as an adopted infant and included sections that marked significant stages of her development. Although the handicaps had sometimes made it difficult for both Jennifer and those around her to notice her growth and changes, this album recorded them for all to see.

When Jennifer arrived at the party, the album was waiting for her as a special symbol of her development. What she still didn't know, though, was that the album was open-ended, and a new section, "Becoming an Adult Woman," was about to be added during the party. After dinner, when people were invited to give their presentations to Jennifer, a moving and unexpected ceremony unfolded. Person after person spoke about how they experienced Jenni and what she meant to them,

and they gave her their own special brand of advice about living.

Her grandma Dena gave Jenni a photograph of Dena's late husband—Jenni's grandfather—down on his knees proposing marriage. She spoke about enduring love and her wish that Jenni would have this in her life. Her aunt Meryle Sue read an original poem, "Portrait of Jenni," and then spoke through tears about what this day would have meant to Jenni's grandfather and how proud he would have been of her. Her cousin Stacey wrote a poem that captured who Jenni was to her and offered words about Jenni's future. Advice about men and what to beware of was given by Jenni's step-grandfather and received with much laughter. Photographs of strong women in history were presented.

Person after person spoke with grace and love and special stories about Jennifer's strengths. Her mother watched as Jennifer took in all that she was to people and the sometimes unknown impact that her own courage had had on family and friends. And then all who gathered wit-

nessed the emergence of Jennifer, the adult woman, as she rose from her seat and spoke unhaltingly and with no trace of her usual shyness, thanking each person in turn for what they had given her in life, and talking about the loss of her grandfather and her wish that he could be with her today. She ended with all that she anticipated next in her life.

The weeks and months following this ritual were perhaps even more remarkable than the ceremony itself. Her family experienced a changed Jennifer, a Jennifer who moved from adolescence to young womanhood—starting a full-time job, auditing a community college course, traveling by herself, making new friends, and relating on a previously unseen level.

AS ALL OF THESE EXAMPLES ILLUSTRATE, rituals ease our passage through life. They shape our relationships, help to heal our losses, express our deepest beliefs, and celebrate our existence. They announce change and create change. The power of rituals belongs to all of us.

Index

Credits/Acknowledgments

Cover design by Charles Vitelli.

1. Varied Perspectives on the Family
Facing overview—© 1998 by PhotoDisc, Inc.

2. Exploring and Establishing Relationships
Facing overview—Dushkin/McGraw-Hill photo by Pamela Carley.

3. Finding a Balance: Maintaining Relationships
Facing overview—© 1998 by PhotoDisc, Inc. 113—*The World & I*
illustration by Marcia Klioze Hughes.

4. Crises—Challenges and Opportunities
Facing overview—© 1998 by PhotoDisc, Inc. 154—Subjects &
Predicates photo.

5. Families, Now and Into the Future
Facing overview—© 1998 by Cleo Freelance Photography.

ANNUAL EDITIONS ARTICLE REVIEW FORM

■ NAME: _____ DATE: _____

■ TITLE AND NUMBER OF ARTICLE: _____

■ BRIEFLY STATE THE MAIN IDEA OF THIS ARTICLE: _____

_____

■ LIST THREE IMPORTANT FACTS THAT THE AUTHOR USES TO SUPPORT THE MAIN IDEA:

_____

_____

_____

_____

■ WHAT INFORMATION OR IDEAS DISCUSSED IN THIS ARTICLE ARE ALSO DISCUSSED IN YOUR TEXTBOOK OR OTHER READINGS THAT YOU HAVE DONE? LIST THE TEXTBOOK CHAPTERS AND PAGE NUMBERS:

_____

_____

_____

_____

_____

■ LIST ANY EXAMPLES OF BIAS OR FAULTY REASONING THAT YOU FOUND IN THE ARTICLE:

_____

_____

_____

_____

■ LIST ANY NEW TERMS/CONCEPTS THAT WERE DISCUSSED IN THE ARTICLE, AND WRITE A SHORT DEFINITION:

_____

_____

_____

_____

*Your instructor may require you to use this ANNUAL EDITIONS Article Review Form in any number of ways: for articles that are assigned, for extra credit, as a tool to assist in developing assigned papers, or simply for your own reference. Even if it is not required, we encourage you to photocopy and use this page; you will find that reflecting on the articles will greatly enhance the information from your text.

We Want Your Advice

ANNUAL EDITIONS revisions depend on two major opinion sources: one is our Advisory Board, listed in the front of this volume, which works with us in scanning the thousands of articles published in the public press each year; the other is you—the person actually using the book. Please help us and the users of the next edition by completing the prepaid article rating form on this page and returning it to us. Thank you for your help!

ANNUAL EDITIONS: MARRIAGE AND FAMILY 98/99
Article Rating Form

Here is an opportunity for you to have direct input into the next revision of this volume. We would like you to rate each of the 45 articles listed below, using the following scale:

1. **Excellent: should definitely be retained**
2. **Above average: should probably be retained**
3. **Below average: should probably be deleted**
4. **Poor: should definitely be deleted**

Your ratings will play a vital part in the next revision. So please mail this prepaid form to us just as soon as you complete it.
Thanks for your help!

Rating	Article	Rating	Article
	1. The Way We Weren't: The Myth and Reality of the "Traditional" Family		23. Parental Rights: An Overview
	2. Feminism & the Family: An Indissoluble Marriage		24. The Myth of Quality Time
	3. Among the Promise Keepers: An Inside Look at the Evangelical Men's Movement		25. Effective Fathers: Why Are Some Dads More Successful than Others?
	4. African American Families: A Legacy of Vulnerability and Resilience		26. The Great Ages of Discovery
	5. Gay Families Come Out		27. Grandparent Development and Influence
	6. Man's World, Woman's World? Brain Studies Point to Differences		28. Sibling Connections
	7. What Makes Love Last?		29. Behind Closed Doors
	8. Back Off!		30. Things That Go Bump in the Home
	9. Choosing a Contraceptive		31. Helping Children Cope with Violence
	10. Staying Power: Bridging the Gender Gap in the Confusing '90s		32. Resilience in Development
	11. Who Stole Fertility?		33. Beyond Betrayal: Life after Infidelity
	12. Missing Children: One Couple's Anguished Attempt to Conceive		34. Sex in America: Faithfulness in Marriage Is Overwhelming
	13. Men, Sex, and Parenthood in an Overpopulating World		35. The Myth of the Miserable Working Woman
	14. The Artificial Womb Is Born		36. Remaking Marriage & Family
	15. What a Baby *Really* Costs		37. Should This Marriage Be Saved?
	16. The Lifelong Impact of Adoption		38. Lessons from Stepfamilies
	17. Fertile Minds		39. Caregiving: Continuities and Discontinuities in Family Members' Relationships with Alzheimer's Patients
	18. Peer Marriage		40. Hard Lessons
	19. For Better or Worse?		41. How Kids Mourn
	20. Receipts from a Marriage		42. To See Your Future Look into Your Past
	21. The Work of Oneness: How to Make Marriage a Sacred Union		43. What's Ahead for Families: Five Major Forces of Change
	22. The Healing Power of Intimacy		44. Rewriting Life Stories
			45. Rituals for Our Times

(Continued on next page)

ABOUT YOU

Name _____ Date _____

Are you a teacher? ❑ Or a student? ❑

Your school name _____

Department _____

Address _____

City _____ State _____ Zip _____

School telephone # _____

YOUR COMMENTS ARE IMPORTANT TO US!

Please fill in the following information:

For which course did you use this book? _____

Did you use a text with this *ANNUAL EDITION*? ❑ yes ❑ no

What was the title of the text? _____

What are your general reactions to the *Annual Editions* concept?

Have you read any particular articles recently that you think should be included in the next edition?

Are there any articles you feel should be replaced in the next edition? Why?

Are there any World Wide Web sites you feel should be included in the next edition? Please annotate.

May we contact you for editorial input?

May we quote your comments?

ANNUAL EDITIONS: MARRIAGE AND FAMILY 98/99